VIETNAM'S NEW MIDDLE CLASSES

GENDERING ASIA
A Series on Gender Intersections

Gendering Asia is a well-established and exciting series addressing the ways in which power and constructions of gender, sex, sexuality and the body intersect with one another and pervade contemporary Asian societies. The series invites discussion of how people shape their identities as females or males and, at the same time, become shaped by the very societies in which they live. The series is concerned with the region as a whole in order to capture the wide range of understandings and practices that are found in East, Southeast and South Asian societies with respect to gendered roles and relations in various social, political, religious, and economic contexts. As a multidisciplinary series, *Gendering Asia* explores theoretical, empirical and methodological issues in the social sciences.

Series Editors: Wil Burghoorn, Gothenburg University; Cecilia Milwertz, NIAS; and Helle Rydstrøm, Lund University (contact details at: http://www.niaspress.dk).

1. *Working and Mothering in Asia. Images, Ideologies and Identities*, edited by Theresa W. Devasahayam and Brenda S.A. Yeoh

2. *Making Fields of Merit. Buddhist Female Ascetics and Gendered Orders in Thailand*, by Monica Lindberg Falk

3. *Gender Politics in Asia. Women Manoeuvring within Dominant Gender Orders*, edited by Wil Burghoorn, Kazuki Iwanaga, Cecilia Milwertz and Qi Wang

4. *Lost Goddesses. The Denial of Female Power in Cambodian History*, by Trudy Jacobsen

5 *Gendered Inequalities in Asia. Configuring, Contesting and Recognizing Women and Men*, edited by Helle Rydstrøm

6. *Submitting to God. Women and Islam in Urban Malaysia*, by Sylva Frisk

7. *The Authority of Influence. Women and Power in Burmese History*, by Jessica Harriden

8. *Beyond the Singapore Girl. Discourses of Gender and Nation in Singapore*, by Chris Hudson

9. *Vietnam's New Middle Classes: Gender, Career, City* by Catherine Earl

NIAS Press is the autonomous publishing arm of NIAS – Nordic Institute of Asian Studies, a research institute located at the University of Copenhagen. NIAS is partially funded by the governments of Denmark, Finland, Iceland, Norway and Sweden via the Nordic Council of Ministers, and works to encourage and support Asian studies in the Nordic countries. In so doing, NIAS has been publishing books since 1969, with more than two hundred titles produced in the past few years.

UNIVERSITY OF COPENHAGEN

norden

Nordic Council of Ministers

VIETNAM'S NEW MIDDLE CLASSES

Gender, Career, City

CATHERINE EARL

Nordic Institute of Asian Studies
Gendering Asia series, no. 9

First published in 2014 by NIAS Press
NIAS – Nordic Institute of Asian Studies
Øster Farimagsgade 5, 1353 Copenhagen K, Denmark
Tel: +45 3532 9501 • Fax: +45 3532 9549
E-mail: books@nias.ku.dk • Online: www.niaspress.dk

A CIP catalogue record for this book is available from the British Library

ISBN: 978-87-7694-145-1 (hbk)
ISBN: 978-87-7694-146-8 (pbk)

Typeset in Arno Pro 12/14.4 Typesetting by Lene Jakobsen
Printed in Great Britain by Marston Book Services Limited, Oxfordshire

*Cover illustrations: (behind) '300th anniversary of Saigon/Ho Chi Minh City',
a billboard designed by Phan Hoai Phi (from 'Tranh cổ động' [Propaganda
posters], Trường Đại học Mỹ thuật Thành phố Hồ Chí Minh, 2000); and
(front) reworking of an image by an unknown artist (all efforts to locate the
artist have failed but we would be happy to hear from him/her).*

Contents

Acknowledgements

This research began as a doctoral project at Victoria University in Australia. The fieldwork was funded by grants from the Department of Asian and International Studies and the Secomb Travel Fund at Victoria University, and the Australian Federation of University Women E. M. Hinder Bursary for Research in Southeast Asia. In Ho Chi Minh City, my research was hosted initially by the Faculty of Oriental Studies and later by the Department of Sociology at the University of Social Sciences and Humanities, Vietnam National University. The Nordic Institute of Asian Studies hosted me during the preparation of the manuscript. I am indebted to Mark Stevenson, Marc Askew, Phan Văn Giưỡng, Bùi Khánh Thế, Philip Taylor, Ngan Collins, Nguyễn Hồng Xoan, Trần Phi Phượng, Irina Vasilenka, Anastasia Sai, Noni Basalama, Minna Hakkarainen, and Adam Fforde who provided inspiration, motivation, criticism and humour throughout the project. My thanks go to my fabulous editors at NIAS Press Gerald Jackson and Leena Höskuldsson who made the process seamless. Most importantly, I acknowledge my informants in Ho Chi Minh City and the willingness with which they participated in the research. I am grateful for the support of my family and friends in Australia, Vietnam and Denmark who accommodated and sustained me throughout the project.

Earlier versions of sections in chapters 1, 2, 4, 5 and 7 have appeared in 'Cosmopolitan or Cultural Dissonance? Middle-Class Encounters with the Other', in Marika Vicziany and Robert Cribb (eds), *Proceedings of the 17th Biennial Conference of the Asian Studies Association of Australia, Melbourne, Australia: Is this the Asian Century?* Melbourne: Monash Asia Institute, Monash University, 2008, pp. 1–15; 'Post-War Mobilities: Gender, Poverty and Opportunity in Vietnam's Third Wave of Mass Urban Migration', *Children in War: The International Journal of Evacuee and War Child Studies*, Vol. 1, No. 10, May 2013, pp. 71–6; and 'Vietnam's "Informal Public" Spaces: Belonging and Social Distance in Post-Reform Ho Chi Minh City', *Journal of Vietnamese Studies*, Vol. 5, No. 1, February 2010, pp. 86–124.

CHAPTER ONE

Middle classes in post-reform Ho Chi Minh City

*I*n 1998 I arrived in Ho Chi Minh City for a Vietnamese language course and was immediately struck by the number of communist slogans in yellow capitals on red banners strung across the major streets. The banners were not an everyday decoration but celebrated 300 years of Vietnamese settlement in Saigon. A number of colourful billboards also decorated the street corners at major intersections. Waiting on my bicycle in the traffic, I noticed a billboard that depicted Vietnamese society on the occasion of the 300th anniversary. A line of eight citizens facing a sketched cityscape – modern and progressive concrete buildings and a parked car – exemplified Ho Chi Minh City society. At the back stood a young trio: the men in a shirt and tie and the woman in a plain blue *áo dài* traditional dress, the typical uniforms of state employees at that time. In front of them, in the middle of the group stood a male civil servant in a khaki uniform and a female agricultural worker in a black *áo bà ba* peasant blouse, a sheath of rice in her arms. At the front of the group stood a construction worker in an orange boiler suit, a scientist carrying his technical books, and a schoolgirl in a blue uniform with a knotted red neck scarf. It was the prominence of the skilled and educated at the forefront of society and the centre of the billboard that was striking. In the 1990s, contributions of educated young women had become so important in the post-reform urban economy that positive aspects of *đổi mới*, the nation-wide macro-economic reform introduced in 1986, were symbolized by images of middle-class urban schoolgirls (*nữ sinh*) representing youth, mobility, modernity, cultural vitality and pride (Werner 2002, p. 41).

Symbolizing the future progress and development of Vietnamese society through the image of a hard-working studious girl was striking for a nation whose past national narratives had ideologized a patrilineal sexual division of labour and a socialist expectation of the participation of women in society. This symbolic shift corresponded with the opening of Vietnam's economy and the widespread social and economic changes that reform is assumed to have instigated. While some scholars, notably Martin Gainsborough (2010), have questioned an assumption of widespread change led by reform, there have been noticeable transformations in Vietnamese social life. Among these are increasing social differentiation, globalization and urbanization.

Since the economic reforms of the mid-1980s, millions of young women in rural Vietnam have left their homes. The majority have flocked to Vietnam's cities. Apart from the hundreds of thousands of girls and young women who relocate from their natal homes to their husband's house after marriage, each year hundreds of thousands of other young women – many not yet married – move to Ho Chi Minh City for work and study. Of those working, tens of thousands are employed in factories, hotels and other work sites. Tens of thousands of others find themselves informal positions as housekeepers, nannies and cooks. Selling goods at local markets, from street stalls and in portable baskets provides income for an additional, unestimated number of young migrant women. Of those studying, thousands complete secondary school while boarding with relatives and working in their houses. Thousands of other young women move to the city each year for the purpose of university education and professional work. This wave of post-war mass migration dominated by women is an impact of reform in Vietnam that has been crucial in the development of urban middle classes.

This book investigates Vietnam's emerging urban middle classes through an exploration of the lifeworlds of educated urban migrant women – women who are young, unmarried, university educated, professionally employed, and living away from their natal homes – in Vietnam's mega-urban Southeast, the industrializing region that incorporates Ho Chi Minh City and neighbouring Đồng Nai and Bình Dương provinces. The research presented in this ethnography is among a handful of recent studies that deal with urban social life in Vietnam and the first monograph study to date to explore new middle classes in Ho Chi Minh City.

It offers a unique approach among studies on Vietnam in utilizing a framework for analysis that draws on the sociology of Pierre Bourdieu with important modifications stemming from feminist analysis, migration studies and cultural studies literature. This book adds to a growing number of studies that consider urban culture in Pacific Asia and in the postsocialist world. The approach I take enables me to explore influences of change and continuity in daily social life as middle classes re-emerge in post-reform urban Vietnam. By entering the lifeworlds of informants, it is possible to explore what it is like to live in middle-class Ho Chi Minh City. In doing so, my aim, firstly, is to explore the extent of change experienced by young educated women in their daily lives in post-reform urban Vietnam. Secondly, I seek to investigate the nature of middle-class formation in contemporary urban Vietnam and, thirdly, to analyse similarities and differences between middle classes in post-reform Ho Chi Minh City and those recorded in literary memoirs of life in postcolonial Saigon as well as those researched across contemporary East and Southeast Asia. Overall, through my approach I aim to redress to some extent the gender blindness of past studies of middle classes in Asia. I recognize that a study such as this one that focuses on depth of analysis is limited in terms of its ability to produce generalized findings.

VIETNAM'S TWENTIETH CENTURY

In any study of social life, it is important to provide a historical contextualization for the research that reflects its underpinning social world. The setting for this research is Ho Chi Minh City, the largest city in Vietnam. I assume a number of broader contextual frames regarding the southern capital and it is important to acknowledge at the outset that the specificity of a study in Ho Chi Minh City is not representative of all Vietnam. My approach assumes that Vietnam is not now, and has not been at any time in the twentieth century, isolated from international contact. That is to say that when Vietnam's contact with the 'west' (US, Western Europe, Australia) was limited, other international networks operated in the Soviet and post-Soviet worlds. Further, in unofficial networks, Vietnamese maintained contact internationally through extended family networks, various religious organizations and affiliations in Buddhist, Catholic and other doctrines, as well as other informal or even illegal systems of contact, exchange and trade. These external networks and affiliations are significant in Vietnamese social life as the Vietnamese post-war diaspora extends across every continent. Although contact has not been consistent, the diversity of the social landscape and cultural space in Ho Chi Minh City has developed from a long history of contact with outsiders from foreign countries, and also from other regions in Vietnam, contacts which influence the lives of the middle-class women at the centre of my study. The focus on Ho Chi Minh City is not driven by a preoccupation with any perceived underlying political perspective, but is a means to identifying continuities and changes in a particularized regional social and cultural life.

At the turn of the twenty-first century the Socialist Republic of Vietnam appeared to be a politically stable and economically developing nation. The significance of this unification and stability was in contrast to its twentieth century which was characterized by a succession of foreign and foreign-backed regimes as the nation emerged from colonial annexation to become an independent communist state. The story of this instability differs when told in Vietnam and outside. In summary, the nine-year First Indochina Conflict (1945–1954) broke out after decades of anti-colonial uprisings and interludes of Japanese and Chinese occupation in the final years of the Second World War (Lawrence and Logevall 2007; Marr 1971, 1995). Colonial power officially ended in Vietnam with the 1954 Geneva Accords, an agreement to withdraw troops and divide Vietnam into two states: Ho Chi Minh's communist Democratic Republic of Vietnam in the North and the Republic of Vietnam, the American-backed capitalist democracy in the South. The instability of postcolonial peace in the two Vietnams soon gave way to the Second Indochina Conflict (c.1962–1975), which is known in Vietnam as the 'American War' and outside as the 'Vietnam War' (Bradley 2009; Elliott 2003; Heberle 2009). In 1975 the two Vietnams were reunified into the current Socialist Republic and the southern capital Saigon was renamed Ho Chi Minh City.

While the Socialist Republic of Vietnam's national narratives have centred on socialist experiences including those of the postcolonial North, the contrasting experiences of everyday life in the alternative postcolonial southern Vietnamese state remain within living memory, particularly in Ho Chi Minh City and the Vietnamese post-war diaspora. The postcolonial South before 1975 was highly urbanized and supported an expanding middle class of educated professionals in the wartime capitalist economy. This heritage remains alive in public discourse and memory and it informs the direction of this research as it is embedded in the lifeworlds of Ho Chi Minh City's middle classes. To highlight this alternative history of Vietnamese postcolonialism, one centred on urban middle-class culture, I draw on the published memoirs of expatriate middle-class Vietnamese women, such as Mai Elliott, Nguyễn Thị Thu-Lâm and others (see Chapter 2).

As middle-class women's memoirs illustrate, Hanoi and the postcolonial North were de-urbanized during wartime and village culture dominated, while the postcolonial South had been rapidly urbanized through two waves of mass migration. Wartime urbanization saw Saigon's population quadruple to 1,776,000 by 1958 with the mass migration of refugee families – middle classes, Catholics, former colonial civil servants, and intellectuals – from the North. By 1975 Saigon's population had further increased to almost four million with the mass migration of southern peasants particularly from the Mekong Delta (Nguyễn Quang Vinh 1996, p. 91; Thrift and Forbes 1986). The impact on Saigon was significant with overcrowding straining infrastructure and hostility directed towards the middle classes arriving from the urban North who were seen to threaten residents' existing social positions and jobs. Additionally, lower classes took jobs in Saigon's expanding wartime service industry and they acquired new status based on money rather than education or class cultural credentials, which also threatened to displace the social power of urban middle classes. Such fears – of outsiders and of downward mobility – characterize present-day Asian middle classes (So 2006, p. 32).

Continuities and discontinuities marked late twentieth-century Vietnamese history. By 1986, while northern Vietnam had lived with socialism for three generations, southern Vietnam had experienced socialism for only a decade. Before 1975, young people in the postcolonial South had wide access to higher education and professional careers in the wartime service-based capitalist economy. After 1975, urban middle classes in southern Vietnam experienced rapid downward social mobility with a loss of social position, status, assets, resources and wealth. Many underwent socialist 're-education', or fled to rural areas or abroad. Others attempted to camouflage their identities to avoid these experiences. For those who had previously fled Hanoi, it was not the first time they had experienced a loss of assets, status and the future they had expected. In southern Vietnam after reform, experiences of the postcolonial middle class in Saigon – international study, salaried professional work, social segregation, and globalized leisure – remain within living memory even though Vietnam's national narratives are virtually silent on this topic. Van Nguyen-Marshall (2004, p. 157) comments that the South Vietnamese experience is 'conspicuous' by its 'absence'. The social context of postcolonial Saigon that centred on middle-class urban living remains alive in public discourse and memory in Vietnam and underpins the desires for social mobility of those seeking to live in Ho Chi Minh City and Vietnam's urban Southeast where opportunities may be realized. On this basis, I argue that since the 1990s middle-class culture in Vietnam's Southeast has not only been developing but is re-emerging also.

POST-WAR URBANIZATION TO VIETNAM'S SOUTHEAST

Urbanization has been a key factor in the expansion of middle classes across Southeast Asia and in Vietnam. Saigon / Ho Chi Minh City has been a magnet for migrants throughout the twentieth century. The most significant *mass migrations* to Saigon / Ho Chi Minh City have occurred during periods of political upheaval and dramatic social change: firstly, due to an influx of refugees from the North after the displacement of the French colonial regime in 1954; secondly, due to an influx of refugees, most of whom were peasants escaping political unrest, guerrilla conflict and rural unemployment in South Vietnam before 1975; and, thirdly, due to an influx of spontaneous economic migrants and students after macro-economic reform in the 1980s (Thrift and Forbes 1986). This third wave of mass migration is notable as it was dominated by those seeking education and employment rather than those forced to escape war and further because it was dominated by young women rather than families. Its influence on urban life has been significant in bringing new ideas and social practices to Ho Chi Minh City and the Southeast. This post-war urbanization is the context for the re-emergence of Vietnam's middle classes.

While Saigon had been the focal point of postcolonial urbanization, Ho Chi Minh City became post-war Vietnam's urban 'growth pole' (Dang 2008, p. 191). In the 1980s, spontaneous migrants began to flock to Ho Chi Minh City and they came from all but five remote provinces across Vietnam. After a brief decline in 1976–1979, Vietnam's urban population grew faster than its rural population, so that throughout the 1980s on average 264,000 were added to Vietnam's cities every year (Forbes 1990, pp. 3–5; Thrift and Forbes 1986). The introduction of the *đổi mới* program of macro-economic reform in 1986 saw urban migration escalate as employment opportunities in the industrializing zones of the Southeast and other urban centres grew for graduates and unskilled migrants alike. Liên (pseudonym, introduced in Chapter 3) was one of the young women who arrived from the Mekong Delta to Ho Chi Minh City in the late 1980s to study at university. She had plans to graduate and gain secure, well-paid employment so that she could build a better future for herself, her sisters and her mother. She did so by taking up a salaried profession in Ho Chi Minh City in the 1990s.

In the 1990s, Ho Chi Minh City continued to grow and it retained its dominant position in Vietnamese industry where it accounted for just over a third of the nation's industrial output and seven times as much foreign trade as Hanoi (Turley and Womack 1999, p. 74). New factories provided employment opportunities particularly for young women in garment, textiles and electronics production which enabled them to contribute remittances to their natal families back home. Nghiem Lien Huong (2004, pp. 297–8) reports that garment sweatshops were the fastest growing industry in post-reform Vietnam. While employment opportunities were plentiful, a gender division of labour on the factory floor, which saw male and female garment workers conform to conventional gender roles, advanced the careers of men over women (Tran 2004, p. 225). Millions of single Vietnamese women originally from rural areas working in manufacturing were faced with underemployment because they were 'construed as docile, hard working and free of responsibility' making them the preferred type of worker (Bélanger and Pendakis 2009, p. 265). Even with the poor conditions that it offered to workers in general and women workers in particular, the manufacturing industry continued to expand. It was not the only sector of the post-reform economy to offer employment opportunities that were worth moving to the city to pursue.

The expansion of the non-state sector, especially the development of the foreign-invested sector, provided an increasing number of jobs for women with education in administration and secretarial positions, interpreting and other office-based work. Liên and other young rural–urban migrants began to arrive from across Vietnam to pursue education. Equipped with education, they sought more attractive employment opportunities in the salaried professions of Ho Chi Minh City's industrialized labour market. Like Liên, the majority of young migrants arrived in the city from the neighbouring Mekong Delta region (*Dân Số Thành Phố* 2000, p. 7). Throughout the 1990s, urbanization escalated and about 100,000 migrants arrived in Ho Chi Minh City each year. In its second decade, the flow of urban migrants increased to over 200,000 a year from 1999 to 2004 (Hy 2009, p. 1) and over 300,000 migrants a year (1.6 million) from 2005 to 2009 (GSO 2011c, p. 34).[1] Consequently, the Southeast region has become Vietnam's most highly urbanized region and one of the four largest and most rapidly developing mega-urban regions in contemporary Southeast Asia (Douglass et al. 2008, p. 284; Rimmer 1995, p. 150). Mega-urban regions have provided the conditions in which Southeast Asia's new middle classes have risen and flourished.

Liên was one of the migrants who arrived in Ho Chi Minh City to pursue education in the late 1980s. Among the migrants to arrive in the 1990s were Cúc and her sister Hạnh (introduced in Chapter 3), both of whom had come from the Mekong Delta to Ho Chi Minh City to study

---

1   The official numbers estimating urbanization to Vietnam's Southeast are dizzying. With spontaneous population movement and seasonal migration to wage employment in the city, it is difficult to accurately track and quantify numbers of urban migrants in Vietnam. Estimates suggesting that Ho Chi Minh City houses approximately 10 per cent of the national population of 85 million recognize that the city's population growth is substantially under-estimated in official statistics (Dang 2008, p. 185). For example, from 2002 to 2005, official estimates of the population of Ho Chi Minh City saw an increase of 7.5 per cent. At the same time the increase in numbers of workers in Ho Chi Minh City enterprises was 39 per cent (Dapice, Gomez-Ibanez and Nguyen 2010, p. 3). While current estimates put Ho Chi Minh City's permanent population over eight million, official population projections in 2009 saw it approaching 10 million in 2034 (Ministry of Planning and Investment & General Statistical Office 2011, p. 30). One factor complicating the accuracy of population estimates is a presumption that people comply with the official household registration system (*hộ khẩu*) that differentiates between people registered at: the address where they live (KT1); a temporary address in another district of their home province (KT2); a temporary address for up to one year in a different province (KT3); and a temporary address for up to six months in a different province (KT4) (Nguyen Tuan Anh et al. 2012, pp. 1109–10). I heed the warning offered by Jonathan Pincus and John Sender (2008) about relying on official Vietnamese government statistics, such as Vietnamese national census data. While I am conscious of their limitations, I use official figures not for their exact numbers but to contextualize the scope and significance of trends that are apparent in the social world.

at college and train for a 'white-collar' profession. Thu (introduced in Chapter 3) and Minh (male, introduced in Chapter 4) also arrived in Ho Chi Minh City at this time. Having already graduated college in Central Vietnam, they had both migrated to pursue the greater employment opportunities that the city offered. Among those arriving in the 2000s to study at college were Tuyết, the youngest girl in a large village family from the Southeast (introduced in Chapter 3); Nghĩa, the youngest boy in a large village family from the Centre (introduced in Chapter 5), and Vân, the niece of Cúc and Hạnh (introduced in Chapter 7). They were among the individuals whose lifeworlds I shared as I explored the re-emergence of middle classes in Ho Chi Minh City. The pursuit of education and salaried professions as a way to build a better future has not yet been the focus of empirical research in post-reform Vietnam. The analysis of middle-class development in urban Vietnam has also not yet been the focus of an in-depth study. This research on the case of postsocialist Vietnam contributes to the existing literature on class formation in capitalist Southeast Asia, a body of literature that has been evaluated as 'gender-blind' (Sen 1998, pp. 38–9).

FEMINIZATION OF URBAN MIGRATION AND EDUCATION MOBILITY IN POST-REFORM VIETNAM

The Vietnamese state considers the extent of urbanization to the Southeast to have made it Vietnam's 'exceptional destination location for migrants' (GSO 2011c, p. 34). What is especially significant about Vietnam's post-reform urbanization, the third wave of mass urban migration to Saigon / Ho Chi Minh City, is the dominance of young migrant women in both rural–urban and urban–urban migration streams (GSO & UNDP 2001, p. 51). While this pattern has been observed in contemporary migrations across other Southeast Asian contexts (e.g. Piper and Roces 2003b), a feminization of migration to Vietnam's Southeast was one of the 'most notable' findings of its 1999 national population census (GSO & UNDP 2001, p. 98).

One of the central motivations for young women to migrate to the Southeast is to find new opportunities, such as higher standards of living, greater access to education and better employment opportunities that without relocation would be unattainable. Educational opportunities, in particular, are markedly better in urban areas.[2] As members of relatively prosperous village families that have benefitted from socio-economic reform in Vietnam, young women's migrations to the city are shaped around the consolidation, or improvement, of an existing family status and the mitigation of risk associated with attempting to rise socially. Many families, particularly in the Mekong Delta, encourage their daughters to seek opportunities in urban labour and education markets. In contrast to low-skilled labour migrants, aspirational migrants relocate to the Southeast with a long-term goal of achieving self-improvement through education and subsequently through a profession (GSO 2011d, p. 66). In doing so, family resources are directed away from marriage in Vietnam as one of the dominant strategies for young women to advance socially and economically (Bourdieu 1976, 1997). Rather, resources are invested in education as a long-term strategy to achieve ensuring social status and prestige.

Education migration is a family strategy that often involves considerable planning and investments of family resources. The purpose of this type of migration is ultimately to guarantee secure future employment that in turn benefits the natal family, as well as enables individual migrants to improve their own social positions. Văn Thị Kim Cúc (2002, pp. 104–6) suggests that the aspirations of Vietnamese parents for their children's educational success are not determined by gender, with all children in aspirational families pressured from childhood to achieve high grades at school to maintain family prestige and to win a university place. In this quest for betterment, pre-existing access to resources strongly shapes migration strategies through which the family can benefit by further consolidating social position or facilitating upward social mobility in terms of both cultural and material resources.

The pursuit of enduring social status and upward mobility through education and profession is so great that it has caused a 'brain drain'

---

2   In 1999 official figures for high school completion for both sexes in urban areas were more than three times higher than rural areas (20.2 vs 5.9 per cent), but the most substantial difference between urban and rural areas is in the completion of college, university or higher degrees with 6.4 per cent of the urban population graduating compared to just 0.9 per cent in the rural population (GSO & UNDP 2001, p. 73). There continues to be a great disparity between urban and rural levels of education, particularly for women and ethnic minorities who are among the most disadvantaged nationally. In the Mekong Delta and Central Highlands, rural men and women have lower levels of education in 2009 than urban people did in 1989 (GSO 2011b, p. 48).

in the Mekong Delta. Nguyen Pham Thanh Nam et al. (2000, p. 10) observed that the majority of graduates from Cần Thơ University (located in the Mekong Delta's largest city) moved to Ho Chi Minh City for employment after graduation, with only one in five graduates returning to their home provinces. High school graduates also migrated to the city for employment. In official figures that focus on permanent migration, the highest migration rate continues to be for those who have graduated upper secondary school, with more women represented than men (GSO 2011d, p. 73).

Women's education is a starting point in building a more prosperous future. Danièle Bélanger and Katherine Pendakis (2009, p. 280) regard education to be the 'golden passport' to higher paying jobs in the foreign-invested and non-state sectors in Vietnam. One in three women in urban Vietnam have completed upper secondary or higher education (GSO 2011b, p. 43). The expansion of the Vietnam National University, the largest in Ho Chi Minh City, reflects the growing demand for higher education in the 2000s. Its annual student enrolments expanded from 4,835 in 2000 to 17,749 in 2007, with the Social Sciences and Humanities campus increasing annual enrolments from 1,002 to 4,501 students (GSO 2008, p. 305). This campus offers undergraduate courses in foreign languages, English literature and journalism which are particularly popular among young women seeking office jobs in state and non-state companies.

Students from privileged backgrounds have clear advantages over other students outside the classroom. Anecdotal evidence suggests that the younger members of the family, such as Tuyết and Cúc, are often well resourced for the pursuit of education in the city. Working in small agriculture businesses and wholesale trade back home, their older siblings and other close kin were able to support their moves to Ho Chi Minh City by financing their daily needs via a modest allowance and modest city accommodation arranged through their personal and community networks. Their investments were made with an expectation of reciprocity that morally obliges a young person to repay a moral debt to her elders (Shohet 2013).

Many other less privileged students, such as Nghĩa and Thu, both from Central Vietnam, also arrived in the city to pursue careers but with more limited assistance from family. Like Nghĩa, they might live in student dormitories or, like Tuyết, Cúc and Thu, in shared accommodation. Due in part to a tight housing market in Ho Chi Minh City, living alone in the city is unusual.[3] Moreover, for many young people, the idea of being alone, away from home and isolated from family or kin would be unbearable, a theme I explore in terms of belonging in the following chapters.

While initially supported by their families when they arrive in the city, young educated migrants are eventually able to improve their own positions and those of others within their families. But not all members of a family have equal opportunities or abilities to prosper. Different individuals in the family may occupy different class status positions, just as they may occupy different gender or race status positions. Bernard Lahire (2008, p. 174) notes that when an individual does not have the same social status, the same education or the same position within a professional hierarchy as her parents, her experiences will be more varied and as a result 'translate into a heterogeneity of cultural practices and preferences' that can distance her from others within her family. Rather than sharing experiences, members within families can have contrasting and divergent experiences that stem from their individualized interactions with the social world. I explain such contrasts through the concept of a 'multi-dimensional' family, a term that I use to reflect the diversity of experience stemming from qualitatively different socialization, education, employment and other influences on members of a family. Multi-dimensionality within a family, particularly one that has previously experienced downward mobility, enables its members to draw on diverse resources to rebuild lost status.

The majority of educated migrants in Vietnam's Southeast benefit from the investment of resources by members of their natal families, sometimes in addition to student bursaries and stipends they might

---

3   Vietnamese state figures report that the tightest housing markets are metropolitan and Ho Chi Minh City has the highest rate of shared housing nationally with 16 per cent of residents living in shared arrangements (GSO & UNDP 2001, p. 86). Ho Chi Minh City, the South Central Coast, the Southeast, and the Mekong Delta have more than a quarter of households comprising more than 6 persons (28.6, 26.2, 26.7, and 27.7 per cent respectively) (GSO & UNDP 2001, p. 82). The proportion of households sharing an apartment is higher in urban than rural areas and has increased since the 1999 census. In Vietnam's major cities, including Ho Chi Minh City, 17.2 per cent of households are shared, compared to only 6-8 per cent in other urban areas, and housing is much smaller with a much greater proportion of dwellings under six square metres in size (GSO 2011c, pp. 84–5).

have received. Members within multi-dimensional families may combine diversified income sources to provide a secure resource to support the long process of socialization of their urbanized daughters initially to achieve a higher level of education and eventually, through salaried professional employment, into a circumstance where they can ascend to an enduring middle-class position. Their motivation and the long-term financial investments of kin contrast with other migrant groups who draw on limited resources in their quest for greater prosperity. Contrasts are most apparent between educated migrants and urban labourers or manufacturing workers who have no intention of remaining in the city permanently and who engage in seasonal or contract labour with the goal of supporting their families via cash remittances without enhancing their own skills (Ha and Ha 2001, pp. 154–6; see also Jerneck 2010; Winkels 2012).

With the resources committed by family members, a young person may engage with various long- and short-term strategies and different levels of investment of finances and time in order to pursue a better life for themselves but also, in reciprocity of the initial investment, for members of their natal family. While urban migration may be a 'turning point' in their lives (Hardy 2003, p. 331), Vietnamese migrants maintain close relations with their families and do not make a complete break from their past. Rather, the connections within families is characterized by a 'singular field of interaction' (Lee and Piper 2003, p. 126) between members in diverse locations with different levels of education, different incomes and a diversity of social experience. As I explore in the following chapters, self-improvement and individual achievements do not only reflect on the individual but also on their kin.

Educated migrants move to Ho Chi Minh City where they can pursue a professional career, yet they remain active members of their families and village communities by maintaining direct contact. This is a pattern that characterizes various types of labour migration across Southeast Asia (e.g. Mills 1999). However, in Vietnam urban migrants are highly educated. Permanent migrants in Ho Chi Minh City have been found to have higher-level qualifications than non-migrants, with the young being the most highly educated. Almost a third have completed higher education (Dang 2008, pp. 202–3; GSO 2011b, p. 37). In Ho Chi Minh City, migrants also have a higher standard of living than non-migrants and two-thirds of rural–urban migrants there have achieved a *very high* standard of living (GSO 2011c, pp. 43–44, emphasis added).[4] By maintaining contact with their family homes, they can play a role in raising the standard of living of the family and rebuilding lost status also.

Young women, such as Liên, Hạnh, Tuyết and Diễm (introduced below), are attracted to the non-state sector where the majority of employment opportunities for educated and skilled women in the Southeast are located. The three provinces of the Southeast and neighbouring Bà Rịa–Vũng Tàu together account for three quarters of the foreign investment in Vietnam (Dang 2008, pp. 185–6). More than two thirds of employees in the foreign sector and nearly half in the private sector are women. Throughout the 2000s both sectors of non-state employment have expanded dramatically and numbers of women employees have continued to grow (GSO 2008).[5] Besides working, there are other less direct advantages of employment in the non-state sector in terms of accumulating cultural capital and building an enduring middle-class status position.

The feminization of migration to Vietnam's Southeast has social consequences as young educated migrants encounter new ways of living that challenge conventional behaviour and expectations. Fin-de-siècle middle-class women share a background that includes a relatively strict upbringing where, through the socialist education system introduced to southern Vietnam from 1981 (Phạm Minh Hạc 1998), they were taught the social and moral dangers of excess and consumption as well as instilled with a commitment to occupy their free time with productive and socially valuable activities. As children, their training continued in their natal homes, where girls and their sisters were taught to behave as model citizens, displaying the type of behaviour expected in model families.

---

4   Vietnamese state figures record two-thirds (67 per cent) of rural–urban migrants in Ho Chi Minh City having a very high standard of living, compared to half (52 per cent) of non-migrant urban residents and only 15 per cent of non-migrants rural residents (GSO 2011c, pp.43-4).

5   The relative growth of enterprises in state and non-state employment sectors in Ho Chi Minh City in the 2000s contrasts starkly. State figures indicate the private sector expanded from just over 10,000 enterprises in 2001 to more than 35,000 in 2006 with 891,408 total employees, nearly half (41–45 per cent) of whom were women. The number of foreign enterprises increased from 664 to 1,324 with 409,333 employees, more than two thirds (67–69 per cent) of whom were women. At the same time, the number of state enterprises decreased from 727 to 461 with 246,612 employees, more than a third (35–40 per cent) of whom were women (GSO 2008, pp. 87, 91, 96).

For girls, this meant following a strict code of behaviour in every aspect of their lives. They were taught to yield and 'sacrifice' to all male, older and other senior family members. They were taught to dress modestly and behave in a feminine manner whilst working to ensure the smooth running of the household. Despite purported gender equality (*bình đẳng giới*) in Vietnam's communist ideology (Le Thi 1998; Werner 2009, pp. 78–80), their training in both state and familial spheres presupposed the continuation of patrilineal kinship as one of the salient structures for women to advance socially.

After migrating to the city as young single women, they were exposed to new ways of living and experienced relative autonomy from the family which freed them to some extent from the traditional obligations of family life. Delayed marriage is one of the most noticeable outcomes of rural–urban migration for young women in Vietnam. Favourable employment attracts unmarried women to work in the foreign sector where women, such as Thu, delay marriage longest. Thu had graduated university on the Central Coast then migrated to Ho Chi Minh City with an aim to work in a well-remunerated office job in the non-state sector while she completed graduate study. Her salary could help support her small family by supplementing her mother's irregular income which was generated from wholesale trade of seasonal products. For her, education was a long-term strategy to build a more prosperous future. For low-skilled rural–urban labour migrants, as Mary Beth Mills (1999, p. 158) observes in research on Bangkok, it is far less common to commit to a long-term investment in education over the short-term rewards of cash remittances.

For Thu, single life enabled her to maximize her achievements and wealth. Chua Beng Huat (2000a, p. 14) pinpoints the years of single-hood after graduation and before marriage as a 'window' of opportunity for urban professionals. Vietnam's non-state sector offers such a window and it accounts for the lowest numbers of married staff, the highest average marriage ages and the highest levels of minimum qualifications. In Ho Chi Minh City, six in ten (58.7 per cent) female university students and young working women aged 20–24 years old remain single. In the foreign sector, a clear majority of women and men remain single (83 and 84 per cent, respectively) and their average marriage ages are high being almost 30 years for women and almost 28 years for men (GSO 2001, pp.

9–10, 15–16, 19). Urban migrants remain single for longer and urban households are smaller (GSO 2011c, p. 13). The probability of late marriage is greatest in Vietnam's Southeast, where singlehood corresponds with high economic development and post-secondary education (GSO 2011a, pp. 109–10, 119). Salaried and professional employment makes it possible for Thu and other young women to achieve status through strategies other than marriage and family. Leisure also offers young women opportunities to build their social status. With enhanced social opportunities and better incomes in the city, the spaces for recreation, leisure and lifestyling have widened considerably for educated urban migrant women. These areas of practice, like professional work, are largely dislodged from the household and family. While supported by elders in their natal families and living away from home to study or work, young women are able to improve their own positions as well as direct benefits back to their families to improve theirs.

Urbanization of the Southeast is one of the underlying conditions that has had a significant influence on the formation of Vietnam's urban middle classes. Even with official recognition of the third wave of migration to the Southeast dominated by young women, there has been less than a handful of ethnographic or quantitative studies addressing the social impact of urban migration on class formation in contemporary Vietnam. My research addresses the effects of contemporary urbanization on educated young women and their families in the context of the development of class culture in Vietnam and the re-emergence of urban middle classes in Ho Chi Minh City. These phenomena – urbanization and expansion of middle classes – stem from state-led development not only in Vietnam but generally across East and Southeast Asia. Exploring new middle-class women's lifeworlds enables me to investigate in which ways the Vietnamese case corresponds and diverges from its Southeast Asian neighbours particularly considering gendered experience.

ASIA'S MIDDLE CLASSES

Until recently middle classes in Pacific Asia were largely absent from academic discourses. Since the 1990s there has been considerable investigation into class formation and class consumption in Asia. Two major comparative projects offered insights into Southeast Asian middle classes, although they did not explore the case of Vietnam. The first of these was co-ordinated by Academia Sinica. From 1992, a project team of 20 social scientists in Taiwan, South Korea, Hong Kong, Singapore, the Philippines, Malaysia, Thailand and Indonesia carried out the East Asian and Southeast Asian Middle Class comparative surveys. The project drew on Goldthorpe's neo-Weberian schema of 11 occupation-ally-based social classes to devise a schema particularized to Southeast Asia comprising six groups: entrepreneurs, the old, new and marginal middle classes, working classes and an 'agricultural class' of farmers and farm labourers (see Hsiao and Wang 2001, pp. 5–8). While 'old middle class' designated small business proprietors and self-employed business people and 'marginal middle class' referred to low-wage white-collar workers, 'new middle class' became the term to describe first-generation urban migrants who became middle class through long-term resource investment in their self-development and their acquisition of education, assets and power. Typically they worked in salaried professions and as managers or government officials (Hsiao 1993, 1999, 2001, 2006; see also Embong 2001; Li Cheng 2010). In this book, I adopt the term 'new middle class' to signify the group of educated urban migrant women whose lifeworlds I explore, in part because this term neatly combines the influences of migration, education and salaried professions that are crucial to class ascension as I have encountered it in the field. Further, the term 'new middle class' also incorporates an idea of the multi-dimensional family, in which the investment of elders enables younger, more highly educated family members to achieve an enduring relatively higher social position than their elders whilst maintaining close contact through mutually supportive relationships across diverse locations.

Southeast Asia's new middle classes are characterized by their diverse social origins, lack of class consciousness and low barriers to social mobility, which is widely facilitated by state-funded education (Hattori, Funatsu and Torii 2003, p. 136). They have risen since the 1970s and 1980s in each country from different forms of economic development and levels of industrialization, different political systems and rates of political transformation, uneven distributions of religions and faiths, and complex ethnic compositions (Hsiao and Wang 2001, p. 35). In particular, middle classes in Southeast Asia emerged under authoritar-ian rulers who aimed to transform their nations from agricultural econo-mies through rapid economic growth that would raise the majority of the population out of poverty (Embong 2001, pp. 13–14). For example, in Malaysia's Klang Valley 80 per cent of new middle classes are first-generation urban migrants mostly from humble rural origins. Class structure is open and fluid and upward intergenerational mobility is primarily achieved through state-sponsored higher education but is also dependent on family class and education background. While new middle classes are affluent, they are not yet economically secure, and even with high salaries, they rely on loans. Home ownership, an improved material standard of living and education for children are key goals of the new middle class. They are conservative and support the status quo rather than change. Politically, they support the state so long as their interests are maintained (Embong 2006b, pp. 159–61). At first glance it seems that clear comparisons and contrasts can be drawn between Vietnam's new middle classes and those surveyed across Southeast Asia.

New middle classes across the globe have gained considerable attention in the 2000s as both products and promoters of globalization (Lange and Meier 2009, p. v). While middle classes in Asia vary significantly from country to country, they share particular features that distinguish them from western middle classes (Hattori, Funatsu and Torii 2003, pp. 129–130 n. 1). Asian new middle-class identities and lifestyles are shaped not only by globalization but also localization. Hagen Koo (2006, p. 13) observes, on the one hand, middle-class lifestyles in Asia are shaped in a globalized context of highly valued American-dominated commercial culture but, on the other hand, in localized contexts that strongly resist the displacement of traditional cultural forms by westernized commercial influences. Alvin So (2006, p. 32) argues that Asian middle classes seek to become highly educated, cosmopolitan and widely travelled but are threatened by outsiders and motivated by a fear of losing their social positions to participate in anti-globalization or anti-immigration movements. As I explore in the following chapters, Vietnam's new middle class share many aspects of these lifestyles and identities.

Conceptualizations of class culture in Asia extend beyond money, material possessions and consumption to include self-improvement, lifestyling, social awareness and a globalized outlook (Hsiao 2010, p. 253). This emphasis contrasts with a narrower conception of the new middle class as 'new consumers' that centres on purchasing power parity (see Myers and Kent 2003). As Hagen Koo (2006, p. 13) reminds us, class culture involves a long process of socialization not simply the possession of status-making goods. The centrality of consumption and consumerism to middle-class lifestyles in Asia was the focus of the second major comparative investigation into Asia's emerging middle classes. The New Rich in Asia series took the form of a wide-ranging thematic analysis of new status groups and consumer lifestyling in Pacific Asia (Chua 2000b; Hutchison and Brown 2001; Pinches 1999b; Robison and Goodman 1996b; Rodan 1996; Sen and Stivens 1998). As Richard Robison and David Goodman (1996a, pp. 5–7) explain, the term 'new rich' is neither a precise analytical tool nor a defined occupational category. New rich is a 'broad brushstroke' that encompasses new wealthy social groups such as new middle classes and entrepreneurs which have emerged with industrial changes in East and Southeast Asia since the late 1970s. Acknowledging differences exist within and between groups, the basis of new rich social power and position lies with capital, credentials and expertise, rather than with position in the state apparatus or a feudal hierarchy. This focus centres on the exploration of emerging middle classes through lifestyling in the forms of taste, trendsetting and social influence, rather than access to wealth (Chan 2000, p. 127; Goodman 1996, pp. 238–9; PuruShotam 1998, pp. 126–7). Upward mobility for Southeast Asia's new rich, however, is also linked to occupation through increasing levels of education and employment in urban professional or bureaucratic positions (Antlov 1999, p. 189; Ockey 1999, p. 234; Shamsul 1999, pp. 100–1).

Considerations of gender are relegated in the New Rich Series from discussions of mainstream social practices; gender is addressed separately in a volume focused on women (Sen and Stivens 1998). In an isolated example, beyond this volume, Ariel Heryanto (1999, p. 162) recognizes that women play significant roles in emerging status groups, such as the 'new middle class', the indigenous Muslim elite and urban professionals in Indonesia. Because of women's participation, he argues, these new groups are what he terms 'non-gendered groups'. This is a 'gender blindness' that, according to Krishna Sen (1998, pp. 38–9), characterizes class analysis in most societies which fail to analyse different experiences of women, for example, by failing to distinguish between 'working women' and 'working-class women'. Gender is often overlooked as a factor in class analysis. Unlike Heryanto, I argue that because women do play significant roles in the new middle class and because gender is a factor not to be overlooked in the economic conditions that give rise to new middle classes, this requires a gender-conscious approach. The experiences of young educated women, young skilled and unskilled women, and other young urban migrant women, firstly, exert a significant influence in driving new middle-class ascension as workers, migrants and junior members of their families and, secondly, their experiences as lived social relations (see below) differ not only with the experiences of other women but also with the experiences of men.

POSTSOCIALIST ASIA'S MIDDLE CLASSES

The focus of the Academia Sinica and New Rich in Asia projects centred on the capitalist economies of Pacific Asia, which are recognized for their diversity of economic, political and ethnic compositions. Post-reform socialist Asian economies, including China and Vietnam, were assumed to be lagging behind their capitalist neighbours with respect to class formation. Chua Beng Huat (2009, p. 102) observes that, based on criteria for membership of the middle classes in Asia that centre on university education, professional employment and home and car ownership, Vietnam and China have a 'thin layer' of middle classes and, in relation to other East and Southeast Asian middle classes, are 'latecomers'.[6] Nevertheless, as Victor King (2008) suggests, we can question to what extent middle classes in Vietnam and China actually differ from those across Southeast Asia.

Victor King (2008, p. 85) observes that like Southeast Asian middle classes, Vietnam's urban middle classes are aspirational. The formation of Vietnam's middle classes stems from economic growth and was accelerated by reform. They are relatively well-to-do and value education and professional employment as a step toward a better life. Like Vietnam's middle classes, China's middle classes share a broad brushstroke of characteristics. The chapters of Li Cheng's (2010) edited volume *China's Emerging Middle Class* provide a snaphot. China's middle classes are those situated in the

---

6   The 'latecomers' Vietnam and China were overlooked in Academia Sinica's comparative studies of East and Southeast Asian middle classes. China takes a prominent position in the New Rich in Asia Series, but Vietnam is overlooked except for one chapter by Stephanie Fahey (1998) that provided a synthesis of published reports about the position of Vietnamese women in the decade after reform.

middle in terms of income, education and occupation (Hsiao 2010, pp. 255–6). Like Southeast Asia's middle classes, economic growth, urbanization, higher education and white-collar jobs characterize China's 'middle' (Li Chunling 2010, pp. 136–9). Economic reform has lifted the majority of the population out of poverty and with continuing growth, as Homi Kharas and Geoffrey Gertz (2010, p. 43) predict, this potentially enables the majority of Chinese to become middle class within one generation. Expanding the higher education sector in China has enabled middle classes to rise from every family, community and sector of society (Lin and Sun 2010, p. 217). Like Southeast Asian middle-classes, China's middle classes are aspirational; on the one hand, they are contented and optimistic but, on the other hand, they are uncertain and insecure about future income, wealth and happiness (Hsiao 2010, p. 257).

As in capitalist Southeast Asia, in postsocialist Asia the state plays a role in middle-class development. For Victor King (2008, p. 97) the role that the Vietnamese state plays is 'inordinately important' in moulding the social class structure. Lotte Thomsen (2011, p. 647) points out that for private enterprise owners in Ho Chi Minh City a personalized relationship with state officials at various levels within the system is the only way to be allocated resources as the process remains controlled by the state. Annette Kim (2008, p. 32) describes the relationship between entrepreneurs in large companies and the state as 'intimate'. However, there are some signs in Vietnam's major cities of some middle classes being outside government control (King, Nguyen and Nguyen 2008, p. 794). China's middle classes also remain closely aligned to the state. A privileged background and access to resources goes a long way in achieving betterment in Beijing, where 'getting ahead' and 'getting rich' requires a combination of skills and, importantly, access to bureaucratic power (Buckley 1999, p. 210). Middle classes in postsocialist Asia share the diverse origins, different paths to development and aspirational orientation that characterize Southeast Asia's middle classes. This book seeks to explore in greater depth and through a gender-conscious lens which experiences characterize Vietnam's new middle classes.

CONCEPTS OF CLASS IN VIETNAM

In his classic study of middle-class consumption in Nepal, Mark Liechty (2003, p. 64) reflects that class analysis has focused on class categorizations which, when applied to the lived experience of middle classness, fall short. Certainly this has been the case in comparative research on Southeast Asia's developing middle classes. While categories of class are theoretical, they can be useful in identifying salient realms of practice for individuals, social groups and institutions, as well as the state. There has been an expectation that economic development would precipitate class formation. In Vietnam, this focus did not directly centre on the formation of distinct classes but on a more opaque notion of increasing social differentiation.

The problem of class formation in Vietnam was tackled by scholars as a newly emerging phenomenon in the years after reform. Economist Melanie Beresford (1993, pp. 216–17) viewed new social classes to have been emerging since the macro-economic reforms of the 1980s due to shifts in economic and political power within existing social groups. More distinct social inequalities, according to Beresford, resulted from social structure becoming more diversified with concentrations of economic power located outside the Party and bureaucracy. Vietnamese historian Pham Xuan Nam (2002, pp. 37–42) considered that distinct social classes, including landowners and a bourgeois stratum, had begun to re-emerge in the 1990s but had not yet fully formed. Political scientist Martin Gainsborough (2002, p. 700) suggested that the social structure was becoming more diversified, although in his view emerging classes remained quite small and were yet to 'flex their muscles'. Across a range of academic disciplines, scholars expected the influence of reform to generate a new social structure in post-reform Vietnam with distinct social classes re-emerging. Yet it remained difficult to actually describe these new status groups.

While increasing social differentiation and an expectation of change characterized an image of Vietnam in the reform era, past hierarchies of relative social position were determined by occupational categories. Political scientist David Elliott (2003, pp. 459–61) observed that with political and economic change in postcolonial southern Vietnam the rural social hierarchy did not become more diversified, but shifted from one set of classifications to another so that a person who was assigned as a 'middle peasant' on one scale could be classified as a 'rich peasant' on another scale. The result, he concluded, was the impossibility of making clear distinctions between classes based solely on occupations.

The language of class in Vietnam is also problematic. US-based anthropologist Nguyen-vo Thu-huong (2004, pp. 184–5) regards a concept of social stratification in post-reform Vietnam to be new and a means for avoiding the language of class associated with the colonial and postcolonial eras. Pre-revolutionary terminology, such as 'petty bourgeoisie' (*tiểu tư sản*), referred to educated urban professionals (doctors, engineers, teachers) who did not necessarily espouse values associated with middle classes, highlighting a limitation of describing social class only in occupational terms. Similarly, 'middle level' (*trung bình*, indicating an average household income) is ambiguous and does not adequately convey a sense of values held, nor does it provide a sense of educational attainment or occupational status. Nguyen-vo (2004, p. 186) reiterates that class terminology in Vietnam is imprecise and uncertain, explaining that aspirational migrant garment workers in her ethnographic research in Ho Chi Minh City resorted to describing their class dispositions and values through concrete details and images that clarified differences in income, lifestyle and outlook. In another study, Nguyen-vo (2008, p. 31) reflects on occupational criteria for class falling short of lived experience and she found that urban sex workers, judged in terms of income, are like the richest entrepreneurs but, judged by occupation, are working-class.

With a dearth of useful class terminology, scholars have investigated the lived experiences of individuals within new status groups in post-reform Vietnam by referring to social practices connected to income levels, especially the poles of poverty and wealth. Philip Taylor's (2004b) *Social Inequality in Vietnam* is a collection of essays by Vietnamese and international authors who consider challenges to the state and the state's responses in the 1990s and early 2000s. Focusing on regional disparities of development, poverty reduction, literacy, land conflicts, human capital and labour migration, the volume explores the inequalities that have emerged in rural collectives, ethnic communities and cities with increasing social differentiation in post-reform Vietnam. In contrast, Christina Schwenkel and Ann Marie Leshkowich's (2012b) collection of essays, 'Neoliberalism in Vietnam', comprises contributions from the US centring on neoliberal logics of globalization and market society in the late 2000s. The authors make sense of individualized strategies employed by wealthy urban dwellers in postsocialist Vietnam by focusing on a wide range of actual practices such as geomancy, anti-corruption, transnational adoption, IVF, HIV, beauty portraits, urban renewal, and money. Both collections deal with social practices that reveal social differentiation as an interaction of individual agents within structural constraints, although neither defines class-oriented status groups precisely.

Drawing on class categories that centre on income levels or differentiate based on occupation alone offer limited analytical power. Thomas Heberer (2003, p. 64) differentiates four strata within the middle class in postsocialist Asia (Vietnam and China) conceptualized not only on a basis of income or occupation but also including education, political power and social networks to differentiate between political-ideological socialized decision makers, traders and artisans, professional workers, and the new private entrepreneurship. Others have identified new status groups in Vietnam on the basis of social power, such as people in administrative power, people who control economic capital, and people with education, experience and employable skills (King, Nguyen and Nguyen 2008, p. 792). However, studies centring on the emergence of capitalism and entrepreneurs in Vietnam have rarely addressed values, attitudes, outlooks or other indicators of class culture beyond income, spending and consumption (e.g. Heberer 2003; Kim 2008; Leshkowich 2012; Thomsen 2011).

MIDDLE-CLASS CONSUMPTION IN POSTSOCIALIST VIETNAM

Consumption practices and consumer expectations mark out middle-class social identities and lifestyles across Southeast Asia (Chua 2000a). Consumption is also connected to emerging class identities in the postsocialist Asian states, but as Mark Liechty (2003, p. 67) stresses, it is difficult to distinguish between classes on the basis of commodity consumption. Victor King (2008, p. 85) suggests that middle-class culture in Vietnam is expressed through globalized consumerist lifestyling. Lisa Drummond (2012, p. 80) associates a 'recoiling' from the use of the term 'middle class' in Vietnam with the naturalization of the consumer-oriented practices of middle-class lifestyles as the 'urban normal'. Michael Hsiao (2010, p. 253) suggests that consumption is one of the crucial indicators for measuring China's middle class, while Jacqueline Elfick (2010, p. 8) identifies consumption as 'the single most important form of expressing social identity' in urban China.

Much attention has been focused on the consumption practices of Vietnam's new consumers. In *Consuming Urban Culture in Contemporary Vietnam*, Mandy Thomas and Lisa Drummond (2003, p. 3) explore the growing popularity of consumption as a leisure practice among Vietnam's emerging affluent youth. They explain that while few share the 'pleasures of purchasing', consumption has exerted an influence on many and, in doing so, it revealed new social divisions and hierarchies in post-reform urban Vietnam. Nguyen-vo Thu-huong (2004, p. 184) suggests that, within localized contexts of social stratification in Ho Chi Minh City, young working-class women do not simply engage in imitative consumption, but generate new ways of being through their consumption practices. Rylan Higgins (2008) aligns emerging consumption with young consumers whose practices break from traditions of the past. Notably, a number of studies exploring commodity consumption in urban Vietnam have done so through a gender-conscious lens (e.g. Earl 2004; Higgins 2008; Nguyen-vo 2004, 2006, 2008; Leshkowich 2006, 2012; Truitt 2008; Vann 2006).

Focusing on globalized youth cultures of consumption in Vietnam, as these studies have done, mirrors a cleavage proposed by Chua Beng Huat (2000a, pp. 13–14). He delineates the practices, attitudes and outlooks of the young and their elders in consumer cultures in new rich Asia, arguing that consumption is 'generational', divided not by a contrast between nationalism and globalization but by the stages of national development in the contrasting tastes of elders who grew up in a culture of thrift necessitated by economic conditions of underdevelopment and youth whose lifestyles are marked by body adornment, expensive leisure entertainment and foreign travel. While older people may be expected to align themselves with nationalistic and younger with globalized perspectives, it is somewhat simplistic to draw a line based on age without considering other compelling influences such as socialization, education, income and social networks. Pierre Bourdieu (1984) similarly divided consumption practices, but he highlighted a division within the dominant class that separated 'old' fractions, whose claims were conservative and based on national heritage and cultural tradition, from 'new' fractions, whose claims were aspirational and centred on education, youth and tastes associated with globalized preferences.[7]

Paying attention to globalized influences in middle-class culture risks overlooking influences stemming from national culture. For Mark Liechty (2003, p. 67), middle classes occupy the 'space between' the others and in this middling space consumption practices enable new consumers to mark out a 'shared project' of distinguishing themselves from consumer practices of the 'global' oriented national elite and the 'tradition' oriented lower classes. Liechty's middling space, like Bourdieu's class culture, is identified on the basis of actual practices not only age or location.

In Southeast Asia, middle class culture has been regarded to be an urban culture. For example, in *Reinvention of Distinction*, Bélanger, Drummond and Nguyen-Marshall (2012, p. 2) focus on the globalized aspects of consumer practices that mark urban Vietnamese middle-class lifestyles. In arguing that middle-class lifestyles are not only consumption-oriented but also urban, they write:

> It is in the city that the accoutrements of middle-class lifestyles can be obtained and shown off, where what is currently modern is displayed, a model to be learned and copied... [I]t is in the city that these attributes are debated and eventually adopted as markers of middle classness, as attesting to a familiarity with modernity and urbanity.

For them, the 'shared project' of the middle class centres on modern and global influences in urban space, overlooking tradition-oriented national culture. However, it is possible that location in social space may not be such an overwhelming determinant of social position. Hagen Koo (1978, pp. 300–1) points out that upward social mobility in the

---

7   In a study on 'new rich' Philippines, anthropologist Michael Pinches (1999a, pp. 35, 48 n. 43) draws on a contrast between the concepts of 'old rich' and 'new rich' to point out a fundamental difference between the analyses in Thorstein Veblen's (1994 [1899]) *The Theory of the Leisure Class* and Bourdieu's (1984) *Distinction*. Pinches views Bourdieu as dealing with a stable and conservative 'old rich' in twentieth century France, but Veblen as dealing with an aspirational 'new rich' in nineteenth-century America on the basis that the American 'old rich' at the time were located beyond the national culture in Western Europe. It is worth noting that Vietnam's pre-revolutionary 'old rich' are no longer based in Vietnam as they relocated to Western European and Pacific Asian nations, especially the US, France, Canada and Australia, where diaspora communities are characterized by disproportionate representation of educated, middle-class, Catholic, and ethnic Chinese (Viviani 1996, pp. 1–5). This absence of 'old rich' in Vietnam affects how we might think about the values, attitudes and outlooks that underpin the spending choices of the re-emerging urban middle classes.

developing world is contingent on access to resources and durable forms of capital. Rural dwellers with access to resources and capital may be more able to achieve a new social position than urban dwellers who lack resources and capital. A villager in the Mekong Delta who has direct contact to Vietnamese relatives living abroad (e.g. in Sydney or Lyon) may have limited contact with a metropolitan area in Vietnam but might possess the means to move up socially. Nevertheless, in Southeast Asia it is cities and mega-urban regions that most readily offer the conditions in which middle classes can flourish.

While consumption is an important aspect of middle-class social practice, my focus extends beyond consumption to explore a range of social practices in new middle-class women's lifeworlds. Like Victor King, I recognize that Vietnam's middle classes share features with their Southeast Asian neighbours, such as a diversity of attributes and a different path to development. In this regard, I argue that Vietnam's new middle classes are not simply 'latecomers'. Like Southeast Asia's new middle classes, they are diverse in origins and have experienced a qualitatively different path involving postcolonial development, post-war set back and post-reform re-emergence. There is not one model of class development, but general trends that can be identified as characteristic of middle classes across Southeast Asia. Certainly some aspects of the Vietnamese case are unique, but others seem to be shared. I argue that the wide-ranging influences of urbanization should be stressed in new middle-class formation. In considering the influences of rural–urban migration, the recognition of a singular field of interaction that operates in multi-dimensional families extending beyond urban Vietnam is important to understanding the lived experience of Vietnam's re-emerging middle-class culture. In this book, I aim to explore the lifeworlds of educated members of the new middle class to reveal how class culture is lived and understood in twenty-first century urban Vietnam. In doing so, I build on earlier research that explored aspects of class through practices of conspicuous consumption among entrepreneurs, labour migrants and other new status groups in urban Vietnam.

ANALYSING VIETNAM'S NEW MIDDLE CLASSES

In seeking ways to analyse the social practices of re-emerging middle classes and new configurations of social differentiation in urban

Vietnam, I am drawn to a neo-Weberian perspective and the sociology of Pierre Bourdieu. With modifications, Bourdieu's sociology provides a useful toolkit for capturing the complexities of social life in post-reform Vietnam because it acknowledges that cultural meanings coexist, compete and are unequally distributed. In particular, Bourdieu's field theory is valuable for analysing social inequality and the production of social distance. It has been used widely in anthropological analysis of post-reform Vietnam by a number of scholars whose research has focused on class or gender. Notably, *Reinvention of Distinction*, edited by Van-Marshall, Drummond and Bélanger (2012), draws on Bourdieu's field theory and his concept of 'hysteresis' to analyse the mismatch between habitus and field in various realms of a globalized middle-class consumer society in twentieth-century urban Vietnam. *Reinvention of Distinction* presumes an underlying coherence and homophily of taste profiles against which the 'exceedingly fragile and often fleeting' lifestyles of the urban Vietnamese case contrasts (Vann 2012, p. 158).

Anthropologists employing a Bourdieusian toolkit in analysis of post-reform Vietnam have often expressed concerns or found limitations in using Bourdieu's sociology without modification. Nguyen-vo Thu-huong's (2008) *Ironies of Freedom* explores neoliberal governance in Ho Chi Minh City's sex industry through a neo-Foucauldian perspective supplemented by an understanding of class as a social phenomenon drawn from Bourdieu's *Distinction*. Nir Avieli's (2012) *Rice Talks* explores central Vietnamese food cultures by drawing on Bourdieu's *Distinction* and its concepts of habitus, taste and social prestige to analyse local identity making through food cultures in the context of a globalized tourist destination. Beyond Vietnam's new consumers, Helle Rydstrøm's (2003) *Embodying Morality* explores the gender socialization of children in a rural northern commune by combining Judith Butler's (1990) perspective on the socialization of sexed bodies in patrilineal contexts with Bourdieu's field theory, particularly an understanding of habitus that is created through processes of embodiment which reflect both individual dispositions and the logic of social structures.

Others have extended the scope of Bourdieu's concepts beyond national culture to transnational fields. Ashley Carruthers' (2002) essay on national belonging among Ho Chi Minh City's returning expatriate Vietnamese centres on their struggles to achieve and maintain relatively higher social positionings analysed in terms of Bourdieu's cultural capital and its convertibility. Hung Cam Thai's (2008) *For Better or Worse* explores trans-Pacific marriages between educated Vietnamese women and working-class or unemployed Vietnamese-American men in terms of Bourdieu's field theory and the convertibility of social worth, measured as forms of capital across transnational fields. The approach that I outline below demonstrates that, like these examples, I draw on Bourdieu's field theory, albeit with important modifications to his concepts which I also apply beyond national culture.

i. Social change and indirect social exclusion

My first modification clarifies the concept of cultural capital to re-emphasize an original dimension of indirect social exclusion that addresses cultural change and social disorder. Bourdieu's model of social change, as presented in *Distinction* (1984), centres on cultural capital as the basis for individual and collective strategies employed to overcome social disadvantages and benefit from the differential exclusion of others. Bourdieu's earlier works defined cultural capital to explain the unequal scholastic achievement of children originating from different social classes (Bourdieu 1997; Bourdieu and Passeron 1979). In this early view, educational achievements are not an effect of natural aptitudes but are dependent on cultural capital previously invested by the family and on inherited social capital used to back it up (Bourdieu 1997, pp. 47–8). Cultural capital is divided into three states. Firstly, the *embodied* state is the form of long-lasting dispositions of the mind and body that are evident via inscription on the individual via, for example, regional pronunciation. This state is the most distinctive and clearly differentiated from all other forms and states of capital. Unlike money and property rights, embodied capital cannot be transmitted instantaneously but becomes, over time, an integral part of the person that can be acquired quite unconsciously and dies with its bearer (Bourdieu 1997, pp. 48–9).

Goods and qualifications are the focus of the second and third states. The *objectified* state encompasses the form of cultural goods which are the 'trace' or realization of distinction. In this state, cultural capital appears in material objects and is transmissible in materiality via legal ownership and not consumption (Bourdieu 1997, p. 50). The *institutionalized* state is a unique form of objectification of cultural capital in the form of academic qualifications that produces a relatively autonomous form of cultural capital. In this state, the academic qualification acts as a certificate of cultural competence that, through institutional recognition, makes it possible to compare qualification holders and even to exchange them by establishing conversion rates between cultural capital and economic capital based on guaranteed monetary values in a strict relationship between qualification, rank and remuneration (Bourdieu 1997, pp. 50–1, n. 10). It is important to understand the acquisition of cultural capital as a process linked to socialization, upbringing and education in a particularized context. Viewing cultural capital in these terms refers not to high culture but to the *highly valued cultural signals* of a particularized social context. Cultural capital, in this sense, may include locally valued tastes that would be regarded as 'low' or 'vulgar' in a different context (Lamont and Lareau 1988, p. 157 n. 5).[8] This modification to Bourdieu's sociology assumes an updated idea of cultural capital which is polysemic, dynamic and flexible.

Bourdieu's understanding of cultural capital evolved over the decades as he adapted and developed his perspective. Michèle Lamont and Annette Lareau (1988, pp. 158–9) track the evolution of Bourdieu's cultural capital from his earliest collaborative works to *Distinction* and propose a clarification to the later definition that re-emphasizes its original Weberian dimension of exclusion divided into four major forms, including direct exclusion and three forms of indirect exclusion. In *self-elimination*, individuals adjust their aspirations to match their perceived chances of success fitting in and exclude themselves when they are not at ease or familiar with specific cultural norms (Bourdieu 1974, p. 35). In *overselection*, individuals with less-valued cultural resources are selected equally and expected to perform equally with those who are culturally privileged, so that they invest more effort than others due to their cultural handicap but never quite 'pass' as equals (Bourdieu and Passeron 1979, p. 14). In *relegation*, individuals with less valued cultural resources end up in less desirable positions and they get less out of their educational investment. Their cultural disadvantage is manifested in early, ill-informed decisions, forced choice and lost time (Bourdieu and Passeron 1979, p. 14). For Bourdieu, because agents are unwilling or

---

8   Annick Prieur and Mike Savage (2011, pp. 568–9) note that the existence of hybrid cultural forms does not mark the erosion of cultural capital as it is no longer understood as centring only on 'high' or 'snobbish' culture. This view contrasts with the 'cultural omnivore' argument (Peterson 1992; Peterson and Kern 1996).

unable to invest the required time and resources to 'catch up', they do not have an appropriate starting position from which to achieve.

Bourdieu's model provides scope for recognizing an individual's agency so long as it is understood within structural constraints. As Bourdieu's social world is organized according to a logic of difference, where functioning social space is characterized by different lifestyles and status groups, social agents are distributed in the overall social space regardless of their gender. Toril Moi (1991, p. 1034) explains that Bourdieu does not provide a discrete 'gender habitus' as gender is part of the whole social field. Yet, feminists have not been deterred from talking about a discrete 'feminine habitus' in which all women share experiences as though they form a unified social group (e.g. Adkins 2004).

ii. Gender as a lived social relation

My second modification involves clarifying Bourdieu's concepts in relation to gender. The model proposed in Bourdieu's *Distinction* has been widely criticized as gender-blind. For example, Elizabeth Silva (2005, pp. 87–8) judges Bourdieu to have overlooked the social origins, trajectories, views and opinions of women. She usefully points out that Bourdieu did not develop his early ideas on gender further than those outlined in 'Family Spirit', although he did extend his schema beyond the family to other fields in *Masculine Domination* (cf. Bourdieu 1998b and 2001). In writing in the 1960s and 1970s, Bourdieu (like most academic feminists of the time) accepted that an actual and real biological difference between the sexes operated in similar ways in all societies to distinguish the male and the female. Bourdieu distinguishes between sex as biological and gender as an accomplishment achieved via the socialization process and expressed through dispositions.

Feminists tend to move beyond Bourdieu's perspective on gender. In a contribution to *Feminism After Bourdieu*, Lois McNay (2004, pp. 175, 185) argues for a recognition of gender as a lived social relation embedded in specific social, cultural, political and economic dimensions. McNay emphasizes the notion of agency in the reproduction of normative identities, through which forms of dominance do not exist passively but are recreated, defended and challenged by agents in practice. In this sense, agency connects identity and social structure, a nexus which allows for the impact of cultural relations upon daily life. McNay (2004, pp. 179–80) places more emphasis on agency but equally values the force of cultural relations, proposing that an idea of agency rethought around a non-reductive notion of experience may account for changes within gender norms over time. In doing so, McNay acknowledges the contrast with Butler's (1999) account of performative agency in which gender is understood primarily as a location within discursive structures. Moving beyond Bourdieu's perspective to view gender as a lived social relation goes a long way toward adequately understanding gender experience in a system of gender complementarity, such as that experienced in Vietnam (see Chapter 4).

iii. Beyond the homophily of a national culture

My third modification extends Bourdieu's concepts beyond national culture to cater to a singular field of interaction within multi-dimensional families where cultural homophily cannot be taken for granted between urban and rural, national and transnational contexts. As Elizabeth Silva (2005, p. 100) points out, contemporary families are fragmented and take many forms which potentially offer greater resources for enhancing cultural capital. This modification enables Bourdieu's concepts to be applied beyond its particularized, historical context to an increasingly globalized and increasingly digitized world, where legitimate culture is qualitatively different from the high culture of Bourdieu's French elites, where increasing numbers of people are choosing to migrate or are experiencing forced displacement, and where social positions – experienced through gender, class and race – are understood in terms of negotiation, flexibility and hybridity.

Revitalizing Bourdieu's model of social change provides a solution to concerns that anthropologists working on social change in Vietnam express. In Bourdieu's social world, interactions between institutions and individuals are used to explain processes of social change. Bourdieu's (1990a, p. 130) *In Other Words* explains that in his social world,

> there will be different or even antagonistic points of view, since points of view depend on the point from which they are taken, since the vision that every agent has of space depends on his or her position in that space... No doubt agents do have an active apprehension of the world. No doubt they do construct their vision of the world. But this construction is carried out under structural constraints.

Dealing with change as a natural part of a functioning social world as Bourdieu does, rather than a disruption to (or end of) that world, enables a more nuanced and culturally contextualized understanding of the continuities and subtleties within a transition society (Szemere 2000, p. 160).

Such a model applied to a transition society, such as post-reform Vietnam, acknowledges that the state does not necessarily have control over individual choices. Eyal, Szelenyi and Townsley (1998, pp. 38–9) regard the outcomes of socialist transition in Central Europe as demonstrating how social actors use 'old' ideas, behaviours and social logics to adapt to 'new' conditions in post-reform society. Their emphasis on continuities with past conditions is important to provide sustained analytical attention to the dynamics of the interactions between agents and social structures, an emphasis that Eyal, Szelenyi and Townsley (1998, pp. 40–1) considered to have been neglected in analyses of post-communism. It is clear that they disagree with a path-dependency model where if the 'right' institutions are implemented, the 'appropriate' behaviours will inevitably emerge. Instead, they argue that the habitus links individual actors to social-structural determinants in an interactive process 'through which *both are likely to be altered*' (Eyal, Szelenyi and Townsley 1998, p. 44, original emphasis).

Continuities between old and new social relations are not completely lost or eradicated as societies reform. In postsocialist societies many features of the socialist past persist. Anthropologist Igor Barsegian (2000, p. 121) points out that these may include an ideologized social life and life-cycle; pervasive state intervention in all spheres of social and private life; extremely ideologized perceptions of 'us' and 'others'; and a society extremely dependent on the state. Continuities between old and new social relations also persist. Anthropologist Carol Nagengast (1991, p. 1, original emphasis) explains that the reinstitution of capitalism in post-reform Poland exposed the continuities between 'earlier, class-based *social* relations that masqueraded as *socialist* relations for four and a half decades'. Scholars of Vietnam have reiterated this theme. Anthropologist Ashley Pettus (2003, p. 12) observes that, as the Vietnamese state liberalized the economy within the framework of Communist Party rule, political priorities of market reform focused on continuity, rather than conflict, with the socialist past. Bélanger, Drummond and Nguyen-Marshall (2012, p. 1) go further in identifying that some continuities are evident in class experience from the French colonial period to the postcolonial and post-reform eras. Martin Gainsborough (2010) also stresses continuities that have been retained in arguing that the dramatic social change assumed to have been generated by reform is over-stated. Like them, I acknowledge continuities with the past in urban Vietnam. In doing so, I adopt this perspective not to consider political discontinuities, but to explore social and cultural continuities in Vietnamese urban middle-class life.

Capitalist Southeast Asia, as anthropologist Michael Pinches (1999a, p. 36) observes, offers a range of more complex and variable models than Bourdieu's France. Postsocialist Asia presents more complex and complicated cases than their capitalist neighbours. Continuities with past socialism add a layer of complexity to the re-emergence of middle classes in urban Vietnam and China. In the contemporary Chinese state, as anthropologist Zhang Li (2001, p. 217 n. 2) reiterates, the single-party system remains in power and the state apparatus continues to expand. Some continuities with past socialism are maintained after reform with privatization officially banned, but new configurations of the post-reform era enable 'an ensemble of techniques that free up not only entrepreneurialism but also powers of the self' (Ong and Zhang 2008, p. 2). Similarly, in the contemporary Vietnamese state, as anthropologist Philip Taylor (2004a, p. 307 n. 1) emphasizes, a modified socialist ideology and nominally socialist political, economic and social structures are retained, without an institutional break from the socialist past. Continuities with past political and social order merged with new conditions post-reform Vietnam have been described as a hybridization (Bélanger, Drummond and Nguyen-Marshall 2012, pp. 5–6; King 2008, pp. 85–6).

Issues of hybridization have been addressed in European studies in terms of social change and cultural continuity to find that 'dissonant' tastes have become more widespread than Bourdieu predicted and that 'escaping' and 'challenging' the habitus are strategies for creating imagined identities among migrants (e.g. Bennett 2007; Friedmann 2002). This approach updates Bourdieu's field theory to regard dissonance not as a mismatch between habitus and field but as new conditions of taste and cultural literacy that operate for all social agents across the field. In this sense, my approach differs from the approach centred on the concept of 'hysteresis', a mismatch between habitus and field, employed by Bélanger, Drummond and Nguyen-Marshall (2012, p. 10) in their collection analysing urban Vietnam's new consumers. In contrast, my research moves beyond consumption to explore a range of practices in the lifeworlds of young educated new middle-class women in Ho Chi Minh City.

RESEARCHING HO CHI MINH CITY'S NEW MIDDLE-CLASS WOMEN:
ENTERING THE FIELD

Entering the field meant entering the lifeworlds of young educated migrant women in Ho Chi Minh City and living among them. Before I arrived in Ho Chi Minh City to undertake a major period of ethnographic fieldwork in late 2000, I was given advice on living in Saigon / Ho Chi Minh City by Vietnamese in Australia. They were expatriate Vietnamese, former members of the Saigonese middle classes. Many had been resident in Melbourne for as long as twenty years, since they had fled Vietnam after the demise of the Republic of Vietnam in 1975. In Melbourne, through getting to know a number of southern families over several years, I had been exposed to Vietnamese social networks, patterns of loyalty and the emphasis on education that characterizes Asia's new middle classes. The advice they offered reflected their own middle-class backgrounds and the daily life they experienced in Saigon-of-the-past. Indicating the significance of the 'second economy' for speedy bureaucratic action in postcolonial and post-war Saigon, they advised me that I would benefit by paying bribes every step of the way. Indicating an underlying curiosity about outsiders and outside places, they advised me that if I left the city, I would be kidnapped by mountain savages and held for ransom, or else snatched by unsophisticated police hungry for English lessons. If I caused any trouble, by carrying foreign-language books, films or other information, I would be deported. If I carried cash, gold, or other valuables, I would be robbed. If I survived these challenges, then I might be the victim of sexual harassment. To avoid these potential menaces, they advised, I should never go out alone, socialize with strangers, or find myself in unfamiliar places. Needless-to-say, I did not encounter such challenging circumstances in Ho Chi Minh City, although I remained mindful that most of the advice warned of dire consequences for those away from family and home. This advice also reflected gendered and classed assumptions about a socially differentiated cultural world that included the perceived role of women as dependent, naïve and vulnerable and their perceived positions as middle classes being economically powerful but, as owners of capital and resources, also vulnerable to financial ruin or exploitation.

Theirs was not the only advice I received. After I arrived in Vietnam, I was given a lot of advice on how best to conduct my research. Foremost was a concern for the accuracy of my representations of contemporary Vietnam to outsiders. One of the most useful observations came, not from academics, but from my Saigonese neighbours, who expressed their concern about the validity of the information I had gathered from books and research reports about urban Vietnamese culture and society. They suggested that a better strategy than going to a library or consulting professors would be to ask questions and have discussions with them and other local people. I understood this as recognition of the value of anthropological practice in revealing the contemporary social world as they experienced it in twenty-first century Ho Chi Minh City.

In pursuing my research, the key methodology I utilized was participant observation. Prior to the 1990s, as David Marr (1997, p. 290) and Hy Van Luong (2006) report, it was virtually impossible for foreign researchers, such as myself, in Vietnam to employ participant observation and travelling fieldwork techniques. Vietnamese state co-operation in the social sciences at that time meant that the research methodologies of foreign ethnographers were strictly monitored and mediated by state-trained and state-employed Vietnamese academic staff as well as other authorities. Foreign anthropologists and ethnographers working in Vietnam throughout the 1990s have reflected on the methodological limitations of state research collaboration, providing accounts of conducting fieldwork interviews with an entourage of accompanying state officials, who were sometimes bored to sleep or eventually distracted by other responsibilities (e.g. Gammeltoft 1999; Hardy 2004; Higgs 2003; Salemink 2003). During fieldwork, I had anticipated a certain degree of official co-operation any foreign researcher could expect. But the stories I heard and read about left me surprised with the ease with which my research eventually progressed.

Exploring feminized lifeworlds during fieldwork was advantageous to the research process. The topic, I believe, made access easier. Like Nir Avieli (2005a, p. 292 n. 8), who suggests that the feminized topic of culinary practices gave him greater access within the field, my topic – young educated women's daily lives in Ho Chi Minh City – was also regarded by most Vietnamese to be not threatening or controversial and I also experienced a widened access within the field. However, my fieldwork was not entirely beyond official scrutiny. Like Annette Kim (2008, pp. 2–3), I benefitted from living locally during my fieldwork, although my movements were monitored by a local policeman in the inner-city laneway where I lived on my first fieldtrip. This monitoring was not covert and may have helped my integration into the close-knit laneway as the residents and their visiting overseas relatives had experienced similar attention (see Chapter 3).

Taking a feminist approach to fieldwork also offered advantages to me as a female researcher. Feminist anthropologists emphasize unequal hierarchies in establishing and maintaining research relationships. Intersubjectivity in research relationships is described in varying terms, such as strategic intervention, negotiation, reciprocity, and idiomatic kin ties. Anthropologists Akhil Gupta and James Ferguson (1997, pp. 38–9) point out that the research area is less a 'field' for the collection of data than it is a site for 'strategic intervention', where knowledge is not 'shared' with those who lack it, but is forged through links between 'different' knowledges. Ethnographic knowledge, in this sense, is 'a process of communication', rather than purely 'a product formed and finished by the participant-observer' (Mills 1999, p. 23). This form of intersubjectivity in research relationships is more closely engaged with everyday social relations.

For feminists, the ability to create 'bonds of solidarity' with informants in cross-cultural research ultimately rests on social inequalities that benefit the researcher, rather than the researched, in unequal hierarchies and in unequal exchanges, where gender, class, status, and ethnic differences are more than the stuff through which culture operates as they are central sources of power inequalities (Wolf 1996, pp. 11–12). Forming bonds of empathy in Vietnamese social relations are crucial and extend beyond kinship to underpin many social networks. Typical bonds include year of birth, rank in the family, place of birth, education level, parent's occupation, and criteria determining social compatibility, such as class background, religion and ethnicity (Phạm Văn Bích 1999). Bonds of empathy resemble East Asian 'particularistic ties', formalized non-kin ties formed between people from the same village, same workplace, or same school class (Jacobs 1979). In Vietnam, non-kin who share comparable social experience are viewed as possessing 'natural' bonds. Such bonds may consolidate research relationships across cultures, as foreign anthropologists working in Vietnam have discovered.

Shared experience can generate bonds between foreign anthropologists hoping to build intersubjective research relationships with informants in the field. Tine Gammeltoft (1999, pp. 46–7) reports that throughout her fieldwork in northern Vietnam her three closest friends were women born in the same year as herself, who thus possessed the assumed bonds that tied their lives together. Yet, for a cultural outsider, overcoming social differences between the researcher and the researched may never be fully possible. Mary Beth Mills (1999, pp. 24–5) reports on the distance assumed by her status 'as a white, well-educated, presumably wealthy foreigner' researching in Thailand. Her status created social, cultural and emotional distance between herself and the community that was expressed when she was addressed as 'professor' or by the same title given to community development workers and other outside 'experts'. While Mills remained an outsider, she was able to develop bonds of empathy with her informants through shared life experiences. Like her, they were young, unmarried and had experienced migration to the city, where they had lived alone, far from home, surviving language difficulties and bouts of homesickness, as well as dealing with the concern their parents felt through their absences. In my fieldwork, I was to discover that in addition to sharing a birth year or the same rank in the family, sharing comparable life experiences – rural-to-urban migration, university graduation, or having worked in similar positions at comparable organizations – could also be a basis for forming bonds of empathy, albeit less secure and enduring than kin relations or directly shared experiences that had endured since childhood. Establishing firm bonds of empathy was what enabled me to enter and share in the lifeworlds of new middle-class women in Ho Chi Minh City.

A PERSON-CENTRED APPROACH TO RESEARCHING
CLASS AND GENDER IN HO CHI MINH CITY

In the field I quickly discovered that the daily lives of young educated women in Ho Chi Minh City were characterized by contradictions and multiple subjectivities and they were highly mobile, frequently travelling not only across the city but beyond its limits as well. The question of how to best collect research data arose: a person-centred approach became a logical choice for my project. The classic approach of Robert LeVine (1982, p. 293) contrasts standard ethnography, being 'a cultural description analogous to a map or aerial photograph of a community', with a person-centred approach that reveals 'what it is like to live there' and identifies 'what features are salient to its inhabitants'. Douglas Hollan (2001, p. 51, original emphasis) builds on this to explain that person-centred ethnographers aim to ask: 'what do people *say* about their subjective experience…; what do people *do* that enacts or reveals behaviourally their subjective experience…; and how do people *embody* their subjective experience'. For Robert Desjarlais (2003, p. 4) the ultimate contribution of a person-centred approach is its sharpening of an understanding of the relation between culture and human subjectivities. He explains:

> You cannot readily tap into the 'lived experience' of cultural subjects, be they in Boston or Calcutta. You can only talk with and live among them…. As I see it, the phenomenal and the discursive, life as lived and life as talked about, are like the intertwining strands of a braided rope, each complexly involved in the other, in time. The [person-centred] work, accordingly… attends both to the specifics of the lives in question – she did this, he felt that – and to the flux of cultural, personal, and interpersonal forces that weighed heavily into the dialogic 'telling' of those lives (Desjarlais 2003, p. 6).

In this project, my fieldwork practice centred on the world of the informants and revealing the complexities of actual living, what was salient to them, what it was like to *live there* and to live through change. To explore re-emerging middle-class culture, I followed the lead of my informants to create a snapshot, rather than an aerial map, of Ho Chi Minh City's new middle classes. This snapshot took the form of a plot, story, or account illustrated by individual cultural portraits. Bernard Lahire (2008, p. 174) points out that in order to understand heterogeneous socializing influences in cultural terms, it is necessary to explore its different dimensions within a social grouping (family, couple, school, professional group) through detailed analysis of 'individual cultural portraits'. George Marcus (1995, p. 109) describes this approach as a 'mode' of multi-sited fieldwork, which enables the researcher to stay within the world of an individual, or individuals, as the subject's practice leads the researcher to scattered locations.[9] Focusing on a snapshot of middle-class culture through the collection of individual cultural portraits connects the theoretical toolkit that I employ with the methodological approach that I pursued.

Following my informants necessarily took me far beyond the city laneways where they lived. Building on Marcus' work, James Clifford (1997, p. 190) challenges anthropologists' conceptualization of sited fieldwork and promotes a metaphor of travelling as a strategy for de-centring conventional notions of the field and staying within the lives of informants without compromising the depth of intensive study. Ghassan Hage (2005, p. 466) also regards fieldwork as travelling rather than multi-sited, criticizing early anthropologists for focusing on bounded location without recognizing mobility and flow between local and international connections. Like other 'travelling' anthropologists in Vietnam aiming to produce a deep interpretation (e.g. Hardy 2004; Kim 2008; Taylor 2004a; Thai 2008), I negotiated a balance between the breadth of contact provided through travelling with the depth of contact provided by dwelling. In this respect, my approach differs from previous anthropological studies that have investigated Vietnam's 'new consumers' – several of which have been *located* in garment factories and cloth markets (e.g. Leshkowich 2000, 2006, 2011; Nguyen-vo 2004; Pettus 2003) – as I took a person-centred approach in following the story of educated urban migrant women, wherever they led.

Through participant observation I gained rich access to contemporary experience, particularly the range of mobilities within women's lives, as well as the contradictions that they faced between their families' expectations and desires and their own. As it turned out, the immersion enabled by the research design provided me with a far greater depth of

---

9   More precisely, Marcus outlines six different modes of multi-sited ethnography. His fourth mode is the most relevant to my project. As a person-centred approach, *Follow the Plot, Story or Allegory* initially requires the identification of a research plot or story and its testing against the reality of ethnographic investigation. The narratives of this mode are a rich source of connections, associations and suggested relationships which shape multi-sited objects of research because processes of remembering and forgetting result in the kinds of plots that threaten to reconfigure the narratives of states and institutions. The lifeworlds of Saigon / Ho Chi Minh City's new middle classes are, in general, not represented in national narratives in Vietnam.

access and of knowledge than I had imagined when originally thinking of a settled fieldwork environment. Participation in highly mobile
women's lives assisted me in conceptualizing with greater clarity, via a
shared experience, how they manage change and negotiate contradictions in daily life.

During fieldwork in Ho Chi Minh City, women in the neighbourhood
where I lived taught me a valuable lesson when they recommended that
I stop reading books to gain background knowledge of urban Vietnam.
In doing so, they acknowledged that culture as they lived it was a legitimate Vietnamese culture, even though it reflected regional variation and
differed from national narratives. Their advice was a significant methodological breakthrough in two ways. Firstly, in recommending that I
talk to them rather than read, the neighbourhood women acknowledged
themselves as 'carriers of culture' (Yuval-Davis and Anthias 1989).
Vietnamese women have been observed as reluctant to volunteer themselves as experts. In separate studies, anthropologists Alexander Soucy
and Ashley Pettus each identify that Vietnamese women do not wield a
comparable authority to male experts, even concerning women's issues
and female behaviour. In an ethnographic study on female religious
practices in contemporary Hanoi, Soucy (2000, p. 185) explains that he
was confronted by a belief, widely held by men and women, that female
key informants 'lack the cultural capital needed to speak authoritatively'.
In an ethnography of urban femininity, also in post-reform Hanoi,
Pettus (2003, p. 20) agrees, citing an experience during her fieldwork
where female Vietnamese research officials selected 'appropriate' female
interview subjects to overcome perceived difficulties caused because
in their view 'many women "didn't understand problems clearly," "were
confused" and "lacked education"'. These examples highlight that some
women in Vietnam seem to share an encultured belief that they should
not act as authorities or experts, especially concerning experiences outside the home. Such beliefs reflect a naturalized femininity which state
reports draw on in blaming women's inherently feminine character for
their lack of participation in decision-making and leadership positions
(Truong 2008, p. 18).

Secondly, the neighbourhood women demonstrated an understanding of the value of qualitative research methods and participant observation – unpopular among Vietnamese state methodologies – as techniques

that drew attention to emic points of view and which acknowledged the 'gap' between public and private commentary. Disruptures between public and private commentary on major social issues is characteristic of postsocialist and transitional contexts, such as Vietnam. In reflections on fieldwork in Soviet and post-communist Armenia, anthropologist Igor Barsegian (2000, pp. 126–7) observes that in the early 1980s Armenians described their daily lives in terms of steady improvement, a position that was in line with state commentary. However, privately, they complained about food shortages, corruption and political tensions. Similarly, the postsocialist era saw Armenians complain in public in line with a new state discourse centred on suffering. But, in private, they confessed to a range of strategies which helped them to cope. Barsegian views this gap between public performance and private behaviour as an important dimension of the postsocialist field that stems from a continuation of the socialist past. It creates a problem of dissonance that demands new interpretive strategies and methodologies to see behind the public 'curtain'. But without new strategies, Barsegian predicts that western social scientists will be particularly vulnerable to remaining on the surface of public performances and, for example, seeking explanations for 'starving Armenians'.

The strengths of a person-centred approach rest with its focus on lived experience and on personal life in the intimate surroundings of family and home, which it values over a broader frame loyal to the simple and uncontested details evident in an aerial photograph of a community. Thus, this book does not aim to present a definitive portrait of Vietnam's middle classes, nor of broad geopolitical change in contemporary Vietnam. Rather, it aims to explore gendered experience of becoming new middle class in the context of a developing mega-urban region from the points of view of a group of educated urban migrant women living in the socially differentiated context of Ho Chi Minh City.

RESEARCH DESIGN

The project design required that I live among and socialize with new middle-class women in Vietnam's urban Southeast, as well as accompany them on visits to their families and friends in the city and beyond. The fieldwork was conducted in multiple visits starting with a year-long stay from October 2000 until September 2001 with six additional trips of one to six months carried out between 2004 and 2012.

During fieldwork, I established and maintained close research rela-tionships with 37 individuals who were members of a range of social institutions including seven extended family groups, one university, one professional workplace, and three social groups that met weekly. Many of the interactions involved group discussion, or conversations with more than one person present. This set of central research relation-ships took me to various locations in Ho Chi Minh City, most of which were private homes and places of recreation, and away from Vietnam's Southeast to provincial cities as well as villages. I maintained regular contact with members of their families and broader social networks, and also met others involved in social groups who were more distantly related or less frequently contacted.

In addition to the central research relationships, I kept in regular con-tact with people (mostly women) in the neighbourhood near the houses where I stayed in laneways of the inner city and newly urbanized areas of the suburban fringe. Living next door, I had opportunities to keep in touch with their families, friends and colleagues. This contact enabled me to more clearly contextualize specific data within a broader social milieu. In some cases interaction between the informants and those in the neighbourhood provided valuable insights into my lines of inquiry as well as my position as a cultural outsider. Additionally, I learned a great deal from significant in-depth meetings, most often with small groups at various social gatherings. If not regular such meetings were at least numerous and provided opportunities to confirm or unsettle pre-vious findings. Outside these interactions and meetings, on each of my fieldwork trips I talked with hundreds of people of both genders, all age groups and varying social backgrounds. The majority lived in Ho Chi Minh City or had direct connections to people in the city. Most were past or recent migrants to Vietnam's Southeast and few, such as Diễm, described themselves as '100 per cent Saigonese', an increasingly rare identity that involves having no kin roots outside the city.

ABOUT THIS BOOK

This book provides a snapshot of what it is like to live in middle-class Ho Chi Minh City, a city of migrants. Its eight chapters offer the first ethnography of Vietnam's new middle classes through a focus on the lifeworlds of young educated professional women, such as Diễm. She was the eldest daughter in a Saigonese family. She had graduated from university in Ho Chi Minh City and started working in a foreign company. Like her, Liên, Cúc, Hạnh, and Tuyết had each graduated from Ho Chi Minh City universities and established professional careers. Unlike Diễm, these young women were first-generation rural–urban migrants. Their families had sent them to the city for education and future employment. Thu was also an urban migrant but had graduated from university prior to arriving in Ho Chi Minh City where she worked in a foreign company (see Chapter 3). They were part of a feminization of migration in Vietnam that centred on the mega-urban Southeast. In the course of the research, these women and other informants changed jobs, usually within the non-state sector, and moved house, often from the inner city to the suburban fringe. Some married and raised families, while others travelled abroad for study, vacation or marriage. As I explore in the following chapters, their circumstances facilitated their upward social mobility and they improved their material standards of living and developed through a long period of socialization the lifestyles influenced by globalized and other highly valued cultural influences that mark middle-class culture. Importantly, they were members of multi-dimensional families, in which their own social positions came to outrank those of their elders. Social mobility did not restrict their connections to kin and they maintained social and economic relationships with their natal homes even after marriage.

Their experiences as new middle-class women mirror many aspects of middle-class life in the postcolonial past. Autobiographies and literary memoirs of middle-class Vietnamese women provide a snapshot of urban middle-class life in postcolonial Saigon. In Chapter 2, I explore published self-writing to establish a foundation for the contemporary ethnography and to identify continuities and disjunctures between the past and post-reform society. In understanding middle-class experience in twentieth-century Vietnam, this chapter demonstrates how social actors in Saigon / Ho Chi Minh City might use 'old' ideas, behaviours and social logics to adapt to 'new' conditions (Eyal, Szelenyi and Townsley 1998, pp. 38–9). The discussion traces a thematic history of education, career, embodied femininity, comforts of middle-class life, popular entertainment and attitudes to outsiders in postcolonial Saigon as they are expressed in the autobiographical sources. Identifying a history of

Vietnamese urban middle-class life in this chapter is important because, although the political and economic contexts are qualitatively different, I argue that there remains relatively little change in many aspects of social practice among new middle classes whose social positions are achieved and maintained through relying on cultural capital associated with education credentials, professional employment and embodied practices and attributes which retain an enduring value.

While the contexts of wartime postcolonial Saigon and post-reform Ho Chi Minh City are readily differentiated, comparisons can be drawn in the use of urban space by newly arrived migrants. Chapter 3 introduces the contemporary fieldwork context and provides vignettes about selected informants around whose practice the ethnographic themes of the following chapters take shape. In introducing the ethnography, this chapter establishes the social context of new middle-class experiences in inner-city and suburban fringe neighbourhoods of contemporary Ho Chi Minh City. I introduce urban residents (under pseudonyms) including a neighbourhood shopkeeper Xuân – a woman from an educated urban migrant family – and other residents of an inner-city laneway where I stayed and conducted part of the research. I also introduce five informants: Liên, Cúc and her sister Hạnh, Thu and Tuyết. These young women are educated urban migrants who choose to remain in Ho Chi Minh City after graduation to establish a professional career. Their brief biographies enable me to highlight that their experiences and choices affect not only their own lives, but also others in their families. The purpose of these narratives is to provide a snapshot of life as lived across the urban Southeast. It builds on Chapter 2 to demonstrate a range of similarities between twenty-first century urban middle-class life and life as it was for middle classes in postcolonial Saigon in terms of their relative standards of living and lifestyles.

Across Southeast Asia, education credentials and a salaried profession provide a stepping stone to a better standard of living. Chapter 4 explores the relationship between professional career and social mobility among educated urban migrant women in post-reform Ho Chi Minh City. It examines lifestyles surrounding non-state workplaces in terms of educated women's aspirations, achievements and status production. I consider how, with certain conditions, femininity can operate as effective cultural capital to better one's own position and enhance one's family's status for women as well as men. To illuminate this process, the discussion begins with a continued focus on the experiences and choices of Cúc and Hạnh, before exploring the practices of other educated young women who work in professional non-state sector positions, including their sister Thảo, young graduates Tuyết and Diễm, and a manager Minh (male). The narratives of these urban professionals reflect not only the unstable characteristic of urban professional work, but also that a relatively better social position stemming from education and other transformable cultural capital has an enduring value despite social change. Through their experiences I explore how competition in the job market and the differential valuation of qualifications increases the minimum standards for entry and value of cultural competencies gained through direct experience.

Leisure and consumption are important realms of practice in middle-class culture. Chapters 5 and 6 deal with new middle-class lifestyling and its influences on individuals and other members in their multi-dimensional families. Chapter 5 focuses on the leisure practices of educated young women through recreational food practices which have been part of middle-class lifestyles in Saigon / Ho Chi Minh City and which remain widely popular across the urban community. Importantly, such practices are oriented not only to globalized but also localized cultural signals from various regions of Vietnam. It considers the specific examples of Liên, a migrant from the Mekong Delta; Tuyết and Nghĩa (male), young graduates from the rural southeast and centre of Vietnam; and Thu, a young professional from Central Vietnam. The analysis demonstrates that women's leisure options have widened after reform and urban leisure has become increasingly diversified with influences from regionalized Vietnamese cultures as well as a globalized culture. Fusion of popular leisure practices with exclusive spaces also helps distinguish elite and aspirational people from the rest. This chapter demonstrates that a new aesthetic language employed by socially mobile urbanites draws on diverse processes of social exclusion and belonging which challenge social convention to produce or mitigate social distance for members of an emerging status group whose realm of practice is located between localized and globalized influences.

Urban leisure practices centre on individualized social positionings; however, new middle classes not only focus on their own futures but also foster the material and cultural horizons of others within their natal families. Chapter 6 explores the relationships between first-generation urban migrants who have pursued education and professions in the city and other members of their families who remain in rural areas. Spatial distance can facilitate social mobility and the absence of a family member can consolidate claims on relatively higher social status in multi-dimensional families. They are characterized by a 'singular field of interaction' (Lee and Piper 2003, p. 126) that operates between members with different levels of education and income across diverse locations. The intergenerational transmission of dispositions flows between family members, not simply trickling down from one generation to the next. The discussion explores how consumption practices and the transmission of knowledge and experiences shape the future prospects not only of educated urban migrant women, including Cúc, Liên, Thu and Tuyết, but also members of their natal families. This chapter suggests the roles of urbanized daughters in the natal family in Vietnam's Southeast are changing as new middle-class women question their earlier subordination and explore new configurations of gender status that they achieve through remittances of cash, assets and knowledge. They can become agents of change as their influences across their natal families enable willing family members to experience differential benefits of social mobility.

Changing family values are reflected in the choices new middle-class women in Vietnam's Southeast make about marriage and family life. Chapter 7 deals with these choices which are made to establish and maintain relatively higher social positions but which may create anxiety and attract a degree of social stigma associated with women who remain unmarried and childless, or at least delay marriage and childbearing. The discussion considers how the symbolic privileges of cultural capital among educated urban migrant women are so effective that they displace the differentially valued privileges of emotional capital associated with conventional maternal roles in reconfigurations of gendered expectations. To illuminate this process, the discussion returns to the experiences and choices of educated professionals Liên, Hạnh and Cúc, and introduces brief biographies of Cúc's village school classmates Huy (male), Huệ, Mỹ Trân, Tấm and Thiệu (male), each of whom has experienced single life and/or marriage differently. Extending this exploration of marriage, the discussion introduces Cúc's adult niece Vân, Minh's sister Hương, the shopkeeper Xuân's sisters Chi and Yến, and Diễm to explore solutions to stigmatized social positions experienced by women who do not conform to gender norms. The diverse range of experiences represented in this chapter suggests that urbanized daughters invest considerable resources in creating opportunities to maintain newly acquired social, economic and gender status and they do not exclude the possibility of leaving Vietnam to do so. Transnational marriage, for some, can offer a unique solution enabling them to evade cultural expectations that oblige their subordination to oppressive gender norms.

Finally, Chapter 8 offers conclusions and comparisons of Vietnam's new middle classes with new middle classes in mega-urban Southeast Asia. It provides a snapshot of Ho Chi Minh City's new middle classes based on the experiences that I explored in the lifeworlds of educated urban migrant women. Their experiences are contrasted with those of urban middle-class women in postcolonial Saigon, as reported in the autobiographies explored in Chapter 2. The snapshot of Ho Chi Minh City's new middle classes is analysed with respect to examples from across Pacific Asia to investigate to what extent the case of Vietnam is a latecomer and how significant gender as a lived social relation can be in class formation

CHAPTER TWO

Urban middle classes in postcolonial Saigon

*A*s I began to move within the lives and worlds of young women in Ho Chi Minh City in the early twenty-first century, it occurred to me that many of their attitudes and experiences were not entirely new to Vietnam. I began to wonder how they could be drawing on memories or on images and symbolism of earlier decades and what similarities there were between their experiences and the past. Certainly, these questions alerted me to the relevance of historical context to an ethnography of social change. In this chapter I explore middle-class culture in urban Vietnam through the experiences of middle-class migrant women in Saigon during the postcolonial period (1955–1975), a period of intense urbanization caused by two waves of wartime mass migration to the southern capital.

In the two decades following the end of French colonialism in 1954, many girls and young women from the North, the Centre and the Mekong Delta relocated with their families to Saigon, leaving behind their friends, their schools and their ancestral homes. Some of those who relocated have reflected on their experiences of middle-class girlhood and womanhood in Saigon during this time in their self-writing, the autobiographies and literary memoirs that I draw on in this chapter to explore middle-class life in Vietnam's postcolonial past. While ethnographic records of encounters with Saigon / Ho Chi Minh City are few, the sources that I have collected are autobiographical accounts centred on migration to postcolonial Saigon which detail not only encounters with the cosmopolitan city, but also the resulting changes to the authors' attitudes and prospects. It is the authors' descriptions of their daily lives as they come of age that I find most valuable in providing insights into Saigonese middle-class culture.

These accounts detail the emphasis that middle-class families placed on education for both sons and daughters, as well as the opportunities for social mobility provided by professional and urban workplaces. In descriptions of daily life, they shed light on a developing urban leisure culture that offers new types of entertainment, recreation and social contact. These accounts draw attention to changing family roles for women and the consequences of breaking from social convention, while emphasizing the importance of belonging to a good or ideal family.

In this chapter, I introduce Vietnamese women's self-writing and their rich recollections of experiences which reveal a snapshot of the middle-class social world of postcolonial Saigon but, in line with a person-centred approach, they do not provide an overall picture – or aerial map – of postcolonial Saigonese society. This snapshot provides a meaningful context for comparison with the ethnography of Ho Chi Minh City's new middle classes that follows. It offers a foregrounding for continuities and discontinuities that characterize an alternative narrative of twentieth-century urban Vietnamese life.

A DESIRE TO PRESENT THE SELF: VIETNAMESE WOMEN'S SELF-WRITING AS SOURCES

The set of autobiographical sources that I draw on comprises 11 autobiographies and one biography of middle-class women living in Saigon between the late 1950s and early 1980s. Most of the subjects (introduced below) migrated to Saigon where they were educated or were working before 1975. Political events caused almost all to subsequently leave Vietnam, most as refugees. The autobiographies are relatively recent and were, with two exceptions, written after 1975. Considering that there is a general absence of middle-class Vietnamese women's self-writing in Vietnamese, it is necessary to question what motivates these middle-class women to record their autobiographies.[1] Overall it is generally unstated exactly what motivates the authors of the autobiographies to write. Only one author is explicit in her motivations, stating

---

1   While middle-class women's autobiographies are not well represented in twentieth-century Vietnamese literature, women in Vietnam did engage in literary activity. Historian David Marr (2000, p. 787) reports that a minority of Vietnamese women (who must have been literate, likely educated, urban, and free from family or labour market burdens) had been writing fiction and non-fiction in the 1920s and were influential in experiments in language at that time.

that her book was 'written with passion in the early morning hours and late night, and at the time it was written [after she arrived in the US] it served as a lifeline not only to the past, but to a hoped-for happier future' (Nguyễn Thị Thu-Lâm 1989, p. vii).[2] Her words suggest that for Vietnamese transnational migrants, particularly refugees, the conservation of the former social world in diaries and memoirs may have helped to minimize the sense of loss and re-establish a sense of belonging. Historian Nathalie Huynh Chau Nguyen (2001) views Francophone Vietnamese women's autobiographical novels as 'trauma narratives' that 'heal the loss' of their social world, a world that is virtually invisible in official Vietnamese history. Nguyen's interpretation of this motivation to record social experience in biography and autobiography represents, in Bourdieu's (1993a, p. 74) terms, an interest in conserving an agent's social world.

With political realignment after regime change, it is not necessarily possible to conserve narratives of the past within Vietnam. As historian Patricia Pelley (2002) observes, in the past Vietnamese social history has been rewritten in line with the new ideological perspectives of the new regime. Any positive aspects of Saigonese middle-class society were omitted from revised national history after 1975. Anthropologist Ashley Pettus (2003, pp. 198–9) briefly discusses the ideological demonization of the southern capital in the national post-reunification mass media targetting women. She points out that the Vietnamese socialist state emphasized negative aspects of Saigonese life including successes in petty commerce, consumerism, wealth and infinitely higher – 'decadent' – standards of living than experienced in the northern capital. This context offers some explanation for an absence of middle-class women's memoirs in Vietnamese.

Vietnamese-language memoirs dealing with Vietnamese women's personal lives and targetting a popular audience take the form of revolutionary hagiography, a genre distinct from revolutionary prison memoirs.[3]

---

2   A direct contrast in motivation to write a revolutionary memoir is put forward by communist revolutionary leader Le Thi (pen name of Duong Thi Thoa) who states that her aims were primarily as a record for herself and that she chose to rely on comrade historians to judge whether her words should be used or not used (Duong and Sidel 1998, p. 1021).

3   One of the new popular autobiography genres to emerge in Vietnam in the first decades of the twentieth century was revolutionary prison memoirs. As Peter Zinoman (2001, pp. 9–12) explains, prison memoirs were the autobiographical works of imprisoned intellectu-

Revolutionary hagiography is commonly found in school textbooks. These narratives elevate selected female and male freedom fighters to the status of national heroines and heroes in stories which are often composed with great literary imagination. In this genre, revolutionary women's stories focus as much on their daily lives, personal feelings and family circumstances, as on their revolutionary achievements (Lê Minh Quốc 1999, 2001). Stories about the lives of iconic communist women Nguyễn Thị Định and Nguyễn Thị Minh Khai are popular examples (Lê Quốc Sử 2001; Nguyen Thi Dinh 1976; Nguyệt Tú 1976; see also Pelzer 1993). Some Vietnamese women's self-writing and biography mirrors revolutionary hagiography in dealing with experiences of teenage runaways who reject their bourgeois families to join the revolution as well as experiences of motherhood on the frontline (Duong and Sidel 1998; Đặng Thùy Trâm 2007; Nguyen Thi Tuyet Mai 1994; Tai 2010; Xuan Phuong and Mazingarbe 2004).

Autobiographies of Vietnamese urban middle-class lives seem almost exclusively to have been published by women. Their female authorship makes these accounts a unique set of sources, although other features are equally distinctive. Unlike other Vietnamese autobiographical genres, including styles deriving from classical Chinese traditions of autobiography, modern women's autobiographies use personal narratives to focus on the city and urban life. Like Chinese autobiography genres, earlier Vietnamese autobiographies followed conventions in form, style and subject matter which excluded inner feelings, personal motivations and interactions with family and did not usually address city life.[4] It is also

---

als and activists, which were written with an aim of reshaping public perceptions within the emerging anti-colonial movement. In this book, I do not address the theme of incarceration in the autobiographies of middle-class lives, even though two women and one man tell of the ordeals of political prisoners in the postcolonial South (Hayslip 1989; Loewald 1987; Nguyen and Knight 2004). Additionally, in *Hanoi, Adieu*, a biography of colonial French career officer and Hanoi resident Michel L'Herpinière, Mandalay Perkins (2005) provides an account of his detention in colonial Hanoi.

4   Appealing to a wider audience, contemporary male Vietnamese authors have imitated traditional Chinese autobiographical genres in their memoirs. The opening chapters of *Journal of a Vietcong* portray the author's upbringing and middle-class family life in a style that closely resembles this genre (Truong Nhu Tang 1985). Another example is a short story titled 'The Autobiography of a Useless Person' which imitates the format of a classical autobiography but the content is entirely subjective and personal, detailing family strife as a metaphor for national turmoil (Nguyen Xuan Hoang 1995). Nguyen Trieu Dan (1991) employs a conventional family chronicle format to trace twelve generations of his ancestry and his own life as a diplomat but narrates in a popular voice and incorporates personal anecdotes. Nguyen Dinh-Hoa (1999) traces his life story from colonial Hanoi to

worth noting that contemporary Vietnamese women's autobiographies share some features with women's self-writing in East Asia, including a focus on personal life.[5] The intended audience of middle-class women's self-writing can be assumed to be popular rather than scholarly and located outside Vietnam in the Anglophone world.

Just as middle-class experience was once obscured in collective nation-building projects throughout Southeast Asia (see Robison and Goodman 1996b), the middle-class past has been for the most part overlooked by the Vietnamese state. There are few exceptions to this silence. One is the Vietnam Women's Union-run Museum of Southern Vietnamese Women (*Bảo Tàng Phụ Nữ Nam Bộ*) in Ho Chi Minh City, an institution that highlights not only mythic and revolutionary hero-ines of official Vietnamese history, but also draws attention to educated and elite Saigonese women who made, or are making, a contribution to (colonial, postcolonial, socialist, post-reform) Vietnamese society in sci-ence, manufacturing, fine arts, journalism and diplomacy among other areas (Lê Tuyết Thanh 1993). Another is a compendium titled *Nữ Sinh Sài Gòn* (2002) that celebrates the contributions of alumnae of Saigon's elite private girls' schools in Vietnam and the Vietnamese diaspora.

Autobiographies of middle-class women are valuable sources for recovering history. One of the contributions of narrative accounts of a Saigonese middle-class world is in their making it possible to under-stand – following the aims of person-centred ethnographers – what it was like to live there. In understanding what life there was like, it is possible to realize continuities with life in the present despite significant social changes of the post-war and post-reform eras. This is useful for

_____

postcolonial Saigon and the US in a context of contemporaneous political events. Similarly, Andrew Pham's (2008) biography of his father *The Eaves of Heaven: A Life in Three Wars* narrates his experiences of evacuation from Hanoi to Saigon to the US. While Vietnamese autobiographical genres did not tend to focus on the city, urban life had captured the romantic imagination of poets and novelists in the 1930s, as the urban world offered a new set of collective identities to explore (Marr 2000, pp. 782–4).

5   In contemporary Japanese and Chinese women's self-writing, a focus on the personal has been viewed (by at least two recent scholars) as a feminist concept redefined as a material 'site' or 'historical marker' where diverse historical, political, social, and intersubjective forces interact in struggles for modernity. Wang Lingzhen (2004, p. 1) points out that Chinese women's self-writing has been contextualized in dominant discourses and prac-tices of Chinese nationalism, individualism, state socialism, and postsocialist reform, while Ronald Loftus (2004, pp. 16–18) observes that Japanese women's self-writing illustrates how gender can be an important variable and disruptive force that challenges and subverts dominant discourses.

understanding re-emerging middle-class lifestyles. Although generally unstated in each of the autobiographical sources, there seems to be a desire to conserve a lost social world through a journey of the self. Each account provides rich descriptions of, and unique insights into, middle-class Saigonese life as it was encountered by the female subjects during the mid to late twentieth century. In reporting on their social world and describing their experiences of that social world, the authors bring their pasts to life. Their stories are punctuated by war, where conflict interrupted, dislocated and often destroyed the dreams and aspirations that they held for themselves and their families. Political crises of mid-twentieth-century Vietnam forced whole families to migrate and adapt to new ways of life in Saigon. Needless to say, each of the autobiographies tells of successes, which in most cases reached far beyond their child-hood dreams. These successes may be described, in Bourdieu's (1993b, p. 193) terms, as 'retrospective illusion', a descriptor of predestination that assumes that life is ordered like a story that unfolds from a point of departure or cause and that subsequent events are part of the overall goal. In this chapter, I draw on the autobiographies as sources of subjective experience to create a snapshot of middle-class life.

It is necessary to acknowledge various problems with the use of evidence based on personal memory and self-writing as a basis for research. The value of these narratives centres on the glimpse that they provide of middle-class Saigonese life, a world which is largely absent from Vietnamese official history for political and other reasons. This set of autobiographical sources, like autobiographies and memoirs in general, represents a type of 'secret history' that, as pointed out by anthropologist Rubie Watson (1994, p. 4), takes on added significance when we consider that many of these unapproved rememberings are the stuff from which new histories and new states are created. The following anecdotal snapshot of middle-class Saigonese life provides a historical context for the re-emergence of middle classes in post-reform Ho Chi Minh City and offers comparisons and contrasts of Vietnamese middle-class culture within a qualitatively different political context.

MIDDLE-CLASS WOMEN'S AUTOBIOGRAPHIES: THE SOURCES

Postcolonial Saigon was a rapidly urbanizing cosmopolitan metropolis. Triggered by war, urban migration to South Vietnam – from the

North in the 1950s and from the Mekong Delta, the Central Coast and the Central Highlands in the 1960s – centred on Saigon and it became the major site for population growth (Dang 2008, p. 191).[6] The expansion of Saigon transformed urban ways of living. In the 1960s, the evacuees settled in inexpensive areas, including Tân Định located on the edge of the Saigonese downtown (see Chapter 3). The 'living memories' of Saigon's well-to-do are perhaps better known outside Vietnam, as autobiographies and memoirs published in English or French would suggest. These recollections of middle-class life in postcolonial Saigon provide an alternative trajectory of a Vietnamese past that, even now, is seldom married with a lived reality in Vietnam's present.

The set of a dozen autobiographies explore a qualitatively different world of urban middle-class life to the one that is now re-emerging in post-reform Ho Chi Minh City, but middle-class women in both contexts share some experiences. The autobiographical sources portray the lives of young middle-class women who arrived in postcolonial Saigon as part of a wave of mass urban migration. Most arrived with their families as refugees escaping war. The young women, in general, had no control over the decision to migrate. Their families experienced significant downward mobility, which fostered their aspirations to regain their lost status, assets and wealth. This first wave of mass urban migration, like following waves, would exert considerable influence on urban culture. The arrival of migrants was as highly influential on the development of new ways of living in the postcolonial past as it is in twenty-first century Ho Chi Minh City.

Comparing the autobiographical sources in greater detail reveals several interesting patterns in middle-class Vietnamese women's lives. Foremost, the narratives show that a sense of home is essential to a Vietnamese sense of self. Mai Elliott's (1999) clan history, *The Sacred Willow: Four Generations in the Life of a Vietnamese Family*, traces a century of family life to provide a context for her memoir set in the political and social instability of the postcolonial era. Le Kwang Kim's (1963)

---

6   As noted in in Chapter 1, Saigon's population of 450,000 in 1945 had almost quadrupled by 1958 to 1,776,000. By 1975 the city's population had increased almost tenfold to four million. During this period the urban population of South Vietnam increased steadily from 16 per cent of the national population in 1958 to 43 per cent in 1971 (Nguyễn Quang Vinh 1996, p. 91; Thrift and Forbes 1986).

'A Woman of Viet-Nam'; Uyen Loewald's (1987) *Child of Vietnam*; and Nguyễn Thị Thu-Lâm's (1989) *Fallen Leaves: Memoirs of a Vietnamese Woman* each deal with the consequences of losing home and family. A consistent message in the autobiographies is that a sense of belonging to a family, a birthplace and a nation is a foundation for Vietnamese identity-making.

For Vietnamese, food preparation and participation in family meals are among the most important ways of demonstrating belonging in family life and to a particular place as home. The significance of food to Vietnamese identity is stressed in two autobiographical accounts which appear with recipes for 'traditional' Vietnamese cuisine. The first is an introductory section titled 'Autobiography' in Duong Thi Thanh Lien's (1973) *Vietnamese Dishes*. Her stresses the importance of sharing food in family life, and describes meals as an essential form of communication with the living and with the ancestors. So essential is eating to Vietnamese identity that it is said that Vietnamese can survive only a week without Vietnamese meals. The second, *Green Papaya*, is an autobiographical memoir of restaurateur Lien Yeomans (2001). Her life story is peppered with recipes made from local and seasonal produce that connects her to a family and a place. These sources show that using food to communicate love and belonging is an important part of women's identities, demonstrated in the kitchen and household through their role as mothers, a role for which girls are socialized from a young age. A sense of home and the significance of family meals or regional cuisine are important contributions of migrants to new urban lifestyling.

Wartime migration deprived young women of growing up to lead the lives that they had imagined since childhood and forced them to adapt to a new way of living. Like most of the other autobiographies, Anh Vu Sawyer's (2003) *Song of Saigon: One Woman's Journey to Freedom*; Thinh Hoang's (1989) *My Long Journey: A Vietnamese Woman's Story*; and Le Ly Hayslip's (1989) *When Heaven and Earth Changed Places: A Vietnamese Woman's Journey from War to Peace* each centre on transformations of the self caused by migration. By moving from the postcolonial North to the postcolonial South, or across South Vietnam, it was possible to enter a new social world with new responsibilities and challenges as long as the familiar old world of family, home, position and wealth was left behind. One account, *The Dragon's Journey*, combines a detailed biography of the author's murdered mother and descriptions of her middle-class world that was lost through forced migration (Nguyen and Knight 2004).[7]

As memoirs, the autobiographies bring the past to life. However, many of the authors also draw attention to their desires to contribute to the betterment of Vietnam in the present through their participation in not-for-profit charitable foundations and academic programs based in the US and Australia (Elliott 1999; Hayslip 1989; Nguyễn Thị Thu-Lâm 1989; Sawyer and Proctor 2003; Yeomans 2001). For others, who remain in Vietnam, their contributions are made through commitments to practice medicine and develop new public health programs (Duong Thi Thanh Lien 1973; Le Kwang Kim 1963). Except for Uyen Loewald, who worked with refugees in Australia, these authors have become well known and highly regarded for their philanthropy in Vietnam. In contrast, two remaining autobiographical accounts are published under pseudonyms. One anonymous account is a self-titled autobiography 'Ngàn Hac Tráng' (1995) and the other 'Weaving a Double Cloth' is a brief account of transmigration and subsequent identity dilemmas after leaving middle-class Vietnam (Ho Xuan Huong 2002).[8] While pseudonyms may reflect a reluctance to put oneself forward as a cultural authority, their use may also indicate the longevity of political sensitivities that leave exiles unwilling to associate themselves openly with South Vietnam's postcolonial past. Identity dilemmas encountered by middle-class women living outside Vietnam arise in several autobiographies, including Nguyễn Thị Thu-Lâm's *Fallen Leaves*; Anh Vu Sawyer's *Song of Saigon*; Thinh Hoang's *My Long Journey*; and Lien Yeomans' *Green Papaya*.[9]

---

7   Two supplementary sources that I rely on are Swiss-Australian woman Iphigénie-Catherine Shellshear's (2003) *Far From the Tamarind Tree,* a memoir of growing up in colonial urban Vietnam, and 'To Serve the Cause of Women's Liberation' on women's daily lives in Ho Chi Minh City the 1980s (Hoàng Ngọc Thanh Dung 1988).

8   The selection of 'Ho Xuan Huong' as a pseudonym is worth comment. Hồ Xuân Hương, whose name means 'Spring Essence', was a highly educated and talented poetess of nineteenth-century northern Vietnam. Her talent at classical composition reportedly sent imperial examination candidates into raptures and, although she is remembered for her wit, her poetry – critical of husbands and ridiculing men – is associated with women's autonomy and breaking from social convention (Balaban 2000, p. 7; Lê Minh Quốc 1999, pp. 74–91; Lũ Huy Nguyên 2004, pp. 5–10).

9   Other sources on middle-class women's identities in the Vietnamese diaspora in Australia include Carina Hoang's (2010) *Boat People*, a large-format oral and artefact history, and Nathalie Huynh Chau Nguyen's (2005) *Voyage of Hope* and (2009) *Memory is Another Country*. Among the many volumes on Vietnamese refugees' identities in the diaspora in

With the exception of Le Ly Hayslip (1989), a peasant girl from Vietnam's Central Coast who provides a valuable 'outsider' perspective on urban middle-class life through her work in a Saigonese household as a servant, each of the authors come from comparable middle-class families and the majority of their fathers were civil servants or businessmen rather than military officers. Almost all share experiences of migration to Saigon, except for pharmacist Le Kwang Kim (1963) who was born and raised in a middle-class Saigonese family, and the pseudonymous author of 'Weaving a Double Cloth' who grew up in a Mekong Delta city and never visited Saigon (Ho Xuan Huong 2002). The rest of the women migrated to Saigon in the 1950s and 1960s. The majority were themselves born in or near Hanoi, or to northern parents in the Centre, arriving in Saigon as children (Elliott 1999; Loewald 1987; Ngàn Hac Tráng 1995; Nguyễn Thị Thu-Lâm 1989; Sawyer and Proctor 2003; Thinh Hoang 1989; Yeomans 2001). Another originated in Huế, the former imperial capital in central Vietnam, and came to Saigon as a wife and mother (Nguyen and Knight 2004), while one other was born in the Mekong Delta and moved to Saigon as a student (Duong Thi Thanh Lien 1973).[10] Migration marked a turning point in their lives. These distinctions in origin are historically important as, unlike a move from the Centre or the Mekong Delta to Saigon before 1975, migration from the urban North to postcolonial Saigon from 1955 to 1975 constituted a transnational migration.[11]

While transnationalism during, and since, the postcolonial era is important, in this chapter I review life in postcolonial Saigon with a focus on middle-class experience through a gendered perspective sourced

---

the US are the second volume of Le Ly Hayslip's (1993) memoir *Child of War, Woman of Peace*; G. B. Tran's (2010) poignant graphic novel *Vietnamerica*; Andrew Lam's (2005) *Perfume Dreams*; Dana Sachs' (2010) *The Life We Were Given*; and Trin Yarborough's (2005) *Surviving Twice*. I have not relied on these sources as each deals with problems encountered after leaving Vietnam.

10   A French biography, *Une Famille de Saigon* (A Saigon Family), tracks a similar journey made by Tran Thi Phuoc Sang, the wife of the patriarch's son, from her home in the western Mekong Delta to Saigon to study pharmacy (Nguyen-Rouault 1999). I have not found this source especially useful due to its genealogical rather than social focus.

11   There remains virtually no research on urban-to-urban migration in Vietnam, although social research on Vietnamese transnational migration is growing (e.g. Thai 2008). Certainly most of the autobiographical accounts that I consult detail issues of transnational migration between the two Vietnams, or from Vietnam to a western host country (Australia, US).

from women's autobiographies in line with a person-centred approach. Much of this literature concentrates on individuals and micro-level institutions, so I do not engage in depth with the women's self-writing about revolutionary experiences nor the vast literature that examines the wartime economy and related political situation. Equally I pay little attention to Saigon's concurrent reputation then, or since, as a centre of military entertainment and male-focused recreational pleasures. My focus centres on social practices to highlight what was salient to middle-class women and what it was like to live there. I do this to establish historical roots for the ethnographic project on new middle classes in contemporary Ho Chi Minh City, but also to expose the overshadowing of middle-class experience in late twentieth-century Vietnam.

Middle classes flourished in wartime postcolonial South Vietnam, although life was not necessarily easy. Social differentiation, cultural diversity and aspirations for betterment characterized Tân Định and other inner-city areas where middle-class and other refugees settled in the postcolonial era. Having lost the assets and resources that facilitated middle-class life, families were faced with re-establishing their desired social positions in these densely populated areas. *Sacred Willow*, Mai Elliott's family history, provides one of the most compelling examples among the autobiographies of the impact of urbanization on city life in postcolonial Saigon. Elliott portrays Saigon in the late 1960s as a place where the tempo of life quickened and young people lived hurriedly and hedonistically. Around them, society crumbled as peasants and beggars flocked into the city. She describes stinking urban alleys clogged with refugees, homeless children, garbage and vermin (Elliott 1999, pp. 313–15). Overcrowding and temporary downward social mobility characterized the experiences of new city residents. At its peak, the population density in the Prefecture de Saigon was 27,264 people per square kilometre (Le Van Hòang and Truong Nhu Hien 1965, p. 9). The inner city remains similarly dense today (GSO 2008, p. 23; Hy 2009, p. 2). The origins of the mega-urban development of Vietnam's Southeast are located in wartime urbanization occurring over a quarter of a century.

Wartime Saigon offered relatively liberal conditions to build a new future. Young women benefitted from the wartime conditions. Mai Elliott was one of the educated young women who flourished in the liberated social world of wartime Saigon. Saigon's wartime growth was supported by an expanded civil service and service industry. Schools and universities also expanded to train the workers required, many of whom were women. The recognition of women in Article Five of the Constitution of the Republic of Vietnam in 1956 had greatly advanced women's official status beyond the family. Open-minded parents saw value in educating daughters. With the increased availability of school places during the war, girls soon equalled boys in school enrolments and outnumbered them in universities (General Civil Service Commission 1967, p. 3). An economic need also enabled young women to gain employment outside the home, particularly in the growing civil service.[12] Increasing numbers of nuclear households across Saigon further freed women from responsibilities in an extended family but also generated a shortage of servants which created additional employment opportunities for young women from the countryside (Hoskins 1976, p. 136). Postcolonial Saigon offered opportunities for young people to become economically and socially independent salary earners and to begin rebuilding social status lost after their families had previously been forced to abandon their homes and assets.

CHANGING ATTITUDES TO WOMEN'S EDUCATION

Middle-class Vietnamese women's autobiographies emphasize the significance for Vietnamese middle classes of higher education and salaried professional careers for improving social status. Changing attitudes to women's education since the late colonial period are evident in each family's aspirations for their daughters' schooling. With the wider availability of education for girls, many urban middle-class girls became not just literate but highly educated. In postcolonial Saigon in particular, the emphasis on women's higher education helped determine future success and achievement. So important was education for the urban

---

12   The 1960 census revealed that the growing numbers of women working in the civil service were young: one in four (26.9 per cent) women employees were aged 21–25 years and one in three (31.7 per cent) were 26–30 years. Half (50 per cent) the women employees in their twenties were single (General Civil Service Commission 1967, p. 7). From 1958 to 1962, new positions were created and the proportion of technicians and office workers expanded from 3.9 to 5.4 per cent and from 7 to 8.1 per cent, respectively (Le Van Hòang and Truong Nhu Hien 1965, p. 26).

middle classes that when Mai Elliott's family was fleeing a house fire, her mother saved books not jewellery (Elliott 1999, p. 253).

Reasons given in the autobiographies for changing attitudes to women's education in twentieth-century Vietnam vary, but often focus on increasing rights for women and female emancipation, especially within families that lacked or had lost sons. The purpose of girls' education was also to equip them to help support families that had lost resources and households that lacked a male breadwinner. Further, educated women could expect better marriage prospects deriving from a greater reservoir of accumulated cultural capital. Pharmacist Le Kwang Kim attributes the increasing emphasis on education for daughters to the fragmentation of the extended family in postcolonial Vietnam, a situation that mirrors contemporary urban Vietnam. In 'A Woman of Viet-Nam', Le Kwang Kim (1963, p. 467), who was herself married in her teens and widowed in her early twenties, stresses the importance of education for girls as, in her opinion, young women in the 1950s and 1960s could no longer succeed simply through marriage. Other autobiographies offer explanations that emphasize financial independence and autonomy for women. In *Fallen Leaves*, entrepreneur Nguyễn Thị Thu-Lâm (1989, p. 114), who made up her mind to become financially independent so she could leave her husband, suggests that women require at least a minimum of opportunities and skills training, if not formal education, to earn a living and achieve successes without relying on in-laws. Like her, Ngàn Hac Tráng's (1995, p. 71) mother saw advantage in women's education, even though she herself had never been treated equally (in line with Vietnamese tradition). She fought for her daughters to be educated, believing that if people had equal education, they would have equality.

Institutions of education became important in the socialization process for young women as they moved outside the home and were offered new opportunities and new experiences. Middle-class girls were educated at Catholic boarding schools near Saigon, Đà Lạt, Hanoi and Huế. Boarding schools allowed them opportunities to mix with European and elite Vietnamese students and to be exposed to their cultural practices and behaviours. Especially at boarding school, the responsibility for socialization of children shifted from the parents to the institution (Bourdieu 1996). Additional to academic goals were social and spiritual aims for the upbringing of 'well-bred, well-spoken and well-behaved young ladies' (Shellshear 2003, p. 76). However, not all middle-class students fitted the model. During her childhood in Hanoi, Nguyễn Thị Thu-Lâm (1989, p. 87) was sent to a Catholic boarding school in order to control her tomboyish behaviour. Behaviour problems were not only dealt with in the Catholic education system. Anh Vu Sawyer was expelled from Lê Văn Duyệt Girls High School in Saigon due to inappropriate and unladylike behaviour (Sawyer and Proctor 2003, p. 162). For other girls, behaviour problems began at school but extended to the home and beyond. Ngàn Hac Tráng's (1995, pp. 73–4) problems arose when she started to 'think against' what her father had taught her to become independent and disobedient. Her father did not value or encourage these developments, even though her 'unladylike' behaviour did not affect her academic results.

Saigon's elite girls' schools, including Gia Long School for Girls, Marie Curie School, Petrus Ký College, and Lê Văn Duyệt Girls High School, shaped scores of young middle-class women each year (*Nữ Sinh Sài Gòn* 2002). Schooling provided young women – at least those who were not yet betrothed to marry – with education that could lead to professional employment as well as further academic training that would build their careers (Duong Thi Thanh Lien 1973, p. 4; Le Kwang Kim 1963, p. 462; Loewald 1987, p. 143; Sawyer and Proctor 2003, p. 160). After graduating from secondary school, many aspiring middle-class girls aimed to enter university in Saigon or abroad. To do so, they required the support of their families. In 'A Woman of Viet-Nam' pharmacist Le Kwang Kim (1963, p. 462) reports that, in the mid-1940s, 'courageous – or foolhardy – young women' who wanted to study after primary school had to attend the 'men's college'. Even with changing attitudes to women's position in society and wider access of young women to education, university courses continued to be dominated by men in the postcolonial period.[13] In the early 1960s, Uyen Loewald (1987, pp. 198–9) was one of eight girls studying pure science in a class of 800 and Mai Elliott (1999, pp. 271–2) was the only girl in a preparatory English class for students going abroad to study. Later, in the US, she was one of

---

13   Two Anglophone memoirs by Janice Tait (2005) and David Hess (1977) centre on their teaching posts at the University of Saigon and record teaching conditions there in the 1960s.

15 women in a class of 900. In pursuing higher education, these young women were breaking firmly held patrilineal social conventions about appropriate activities for young women.

Changing attitudes to women's education were an important development in postcolonial Saigon. Schooling and education outside the home provided a range of opportunities for young middle-class women that were historically unavailable to daughters. Attending school allowed girls and young women to enter a new social circle and meet people outside the family, including teachers, classmates and their families. With this contact, they were able to develop relationships beyond kin networks through which an alumnae of fellow elites could enable them to foster personal, business and labour market opportunities or even, in times of trouble, help them to hide or escape. In the 1960s, many of Saigon's middle-class students, like Mai Elliott, were offered opportunities to go abroad to continue their studies, travelling by various means on scholarship programs. Duong Thi Thanh Lien (1973) records her experiences in the US in the early 1970s as postgraduate students on scholarship, and Lien Yeomans (2001) recounts her experiences as a Colombo Plan student in Sydney in the 1960s.[14] Few students were privately funded. In 1954, Le Kwang Kim (1963, p. 468) was able to sell family possessions and valuable 'trinkets' to raise enough money to study in France the following academic year. Transnational experiences widened the girls' horizons in a number of ways (discussed below).

Student life, in Vietnam or abroad, provided young women with new opportunities and experiences. Attending school or university was a way to meet boys and men without the intervention of a matchmaker. Nguyễn Thị Thu-Lâm (1989, p. 107) was at one time 'promised' to her biology teacher. In her memoir, Uyen Loewald (1987, pp. 159, 162) makes much of taboo sexual relationships between teachers and students at the Gia Long School for Girls' boarding house, telling tales of teenage abortion, the suicide of a pregnant student and same-sex liaisons. In contrast, Mai Elliott (1999, pp. 264–5) complains that attending a girls' school provided no opportunities to meet boys, to get to know them, or to fall in love.

---

14   The Colombo Plan for Co-operative Social and Economic Development in Asia and the Pacific, an aid program of the British Commonwealth, operated from 1951 to draw attention to regional needs and improve living standards through human resources development, particularly education and training (Megarrity 2007).

An idea that education could provide new opportunities for women consolidated their new social power, but for middle-class young women, a concept of fate continued to play a significant role in making major decisions. Before Lien Yeomans' (2001, pp. 2–3) mother would permit her to accept a scholarship that she had won to study in Australia, she insisted on consulting a fortune-teller, and Mai Elliott's (1999, pp. 272, 306) mother resigned herself to her daughter's marriage to an American due to an earlier prediction from a fortune-teller. A belief in fate was also a dominant force in daily life. Teacher Thinh Hoang (1989, p. 3) explains that she coped with the dangerous journey to and from the remote school where she was eventually posted, travelling along roads filled with landmines, because of a strong belief in fate that helped her to accept the worst situation and cope with its consequences. New social conditions encouraged, or forced, young women to take up new opportunities that had not been part of a conventional daughter's life. Yet some continued to value selected aspects of a familiar parochial culture learned in childhood, such as Vietnamese fortune-telling.

A WINDOW ON THE WORLD: WORK AND CAREER

Middle-class women's autobiographies demonstrate that, in postcolonial Saigon, education credentials were highly sought after to distinguish candidates in the increasingly competitive wartime labour market. To Ngàn Hac Tráng's (1995, p. 75) father, at this time, 'a university degree was some kind of defence' for employment, even for daughters, and the cultural capital (not his term) that his children's individual qualifications conferred was a family achievement that gave him some status. The widespread pursuit of higher education and book-based knowledge in wartime Saigon resulted in a 'growing army' of graduates with little work experience or any practical skills and created a shortage of managers, entrepreneurs, civil servants, technical and 'blue collar' workers (Nguyen Anh Tuan 1987, p. 375). Language, office and business skills became increasingly valuable at this time and women seemed to be at an advantage in these areas. Many urban middle-class girls with secondary or university education worked in downtown offices or businesses. In Saigon in the 1960s, educated women found that working casually or part-time in teaching or for a foreign organization provided sufficient income to support their households, although their employment may have caused problems at home. Ngàn Hac Tráng (1995, p. 74) explains the advantages and disadvantages of office work for educated young women:

> A lot of women were working for the Americans. There were two types of work. Some women were imported straight from the countryside, and ended up as prostitutes... Other women worked for the Americans as interpreters or secretaries. They were paid a lot of money, more than the men could earn. That created a lot of problems, especially if the women were married. There was pressure on the women to get those jobs, because the economic situation was so bad; but in Vietnamese life the husband traditionally supplies everyone in the family, and if you let your wife do that kind of thing, it means you cannot take care of your family. You become ashamed. The husbands agreed to let their wives work for the Americans, because the families needed the money. But the family traditions broke down.

While education had prepared some girls for careers, the financial needs of the household in times of wartime hardship forced others to find work, sometimes for the first time in their lives.[15]

After her husband's death in the 1950s, pharmacist Le Kwang Kim (1963, p. 468) took deliberate action to become the 'man of the household' in order to support her mother, her brother and her son. Remarriage was for her 'out of the question'. Like her, Nguyễn Thị Thu-Lâm (1989, pp. 115, 129) had never dreamed of working after marriage. However, when her circumstances changed due to the war and separation from her husband, she found herself unable to secure professional employment without English, typing or office skills. In contrast, her sis-

---

15 Salaried women did not emerge just with the wartime economy in Vietnam's urban Southeast. Among the first career girls to be recognized in the late colonial era were those who emerged from privileged Cochinchinese families. A 1943 handbook of notable individuals in French Cochinchina included 141 Vietnamese of whom eight were women: five of the notable women were wives of elite men and the remaining three, in addition to being well connected, were career girls. Their professions included medical doctor, teacher (at the *École de Jeunes Filles,* a Saigonese girls' school), and *cải lương* theatre actress (cited in Smith 1972, pp. 473–4). Richard Coughlin (1950, p. 9) explains that as career girls, such as these three women, represented the beginning of a trend that developed throughout the latter twentieth century for young women to leave home before marriage and be educated for an independent career. As early as 1929, Ngo Vinh Long (1974, pp. 11, 14–15) notes, there is some evidence that upper-class women were supporting their families through trade and, throughout the French colonial period, bourgeois women dominated the domestic economy as entrepreneurs. Women's employment conferred benefits for the individual and the family.

ter earned three times her own husband's salary typing for a US business firm. Education had prepared other young women's skills and attitudes for work. Before being imprisoned on political charges, Uyen Loewald (1987, pp. 176, 185) was able to live independently, supporting herself by working as a freelance reporter, teaching foreigners and tutoring rich Vietnamese girls. After graduating, Mai Elliott (1999, pp. 301–2) worked as a broadcaster at Radio Saigon, where the office in the 1960s was full but 'hardly humming with purposeful work', with her male colleagues reading newspapers and drinking tea and her female colleagues knitting, gossiping, or 'pecking at their typewriter keyboards with a pencil so as not to chip their nail polish'.

The expansion of the wartime civil service offered new opportunities to young women. By the 1960s, work available to women in the civil service in postcolonial Saigon was more likely to be part-time and irregular, with low job security. Employed single women were highly mobile within and between workplaces, where a lack of stable conditions and a gender-based 'glass ceiling' caused them to quit their jobs more often than married women. In the Saigonese civil service, only 3 per cent of female employees held executive positions with no woman occupying a position higher than division chief or director. However, wage inequality was not as pronounced for single women as employers had a bias towards hiring unmarried women to minimize absenteeism due to family commitments (General Civil Service Commission 1967, pp. 10–11, 15–16). In the 1960s, such restrictions on a woman's career or education were evident not only in Saigon. As a postgraduate student in the US, Mai Elliott (1999, p. 283) was disappointed to encounter the familiar 'glass ceiling' and male-dominated world, where a handful of female staff worked in administration or language instruction and, except for the Dean of Women, held no positions of responsibility.

Changing attitudes to education and careers for women were widespread in urban areas, although conventional ideas of women's roles also persisted. Mai Elliott's (1999, pp. 271–2) motivation to study abroad had been to join the foreign service and travel the world learning about other cultures. By the 1970s, a desire for adventure had become more widespread across the middle classes. For a young middle-class woman in South Vietnam, leaving the security and protection of home was a necessary first step in exposing herself to the world and gaining independence. Teacher Thinh Hoang (1989, p. 3) explains:

[A]fter twenty-one years of living in a strict and traditional family, I desperately wanted to move out from my parents' house and their protection to see the world outside and to start my own life. Tradition forbade me to leave home unless I got married, otherwise I would be considered immoral by society and my parents might disown me to retain the family's honour. I didn't want to be married yet, so a faraway official job would be an excellent excuse for my adventure.

In the 1960s and 1970s, an important step in achieving autonomy and independence for a young middle-class woman was securing professional work that ranged from taking up a short-term position in an international organization, like Mai Elliott, to developing a career in teaching, like Thinh Hoang. An alternative path to adventure and independence for young middle-class women was to join the revolution, as Nguyễn Thị Thu-Lâm's older sister Tuyết Mai, Xuan Phuong, Bao Luong and Le Thi did (Duong and Sidel 1998; Nguyen Thi Tuyet Mai 1994; Tai 2010; Xuan Phuong and Mazingarbe 2004).

With the expansion of the civil service and impact of wartime labour shortages, government propaganda encouraged women in Saigon to work outside the home. One means for encouraging middle-class women to work was circulating a belief that women who worked outside the home experienced greater psychological well-being and more 'balance' in their lives. As outlined in a Saigonese civil service magazine, female government employees – in contrast to 'idle' housewives – were considered to be less interested in appearing and behaving in an overtly feminine manner and, as a result, would make better wives and mothers due to a well-informed mind and stable emotions (General Civil Service Commission 1967, pp. 6, 20). In a similar vein, US-trained Assistant Professor Nguyen Thi Huo (1967, p. 60) encouraged women, via a newspaper interview, to work in the wartime economy, explaining that without paid employment women's lives would be 'out of balance'. This emphasis on balance in women's lives suggested not only that there would have been a negative impact on the wartime economy, but also that social isolation and a lack of a useful occupation were viewed as having a negative effect on women.

Westernized concepts of the self such as these were not new in postcolonial South Vietnam, having been first addressed in the colonial era by Vietnamese intellectuals in the early 1920s. At that time, views of the self incorporated a sense of independence from one's family as well as an ambition to strive and achieve one's full potential (Marr 2000, p. 777). Pharmacist Le Kwang Kim (1963, p. 469) describes herself in these terms as a result of transnational experience. After financial difficulties in the family forced her to find a profession, she undertook seven years of professional training in France where she was exposed to different cultural values. She explains the result:

> The culture I had partially acquired, now freed from the inhibiting influence of the family, gradually developed and took root in me, soon permeating me entirely. I became completely adult, in the western meaning of the term; making decisions for myself, assuming responsibilities, engaging in undertakings, discussing, persuading, settling questions, becoming daily more sure of myself and of my capacities and my potentialities... I believed myself to be trained for life.

As a young widow with dependents to support, Le Kwang Kim highlights her abandonment of the strict codes of 'traditional' Vietnamese womanhood as a maturation and personal development which implies a lack in women who do not work. Her views were equally influenced by transnational and traditional Vietnamese cultural forces.

MIDDLE-CLASS IDEALS OF EMBODIED FEMININITY

A generation of more worldly-wise young women in postcolonial Saigon influenced popular ideas about social convention and new forms of acceptable behaviour. Etiquette manuals became especially popular at this time, reflecting both the importance of controlling women's embodied practices and the widespread popularity of reading as a pastime. A 1960s-era etiquette manual, *Cẩm Nang Để Trở Thành Người Phụ Nữ Đẹp* (Manual for Becoming a Beautiful Woman), was published for women of all ages (*loại sách cho mọi lứa tuổi*), but, judging by its contents, targetted an audience of young, urban middle-class women. The text emphasizes that a middle-class woman – a mother – has a responsibility in raising her children to insure that they create a successful future through opportunities provided by a broad education and study rather than simply a future based on inherited family legacy (Minh-Loan 1969, pp. 109–10).[16] Unlike

---

16 My attention was drawn to this passage by a previous owner of the etiquette manual who had underlined the passage with neat blue ink. No underlining appears on any other pages

other and earlier etiquette guides, the new concept of 'balance' within a woman's life is emphasized in a long passage dedicated to finding an acceptable medium between the roles of a woman at home and in society (Minh-Loan 1969, pp. 142–5). In addition to conventional sections that focus on physical beauty and social graces, education and outside interests are stressed as necessary requirements for a woman's life.[17] Although urban culture allowed women more latitude in their appearances and behaviours, traditional models of femininity also persisted. This integration of existing practices with new ideas characterized the development of middle-class culture in postcolonial Saigon.

Much of the advice contained in other etiquette guides does little to break the conventions of women's behaviour. Another guide published in Hanoi at the same time focuses only on the domestic role of women. Produced by the former Hanoi governor's wife and with profits benefitting Hanoi bomb victims in the late 1960s, *Nữ Lư[u] Phận Sự* (The Duties of Vietnamese Women) is divided into three sections corresponding to adolescence, marriage and child-rearing.[18] The text focuses almost entirely on physical well-being and behaviour, but also includes a detailed section on becoming an urban housewife. Unlike Minh-Loan's manual, there is no mention of education for a young woman or for her offspring in the chapter on raising obedient children (Lê Trưng Ngọc [n.d.196?], Chs 11, 19). Similarly, *Thanh Lịch* (Refinement and Politeness), an earlier guide produced in colonial middle-class Hanoi and reprinted in postcolonial Saigon, is based entirely on embodied behaviour at social

---

in the volume. Minh-Loan's etiquette guide is widely available in second-hand stores. The place I bought it in Ho Chi Minh City's District Three stocked half a dozen other identical copies. A Vietnamese acquaintance informed me that books like these were no longer popular in Ho Chi Minh City and thus were widely available despite having been banned after 1975.

17 Minh-Loan's manual includes conventional topics on physical beauty including 'protecting beauty', 'personal hygiene', 'looking after hair', and 'looking after eyelashes', among other things. Sections on dress and posture emphasize the importance of personal grooming and youthful appearance. Emotional control dominates detailed passages recommending correct and appropriate behaviour in the psychology of love, especially in dealing with jealousy, as well as the discrete conduct of an unfaithful wife. The responsibilities of women within the family can be summarized into broad categories that address the relationship with a mother-in-law, the art of cooking, a husband's nutrition and health, his status, his sexual interest and satisfaction, as well as the education of children (Minh-Loan 1969). It is noteworthy that middle-class women are portrayed not as single but as wives and mothers.

18 The copy that I viewed, bound in gold leaf paper, included a typed letter of introduction from the author to the volume's owner which clearly stated her philanthropic intentions.

occasions and with material objects, including receiving guests, serving tea and giving gifts (Vân-Đài 1968 [1940]).[19] These conventional guides emphasize the important role of women in middle-class families in bearing family cultural capital in their appearances and embodied practices, a process that especially affects the socialization of girls (Bourdieu 1998b, p. 68). It is useful to note that postcolonial etiquette guides did not only target women. *Người Lịch Sự* (Refined Individuals) addresses the behaviour of urban elite men and focuses on appearance and social interactions, but not on family relationships (Phạm-Cao-Tùng 1954).[20]

While etiquette books may reflect desired expectations, the realities of young middle-class women's behaviour are described in Vietnamese women's autobiographies, especially in *Fallen Leaves*. In line with traditional codes of embodied femininity, middle-class girls were taught from a young age to pay attention to their appearance and behaviour. Nguyễn Thị Thu-Lâm's (1989, pp. 66, 158) mother had always stressed that women should dress and look attractive under any circumstance, perhaps because women embodied the family's status position. Reflecting this, after her family lost everything, her mother's physical appearance changed from 'pampered' to 'calloused'. Most important to a sense of

---

19   The author Vân-Đài is a poetess, born in the first decade of the twentieth century in the Mekong Delta province of Trà Vinh. In her youth, she ran away from her family of civil servants to join the Viet Minh in the north. She produced the etiquette manual to explain the northern middle-class behaviour that she had observed for more than a decade and published it from Luang Prabang in 1940. The text was recently reproduced as an appendix to a volume of her poetry. Although recognized as a national poetess, Vân-Đài's poetry is not as popular as some of her peers' works due to her focus on transitory and uneventful happenings in women's everyday lives (*Nữ Sĩ Vân Đài* 1999; Phương Lan [n.d. 1975?–1985?], pp. 260–1).

20   Reading Phạm-Cao-Tùng's manual, I was again attracted to the underlinings of a previous owner. The section underlined in red pencil focuses on body language and conversation, leading me to conclude that the owner had an upcoming audience with an important, high-ranking man. This owner's reading focused on three sections. Part 1, Chapter 8 'Visiting a Private House' recommends that it is best to make an appointment to visit, but it is not polite to be overly curious or to stare at the belongings in the guest room. Part 2, Chapter 2 'Conversation' advises to dress elegantly and avoid speaking too fast or using overly familiar gestures, such as slapping someone's shoulder or thigh. Part 2, Chapter 8 'Company' describes a refined person as a gracious person who reciprocates and acknowledges worth (Phạm-Cao-Tùng 1954, pp. 60–2, 76–7, 113). The manual is dedicated to all children (*tặng các con*), but clearly targets adult men, by addressing the reader as *ông* (Mr, Sir). Throughout the text, the reader is initiated into elite and westernized social and business circles in a variety of contexts and scenarios, including model conversations and sample outfits (co-ordinated shirt, tie, socks and shoes). Much attention is paid to embodied masculinity, an area that is attracting growing research attention in studies on Vietnam (e.g. Avieli 2011; Horton and Rydstrøm 2011; Martin 2010).

beauty was a light complexion. Nguyễn Thị Thu-Lâm (1989, p. 79) had been raised to be 'very conscious' of skin colour. While she did not mind hearing her mother described as a 'nymph' due her 'pale, fine-boned, well-cared-for face', she could not bear to hear her father called a 'devil', or a 'darkie', due to his dark complexion resulting from his outdoor work as an engineer. In addition to having a light complexion, having long, dark hair was a symbol of youth and bourgeois femininity. Cutting long hair short symbolized a break from these expectations; her older sister cut her hair short 'like a man' on joining the revolutionary Viet Minh (Nguyễn Thị Thu-Lâm 1989, p. 22; see also Nguyen Thi Tuyet Mai 1994).

Other autobiographies also record changes in appearance reflecting a break from expectations. An increasingly westernized appearance linked young women with a modern middle-class culture and, in particular, hairstyle was representative of a rejection of traditional embodied femininity. Uyen Loewald (1987, p. 143) describes her middle-class classmates at Gia Long School for Girls. They arrived on new bicycles or in taxis and their fathers' official cars. They compared brand names and boasted about their fathers' positions and intelligence. They wore sophisticated white *áo dài* (traditional long dress) and permed hair, rather than simple colourful printed suits (*bộ*) and a natural hairstyle. Mai Elliott had made 'no effort to look alluring' before travelling abroad, choosing to dress plainly and wear no makeup with her permed hair. When she returned, her relatives had trouble recognizing her as a 'mature and cosmopolitan' woman with a bouffant hairdo, makeup and stylish western clothes (Elliott 1999, pp. 271, 295). Similarly, having left Vietnam for another country, one middle-class student was prompted to break with her past and cut off her long black hair which was for her 'a symbol of being Vietnamese' (Ho Xuan Huong 2002, p. 8). For middle-class young women, a cosmopolitan outlook could be embodied in clothing and appearance.

Young women's behaviour was more closely monitored as girls were growing up. Some middle-class girls avoided traditional and modern urban ideals of femininity. Lien Yeomans (2001, p. 41) described herself as a 'tomboy', who preferred bicycle racing to chasing after boys. Like Yeomans, Nguyễn Thị Thu-Lâm (1989, p. 87) also described herself as a tomboy. She reflects on her mother's intervention:

Mother had always demanded perfection from her children. Now [in late 1953], disillusioned with the Việt Minh and the probable outcome of the war and discontented after years of insecurity and deprivation, she began to direct all her energies towards me. Nothing I did met with her approval. According to her, I was too skinny; I acted like a tomboy; I did not eat or walk properly; I needed reforming.

Nguyễn Thị Thu-Lâm's mother saw it as her responsibility to teach her child to behave correctly in line with traditional codes of feminine behaviour. Other girls also learned how to behave in the home. Mai Elliott (1999, p. 244) was taught that women should 'eat daintily like kittens'. Uyen Loewald (1987, pp. 8, 28) was exposed to correct manners for eating and correct manners for ladies. Additional to perfecting their manners, some young women were expected to gain knowledge and experience of customary rituals. At home, Lien Yeomans (2001, pp. 6, 38–9) learned traditional tea making and herbal medicine from her Confucian-educated grandfather as well as the details of preparing family ritual feasts and anniversary celebrations (e.g. *ngày giỗ*), which included catering for large groups. Middle-class girls' appearances and behaviours reflected their families' class values and investment of resources. As bearers of family cultural capital, daughters were judged by recognizable norms and ideals that held value so long as they were deciphered by others.

One of the most important tests of a young woman's appearance and behaviour came at her marriage. In postcolonial Saigon, a daughter's success lay with her achievement in bearing cultural capital on behalf of the family by marrying a man with the highest possible status to combine the power and wealth of the two families (Hoskins 1976, pp. 131–2; see also Bourdieu 1976). Le Kwang Kim (1963, p. 464) demonstrates this situation. On the eve of her marriage, she considered herself to exist 'not in her own right', but in relation to her family. Without consulting her, her father had selected her husband and arranged her marriage, organized her conversion to Catholicism, and withdrawn his daughter from school. Three of Mai Elliott's older sisters were married before they were 20 years old and before they finished school, but Elliott herself had been 'too tall' and 'too smart'. Like other older and well-educated girls, she was viewed as 'arrogant', 'demanding' and lacking submission (Elliott 1999, pp. 269–70). By the 1960s, educated, economically independent career girls were reported to be less inclined to desire a family but instead to exhibit antagonism towards men ('Women and their New Responsibility' 1967, p. 27). In line with this belief, Elliott's family did not pressure her to marry but permitted her to go to university and establish a career.

Whether or not such changes created space for more balance between old and new, inside and outside practices in women's lives, social changes were evident within a generation. Throughout the postcolonial era, as levels of education for daughters increased, marriage ages also began to increase and the accumulation of cultural capital depended not only on women's capital-bearing roles but also on capital-accumulating roles. In other words, women were able to accumulate cultural capital on behalf of the family outside the home through schooling and workplace achievements as well as within the home through emotional capital, the unique form of cultural capital associated with the work of wives and mothers who create a loving disposition in the family (Bourdieu 1998b; Nowotny 1981; Reay 2004).

SAIGON AND THE COMFORTS OF MIDDLE-CLASS LIFE

For many educated young women, it was opportunities in postcolonial Saigon that made change in their lives possible. Saigon's reputation drew migrants seeking a new start and a better future. Modern Vietnamese literature has adopted this theme, portraying Saigon as a place of opportunity. The name 'Saigon' became a powerful cultural symbol in twentieth-century Vietnamese short stories employed to represent a destination that characters desire to reach to make a new start or succeed in business (Balaban and Nguyen 1996; Pham Thi Hoai 1997; see also Nguyen-vo 2006). Accounts by foreign visitors and expatriates often described Saigon as a place of pleasure and centre of decadence (Edwards 2003). Middle-class women's autobiographies describe Saigon as a place of refuge and opportunity, but also as a place of hostility and rejection.

The reputation that Saigon held in the romantic imagination of visitors, temporary residents and migrants alike in many cases preceded their contact with the southern capital. Mai Elliott (1999, pp. 246–7) recalls hearing about the 'tropical cornucopia' and the natural wealth of the south, in contrast to her home in the overcrowded northern delta. As a frontier land, for Elliott, the South was a romantic paradise that could provide opportunities and refuge, but also held the danger and risk associated with borderlands. The city's reputation as a place of opportunity was still attractive to migrants. Like thousands of other middle-class families, Anh Vu Sawyer's family had also left the deprivation of the war-torn North to head for Saigon where they believed they could make 'new lives of hope' (Sawyer and Proctor 2003, p. 156). In *My Long Journey*, Thinh Hoang (1989, p. 1) describes her parents sharing similar hopes which led them to give up all their property in the North – including an enormous house, a shopping centre and a weaving factory – to head south, comforting themselves by saying: 'As long as we are still alive and healthy, we can start our life all over again'.

Meeting returnees from Saigon also coloured the city's reputation in the eyes of prospective migrants. Before moving to Saigon to work as a housekeeper in a middle-class household, peasant girl Le Ly Hayslip remembers her idea of Saigon as 'every country girl's vision of nirvana'. In *When Heaven and Earth Changed Places*, Hayslip explains that her own image of Saigon was moulded by her sister's glamorous friend, who returned home to central Vietnam, 'as if she had returned from another planet' with her hair 'piled up like a beehive on her head and made brittle as a bird's nest with hair spray'. She wore clothes that shocked the young Le Ly by leaving her shoulders, arms and thighs 'exposed'. The image of Saigon represented by this girl in Le Ly's mind was decorated with women who 'wore *makeup* and brassieres and high-heeled shoes' (Hayslip 1989, pp. 112–13, original emphasis). Migration had caused the country girl to be transformed into a modern urban woman who embodied the alien world of the city and symbolized the effects it could have on one's appearance, attitude and self.

Life in the southern capital, for Le Ly Hayslip, Mai Elliott and others, was modern and westernized. Saigon was a place where both lifestyle and the built environment were artificial and modernized. On arrival, encounters with the built environment, rather than the people, were initially confronting. Le Ly Hayslip (1989, p. 115) was overwhelmed by city streets crowded with 'miles and miles of traffic – cars, trucks, buses, convoys, taxis, jeeps, motorbikes, *siclo* pedicabs, and bicycles – in front of the bus and behind it, beside it and on the sidewalks, in the alleys and on the curbs – some even driving into the buildings beneath giant garage doors!' Like Hayslip, migrants arriving from northern cities were equally confronted by the urban landscape. Although Hanoi was also a capital city at the time, its contrast with Saigon was dramatic. Mai Elliott (1999, p. 247) compares 'serene' and 'green' Hanoi with the 'sprawling' and 'bustling metropolis' of Saigon which lacked Hanoi's 'charm'.

The living conditions of middle-class families indicated much about their wealth and social position. Le Ly Hayslip (1989, pp. 121–2) records her experiences working as a servant in an urban middle-class household, where there was a cleaning girl for every floor, a cook and scullery maid, a handyman, and two chauffeurs. Having difficulties ne-gotiating her way in the European bathrooms and modern kitchen with gas and electricity, she felt unaccustomed to the domestic luxuries she encountered. Hayslip waited on her 'frail, intelligent-looking' mistress, accompanying her in a Mercedes to go shopping or to take tea with the rich ladies of Saigon. Still a young girl, she daydreamed that she would become a middle-class lady 'commanding servants and buying clothes and having beautiful babies'.

The household conditions that Hayslip describes are not especially extravagant. In the 1960s, the average Saigonese family could afford to hire at least one servant (General Civil Service Commission 1967, p. 21). In the early 1970s, meal preparation in middle-class Saigon became even less time consuming as kitchens had a refrigerator, gas, electricity, a rice cooker and other appliances (Duong Thi Thanh Lien 1973, pp. 11–12). *Fallen Leaves* shows that Nguyễn Thị Thu-Lâm's (1989, p. 6) family home was a typical middle-class household which included household staff and a car. A passage in *Sacred Willow* tells that after a house fire destroyed their home, the Elliott household (comprising five sisters, two maids, her mother and herself) moved to another house on a leafy street that boasted electricity, running water, a toilet and a separate servant quarters (Elliott 1999, pp. 248, 255). Even middle-class households in rural areas were well-off. *The Dragon's Journey* describes Teresa Nguyen running a household in Pleiku that boasted attendants, a cook, a jeep with a driver, a tap with a reservoir, and fruit trees (Nguyen and Knight 2004, pp. 10–12).

The labour of household staff freed middle-class wives from manual work at home, enabling them to spend time on other activities. As a child, Nguyễn Thị Thu-Lâm (1989, pp. 9–10) saw little of her mother except at mealtimes and bedtimes. Her mother was one of the 'new afflu-ent westernized generation' whose social role kept her out of the house doing charity work, leaving the servants to run the household. Uyen Loewald's (1987, pp. 54–5) mother had been a housewife, who had complained after losing her servants and their labour, although Loewald herself did not miss them or the lice they shook from their heads. Lien Yeomans' mother was also a housewife. After sending the children to school or work in the mornings, she dozed until her servant arrived to clean the house and prepare the meals. Each of Yeomans' sisters, living in Saigon in the early 1970s, had at least one full-time domestic helper responsible for childcare, freeing time to spend at the gym training their bodies and maintaining their figures (Yeomans 2001, pp. 28–9, 91). The relatively higher standards of living reported in middle-class households in postcolonial Saigon indicate that displaced middle-class families were able to capitalize on education and employment opportunities in wartime Saigon to improve their prospects and build their new lives of hope.

GLOBALIZATION OF POSTCOLONIAL MIDDLE-CLASS LIFESTYLES

Among middle classes, leisure and consumption demonstrated afflu-ence. In middle-class homes, embodied practices and material goods particularly marked relative status, although the value placed on them varied considerably. Despite the difficulties of war, Saigon in the 1960s was a broadly globalized place where higher incomes and more free time allowed urban culture and popular entertainment to flourish. Imported products gained in popularity, enhancing foreign influences in urban culture and impacting on lifestyle and home decoration choices. In *When Heaven and Earth Changed Places*, Le Ly Hayslip (1989, p. 199) explains that she became aware of an increasing range of American goods (including motorbikes, cars, TVs, stereos, refrigerators, air-conditioners, cigarettes, liquor and cosmetics) that were being imported for the postcolonial Vietnamese elite and which were helping to create a new privileged class who were worshipped for their newly acquired wealth. Hayslip suggests that the display and use of goods played a role in distinguishing betterment among elites, but also affected how elites were regarded by others. Even though foreign goods have been valued both positively and negatively, historian David Marr (1993, p. 337) has concluded that, in the twentieth century, there has consistently been a great curiosity among Vietnamese about things foreign.

Entertaining at home had long been popular among Vietnam's middle classes and was a means for showing off relative wealth and status. In the heart of colonial Hanoi, Uyen Loewald (1987, pp. 28–9) spied on her mother's extravagant dinner parties from behind a curtain. At these parties, her mother was elegant and beautiful in 'perfect makeup and dresses' while her father wore a suit and tie to 'look like a foreigner' and 'spoke French in the middle of a Vietnamese sentence'. Although in some circles imitating a foreign appearance was positive, to others physical appearance was directly linked with moral character, so that a foreign appearance could reflect negatively on the self. Le Ly Hayslip (1989, p. 113) recalls consciously learning to recognize the differences between the westernized fashion styles of urban women and prostitutes. Her attitude to a westernized appearance demonstrates a connection between foreign influence and moral deficiency which reflected negatively on outsiders and also indicates an ongoing tension concerning a displacement of Vietnamese culture by imported cultural influences.

An important dimension of exposure to outside cultural influences is the indirect contact experienced through reading and conversation with people who have direct experience, as well as through other pastimes that provide exposure to imported cultural influences, such as foreign cinema, theatre, music and sport. Reading in particular played a significant role in introducing middle-class women to foreign ideas. Urban middle-class culture in twentieth-century Vietnam was a highly literate one, producing and importing a wealth and diversity of literature and reading materials (Võ Phiến 1992, p. 46). Reading tastes among girls in middle-class families ranged from Chinese literature to French philosophy and romance literature, but also included serialized romances in Vietnamese newspapers (Ho Xuan Huong 2002, p. 13; Le Kwang Kim 1963, p. 462; Loewald 1987, pp. 125–6; Sawyer and Proctor 2003, p. 214).

While reading provided middle-class girls with an introduction to the outside world, some young women were privileged to know someone who had travelled abroad. Returnees conveyed first-hand experience and valuable cultural knowledge. In the years before she travelled abroad herself, Mai Elliott's (1999, pp. 262, 265) contact with things foreign increased through her brother who was sent to the US for a year of military officer training, but reportedly spent his time there shopping, sightseeing and socializing, and eventually returned to Vietnam with a stack of popular music recordings and a gamut of stories to tell. Before she travelled abroad, Nguyễn Thị Thu-Lâm (1989, pp. 26, 76, 100) gained knowledge of foreign culture from her sisters who were educated on scholarship at a Catholic college in Chicago and her brother who was fluent in Japanese, Chinese and French. Other middle-class families also sent their children abroad to study: Lien Yeomans' (2001, p. 38) brother studied in Europe, while Anh Vu Sawyer's sister studied chemistry in Germany and her brother engineering in the US (Sawyer and Proctor 2003, p. 216). These four young women eventually studied abroad themselves and later migrated from Vietnam after marrying foreigners. Their exposure to imported and foreign cultural influences contributed to the development of their cosmopolitan outlooks.

In addition to personal connections, postcolonial Saigon provided a wealth of imported entertainment that was accessible to middle classes. Foreign popular culture, cinema and music were widespread sources of entertainment. Window-shopping and café culture were typical pastimes of urban young people. During free time, Nguyễn Thị Thu-Lâm (1989, pp. 113–14) used to meet her friends on fashionable 'Freedom' Street (Tự Do, now Đồng Khởi) in downtown Saigon, where an afternoon outing would begin with window-shopping and flirting with young men. Afterwards, the young people would sit in an ice cream parlour listening to American pop songs. Although none of them spoke English at that time, they had memorized the lyrics. On top of listening to imported music, going to the theatre and cinema were also popular activities for young people. Mai Elliott (1999, p. 264) used to go out to the cinema with her sisters to see American films and buy ice cream after the show. However, some outings were not so much fun. While on a date with her boyfriend to see *South Pacific* at Saigon's Rex Theatre, Nguyễn Thị Thu-Lâm (1989, p. 169) was heckled by Vietnamese men for fraternizing with an American.

In contrast to cultural activities, sport was not a widely popular pastime among middle-class girls in Saigon, although elite ladies played tennis. Uyen Loewald (1987, p. 129) describes watching the mistresses of the emperor, the prime minister, and other senior ministers playing tennis in expensive new shoes and using new balls, which they left behind for children including her to take. Other sports, such as horse racing and sports hunting, were more popular among French colonial circles (Perkins 2005, p. 26). In postcolonial Saigon, outside middle-class circles, cock-fighting and other street sports continued to be popular among them. To Teresa Nguyen's distress, as a boy, her son Longy developed an enviable cock-fighting business that serviced the underside of Saigon's street culture (Nguyen and Knight 2004, Ch.11). Tomboyish middle-class girls enjoyed activities such as swimming in the river or riding a bicycle (Nguyễn Thị Thu-Lâm 1989, pp. 5, 97; Yeomans 2001, p. 41).

Family vacations offered middle-class children other opportunities for sport and outdoor activities. During the war, Saigonese paediatrician Duong Thi Thanh Lien (1973, p. 2) fondly recalls vacations taken to the highlands, the seaside, or her grandmother's farm, where the children ran free, ate copiously, and spent rare time with their father. Despite wartime hardships, taking trips to the mountains or seaside continued to be typical vacations for the urban middle classes. Mai Elliott's (1999, p. 264) family took an annual vacation to the beach at Nha Trang or the mountains at Đà Lạt, whereas on the weekends, Nguyễn Thị Thu-Lâm (1989, p. 161) flew with her American boyfriend to resorts in Đà Lạt or Danang.

Lifestyle differences in postcolonial Saigon emphasized social distance between members of the middle classes and differentiated those who had contact with the highly valued cultural signals associated with cosmopolitan and elite tastes. The different cultural influences within popular entertainment in postcolonial Saigon conveyed association that could also be used to distinguish between members of the middle classes.

URBAN SOCIAL DIFFERENTIATION AND A FEAR OF FALLING

The autobiographies show that middle classes had an outward-looking perspective and interest in certain foreign cultural influences but differentiated themselves from the majority of others, particularly lower classes, peasants and foreigners. Anh Vu Sawyer recalls the hostility that her father's family directed towards her mother, whose land-rich peasant background was socially beneath her father's own elite educated family. Although her mother conformed to the role of a daughter-in-law as a virtuous and beautiful mother who gave birth to sons, her parents-in-law continued to look down on her due to her lower social background (Sawyer and Proctor 2003, p. 37). Similarly, Le Ly Hayslip (1989, p. 115), who moved from a peasant village on the Central Coast to a job arranged through family connections in Saigon, was conscious of her different social background. In Saigon, she felt as though she 'was in the house of strangers – made stranger still by their city ways' and where life was cramped and crowded, characterized by their 'impiety for their ancestors' and the 'impoliteness of their children'.

Middle-class outsiders were not welcomed either. Many northern middle-class families arriving in Saigon after 1954 found it difficult to integrate. Thinh Hoang (1989, p. 1) reflects that after her family's arrival, misunderstandings, hostility and suspicion made their first years in Saigon very difficult. Similarly, Mai Elliott (1999, pp. 248–9) recalls that she felt she was an 'outsider' in Saigon and felt that the Saigonese were 'far from welcoming', hated the northerners and feared the security of their incomes and meals. At school, Elliott and her sisters were greeted with 'resentful stares' and surrounded by 'hostile' students. Experiencing similar rejection, in Child of Vietnam Uyen Loewald (1987, pp. 122–3) describes the hostility her mother faced at the food market and the 'vicious attitude' that prompted her to learn the local dialect and customs. These episodes reflect an issue observed in contemporary Vietnam, where the position of expatriate Vietnamese returning home closely mirrors that of the arrival of northern migrants in the past. Anthropologist Ashley Carruthers (2002, p. 428) points out that, although Vietnamese returning from a diaspora community (in a more industrialized country) can 'create social envy' by displaying relative wealth, the conversion of their successes abroad into 'durable status within local Vietnamese social hierarchies' is not achieved automatically. Carruthers observes that the typical returnee's experience in contemporary Vietnam is loaded with 'incivility, exclusion, extortion, and refusal of social honour'. The hostility experienced by outsiders in Saigon was repeated across social levels.

Foreigners, especially westerners, were also rejected by Vietnam's postcolonial middle classes as less worthy, less educated and socially lower ranked than themselves. In Sacred Willow, Mai Elliott (1999,

p. 307) describes the tension caused by her intended marriage to an American:

> My father was more distressed by the shame that my marriage to an American sergeant would bring to our family than by my breach of filial piety [in choosing my own husband]. He told me that only prostitutes and bar girls got involved with foreigners, and that if I married an American, everyone in Vietnam would take me for a whore. My relatives would despise me, and my family's honor would be stained. He also told me that by marrying beneath my station I would make him and my mother a laughingstock. In his mind, an American sergeant was no better than the orderlies he used to have at his beck and call in his mandarin office – to fetch him his pipe and bring him his tea. He could already imagine the sneers and snide remarks of his relatives and acquaintances.[21]

In *Green Papaya*, Lien Yeomans (2001, pp. 72–3) expressed her discomfort at seeing Vietnamese girls with American soldiers on a return trip to Saigon from abroad in the mid-1960s. Although Yeomans herself also eventually married a foreigner, she at first shared the views of the middle classes, including Elliott's parents, who felt their positions threatened by the presence of outsiders.

As the war escalated in the 1960s hundreds of thousands of foreign officials and troops arrived in Saigon. Their presence created new economic opportunities for the lower social classes in the service industry, which consequently threatened the stability of social structure and the privileged position of the middle classes. Elliott (1999, p. 314) reports becoming conscious of how rapidly acquired wealth destabilized the existing social order in 1960s Saigon and displaced traditional social values by turning society upside-down so that 'money, not intellectual achievements or social usefulness, had become the yardstick of success'. Attitudes to wealth acquisition in Vietnamese folklore indicate that, as Bourdieu (1984) has argued, the rapid acquisition of wealth is mocked through popular beliefs that the achievement of new economic power and position may be somehow underhand. In Vietnam, a desire for upward mobility and a fear of downward mobility generated comparable sentiments. According to the folklorist Huỳnh Đình Tế (1962, pp.

---

21 Mai Elliott's extract touches on the issues of transnational and inter-racial marriage which I do not explore in this chapter. For my discussion of transnational marriage in post-reform Vietnam, see Chapter 7.

138–42), in Vietnamese folklore there is little evidence that financial prosperity can confer prestige upon the individual, with the rich who respect money and belittle human dignity condemned. Similarly, those who get rich dishonestly or become slaves to money are also condemned. While folklore warns that money is believed to exert a great influence on one's character and personality, and to 'add charm to one's physical appearance', it also can bend the law to one's will, conceal one's stupidity, provide company and servants, and whatever else one likes. However, money may also lead one astray, part friends and estrange relatives. Other proverbs urge Vietnamese to live within their income, to avoid debts and save money for hard times. Such advice on wealth and poverty may have been useful for those trying to maintain existing status when under threat from the newly rich who had found wealth in the wartime service industry in the 1960s.

Any potential threat of new wealth against stable social structure most affects the established middle classes, as it is their continued access to resources and capital that is most at risk of displacement when social values begin to change with changing economic conditions. With the threat of social displacement comes a fear of downward mobility. For Vietnamese, becoming wealthy should occur via education and moral manners, not the 'wild' lifestyles of the newly rich (Pham Xuan Nam 2002, p. 40). The threat posed by rapid wealth acquisition without the development of cultural sophistication still looms over middle classes in contemporary urban Vietnam. Contradictions that existed within Saigonese life between middle classes and foreigners demonstrate that, on the one hand, outside influences are valued and imitated, but on the other, are rejected or mocked because of a direct threat to the social position and prestige of the middle classes. This contradiction resembles the dual façade of Asia's new middle classes which are optimistic and liberal on the one hand, but security-oriented and anxiety-laden on the other hand (Koo 2006, p. 15).

The lifestyles of urban middle-class youth in postcolonial Saigon were greatly influenced by western popular culture and perpetuated an association of classiness with 'outside' that had originated in the colonial era. At this time, social distance was not exclusively associated with foreign cultures, as relative social positions within middle classes and between different social classes were also determined by dispositions, attitudes and behaviour in line with Vietnamese cultural traditions. Nor were outside influences in urban middle-class life always seen in a negative light. However, as urban, educated and elite young people became increasingly fascinated with things foreign throughout the colonial and postcolonial periods, outside influences in postcolonial Saigon were regarded by some as threatening to Vietnamese tradition. These opposing trends produced a comparable contradiction to one experienced in the post-reform era.

In the 1960s, Mai Elliott (1999) reflects on her own upbringing to highlight a displacement of Vietnamese values by the pervasive influence of American culture in postcolonial Saigon. As a university student, Elliott was so familiar with western popular culture that she was at a loss to answer the most basic questions put to her about the Confucian heritage in Vietnam. Throughout her childhood and years at school, she had regularly attended cinema screenings and listened to American pop music in preference to paying attention to Vietnamese cultural traditions and entertainment (p. 264). Elliott describes the 'individualist' influence believed by many Vietnamese to stem from foreign sources as a threat to Vietnamese cultural heritage, claiming that foreign influences in urban middle-class lives had become so dominant that the wealthy had become like 'tourists' (pp. 344–5). Indeed since the late French colonial period, bourgeois women had been described living 'like outsiders in Vietnam' speaking French and socializing with French people, as well as spending excessive amounts of money to lead a 'modernized' lifestyle (Ngo Vinh Long 1974, p. 16; see also E. Peters 2012).[22] This 'individualist' influence can be viewed, in part at least, to result from aspirations to regain social position that was lost due to political upheaval and economic restructuring.

Intergenerational downward mobility in twentieth-century Vietnam affected most the elites and middle classes, who had pursued the cultural

---

22 Ironically, French views of Vietnamese and Indochinese indigenous elites in the late colonial period were less than flattering. For example, Gail Kelly (1984, pp. 538–40) describes, in colonial era Indochinese school curricula and textbooks, a dominating focus on French culture and society as well as French buildings and environment in lessons that position Vietnamese infrastructure as economically backward, underdeveloped and poorly maintained. A secondary strategy to discredit the Vietnamese was made through French-language teaching materials that dealt solely with pre-colonial Vietnamese society – ignoring Khmer, Lao and other cultures in Indochina, as Kelly pointed out – to clearly distinguish between indigenous society and French society.

influences most dominant under each regime. In the colonial era, elites and middle classes had familiarized themselves with French culture in order to secure relatively higher social positions, education opportunities at home and abroad, better employment postings and family connections with foreigners through marriage. Mai Elliott's (1999, pp. 42–3) grandfather recognized the value of following the dominant cultural influence. Once the French colonial authorities had announced the end of the Vietnamese imperial examination system, he insisted that his younger sons (Elliott's father and uncle) obtain a French education to have some hope of making a future for themselves. Later, in the postcolonial South, familiarization with English language and American cultural influences lead to higher social positions, lucrative jobs, overseas training and, potentially, transnational marriage. Even though the advantages were obvious to those who could gain access, attitudes in the 1960s were still divided. While Mai Elliott had not been concerned about her lack of traditional Vietnamese cultural training, Saigonese pharmacist Le Kwang Kim (1963, pp. 469–70) felt torn between Vietnamese and outside cultural influences. After years studying abroad, re-adapting to the changed conditions in postcolonial Saigon was for her like being 'divided between two opposing trends' where 'one is conscious of being at once strong and weak, at home and at the same time foreign, doubtful and also assured... between the frenzied urge towards westernization and the simultaneous need to cling passionately to the old traditions'. Desires for betterment and interests in outside influences presented real identity dilemmas that not only affected young middle-class people individually but also impacted on urban Vietnamese culture.

FINDINGS

Successive waves of urban migration have exerted a diverse range of influences on the city and its people. Urban migrants to Saigon / Ho Chi Minh City have been confronted with new conditions that transform self-identity as well as new opportunities for education, work and a future prospects that can improve their individual and their family's relative social positions.

By presenting a snapshot of the social practices and values associated with urban middle-class life in the postcolonial past, this chapter has established a historical foundation for the following ethnographic chapters. This foundation has outlined the 'old' ideas, behaviours and social logics of postcolonial urban middle-class social practices and highlights that there has been relatively little change in many aspects of the social orientation of urban middle classes in Vietnam notwithstanding the qualitatively different geo-political contexts of postcolonial and post-reform eras.

What has emerged in this chapter is that family culture remains important in the lives of middle-class young women. Unlike other social groups who do not share access to resources and social networks, middle-class young women struggle to find a balance in their lives between conventional family roles and new values and behaviours influenced by imported trends and cultural practices. This chapter highlights that a concept of class is contested in twentieth-century Vietnamese social and cultural life and that twentieth-century urban womanhood is comparatively contested and characterized by shifting representations of women as urban and as middle-class. Through their memoirs, the experiences of postcolonial urban middle-class women have exposed a series of contradictions in various aspects of social life. Urban middle-class women were able to attain high levels of education and, as a result of working in white-collar professions, they were able to support themselves and their households rather than depend only on men. Unlike prostitutes and bar girls, educated middle-class women were able to gain access to lucrative and high status positions in foreign-invested and private sector employment markets through their social networks and using existing family resources. Yet their work was unstable and they were restricted by a gender-based 'glass ceiling'.

Not only migration but also contact with foreign influences in westernized workplaces and popular culture enabled young middle-class women to explore new ways of living which resulted in challenges to conventional social roles and to expectations that girls and women should conform to a range of genderized social norms. Changing social conditions experienced as a result of migration also impacted on their capacity to explore new ways of living, which they demonstrated through shifting norms of embodied femininity, behaviour and appearance as well as their participation in commodity consumption and leisure culture. While some struggled to find a balance between Vietnamese and imported influences and a sense of belonging after migration, others were able to adapt to new social conditions in ways that benefitted themselves and their families.

The snapshot of urban middle-class culture in postcolonial Saigon in this chapter reflects that experiences of migration and the accumulation of enduring cultural capital are among the most influential factors in maintaining and producing status during a period of transition and social change.

CHAPTER THREE

Living in twenty-first century Ho Chi Minh City

Unlike postcolonial middle classes, who fled war and were faced with reclaiming and rebuilding status lost during their lifetime, middle classes in post-reform Ho Chi Minh City are aspirational and migrate to urban areas with a goal to move up socially and achieve a new status position not yet experienced during their lifetime. Moving to Ho Chi Minh City is one of the initial steps in a long-term strategy to claim an enduring new middle-class position and realize the privileges that it can confer.

The women I introduce in this chapter share many of the middle-class values and attributes found in autobiographies discussed in the previous chapter. As a group they differ in one important respect: they all left their families to relocate by themselves to Ho Chi Minh City and they maintain direct connections with their natal homes outside the city. Living away from home can present challenges. For a young Vietnamese woman to leave her family after graduating from high school was not uncommon. But for her to leave her family without then arriving in a new family – in her husband's home – was less common. Increasingly, in the latter twentieth century, young Vietnamese women left their natal homes for education and work (including revolutionary training and fighting). While some young women were able to choose to leave, many others were sent or forced to go due to financial hardship. After the war, economic development attracted migrant women to work in Vietnam's cities. The United Nations estimates that as many as a third of young Vietnamese women have lived away from home for work or study for at least a month (Marx and Fleischer 2010, pp. 31–2). While many young women migrate temporarily, others relocate to Ho Chi Minh City permanently.

This chapter explores the new social worlds of young educated women who migrate permanently to Vietnam's Southeast by focusing on their living conditions and life in their neighbourhoods. In doing so, it highlights some of the influences of urbanization on Ho Chi Minh City's urban heart and on its suburban fringes. In describing the neighbours and the neighbourhood in a laneway in the urban heart and a small street in the urban fringe, I attempt to capture the social diversity that exists within contemporary Ho Chi Minh City. Six significant informants emerge who, with their families, friends and colleagues, are central characters in the ethnographic chapters that follow. I introduce Xuân and Liên, who live in the urban heart, as well as Cúc, Hạnh, Thu and Tuyết who live in the urban fringe. The purpose of this chapter is to open up a world of new middle-class women, a group who – in contrast with many of their neighbours – are well resourced, relatively independent and highly mobile in their daily lives. The style of ethnographic description is intended to illuminate daily life in Ho Chi Minh City by exposing the reader to the sensory and embodied experiences that characterize urban Vietnamese social life particularly in residential laneways. Introducing the social context of the research in this way reflects a person-centred approach in that it aims to capture what it is like to live there.

TẦN ĐỊNH: THE URBAN HEART

Urban migrants often settle in inexpensive commercial or developing areas and in the 1980s and early 1990s they favoured Ho Chi Minh City's inner urban areas, including Tần Định located in District One in the heart of the city. Since the 1960s Tần Định had been crowded with refugees and young economic migrants seeking a better life in the city. Huỳnh Ngọc Trảng et al. (1997, pp. 95, 103) report that urbanization of Tần Định began in the colonial 1930s when paddy fields were drained and roads in the area surveyed. By 1965, the Tần Định area had become densely populated and socially diverse. During the war, Marilyn Hoskins and Eleanor Shepherd (1965, pp. 9–10) found Tần Định to be an 'up-and-coming' neighbourhood with a 'smooth blending' of Northerners, Southerners, people from the Centre, Chinese, Catholics and Buddhists who had been forced to flee war. Social tension and other problems were reported by residents as being caused by outsiders, strangers and those without relatives in the area. Just one family was an established local family, so most residents were new arrivals and many of them were refugees who had experienced downward mobility and were aiming to regain their social and economic positions (Hoskins and Shepherd 1965; see also Hess 1977).[1] In 1991, Tân Định remained an area of great social diversity, primarily based on a market economy dominated by street selling and informal commerce. Tân Định was typical of inner-city life and deemed as being representative of contemporary urban society in 1991 by members of the Vietnamese Institute of Sociology seeking a location for a small-scale household survey commissioned to gauge the immediate effects of macro-economic reform on the social and material well-being of city residents.[2] Like other inner-city areas, the majority of the Tân Định population were migrants who came to the area in the second half of the twentieth century.[3] Other families had also arrived in the 1980s. Most of the new families who came to Tân Định were poor and from southern provinces, having arrived in the city for labour programs, petty trading, or having stayed after completing education or training (Trịnh Duy Luân 1996a, p. 101).

The researchers found that Tân Định was overcrowded and housed three to four times as many residents as other parts of the city. Over half

---

1   It is important to acknowledge the methodological limitations of this study. In a preface, Hoskins and Shepherd admit that none of the residents in the neighbourhood were aware that they were the subjects of the major study in 1965, nor of follow-up interviews in 1966. Nevertheless, in each example each example they reported, Hoskins and Shepherd suggest that moving to the city had followed downward mobility through losses of highly valued economic, social, and cultural capital, which are described in terms of household income, family wealth, status, educational credentials, employment, material possessions and the quality of housing. In assessing the residents' potential to regain social position, they stress class attributes and social differentiation expressed through embodied cultural capital (not their term) among women, men and children, giving examples of speech, deportment, behaviour, attitudes, beliefs, and related interactions within families and in the neighbourhood between people from different origins (Hoskins and Shepherd 1965, pp. 103, 118, 171, 190, 202).

2   The Tân Định household census results focus on the situation after *đổi mới*, although much of the supplementary material used by the research team relies on unpublished Vietnamese research materials that coincide with or predate the introduction of economic reform in 1986.

3   The local household census revealed that four in six (70 per cent) of Tân Định residents were born in the southern provinces and 'old Saigon' (*Sài Gòn cũ*) before 1975, one in six (12 per cent) came from the central provinces and one in six (13 per cent) were born in Hanoi and were displaced by war. Residents categorized under 'other origins' (*người từ nguồn gốc khác*) included those born in China before 1955 who came to Vietnam for business, as well as Vietnamese born in Cambodia or Laos during the colonial era (Trịnh Duy Luân 1996a, p. 101).

of its population was female and more than three quarters were under 40 years old, reflecting typical demographics of post-war societies. Even though more than a quarter (25 per cent) of Tân Định households were considered 'well-off', the area was relatively disadvantaged and marked by higher than average rates of unemployment and lower than average levels of higher education. Nearly a third of residents were out of work, two thirds had only a primary school education and only 5 per cent of Tân Định residents possessed university degrees (Trịnh Duy Luân 1996a).[4] As a representative area of Ho Chi Minh City, Tân Định's social diversity confirmed the difficulty in generalizing about what constituted an urban way of life (Trịnh Duy Luân 1996b, p. 160). Cultural dissonance characterized daily life in inner-city areas of Ho Chi Minh City.

Tân Định offered me an excellent location for research on urbanization and social mobility. The house where I stayed in Tân Định with a woman named Liên (introduced below) was one of two small laneway houses that she owned in the inner-city area. This house was at the end of a laneway (*hẻm*) just wide enough for motorbike handlebars, as long as the mirrors were removed or turned in. Despite its limited dimensions, the laneway provided access for a number of resident families, each of which had arrived in Ho Chi Minh City hoping to build a more prosperous future. This laneway became the starting point of my research and it is from here that I begin to introduce the social context of Ho Chi Minh City's new middle classes.

The laneway in Tân Định was separated from the street by a wire gate, located between a grocery shop and a jewellery counter. The gate was usually open during the day although only those with a purpose entered as it was awkwardly narrow. The laneway ended abruptly with a blue door above a square drainage grate. The grate especially posed a danger to coasting bicycle wheels. Whenever I came back to Liên's house on my bicycle, I always had one foot on the pedal and the other ready to hit the ground and stop to avoid damage to the bike, to me, or to the blue door.

---

4   The Institute of Sociology research team found that the population density of Tân Định (61,566 people/km^2) was more than three times the Ho Chi Minh City average (20,000 people/km^2) with Ward 6 housing more than four times the city's average (87,039 people/ km^2). Of its population, 54 per cent was female; 77 per cent were under 40 years old; 29 per cent were unemployed; and 70 per cent had a primary school education (Trịnh Duy Luân 1996a, pp. 99, 101, 104–5, 107–9). While only 5 per cent of Tân Định residents possessed university degrees, graduates and postgraduates made up almost 14 per cent of Ho Chi Minh City's workforce in 1990 (Nguyễn Quang Vinh 1996, p. 95).

The blue door led to a concrete courtyard and two houses, that of the neighbour and Liên. The concrete courtyard was neatly swept each morning and afternoon by the neighbour, who let her dogs loose to exercise there in the quiet afternoons. The two dogs – one black and one white – were the size of rats. Their claws scratched on the concrete and their teeth gnawed on bones and each other. They yapped, pissed, barked, and rummaged in any garbage waiting for collection. Each time the neighbour was out there, she helped herself to the refuse she could use and organized the piles of rubbish and recycling neatly along the whitewashed courtyard wall. She inspected the contents of my rubbish bags, ensuring fruit peels were wrapped in newspaper and any paper, metal, cloth, glass, string, or plastic was retrieved and separated for reuse or resale to peddlers. After organizing the rubbish, she locked her nipping dogs back in their cage and opened the courtyard tap to fill her bucket. She left the bucket under the tap, filling it by listening to the pitch as the water trickled in. Although Liên's house had running water, that tap was the only source of water the neighbour had. Bucket full, she sloshed the courtyard, washing away streams of raiding ants and dog smells, to leave the concrete wet so our shoes and tyres made dirty tracks inside the house.

It was a long time after moving in before I saw the neighbour's face. She only seemed to go out when her husband was home in the early mornings. No matter how quickly I came to the window, I was too late, managing only to catch a glimpse of her colourful cotton suit (*bộ*) or a rusty bicycle wheel disappearing from the courtyard as the gate snapped shut. I guessed she went outside to the market as I could see the twisted piece of wire near the gate where her *nón lá* (triangular reed hat) usually hung. Like the hat, her double-storey wooden house seemed to hang from the courtyard wall. Her house was always locked during the night, effectively placing a curfew on her husband and son. Sometime before midnight, she locked up with a set of heavy padlocks. The house gate was padlocked. The house door was padlocked. Sometimes the court-yard was also padlocked, regardless of whether we were in or out. There had been several disputes about the need to lock the courtyard because the laneway gate outside was also shut at night. Despite these locks, her balcony was enclosed under a web of wire fencing and curls of barbed wire. It was also padlocked. Whenever anyone moved inside their house, the floorboards and the walls also moved, and the structure seemed to be held together by twisted wire and the series of padlocks.

At the back of our house, where I slept on a mezzanine above the kitchen, I could easily hear what happened next door. At night, after a few steps and creaks, the clicking of a lock opening and the sliding of a door bolt was usually followed by the husband's pissing and his rasping cough. During the day, he was quite social and talkative, his hair white, teeth askew, knuckles protruding sharply. He smelt like the tobacco he sold on our street corner and, even though I passed daily, it was months before I could single him out from the others. Once, in the house he and his wife had argued all evening and into the night. Maybe he beat her. It was impossible to tell if the violent sounds were directed against her or against objects in the kitchen. Either way, clatters and crashes punctuated their dispute.

The neighbour's kitchen more often clucked, thudded and sizzled. She usually cooked in the late mornings. After some weeks I could determine by aroma what the family would be eating that day. I could also determine by perfume when they bathed each day, in the evenings, after she carried the water from the courtyard tap. The soapiness briefly masked the reek of their latrine. Their lack of facilities may have been because their place was unrenovated, making it older than any of the other neighbours' houses. That was not their only difference with the neighbours. Even though their adult son was obsessed by football, he did not join the laneway neighbours in a nearby café to watch games.[5] The son watched at home regardless of the broadcast time, cheering and protesting boisterously. He worked somewhere, socialized elsewhere and seemed to come home only when there was a match.

While they had a television, there was no telephone. One week the neighbour received several calls on our phone. She did not say much when she appeared in the doorway. She was wearing a printed cotton suit as usual, with long pants and short sleeves, and *dép* (slip-on plastic shoes) scrubbed clean. She pointed across the room and smiled at me. She stood just outside the doorway hesitating. She held the ends of her long hair, still dark, which was tied back neatly but reached her

---

5   Watching television had been as popular a pastime as reading among Tấn Định's young people since before reform with 92.9 and 91.5 per cent respectively enjoying these pastimes in 1985 (Đặng Thanh Trúc 1996, pp. 183–4). A local café rather than a private home would have been the typical venue for television watching.

hips. Looking at her face, it was impossible to know her exact age but she must have been between 40 and 60 because her son was already an adult. She still had her teeth and a wide smile. Almost immediately after she appeared in our doorway, the phone rang. Kicking off her shoes, she rushed towards it, holding her hand out to stop me taking her call. Soon after the phone calls, a second-hand Honda Cub motorbike appeared inside her gate. It was not long after that when a niece arrived to help inside the house. The niece worked in exchange for lodging and studied at one of the city's schools.

It seemed that everyone along the laneway was studying. Even babies and toddlers came in from outside to classes at the laneway's nursery school (*trường mầm non*). No matter how sour our neighbour's mood, she always smiled at the children whose limbs poked through the window bars into the laneway. The school – although soon to close – had been a fixture of the laneway for years and provided most of the morning and evening traffic. The courtyard neighbour had been there when the nursery school family first arrived in Saigon with their eight young children.

The matriarch of the nursery school was a large woman in a printed satin suit with styled hair streaked with grey. She spent her days supervising the kids as they laughed and occasionally cried. Her voice was usually gentle and sometimes sang, but also scolded. Close to lunchtime, the sizzle of the kids' meals made the courtyard dogs yap. After lunch, all became quiet as the kids slept on mats in front of an altar on the floor, its psychedelic halo of LEDs twinkling silently. The children were the centre of the nursery school family's activities. An unmarried daughter helped at home running errands and hanging out washing. She showered a favourite child in cuddles or just stood in the doorway waiting, where she seemed hopeful that something or someone would come along one day. At the end of each day her brother, shirtless and smoking, squatted on the doorstep at her feet to remove his splinters and treat his blisters. Upstairs on the balcony, the grandfather – wispy grey beard, thin grey cotton suit – shuffled between his cactuses and orchids. He twittered to his caged birds and he checked the washing drying on the balcony rail. Downstairs, a pregnant daughter-in-law rolled along the laneway back and forward between the gate and her door. After the appearance of her babe, which her sister-in-law could show off, the new mother rested in a hammock strung up across the nursery school room. During the day, there was no evidence that the family slept in this room. At night, their rolled out sleeping mats were separated by billowing white mosquito nets strung from picture frames, light fittings, door frames, or an invisible nail.

Opposite their busy place was a small home housing the remnants of another large family, who had also arrived in Saigon when their six boys were small. The family had grown up in a multi-story brick house on the street, but a desire for education had led to its sale. Four of the sons had since left; two were studying in the US. The two youngest remained at home fostering plans to study abroad. They shared a disenchantment with Vietnam's education system that was growing among Ho Chi Minh City's middle classes. With overseas Vietnamese relatives in the US willing to host them, the boys would be able to realize their education plans. The two youngest boys – and sometimes their classmates – spent the evenings glued to their monitors, where they played online games or, when their mother was home, listened to English conversation in electronic American accents.

Outside, their retired father paced up and down the laneway, directing visitors, opening and closing the laneway gate, noting through his owl-like glasses who went in, who went out, and when they came back. He loved to hate two bony kittens tethered at the base of someone's kitchen door and hissed threats to them as he passed. His wife, the jeweller, was set up near the laneway entrance out in the street. At her sales counter, she traded gold and cash, but also looked after visiting grandchildren and ate her meals. Like her neighbour, she was well dressed in a printed satin suit, but her hair was dyed reddish-brown and permed. Her makeup gave her dark eyes and rosy lips, her heels gave her height, and gold jewellery gave her a jingle as she polished her glass display case. While she rarely left her post unattended, her shrill voice organized her children, grandchildren and the other neighbours.

These neighbours, who had long established their families in the laneway, highlight the diversity of urban life. Their daily lives reflect their ongoing aspirations for betterment and some of the strategies they use, and have used, to regain status, position, assets and wealth lost, or not achieved, before migration. Other neighbours also shared aspirations for betterment and aimed to improve their existing positions.

MEETING XUÂN

Adjacent to the jewellery counter, Xuân ran her own shop in the front room of her simple house. She sold cosmetics and household goods, as well as tools for repairing the electricity supply and all kinds of lights and fittings. In the evening, she became too busy to talk as customers came to buy light bulbs, shampoo and soap. After carefully giving change for each sale, she stashed her profit with a wad of cash in the front pocket of her *áo bà ba* (southern-style peasant blouse). When she needed to, she changed large notes from a cash box she kept somewhere away from the street. Her husband did not have a key to her cash box. Without it, he could not make a sale on her behalf. One day when she was out the back bathing her son, he had me chat with his sister-in-law while I waited. Other times he would tell me to return in a short time to make my purchase.

Xuân looked after her toddler while she ran the shop. She fed him on the pavement, chasing his dribbling mouth with a spoon. Her eye followed him as he roamed between stock, the family's motorbike, and the small plastic stools where Xuân's sisters sat when they visited. Xuân was typical of women in Vietnam's Southeast; almost all were literate and married by their mid-twenties, and almost half (45.7 per cent) of the first-generation migrants in the Southeast had completed upper secondary or higher education (GSO 2011a, p. 108; GSO 2011b, pp. 27, 44). Xuân's home was also typical of urban households as it housed a nuclear family who owned a television, motorbike and refrigerator, but not a washing machine or air-conditioner (GSO 2011c, p. 87). Like her sisters, Xuân lived close to her mother's house and remembers the move to Saigon. The family had migrated from Huế, the former imperial capital on the Central Coast when Xuân, the youngest, was a child and their father, a Catholic scholar, was still alive.

Mid-morning most days, Xuân took lunch to her mother at her market stall several hundred metres along the street. She steered her husband's Honda Cub one-handed and balanced the meal with the other hand. It was the only time she took the motorbike out without her husband. During the afternoons, Xuân could not be found. Like the other neighbours in steamy Ho Chi Minh City, she took a rest (*nghỉ trưa*) on a bed, a sleeping mat, on a deckchair, or in a hammock. Customers, if any, were ignored. Appliances were turned off. The laneway slept. The rest of the time, Xuân was there waiting for customers and, like the jewellery seller and her husband, monitoring the laneway. This way, it was easy for her to keep up with what was going on and find out whatever she wanted to know.

Xuân had a curious mind. If I stayed out late, the next day she wanted to know where I had gone, whom I had gone with, what I had done, had I been safe, and had anything happened to me. We most often met in the late afternoons. Before it came time to prepare dinner, with her hair still wet after her bath, she related interesting articles from *Phụ Nữ* (Women) newspaper and I told her what I had seen. When Xuân found out that I was staying at Liên's house, she revealed that she knew Liên sometimes went out very late wearing a western dress (*aó đam*) and makeup. Xuân herself had never been out late and was surprised that when I went out I had seen respectable women out late. All the same, she happily sent her husband into Liên's house to fix a broken light fitting and later report his findings to her sisters when they dropped by to visit. Xuân had noticed that, like herself, I did not wear makeup. In our likeness we were unlike her American relatives, the jewellery seller and Liên, who were glamorous and well made-up. Xuân had been pleased when one of her sisters found out we were born a few months apart (*bạn cùng tuổi*), giving us something in common and a bond. Xuân's values mirrored a traditional ideal of middle-class women as submissive yet accomplished and sophisticated (Công Huyền Tôn Nữ Thị Nha Trang 1973; see Chapter 7 below). Although she was now a modest laneway shopkeeper, as a scholar's daughter, she had learned these views from her mother and elder sisters during her childhood.

Each evening, I stopped at the laneway entrance for Xuân's report on the day's happenings. Her reports focused on interesting activities in the neighbourhood, including what I had been doing each day. Often in collaboration with the jewellery seller, she recounted which meals I had taken and where, what I had said, whom I had met. She knew what I had bought, how much I had paid, and whether the price was too high. Sometimes she inspected my goods, particularly new clothes or new photographs. She kept track of who visited me, noting who they were, where they came from, and what business they had with me. She remembered what time they came, what time they left, and if they had visited before. It was in this manner that Xuân monitored those of us who left the laneway during the day. She did not seem concerned with the ones who remained under her nose, but only with those who disappeared going places and doing things that she did not know about and could only imagine. Of all the things about Xuân that Liên disapproved of, it was Xuân's imagination that especially annoyed her.

MEETING LIÊN

The first night I stayed at Liên's place in the laneway, it had not taken long to settle in. It was late when Liên had finished cleaning and I had finished unpacking my things near where I would sleep on the mezzanine. Neither of us had eaten an evening meal as I had arrived soon after the afternoon rain, but we sat for a long time in the main room, chatting and peeling oranges. Liên handed me a knife I thought of as a machete, but quickly retrieved it from my uncertain hand with a laugh. She dug its blade into the richly green skin of a ripe orange and twisted it so that the peel came off in one long curl. She nicked the top and the bottom of the orange with the knife to remove its ends. Apologizing and reassuring me that her hands were clean, she broke the orange open with her thumbs, but cleaned the threads of pith from its centre with the tip of the knife. After inspecting each half, she offered me one and took the other herself.

With our palms full of delicately expelled orange pips, we compared our lives and lifestyles. We had both grown up in the countryside and had moved to the city to study at university, both loved studying French as schoolgirls, and both liked to sleep late whenever possible. As students living on scholarships, we both had each retrieved our neighbours' discarded furniture from the street to use in our houses. It was on a reclaimed single bed used as a sofa that we sat. The missing leg of the sofa-bed was replaced by a brick and some old textbooks, which were camouflaged by a slippery floral bedspread. Liên handed me half of another peeled orange and we learned more about each other. But, like the sofa, the conversation became uncomfortable. Liên's eyes flashed. With a flourish of the machete, she highlighted the differences between her Vietnamese life and my Australian life. She pointed out that, unlike her, I had the freedom to choose a partner for love even against my family's wishes. More importantly, I could decide when to have a child with or without a husband and, without a strict one-or-two-child state family planning policy (introduced in 1989, recently relaxed), I had the opportunity to have many children. She paused, then continued to contrast our experiences. Outside the home, I had the legal right to gender equality in the workplace. In job hunting, my employers could not legally specify the desired physical appearance and personal characteristics of an applicant. In Vietnam, she warned me, regardless of her qualifications, if a Vietnamese girl was not tall enough or not pretty enough, she might not be employed.

Liên had first arrived in the city from the Mekong Delta to study at university in the late 1980s. Her move was part of a growing brain drain of rural students drawn to urban education opportunities. In the early 1990s, Liên had begun working in the lucrative and rapidly developing tourism sector, before winning a scholarship to study abroad. By her early thirties, she had risen to become a manager. Liên had worked hard to achieve her position and was committed to her career. She was one of the first Vietnamese women that I had met who openly articulated a desire for gender equality and autonomy. She was also one of the first privileged urban women I had met. She seemed full of contradictions. Although Liên cultivated an outward-looking personality by seeking new and foreign things in her urban lifestyle, she also fostered a traditional pathway by looking after her family in the countryside and paying particular attention to her mother's well-being. Perhaps it was the experiences that she brought back from postgraduate study abroad that informed her views about autonomy, independence and gender relations, which so differed from the state's ideological position regarding the submissive role of a good woman as a wife and mother (Rydstrøm 2010).

Unlike Xuân who ran a home-based business and cared for her child and mother, Liên left the laneway each day to work. Liên's mornings were strictly timed so she would not be late. She got up around 7 am, folded up her mosquito net and smoothed her bed back into a sofa. She then washed her face, drank a flavoured yoghurt drink and got dressed. Usually, she wore imported clothes which she had ironed the evening before. Next, she sat by the computer on a pile of economics training manuals stacked in front of the dresser which was directly under the window where the light was good. She balanced there while applying her makeup and styling her short spiky hair. Her cosmetic bottles and tubes were neatly lined up on the dresser, their French and Japanese labels visible. Taped to the dresser mirror was an old photo, a hand-colourized black and white portrait, showing her in a flower garden wearing an *aó dài* (traditional long dress), long hair flowing down her back and her face shaded by a parasol. Next, she chose a pair of shoes from the rack near the door. She put her handbag and often a folder of papers in the basket of her motorbike, a fully imported Japanese model and clearly her most valuable asset. She cherished it and the independence it allowed her. With it, she could go wherever she desired, whenever she desired (see Chapter 6). She attended to it with a worn polishing cloth after removing water and mud with a towel. The motorbike stand rested on an old mouse pad, a forgotten promotional item, which prevented it from scratching the bright geometric floor tiles. After opening the screeching metal door, she manoeuvred the heavy motorbike outside. It took several minutes for her to make her way from the courtyard to the laneway and lock up, before zooming off.

MEETING CÚC AND HẠNH

Whenever anyone entered the laneway, the echo of their motorbike engine alerted the residents. If there was a visitor for one of us, the engine would cut out in front of the blue door and a brief conversation might strike up with one of the sons smoking in the laneway. A hand would reach through to unlatch the door and it would begin to open, slowly, until it was clear the yapping dogs were caged. The visitor would then call out their greeting as they entered. One such commotion in the laneway brought two young women into the courtyard. The passenger, taller, was holding the door open as the driver manoeuvred a Honda motorbike into the courtyard. They both wore long-sleeved dark jackets and riding gloves. Their identities were obscured by cotton face masks worn to minimize the impact of air born pollution in traffic.

By the time their motorbike was secured in the courtyard, Liên was in the doorway welcoming them in. The sisters had travelled from the house that they shared in the city's north to meet me. Liên made the introductions. The taller one was her colleague Hạnh and the driver was her younger sister Cúc. Like Liên, both sisters were from the Mekong Delta and had come to the city for university study. Their move to the city had been supported by their older siblings – a brother who operated an orchard, a sister who traded rice. Like the shopkeeper, Cúc was born in the same lunar year as me, making us as compatible as school classmates (*bạn cùng lớp*).

Liên gestured them both onto the stiff settee decorated with thin Mickey Mouse cushions and picked up a thread of previous conversation with Hạnh. The four of us sat in the sleeping area which, by day, was the main room of the house. As usual, Liên sat on her sofa-bed between the motorbike and the television, I was between the television and the telephone, and opposite Liên, the sisters were between the telephone and the computer. A collection of cords and cables providing power, light and email snaked across the wall above their heads. Liên and Hạnh discussed renovations to Liên's mother's old wooden house in the countryside. Liên's mother had been avoiding decisions about repairing flood damage and glazing windows. Her mother's neighbours were very critical that one of the mango trees would have to be removed to make room for a new brick extension (see Chapter 6).

It was not long before the afternoon rain started and in seconds it drowned out their voices. The rain had started suddenly as always, but was heavier than the previous day. At the back of the house, a stream of cockroaches began to flow out of the bathroom warning us that the drains were filling up. At the front of the house, the courtyard soon filled with water flowing back up the laneway drain. Rubbish and mud spilled out onto the concrete. Water cascaded from the roof tiles, making a waterfall that blocked the front door. We sat through the downpour. The three of them sat with their backs straight and their knees together. Their smiles were wide revealing sets of uneven white teeth. Their hairstyles were short and fashionable. At home Liên usually wore a matching printed suit (*bộ*). The visiting sisters were well dressed in street clothes. Cúc wore a close fitting pastel blouse tucked into cream jeans. Hạnh wore a white lacy business shirt tucked into black pants. Both had left their low-heeled black sandals at the door. Neither wore nail polish. Both had pierced ears but Cúc wore only one gold earring, the partner lost. All three wore greenstone pendants on gold chains around their necks and marble bangles on their left arms, as they had since childhood. The bangles fitted so snugly that the only way to remove them would have been to break them off. The rain stopped as suddenly as it had started. After the rain, the sisters invited me to visit their family and then left for English night classes. Over the months that followed, these three women opened up to me a world of urban middle-class culture. Through this initiation, I began to explore how educated urban migrant women adapt to life in the city and how they live away from home.

HO CHI MINH CITY'S URBAN FRINGE

The northern fringes of Ho Chi Minh City, where Cúc and Hạnh lived, had been recently settled by migrants attracted to opportunities in the post-reform urban economy. Labour migrants to Ho Chi Minh City in the 1990s and 2000s settled on the city's fringes in developing urban districts such as Gò Vấp, Tân Bình and Thủ Đức as well as in rural-zoned peri-urban districts such as Bình Chánh and Hóc Môn (see Harms 2011). Settling in the urban fringes is advantageous for migrants due to cheaper land prices and the greater availability of relatively affordable housing.

One of these recently settled areas is Gò Vấp, a residential district on the northern fringes of Ho Chi Minh City that has urbanized from a semi-rural area since the 1990s. Based on a random household survey conducted in 2000, half of the residents of Gò Vấp arrived in 1997–1999, with two-thirds arriving from 1994–1999. Initially men dominated migration flows to Gò Vấp but after 1997 women made up the majority of migrants. As across other districts of Ho Chi Minh City, more women than men now live there. Contrary to national trends, more women than men in Gò Vấp hold university degrees (6.4 to 4 per cent), although in line with national trends, Gò Vấp women earn less than men receiving around 82 per cent of male wages. In 1999 half of Gò Vấp households had the bare necessities with only 6 per cent considered rich. At that time, four in five Gò Vấp households had their own motorbike and a colour television, and one in three had a refrigerator (Long et al. 2000, pp. 53–4, 56, 64, 66, 70–1). By 2009, almost all city households owned these assets (GSO 2011c, p. 86).

Like inner-city Tân Định, Gò Vấp was initially settled by inter-provincial migrants. But in Gò Vấp and the urban fringe intra-urban mobility accelerated its settlement as families began to leave Ho Chi Minh City's overcrowded inner districts to be closer to work, to own their own property, and to find larger and more affordable homes (Gubry et al. 2010, pp. 75–6). Since 1989, the population of Ho Chi Minh City's inner city has remained stable and growth has taken place on the northern urban fringe, with a population explosion of 2.25 million in the newly urbanizing districts of Gò Vấp and Tân Bình (Hy 2009, pp. 2, 26 n. 3). In a decade, the population of Gò Vấp had become as dense as Ho Chi Minh City's District One (26,065 and 26,289 people/km² respectively) and Tân Bình District in the urban north was on its way to becoming as overcrowded (17,871 people/km²) (GSO 2008, p. 23). Both districts were also rapidly becoming as unaffordable as the inner city.

Thu (introduced below) was an inter-provincial migrant who lived in Tân Bình District in a rented room in a rooming house in the proximity of the Maximart supermarket on Cộng Hòa Street. She invited me to spend the day with her and I caught the public bus to her place. As she was running late, she sent me a text message asking me to wait at the front of her building for her to return. This delay gave me an opportunity to relax in her neighbourhood which was much like an inner-city laneway.

Outside Thu's building in Tân Bình, a *nước mía* (sugarcane juice) vendor and a coffee shop both sustained successful businesses. Mai, the sugarcane juice vendor, greeted me in her thick Mekong Delta accent when I arrived, having recognized me from before. She invited me to order a drink and gestured to the nearer of a pair of black and green plastic strap chairs set up beside a small table. I did not hear the machine grind so I knew the plastic cup of iced sugar cane juice she placed on the table came from a jug of prepared juice. It was sweet, cool and delicious, reviving me after the stuffy thirty-minute, nine-kilometre ride from the Bến Thành bus terminal and the sunny ten-minute walk on bitumen tarmac and cracked concrete through a maze of side streets from the main road to Thu's place.

Behind me the vendor's kid pulled on the back of my chair and chanted, 'bà Tây, bà Tây …' (Mrs western lady). She was about four years old and usually wore hot pink or pale pink or both. Her hair was tied into pigtails and she chanted rhythmically as she played in the front room of their house behind the chairs, or skipped on the pavement in front of the chairs, near where her mother worked. Mai scuffed in her thick foam *dép* and her long ponytail swung across the back of her candy-coloured sleeveless shirt that, unlike the *áo bà ba* blouse that Xuân the laneway shopkeeper wore, was quite popular among modern young city women.

Only once did Mai leave her station to settle the bill at a far table against a wall on the opposite side of the intersection to her cart, where a group had been resting for several hours amongst their motorbikes. She took a round tray in one hand and dropped a *nón lá* on her head before diagonally crossing the road intersection into the shade of the wall opposite. The street was virtually silent, but not still. The leaves of the tall trees that shaded the street glinted in the sun. The piles of rubbish that lined the street sometimes shuffled as a rat or dog investigated. All the while, mobile vendors were passing by the building. Oranges were in season; a man riding a bicycle cart of oranges passed a woman pushing her cart of oranges. An older man pushed a huge cage cart containing all sizes and colours of plastic basins, buckets and pans as well as brooms, mops and brushes, topped off with a bundle of brown feather and colourful synthetic fibre dusters. None of these vendors called out as inner-city vendors typically do. They just walked or rode by, their goods displayed on a pole where people – on terraces, in cafés or waiting in front of the local school – could see. Occasionally a woman appeared from a doorway to buy a kilo of oranges, a plastic strainer or a DVD.

The street became more crowded towards 11 am with the arrival of parents waiting to pick up their children from the school opposite. The school parking guard unlocked and unhooked the heavy chain that secured a row of motorbikes. He walked each vehicle in turn from the sidewalk to the street and lined them up facing the road so that the rider could simply show the ticket and leave. The motorbikes did not belong to the teachers but to the senior students and moments after classes were dismissed they were gone. Out of the stream of traffic, Thu arrived. She apologized, having been delayed at the bank where she had sent money home to her mother, and invited me inside.

MEETING THU

Thu unlocked the street gate and pushed her motorbike past a three-metre fish tank into a large room which garaged more than a dozen motorbikes belonging to the other tenants. I had first met Thu when she was completing an MBA through a fee-paying off-shore program, which she paid for using a bank loan and a second higher interest loan from an aunt who traded gold. With the high salary of the job she won after graduation, she soon paid off both loans. The job was at the Ho Chi Minh City representative office of a European company and Thu was the most junior of its three employees. Her role was a Girl Friday.

She had arrived in Ho Chi Minh City from the Central Coast in 2000, eight years after graduating from university in Huế. Her decision to invest in graduate studies had exhausted her earnings and, in the short term, limited her options for housing. Nevertheless, she could afford to live alone in the rented room in Tân Bình.

With her motorbike locked, helmet stowed and shopping in hand, she led us upstairs to her place. Outside, Thu wore her favourite pair of burgundy leather authentic Clarks brand shoes. She kicked these off at the door and entered the sparsely furnished room. The room was cosy, about 20 metres square, but comfortable with one window opening into a light well in the centre of the building. On the floor along one wall was a flat screen TV and a laptop. Thu enjoyed a cable television subscription and broadband internet connection. There was also a knee-high table, a plush chair shaped liked lips and a chest of drawers decorated with a cute metre-high Strawberry Shortcake character. On top of the chest of drawers was a small bracelet of silver tortoises, which Thu had worn until a friend, a more senior colleague, had encouraged her to discard it as, in her opinion, the tortoises – a powerful symbol of longevity – were inhibiting Thu's ability to adjust to the demands of the dynamic workplace and slowing down her career.

On the floor against the other wall was a fridge, a bladeless fan, an induction cook top and a water filter. The few dishes Thu owned were stacked on the tiles under a tap in the corner. The ensuite bathroom housed a flushing toilet, a hot water machine, a small hand basin, a large plastic bowl for hand washing clothes, and a peg rack where her clothes hung. While Thu washed her own clothes, at least once a week she had her hair washed at a nearby hairdresser. She slept on a mat on the tiled floor and kept books and various other items on a mezzanine shelf that crossed half the room. Thu's standard of living was high and her lifestyle comfortable.

The room was rented. Thu's landlady was strict and insisted on evicting tenants who were more than one day late paying rent. Thu carefully maintained the relationship with her landlady which was good on the basis of sharing the bond of a common natal home on the Central Coast and supplying a constant stream of small gifts, usually comprising fruit or a home-cooked meal. While her accommodation suited her budget, Thu was dreaming of purchasing a property of her own, a desire of most Vietnamese to establish roots and also an indication that her move to the city was becoming permanent.

MEETING TUYẾT

The expansion of Ho Chi Minh City was driven by urbanization and intra-urban mobility. A lack of affordability of inner-city housing and a desire to own a home attracted people to the northern fringes in the 1990s and 2000s (Gubry et al. 2010, pp. 74–6). While Thu dreamed of a property of her own, Tuyết already owned her own home. I had first met Tuyết when she was a student living in an inner-city rooming house. Her move to the city had been supported by one of her older sisters who worked in petty trade. Tuyết continued living in the student room after beginning her career and, like Thu, had been dreaming of a home of her own. The strain of commuting and pressure from her large family to be closer to her ageing parents in Bình Dương province led her to hunt for land in Thủ Đức, a newly urbanizing area between Bình Dương and Ho Chi Minh City. In 1997 the expansive rural district of Thủ Đức had been sub-divided into three, and with the new Districts Two and Nine, rezoned as urban (Hy 2009, p. 26 n. 3). These new districts were rapidly urbanizing but not yet crowded. Thủ Đức and Districts Two and Nine still had relatively low population densities (GSO 2008, p. 23).[6] Thủ Đức had become highly desirable as an investor suburb, due in part to its improved infrastructure.

Thủ Đức was considerably more affordable than other districts in Ho Chi Minh City's north, particularly Gò Vấp and Tân Bình. After marrying, Tuyết had purchased land and commissioned her new brother-in-law to build a house. Although she had to wait for a break in his schedule, Tuyết saved about two-thirds of the overall cost of a new home. With land prices rising, over the next five years the value of the home would quadruple. It was tucked away in a small street in a developing area. Getting to Tuyết's house from the highway by motorbike was best achieved with a guide. First the rider turned down a small street, then into a laneway and through the wall of a damaged house into a graveyard at its rear and across a board over a ditch of stagnant water. Next the rider turned into another laneway that led to a series of small internal streets that wound between newly constructed houses and finally opened onto Tuyết's street. Her new house perched on a tiny block of land that the

---

6   Vietnamese state figures record the population density of Thủ Đức in 2007 as 7,706 people/km² and those of Districts Two and Nine as 2,679 and 1,941 people/km² respectively. They compared to District Seven (5,575 people/ km²), which incorporates the exclusive gated communities of Phú Mỹ Hưng (GSO 2008, p. 23).

previous owner had subdivided to sell. In front of the house was a small odd-shaped courtyard with a steeply angled concrete floor and freshly white washed walls. This was where her family's motorbike and bicycle stood when the house was open. In the courtyard there was also a tap for cleaning fish, scrubbing shoes on Sundays, and watering a number of potted plants.

At the front of the house, the guest room was furnished with a sofa and a coffee table that stored traditional medicine, candy, newspapers and books. On the wall above the sofa was a calendar and several artworks. The household's shoes were kept outside the room on the top step where they were out of the sun or rain. Several family portraits were on the altar set up inside the door. On the wall opposite the sofa was a large plasma television. The couple enjoyed cable television; Tuyết's husband improved his English skills by watching documentaries on Australia Network during the day while Tuyết preferred watching Hollywood action films after work. She also enjoyed chatting on the Internet with friends across town. Tuyết had limited opportunities to meet them due to the distance between their houses and also because she worked full-time. Her husband, who was also the youngest in a large family, had been retrenched, was unemployed and looking for a graduate study program in Ho Chi Minh City.

Tuyết employed her older sister as a cook and housekeeper, paying her on a monthly stipend which supplemented her regular work in petty trade. Her sister did the housekeeping in the mornings. The kitchen was at the back of the house joining a neighbour's wall so there was little ventilation or natural light. Throughout the house, the flooring was extravagant black granite which reflected like a pond when clean but easily picked up dust and became gritty underfoot. When she was not cooking or serving food, the sister was usually sweeping.

Upstairs, there were three levels, with three bedrooms, two bathrooms and a home office. Each room was decorated with studio portraits of the young couple in wedding attire. On the roof top terrace, where Tuyết's husband was growing salad greens in a plastic lined basket of soil, the couple could enjoy the fresh river breeze at night. Owning their own spacious home also enabled them to entertain friends and relatives at home. The move across Ho Chi Minh City from a shared rented inner-city room to a home of her own located Tuyết closer to her workplace and her natal family, but also offered her a relatively better standard of living that contrasted with the lifestyles led in the village of her childhood and the modest accommodation of her days as a university student.

FINDINGS

Living in Vietnam's urban Southeast enables educated young women to take up opportunities that they might never have had without migrating to the city. Aspirational migrants arrive in Ho Chi Minh City from across Vietnam, particularly from the Mekong Delta and Central Coast. They grew up in relatively humble conditions and were pressured from a young age to achieve scholastically as a means to securing a better future. Investment in their education was a long-term strategy implemented by the family to realize social mobility in the future. Winning a university place was a first step in realizing the dream to build a more prosperous life. Migrating to the city for university study, or after graduation, and finding a salaried job that involved professional white-collar work was a subsequent step in moving up socially. To realize this strategy, the young women left their natal homes with the support of their elders – parents, older siblings, an aunt or uncle – who contributed resources as they could afford them. Even though they were located away from their families in the city, the young women maintained close contact and regularly visited their families. They made a break from the past, but did not sever all ties. In recalling their relative impoverished childhoods, they remain conscious of the influence they can have on the family back home. A family that becomes fragmented in this way is a multi-dimensional family, where younger members who relocate to the city are able to achieve a relatively higher social position with the support of older members who remain in rural areas.

In the city, young educated migrant women are highly mobile in their daily lives, travelling across Ho Chi Minh City for work, leisure and family commitments, and often journeying beyond the city to return home temporarily, especially for family rituals. They enjoy a relatively high standard of living; most possess the material assets and household technologies associated with urban affluence, some can afford to live alone, and others own their own homes. Housing in the crowded inner city is more restricted than the more spacious properties in the less expensive urban fringe. City life exposes them to new ways of living and new opportunities for education and work, for leisure and recreation, for marriage and social life that would not have been available if they had remained in their natal homes.

CHAPTER FOUR

Lifestyles of professional work

*A*n initial step towards achieving social mobility is gaining an education and associated cultural competences required to build a career as a salaried professional. Education is essential to securing the types of employment that might eventually give access to the conditions for realizing social aspirations. Education and employment also provide opportunities for exposure to the social, economic and cultural markers of success. Building a career requires finding an occupation suitable to one's skills, experience and qualifications. But achieving enduring social status can be difficult in the highly competitive job market of Vietnam's Southeast. Many graduates are unable to secure stable employment. High rates of graduate unemployment in urban Vietnam can also indicate that, when many graduates are unable to make a good match between their skills and occupations, they might settle for a lower-skilled position, or opt out of the salaried professions of the new middle class in preference for small business or homemaking (Leshkowich 2006; Turner and Nguyen 2005). Those who persist may face other challenges.

Certain types of work which have long been considered suitable only for women are increasingly associated with achieving upward mobility as this work is often located in the foreign or private sectors (Fahey 1998, p. 241). Female-dominated fields, such as general office work, secretarial and interpreting positions, are among the fields which provide direct access to conditions that enable an aspiring young woman to better herself and even to become a member of the new middle class. How she might achieve this depends on the connections she makes between career choices and lifestyling options. Conforming to or resisting Vietnamese traditional ideals of femininity may become central to her success.

This chapter explores how young educated migrant women make a living in the mega-urban Southeast. The discussion begins with job-hunting and focuses on types of urban and professional employment in the lives of Cúc and Hạnh, as well as their sister Thảo, a young graduate Tuyết, and others. This chapter identifies how workplace performances of femininity affect urbanite lives for women and men, such as Minh, and in what ways working is beneficial to developing an enduring new middle-class social position.

PROFESSIONAL EMPLOYMENT IN THE MEGA-URBAN SOUTHEAST

Job-hunting in Vietnam's Southeast reveals to graduates how competitive the urban employment market has become, even when they have been forewarned about its nature. Despite the competition, opportunities are promising and continue to attract migrants from across Vietnam. Cúc was one young person who followed her older sister to Ho Chi Minh City for university study and a professional career. Soon after we met, Cúc invited me to visit her rented house to spend the day hanging out. She had hoped my company would distract her sisters from nagging her to find a job. Cúc had not worked since being retrenched from a position at a foreign-owned company two years earlier. She had been recruited for that position, along with several of her classmates, from the graduating class at her university. Cúc was still waiting for an appropriate job to come her way. She was fussy about which positions she would apply for. She had a university degree and certificates in English language proficiency. But her workplace training, undertaken as part of her previous job, was out of date and of little help to her profile of skills.

Cúc was looking for a position that was close to home. She did not want to commute more than half an hour to her workplace as her younger sister Thảo, a supermarket cashier, did each of the seven days a week she worked. Cúc did not mind working hard, but she did not want to work so hard that she never had time to see her friends or visit her parents in the village. She did not want to travel away from home overnight, as her brother regularly did in his position as a national sales representative for a foreign-owned manufacturing company. Cúc did not want to work in the public eye, in reception or customer service, as her cousin did. Her cousin had described the interview process which had involved an assessment of her physical appearance, including facial features, hairstyle, makeup, body shape, weight and height. The cousin had to fit an age bracket (23–28 years old) as well as remain unmarried and childless to keep the job. Cúc desired a specified minimum salary, a suitable wage for a graduate with several years working experience, but one that was relatively high considering her lack of experience and extended time outside the workforce.

As her older sister, Hạnh had the right to advise Cúc. She did this by encouraging her to consider a range of workplace benefits other than salary. Hạnh had found that office work provided a range of advantages. A uniform provided by the company would save her buying new clothes, but also save her ruining her good outfits travelling to work by motorbike and from stains caused by photocopier toner and printer ink. Working in an office had the advantage of air-conditioning as well as work that was not physically demanding. Better still, in many offices staff could benefit from a comfortable chair, individual desk, free phone calls and access to the Internet. With other women working in the office, sharing lunch could break up the monotony of the working day with enjoyable social outings to nearby restaurants and cafés. These conditions might have been readily available in the foreign sector in Vietnam's Southeast but were not necessarily widespread in the private or state sectors.

Hạnh considered that working in a state company would provide guaranteed conditions, including medical checks and maternity leave, and the position would be permanent. Even though the salary would be significantly lower and there would be fewer challenging or rewarding opportunities, a worker could take extended periods of leave to continue studying to improve her skills or even to organize a short-term consultancy position in the non-state sector to boost her income. Hạnh's own work experience had taught her that temporary and short-term contract positions in private companies in Ho Chi Minh City were far easier to secure than permanent jobs. Further, the non-state sector offered more robust opportunities for social mobility with more challenging work, greater opportunities for networking, and higher remuneration.

The expansion of the private sector in Vietnam after reform was regarded by the Vietnamese state to be a solution for the employment of women beyond agriculture (Le Thi 1995, p. 214). But employment for women in professional positions is characterized by instability and wage inequalities. Vietnamese women in general have lower wages than men and more irregular incomes. In 1992–93, women in the Mekong Delta and Southeast region earned just 60 per cent of men's wages (Tran and Le 2000, p. 112). While participation rates are improving, women in

Vietnam on average earn only about 85 per cent of men's wages (Giang 2010, p. 44). Women's high representation in the foreign sector in Vietnam – where two-thirds of employees are women (GSO 2008, p. 96) – contrasts sharply with average incomes as foreign sector jobs are particularly well remunerated in comparison with the state sector. Across Southeast Asia, new middle classes favour the non-state sector for employment. In Malaysia, middle-class parents prefer their daughters to take up positions in the private sector or in their own businesses (Embong 2002, pp. 90–1).

To be successful in job-hunting, it is important to study the competition. Playing the potential employer, Hạnh compared Cúc to each of the graduates in a jobseeker column and pointed out why Cúc was better qualified and more skilled than each of the other graduates. Frowning in concentration, Cúc also studied the column and agreed, questioning why she had not yet found a job.

At this time, graduates and unemployed workers advertised their qualifications and skills in a jobseeker (*người tìm việc*) column in the classified section of newspapers and periodicals with the hope of being approached by an employer. An example in a weekly publication included résumés of 51 jobseekers, 13 of whom did not have university qualifications. Of the 38 graduates, 16 were teachers, ten more were English teachers, six had commerce or economics degrees, and six were IT and accounting graduates. All were seeking employment in an office, enterprise or school. Two knew two foreign languages and none held postgraduate qualifications (*Thế Giới Phụ Nữ*, 11 Nov 2000, pp. N-O). While it is unclear whether these jobseekers were already employed and seeking to better their positions, what it did suggest was that graduates are clear about the type of work and minimum conditions that they desire, and that existing qualifications, skills and experience reflect a competitive urban job market.

Having academic qualifications is a requirement for entry to professional work, even to simple administrative positions. Vietnamese families are willing to invest resources to send their young people to the city to spend years studying for university qualifications. While many rural parents do not have direct personal experience of university education, in sending their children to city institutions, they recognize a connection between university or college education and increased opportunities for their children in the urban labour market and for themselves in the form of remittances of money, goods and knowledge that will flow from their children in the future (GSO & UNDP 2001, p. 25; Ha and Ha 2001, pp. 154–6; Long et al. 2000, p. 119; Nguyen Pham Thanh Nam et al. 2000, p. 10). In multi-dimensional families where young people occupy relatively higher status positions than their parents and older siblings, there is a degree of self-interest and an expectation of reciprocity among the elders in investing in the young people's education (see Chapter 6).

The labour markets in Vietnam's cities are highly competitive. In the major cities, half the population has a college education.[1] Despite studying at university, many urban graduates face difficulties finding secure work in the competitive urban labour market. Ngan Collins (2005, pp. 176, 184–5) suggests that less stable employment continues to be a signifi-cant problem that affects urban employees and especially impacts upon women. The highest rates of unemployment were found amongst young women aged 20–34 in Vietnam's major cities (GSO 2011c, p. 83). But only one in fourteen (7.3 per cent) of Vietnam's unemployed were university graduates (Giang 2010, p. 44). University education provides credentials and possibly skills that enables graduates to find work but the jobs they find are often insecure or outside their professional area. In the 1990s up to a third of graduates in Hanoi were unemployed or working in fields un-related to their study (Marr and Rosen 1999, p. 193). By the early 2000s some of Hanoi's unemployed graduates had turned away from a salaried profession to small business in preference to ongoing under-employment (Turner and Nguyen 2005, p. 1700). An increasingly competitive labour market characterized by less stable employment among graduates in fact stems from greater access to higher education.

Increasing participation in higher education adds to the competitive-ness of the urban labour market by reducing the value of qualifications. When status groups who previously made little use of the school system enter the race for academic qualifications, their presence forces groups whose reproduction was mainly or exclusively achieved through education to step up their investments in order to maintain the relative scarcity of their qualifications and their class positions. As Bourdieu

---

1   Young women are highly educated: state figures report one in three (32.3 per cent) women aged 25–34 and one in seven (15.2 per cent) women aged 35–44 have junior college, uni-versity or postgraduate education. This compares with one in three men (35.4 per cent) and one in five men (20.5 per cent) respectively (GSO 2011c, p. 75).

(1984, pp. 133–4) explains, academic qualifications become key stakes in inter-class competition, generating continued growth in the demand for education and causing an inflation of qualifications. This effect, which is evident among Ho Chi Minh City's graduate jobseekers, occurs when competition among graduates to find suitable employment is exacerbated by the changing value of academic qualifications. Widespread women's education also becomes a significant factor in this kind of effect because women bring qualifications to the labour market which were previously held in reserve. This causes a gradual extension of the monopoly held by those with academic qualifications and a restriction of the types of employment open to the unqualified.

GENDERING WORKPLACES

Vietnamese women have been working in salaried professional positions in Saigon since the wartime boom and after. But types of employment in Vietnam are gendered. Vietnamese do not regard occupations to be gender neutral and an assumed gender divide that exists in Vietnamese social relations extends to 'men's sectors' and 'women's sectors' of employment (Tran and Le 2000, p. 95). Genderizing has applied to almost every sector and occupation in Vietnam. In agriculture 80 per cent of workers are women and women dominate other sectors, making up 70 per cent of workers in textiles production; 100 per cent in pre-schools; 80 per cent in primary schools; and 81 per cent in nursing (Tran and Le 2000, pp. 98–9). Women comprise more than half of workers in light industry, trade, finance, state insurance, and communication services (Hòang 1996, p. 191). Medicine is also viewed as an 'appropriate job for a woman', since former General Party Secretary Lê Duẩn was reported stating 'a doctor is like a good mother' (cited in White 1987, p. 231). Occupations such as these have been considered suitable for women at least since the 1930s, when two-thirds of educated women worked as teachers and headmistresses of district and provincial schools and the remainder were midwives, nurses, secretaries and businesswomen (Coughlin 1950, p. 5; Ngo Vinh Long 1974, p. 15).

In Vietnamese workplaces, the image of a typical woman worker is shaped by Vietnamese beliefs in an inherent feminine 'character' (*tính nữ*). For Vietnamese, gendered characteristics differentiate men's and women's abilities in different occupations and employment sectors.

Helle Rydstrøm (2004, p. 74) observes that a typical female character includes gentleness, obedience, sweetness and being easy to control. Angie Ngoc Tran (2004, p. 212) reports that women workers are expected to be more docile, dexterous, passive, more flexible, conscientious and less likely to rebel than men. Gendering employment amounts to a double message for Vietnamese women, suggests Christine White (1987, p. 231), as they legally have equal access to education and employment in general, but some jobs are believed 'naturally' better suited to women. These beliefs are widely held by women and men but young women, especially those from rural areas, are able to benefit from the availability of 'feminized' low-skill jobs in the industries of the Southeast. In garment, textiles and electronics manufacturing, as Danièle Bélanger and Katherine Pendakis (2009, p. 265) found, unmarried young women who are perceived to be docile and hard working are the most preferred employees.

Different employment fields provide different opportunities to Vietnamese women given an assumed naturalization of workplace femininity. Vietnamese intellectuals in the 1980s used a naturalization of workplace femininity to account for disproportionately fewer numbers of Vietnamese women in leadership positions. They report low participation of women due to a lack of prerequisite education, qualifications and experience, but also due to a female 'inferiority complex' which limited women's capacities to achieve (Lê Thị Nhâm Tuyết 1989, pp. 40–1). While in the early 1980s women occupied 5 per cent of leadership positions in management in Vietnam, by the early 1990s women occupied 10 per cent of leadership positions as managers and government ministers in female-dominated fields (i.e. education, health care). At this time, there were few or no women leaders in economic sectors including planning, investment, finance and banking (Tran and Le 2000, pp. 188–9). Women in manufacturing and in government and the state sector were also expected to defer to the experience, authority and expertise of men. In the state higher education sector, where women were a minority, female academics faced under-employment due to a gender-based 'glass ceiling' that limited further professional opportunities and restricted their promotion. Even though women were employed at universities and colleges in Vietnam's major cities, several of Ho Chi Minh City's institutions had few senior female staff and no women on their management boards (Nguyen Thi Khoa 1997, pp. 262–3, 266). Female academics in Vietnam were disadvantaged by perceptions that women are weaker than men, they are passive in the workplace and they make poor leaders (Le Thi 2001, pp. 140–1). By the late 2000s, women held a quarter (25.7 per cent) of seats in the National Assembly and 12.5 per cent of the ministerial and 9 per cent of the deputy ministerial appointments. However, women's representation as heads and deputy heads of government departments was falling. The under-representation of women in senior positions and absence from decision-making posts was explained in terms of 'women's lack of ability'. Attitudes such as these coupled with a lower retirement age for women, Truong Thi Thuy Hang (2008, pp. 16–19) asserts, underpin Vietnamese employers preferences to hire and promote men.

In contrast, in female-dominated fields that are positively associated with feminine qualities of caring and nurturing, women are able to control their conditions, training and incomes. In Vietnam, four in five employees in pharmacy are women and women workers have had advantages in pharmacy that have not been available to them in other fields. Nearly two thirds of women in pharmacy achieved graduate or postgraduate qualifications, appointments to senior positions including directorships, and opportunities to travel nationally on public health campaigns. Pharmacy has offered women increased opportunities for professional development and career achievement, also unavailable to women in other sectors (Lê Thị Nhâm Tuyết 1989, p. 56).

While occupations have been recognized as suitable for women since the 1930s, urban Vietnamese have challenged the naturalization of workplace femininity since at least the 1960s. Within the constraints of a wartime economy, Saigonese administrators and intellectuals began questioning popular beliefs about feminine characteristics in determining the suitability of women for particular positions in order to meet staff shortages. The Saigonese public administration acknowledged that women's abilities differed depending on their education and experience in a reassessment of whether sentimentality – a characteristic historically associated with Vietnamese femininity – made women unsuitable for leadership (General Civil Service Commission 1967, pp. 18–19). By the mid-1980s, as David Marr (1988, p. 19) observes, gifted young women had begun to avoid teaching and other professions stigmatized as 'women's work'.

After reform, challenges to the naturalization of workplace femininity, which had stunted women's careers, began to escalate. In 2003, an article in *Phụ Nữ* (Women) newspaper questioned whether women could be better managers and leaders than men. Based on an analysis of feminine characteristics, the article suggested that a woman is just as capable of leading a company, corporation or nation as a man and she may even be a superior (*trội hơn*) choice due to her feminine character. Reasons listed include that, although men are physically larger than women and excel at giving and receiving orders, women have better physical reflexes, are more flexible (*mềm dẻo*), and have the advantage of being more open-hearted and more approachable than men in communicating with others. Women can analyse problems more effectively and efficiently than men, and adapt more readily to change because they are not as conservative as men, giving them a flexible (*đa dạng*) management style. Relationships between 'female chiefs' (*sếp nữ*) and their staff are also better because women are more sympathetic, gentle, but also decisive (*Phụ Nữ*, 24 March 2003, p. 9). This article clearly maintains that there are inherent differences between Vietnamese men and women that affect their abilities at work. But it also indicates that some characteristics associated with workplace femininity have been re-evaluated and are viewed more positively by emphasizing the abilities of women, rather than focusing on how women fail to be men.

The Vietnamese state has noted that the private and service sectors of the mega-urban Southeast which attract graduates and other young people value feminized attributes such as flexibility, adaptability and approachability in staff (GSO & UNDP 2001, pp. 88–9). Emphasizing women's abilities allows for the possibility of women occupying higher status positions, a feature feminist sociologist Lisa Adkins (2001, p. 679) regards as a positive consequence of workplace femininity. In Vietnam, this is particularly evident in a female-dominated field such as pharmacy. In other fields, workplace femininity has been used to create disadvantages for women. Linda McDowell (1997, p. 154) observes that workplace practices in London's financial sector naturalize women's performances of femininity through definitions which do not concern skills or competencies but that changing attitudes in employment mean that performances of workplace femininity may become advantageous. Femininity may be an asset in the labour market as it is in the marriage market where it is traded for economic and symbolic advantage (Lovell 2000, pp. 23–5). But, as Beverly Skeggs (2004, p. 22) points out, femininity can act as cultural capital in a way that is not conventional and conforming to gender normalcy can only offer a limited form of capital.

One approach to understanding how femininity can be reconfigured to become an advantage in the workplace is to recognize feminine appearances and behaviours in terms of embodied cultural capital. This focus from western feminist theory on shifts in the value of femininity at work opens up possibilities for understanding how members of the new middle class in Vietnam might reconfigure gender expectations to enhance their careers and lifestyles. Femininity as cultural capital functions along the lines of Bourdieu's first state of embodied cultural capital, where dispositions are inscribed on the mind and body of the individual as a process of self-improvement. Unlike money and property rights, embodied capital cannot be transmitted instantaneously as, over time, it becomes an integral part of the person. Because of this, it is more disguised and predisposed to be unrecognized as a form of capital and recognized instead as a legitimate competence (Bourdieu 1997, pp. 48–9). This recognition is what drives the naturalization of femininity in Vietnamese workplaces and what makes femininity as cultural capital important in producing social distance in professional urban workplaces.

However, as Lisa Adkins (2001, pp. 670–1) points out, an increasing feminization of work and workers does not simply 'undo' conventional understandings of gender, but results in an entirely new configuration. Emerging middle-class positions have been increasingly defined by mobile relationships to gender performance, with more flexible gender codes evident among urban middle classes (Adkins 2001, p. 691). As Bourdieu (1984, pp. 382–3) explains, middle-class women seem to be less pressured to conform to feminine norms of chastity, modesty and docility as socially constituted differences between the sexes 'weaken' when individuals move up the social hierarchy.

WORKING TO FIND LIFESTYLE

Cúc's job-hunting project lasted for several weeks into the new year. The job Cúc eventually won was in the office of a textiles factory located on the northern fringes of Ho Chi Minh City, a rapidly industrializing area providing increasing employment opportunities. The company employing Cúc was a Vietnamese state textiles enterprise that supplied clothing to the export market. Cúc's workplace was a thirty-minute motorbike ride from her home, a journey she undertook six days a week. With six other women, she shared the responsibility of running the factory office. Her main duties centred on accounts and included answering the telephone, taking messages, writing letters, sending and receiving orders, photocopying and filing. Her workplace provided her with access to the Internet and a personal email account, a coup considering her junior level in the company. At work, Cúc used Vietnamese with her colleagues and English with international distributers and wholesalers. She had virtually no face-to-face contact with foreigners.

Like the other company employees, Cúc was required to wear a uniform to work. For women workers in Vietnam, varying formal and informal dress codes apply depending upon the occupational area and work duties. The different status of employees is recognizable in their dress codes. Cúc's uniform was a white shirt embroidered on the breast pocket with the company logo. Cúc and the other young office staff wore the uniform with jeans, or straight skirts, and fashionable shoes, but the older workers and recent migrants from the countryside on the factory floor preferred plain dyed loose slacks in dark colours and *dép* (cheap plastic slip-on shoes). Those uniforms resembled the fitted *áo bà ba* blouse and loose *quàn* pants of traditional southern peasant garments, similar to those worn by Xuân in her shop and women in Cúc's home village. Nevertheless, Cúc and her office colleagues covered the state-company logo on their blouses with their trendy jackets when they went out. Like the other office staff, Cúc had also begun to wear reading glasses. When she was not reading, they were visible on the top of her head or hanging around her neck.

Through her workplace, Cúc had quickly fallen into a social group of other single young women who shared her lifestyle aspirations. Via her contact with this group, she learned to recognize and display urbanite credentials in embodied practices and through markers of social mobility (see Chapter 5). Gradually Cúc's social world began to more closely resemble that of her sister Hạnh, who was then working in the non-state sector.

MOBILITY AND CAREER LIFESTYLE

After staying overnight at the sisters' house, Hạnh offered to give me a lift home on her way to work. By the time we set out, it was after 9 am and late to start a working day in Ho Chi Minh City. Hạnh seemed unconcerned and I wondered if she had taken the morning off, a query that drew a smirk and a denial from her. On the way, she pulled over three times to answer, without removing her riding gloves, the mobile phone which hung on a cord around her neck. It became clear that since I had last met her, Hạnh had changed jobs. Her new job had a higher salary, but required her to travel 45 minutes to and from work as well as travel all over Ho Chi Minh City to meet local suppliers, whose goods her company shipped throughout Asia and to the European Union. Some days she travelled over 100 kilometres between her house, the downtown office and industrial parks on the western, northern and southern city fringes. Because she used her own motorbike, she reasoned it was no problem to cross town to deliver me home on work time.

The advantage of Hạnh's new position was that her duties were very light, involving communication and liaison but limited responsibility. Despite being a full-time employee, she estimated that she spent less than 10 hours per week in the office. Most of that time was spent negotiating on her mobile phone. With little tying her to the office, Hạnh was free to leave as long as she took her mobile phone with her. With the extra time during the week, Hạnh was able to attend classes, an activity encouraged by her boss. She also had enough free time to meet friends during the day and rarely returned to the office after lunch. She admitted she was bored at work and often felt lonely, but aimed to keep the job for a year until she graduated courses in Japanese language and macroeconomics, each of which might assist her to get a better job.

Aspiring to a better job motivates graduates like Hạnh. Un- or underemployment of graduates and professionals enables their pursuit of further qualifications and credentials. Bourdieu (1984, pp. 133–4) dealt with a continued growth in the demand for education and the inflation of academic qualifications as a problem of widespread women's education. In his analysis, the education of middle-class women contributes to a devaluation of academic qualifications through interclass competition that generates an increasing demand for education. Although a more ideal job for Hạnh might be one that made more effective use of her existing skills without requiring additional formal qualifications, investing time to enhance her academic qualifications helped to consolidate her reservoir of cultural capital for a better job in the future. Following Bourdieu's (1984, p. 337) view, her under-employment actually increased her ability to 'take off'.

Yet there are other advantages of graduate under-employment for social mobility. Like most of her friends, Hạnh frequently changed jobs, usually staying a year, or less, in any position. She moved to increase her salary, improve her status at another company or due to boredom. She planned to continue moving between positions as long as she was in demand and able to do so, or until she got married and no longer wished to do so. Constantly moving meant that she continued to meet new people and widen the network of contacts which could help keep her in work. Frequently moving between companies, on the one hand, might limit career development but, on the other hand, could overcome the problem created by a glass ceiling in a particular workplace and offer different, more challenging experiences.

While women bring qualifications to the labour market which were previously held in reserve, their participation also extends the monopoly on academic qualifications and imposes a restriction on types of employment open to the unqualified or lesser qualified. However, academic qualifications never achieve a total acceptance on their own, because a foundation of economic and social capital is necessary to successfully exploit any advantages offered through cultural capital in the form of education credentials (Bourdieu 1984, p. 134). Establishing and maintaining social networks through the workplace becomes as important to graduates as the qualifications through which they first gained access to the workplace. But there is a range of other ways for a graduate to benefit from underlying cultural capital.

ADVANTAGES OF EXCLUSION

Besides salary, Hạnh's position was less advantageous than Tuyết's first professional position, even though Tuyết seemed to be just as under-employed as Hạnh. Tuyết had graduated with a major in English language, but had never before needed to work as her older sister had supplemented a scholarship she had received to move to the city and study. After graduation, Tuyết had briefly tried teaching undergraduates but, given her young age, had found it difficult to control the classes and, feeling disillusioned, had abandoned that career. Unsure what to do, she had consulted one of her former professors for advice. He had suggested that she apply for a position in a foreign company where she would be required to use her English language skills. Having recently been approached by a prospective employer seeking a reliable and responsible young woman, he had taken the opportunity to introduce her with a recommendation. Tuyết had started work the following day.

Tuyết's job was based in a European-owned company's Southeast Asia office located on the northern fringes of Ho Chi Minh City in Thủ Đức district. Tuyết was the only Vietnamese staff member in her section and her duties involved making phone calls to Vietnamese suppliers, translating letters from Vietnamese into English, and filling out supply forms in Vietnamese. Other staff were employed to deal with foreign suppliers and export deliveries. The majority of her duties were office-based, although her boss occasionally took her on a factory visit or to a meeting allowing her the opportunity to work as his interpreter, which was advantageous to him because she had a working knowledge of the company.

When she commenced work, Tuyết was still living in shared accommodation near the university. Six days a week, she travelled outside Ho Chi Minh City for work. Because the distance was too great for her to manage on a motorbike, she preferred to use the new public bus system. The bus journey took around 45 minutes allowing her time for a rest on the way to and from work. The greatest benefit of Tuyết's job was the salary, which was enough for her to live in a downtown district and send her mother a monthly remittance, a modest contribution but one that was higher than any other member of her family could make. The greatest disadvantages were that she found the job exhausting and the workplace foreign. The international staff communicated at work in English, the language each had in common. Tuyết complained about the air-conditioning in the building, which made her so uncomfortable that she began to wear a winter jacket at her desk. She also complained about the foreign food provided (for free) in the staff canteen, although she persisted in meeting her co-workers for lunch. The advantage of attending lunch was that over the meal she had the opportunity to socialize with her foreign co-workers, who encouraged her to study abroad in order to pursue a vocational career, such as accounting. At the end of Tuyết's three-month trial period, her boss, who regularly had lunch with the general staff, agreed to support her to study a one-year vocational postgraduate course of her choice in any Southeast Asian country.

Tuyết's success at work extended to success in her social life. Her shared room was near the university and, even after graduating and starting work, she continued to socialize with a number of undergraduate friends living nearby. They adopted her as an older sister (*chị*) and looked up to her as a role model due to her enviable job, her higher income, her proficient English skills, her better motorbike, her greater experience, and her more advanced age. The group of younger undergraduates also admired her changing appearance, each of her new hairstyles, her more fashionable clothing, and every new pair of shoes she bought. However, although they admired her, Tuyết began to distance herself from them and began to compare herself to her foreign co-workers. She did not report many similarities between herself and her co-workers from Europe, North America and Australia: each was considerably older than her, in superior positions, and male. But she admired the young women from other Southeast Asian countries with comparable qualifications and positions.

Tuyết began to imitate their dress, wearing straight skirts and short sleeved white business shirts with brightly coloured Birkenstock-style sandals, fashions which had only become popular in urban Vietnam in the 2000s (e.g. *Thời Trang Trẻ*, 15 Apr 2005, pp. 34–7; *Tiếp Thị Việt Nam*, 5 Jul 2004, pp. 24–5). She cut her hair short like them and had it layered to encourage a natural wave that she had been brushing out since childhood to avoid being teased for having curly hair. Despite imitating their work fashions, Tuyết did not copy their lifestyles and, after listening to their weekend tales at lunch on Mondays, refused to socialize with them. She dubbed some of the Southeast Asian girls she worked with as *playgirls*, a negative tag to describe their lifestyles adapted from the Vietnamese word *playboy* (borrowed from English), which indicates a (young) man of dubious character who usually has more than one casual girlfriend, drinks excessively, possibly uses recreational drugs, and stays out late gambling and nightclubbing.

In attempting to better her relative social position in the workplace, Tuyết used strategies of indirect social exclusion. She excluded herself from competition with her (male) European, American and Australian colleagues through self-elimination, because she was not familiar with specific cultural and gender norms. Tuyết overcame the cultural handicap that she faced due to overselection in comparison to the more worldly-wise Southeast Asian girls by imitating their sense of fashion in an attempt to equalize her own performance of a globalized professional workplace femininity. Because Tuyết was unwilling to embrace the life-styles of the Southeast Asian playgirls, she was unable to compete with them, especially at workplace lunches. As a result, she was relegated to a less prominent position. However, because she was recognized by her boss as having less opportunity to gain from her educational investment, she was offered incentives and opportunities for postgraduate study in order to 'catch up' and compete with her more experienced colleagues (Bourdieu 1974, p. 35; Bourdieu and Passeron 1979, p. 14; Lamont and Lareau 1988, p. 158). In this workplace, Tuyết benefitted from indirect social exclusion.

Under-employment in office-based occupations may provide benefits to graduates in their acquisition and demonstration of accrued cultural capital beyond the initial prestige of their academic qualifications. Employed graduates are able to extend their social networks to enhance opportunities for permanency or promotion at work and to build a new way of life to support their upward mobility. Graduate employment also offers contact with outsiders, including those from other cultures, but also those from other social classes and status positions. Contact with superiors at work may enable them to move up with greater ease or greater security through opportunities to travel or undertake further vocationally-oriented study, while contact with inferiors at work and outside work allows the consolidation of their existing positions and demonstration of social distance. However, contact with peers and those from within an equivalent social cohort may involve contestation and competition through embodied practices. These advantages, which women are able to realize in the workplace, are widely recognizable to and widely recognized by others.

NEW CONFIGURATIONS OF WORKPLACE FEMININITY

Workplace femininity can operate as a type of cultural literacy. Characteristics regarded by Vietnamese to be feminine – such as being gentle, sweet,

flexible, open-hearted, approachable, adaptable and having excellent communication skills – are among the characteristics valued by management
in foreign companies in Vietnam. Two thirds of the employees in the
foreign-invested sector in Vietnam are women, but unstable employment
and a glass ceiling can limit their career trajectories. Men entering the new
middle classes are faced with increasing competition as more women enter
the workplace, which devalues qualifications and restricts the availability
of jobs. Recognizing the value of workplace femininity can benefit male
candidates, such as Minh, who are prepared to engage with new gender
configurations.

A friend from the university introduced me to Minh. He was a
well-dressed man in his late twenties, who had worked in management
in foreign companies since he graduated with a degree in fine arts and
English. On our first meeting at his home (see Chapter 6) in the guest
room where his family received visitors, Minh invited me to see photos
of his recent work trip to Mũi Né, a popular coastal resort town. Like
many other company vacations, this 'vacation' had taken place over the
International Labour Day (1 May) weekend.[2] The photos were filled
with young people, in fashionable swimming costumes, sunbathing and
exercising together on the beach. Many of the employees were young
women who, to my surprise, wore revealing bikinis. This surprised me
because, at the time, Vietnamese women preferred public sunbathing in
loose body-covering printed suits (*bộ*) or an oversized t-shirt.

Minh corrected the assumption that I had made that the trip was
a workplace vacation, reminding me that he did not work for a state
company. He explained that his company was a major international corporation. Singled out as a potential candidate for promotion, due to his
qualifications, previous experience and foreign language skills, he had

---

2   Companies provide organized vacations for their staff who may be unable to afford lei-
     sure on their meagre salaries. Popular destinations included beachside resorts (e.g. Nha
     Trang and Mũi Né) or mountain retreats (e.g. Đà Lạt) within a day's travel from Ho Chi
     Minh City. The 30 April anniversary of national reunification (the 'Fall of Saigon') had
     been transferred to the International Labour Day holiday, which retained overt socialist
     associations but shifted focus from a partisan parochial celebration to a globalized one. In
     recent years, this weekend has been transformed into an alternative holiday that promotes
     nationalist culture through the commemoration of the death anniversary of the Hùng
     Kings (*Giỗ tổ Hùng Vương*), the cult of which is celebrated on the tenth day of the third
     lunar month (see Nguyen Thi Dieu 2013). Organized private tours to Singapore, Kuala
     Lumpur and other Southeast Asian destinations have grown in popularity as a way to enjoy
     the Hùng Kings anniversary weekend in Ho Chi Minh City.

received a memo from his manager informing him that the goal of the trip was to foster team-building among the Vietnamese co-workers through trust exercises – performed in a relaxed atmosphere on the beach – and leadership tests that were designed to evaluate staff with management potential. The company's Southeast Asia regional manager – a woman – was due to arrive to meet potential management candidates before the end of the weekend. Looking again at the photos, as I handed them on to his mother and brother, the figure of Minh stood out from the crowd of bikini-clad young women – his colleagues – on the beach. In each photo, Minh displayed his management skills, first organizing a small team, then directing a group, and finally making a speech in front of the others. It was clear Minh wanted the promotion.

I commented that his weekend at the beach looked like fun, with so many beautiful girls in a lovely environment. He hesitated before explaining that he did not see them as girls, but as colleagues, and the weekend was not fun, it was work. Prior to his recent promotion, he had met the Southeast Asia regional manager. She had consulted him individually about his aspirations and intentions within the company. He told me that she had insisted that he, along with the other management candidates, undertake a training course in combatting sexual harassment in the workplace which was a requirement within the company. The course lasted for one day. The message that Minh took home with him was that he must feminize his behaviour by adopting the passive, reflexive and flexible qualities that were valued in female employees. These qualities contrast with Vietnamese male 'character' (*tính nam*), as Helle Rydstrøm (2004, p. 74) described it, which includes aggressive and predatory behaviour, 'being naughty', 'mischievous' and 'active' as well as behaviour that is difficult to control.

In the past, harassment of women by men has been tolerated in Vietnam because it is believed to result from men's typical character and bolder temperament. Comparable behaviour in women is viewed as abnormal because it is not associated with female character. Vietnamese gender stereotypes mean that women are assumed to be subordinate to men and are viewed as more reserved and timid, so that men do not expect resistance to harassment. Young women working in the private sector are perhaps the most vulnerable to harassment, which they may endure if they see no alternative and fear losing their jobs (Khuat Thu Hong 2004, pp. 123–4, 134).

If Minh were to survive in his non-state workplace, the Southeast Asia manager had made clear to him, he should not pursue any romantic feelings he might have for any of his colleagues. If he did, his position would be under threat. If they were to pursue him, he should take them aside and explain to them that no relationship would be possible. He would be their 'older brother'.[3] Like their older sibling, he would be someone who protects and guides them. If they persisted, he told me bluntly, he would sack them to protect his own job. In this case, Minh was expected to suppress any masculine character and draw on emotional capital to act in a fraternal or parental role in his relationships with his staff.

By adopting qualities of naturalized femininity in performances of workplace gender, graduate men like Minh are able to improve their relative positions. Lisa Adkins (2001, p. 691) observes a connection made in analyses of work between increasing feminization of workplaces and emerging middle classes. She notes that new status positions have been increasingly defined by mobile relationships to gender performance, with more flexible gender codes evident among urban middle classes. For women, conforming to naturalized femininity may go unrecognized as a strategy as gender normalcy offers them a limited form of capital (Skeggs 2004, p. 22; see also Skeggs 1997).

Performances of workplace femininity draw on the affective ties of emotional capital that correspond to the valued characteristics of a female character. In a work context, emotional capital includes knowledge, contacts and relations, which hold within a workplace characterized at least partly by affective ties (Nowotny 1981, p. 148; see also Hochschild 1983). In Vietnam, the internal operation of a workplace can be regarded to mirror family relations. In this perspective, as Diane Reay (2004, p. 71) points out, emotional capital is a form of capital which is all about investments in others, used in interactions with others and for the benefit of others. In fostering and supporting staff and in assisting in the development of their further education, skills training and future careers, a male manager may benefit by employing strategies

---

3   Minh's female colleagues addressed him with the pronoun *anh* which is used to designate an older brother, a husband or boyfriend, a male colleague of similar age, or a male colleague in a higher status position if, like Minh, he is a similar age.

associated with emotional capital, where a manager guides and advises like a parent or older sibling. While women benefit from performing modified codes of femininity in the corporate workplace, men may be able to benefit from adapting to new configurations of workplace gender. Performances of naturalized femininity by men may be regarded as new forms of middle-class cultural literacy. Workplace femininity may be a valuable cultural competence for men seeking to ascend in the foreign sector.

EDUCATION AND GILDING

As across Southeast Asia, social mobility in Vietnam is connected to education. Formal qualifications and cultural competences underpin graduate employability and act as a minimum criteria to gain entry. Parents in rural and urban areas recognize the social advantages of educating their children. Văn Thị Kim Cúc (2002, pp. 104–6) explains that most Vietnamese parents (almost 80 per cent) want their children to have a university diploma, but few (under 9 per cent) want their children to learn practical ways to make a living. Parents in the Mekong Delta, who themselves have an overall lower level of education, are even more ambitious for their children's educational achievements than their urban counterparts. Phạm Văn Bích (1999, pp. 146–7) observes that rural young people value education and seek future spouses with education who are engaged in non-agricultural employment in order to achieve enduring status. Achieving recognized qualifications can lead to securing better social positions and greater prosperity, although some graduates – especially rural students with limited resources – owe more to schooling and education because they do not have an extensive, or even adequate, underlying reservoir of cultural, economic or social capital (Bourdieu 1984, pp. 80–1).

Education in general is valued in Pacific Asia, but different value is placed on different credentials. Vietnamese degrees and diplomas are differentiated by the varying status and reputation of institutions such as national universities, city colleges and provincial training institutions (Phạm Minh Hạc 1998, Ch. 10). The differing value of credentials has been more acutely apparent among foreign degrees and diplomas, which have always been highly valued in Vietnam, but have conferred different benefits throughout changing landscape of the twentieth century. During the French colonial period, an academic degree – firstly, from France or secondly, from a French institution in Vietnam – was the criterion by which a person's worth was evaluated, enabling him (or her) to gain higher social status and professional employment (Nguyen and Tran 1980, p. 14). Under state socialism, education was similarly ranked and continued to offer an avenue to social mobility. Until the early 1990s, a 'Moscow degree' served as the ultimate status symbol and prerequisite for a successful career in government, the Party or a profession (Hitchcox 1994, p. 203). At this time, other foreign credentials – from socialist Prague, Sofia or Tashkent, for example – were less highly valued, but conferred more status than Vietnamese credentials. A comparable differential valuation of foreign credentials operates among Chinese students studying abroad; those who spent time in Europe and the US were regarded as 'gilded', while those in Japan became 'silver-coated' (Cheng 2002, p. 164). Similarly, in South Korea, qualifications from elite US institutions held more prestige than those from elite Korean schools (Koo 2006, pp. 10–11).

While an emphasis on education for success in contemporary Vietnam is not new, success based on academic credentials depends an underlying foundation of cultural, economic and social capital, as qualifications alone are not sufficient and will not be fully recognized without additional forms of capital, such as fluency in a foreign language (Bourdieu 1984, p. 134). Proficiency in a foreign language becomes a valuable form of supplementary cultural capital that sets graduates apart in the competitive urban job market. In Vietnam's mega-urban Southeast, English language proficiency has become a minimum entry ticket to professional workplaces in the non-state sector. English proficiency has been the most desired skill for work and learning English has been more popular than any other second language among young people (Marr 1997, p. 319; Marr and Rosen 1999, p. 191). The introduction of English to the school curriculum has ensured that young people have familiarity with, although rarely mastery of, English.

Although qualifications are an admission fee to participate, knowledge of English, including the mastery of pronunciation, colloquial speech and cultural nuances such as references to popular culture and humour based on double meanings, indicates a distinctive scarcity value that operates as embodied cultural capital. Developing such mastery requires considerable time and effort as well as direct cultural contact and allows a graduate to set herself apart from others who do not have equal capacities or resources for such mastery (Bourdieu 1997, p. 49). Ashley Carruthers (2002, p. 429) reminds us that it is very difficult for Vietnamese to arrange exposure in order to achieve this mastery. One ambitious student whom I met in 2011 organized a short-term job in a café in the Phạm Ngũ Lão backpacker district of Ho Chi Minh City to improve her English speaking and listening skills. Like many students who cannot afford to live in the heart of the city, she lived in Bình Chánh and commuted 90 minutes to work by public bus. Her day started at 5.30 am and ended at 10.30 pm, with her shift at the café stretching from 8 am til 4 pm and her university classes from 6 pm to 9 pm. This one-month arrangement was her only opportunity to practice English with fluent speakers, usually European travellers.

Having a special skill such as native speaker fluency and accurate pronunciation is especially important when continued demand for graduates with English proficiency causes an inflation of qualifications. Knowledge of English becomes a minimum qualification for entry, creating a restriction on entry for the unqualified, those without English, but an advantage for those with an additional language which acts as a cultural competence possessing scarcity value. English is widely recognized as a basic skill for a graduate jobseeker aiming to work in the non-state sector. The dominance of English as a foreign language has displaced other languages and fewer young people know a second foreign language. In 1999, fewer than 3 per cent of women under 30 years knew one foreign language and only 0.7 per cent knew two. This contrasted with women aged 31–40 years, of whom more than five times as many (15 per cent) knew one foreign language and twice as many (1.4 per cent) knew two (Tran and Le 2000, pp. 159–60). With widespread knowledge of English, knowledge of a second foreign language further distinguishes a skilled graduate in Ho Chi Minh City's highly competitive job market, as Hạnh, who had commenced studying Japanese, had realized.

EVALUATING CULTURAL COMPETENCES

Hạnh's and Cúc's young sister Thảo was a supermarket cashier in a department store located on the urban fringe district of Ho Chi Minh City.

Thảo's duties included restocking the cosmetics department, operating the cash register, and dealing with customers. Although Thảo commuted long distances and worked long shifts seven days a week, her job provided other benefits, including the advantage of access to imported products in the cosmetics department which she could buy with her staff discount card and sell on to family and neighbours.

Thảo was a graduate. Throughout her degree, she had followed the advice of her father and had studied French. Her father had benefitted from reading French in the (American-backed) postcolonial South when French proficiency had been relatively scarce. He hoped she would also benefit from possessing a rare competence. She had. After graduating, Thảo had gained her position as a cashier because, in addition to her university qualifications, she knew French. She was the only cashier who knew French. Two others knew Japanese and the remaining staff knew English. For her, English proficiency was a transportable skill that could serve in a wide range of workplaces, but French had the scarcity value that had initially secured her the job. Thảo's French language skills had acted as a certificate of cultural competence that conferred a conventional and constant guaranteed value required to enter that workplace (Bourdieu 1997, pp. 50–1).

Even so, for the first three years, Thảo did not deal with a single French speaker. In her fourth year, she met a middle-aged French customer who was living in Ho Chi Minh City. He regularly visited the department store because of its air-conditioning and during his visits took time to chat and joke with Thảo. Discussing her sister's employment, Cúc speculated that Thảo had a further advantage over other applicants because, in addition to knowing French, she was tall which was especially valued in jobs working with foreigners who are perceived to be on average taller than Vietnamese. In pointing this out, Cúc recognized an added advantage of embodied cultural capital in consolidating institutionalized cultural capital.

In 2004 and 2005, I began to hear stories that stereotyped urban salesgirls and their assumed aspirational goals negatively. These stereotypes ridiculed salesgirls' achievements by focusing on their appearances and implying that physical beauty was the only asset they could rely on for achieving betterment. As Robbie Peters (2012) argues, physical attractiveness is necessary for entry to a field that requires a 'public face' in Vietnam. But it is not enough by itself. Like education credentials, an attractive and fashionable appearance must be backed up with other forms of capital. Many salesgirls I met seemed aware of the need for education, in particular through credentials and language skills, to consolidate their positions. A desire for betterment was evident in their commitment to gaining formal qualifications and improving their foreign language skills. In the small boutiques on the quieter upper levels of the Diamond Plaza, a luxury department store, I met one salesgirl in a toyshop who was revising her Japanese writing skills, while others were reading or revising exam materials for other evening classes. Salesgirls at the Maximart department store on Ba Tháng Hai Street and at the Nguyễn Văn Cừ bookstore in District Five ate lunch over their college books in the bicycle parking areas. Others at the Co-op Mart supermarket on Nguyễn Đình Chiểu Street ate upstairs in the staff canteen with their study materials for extra classes. Their activities reflect the value placed on educational credentials and demonstrated cultural competences possessing scarcity value.

Foreign language learning is one of the most recognized and recognizable strategies for betterment employed by aspirational young people in twenty-first century Ho Chi Minh City. With foreign language fluency, graduates in urban professional workplaces produce social distance and exclude competition from colleagues and other jobseekers by demonstrating a cultural competence possessing scarcity value. Thảo secured a highly desired position that conferred high relative occupational status. Scarcity value allows graduates to avoid downclassing by entering new occupations that more closely match their pretensions or by refurbishing existing occupations to which qualifications give them access. In doing so, they bring newly desired aptitudes, dispositions and demands to the workplace to redefine and upgrade the position. Those with higher qualifications and cultural competence with scarcity value cause an intensified division of labour that results in autonomous status given to some of the tasks previously performed by less qualified workers. Their influence brings a redefinition of careers related to the emergence of expectations and demands that are new in both form and content (Bourdieu 1984, p. 150). These emerging expectations and demands compound the issues faced by graduates in a highly competitive urban job market and further challenge their abilities to enter and maintain a position in the new middle class.

While foreign language learning is the focus of many graduates seeking professional employment, familiarity with foreign cultural practices also convey scarcity value that can set a graduate apart. But it is difficult to maintain belonging when distinction is successfully achieved, as Diễm experienced. Diễm was educated in Ho Chi Minh City but many Vietnamese assumed she was foreign due to her appearance with dyed permed hair, her perfect English and her behaviour. Diễm worked for a foreign company and had few Vietnamese friends. As a student she had begun adopting foreign cultural practices by imitating her foreign English teachers' dress styles and mannerisms. At twenty, she had a relationship with a Canadian boyfriend and copied his behaviour, such as requesting to take home uneaten food from a restaurant, a practice Vietnamese found unusual. In her late twenties, Diễm continued to socialize with a group of expatriates. She spoke excellent American English and complained that at work, although she passed as a foreigner, she was paid as a Vietnamese national earning a tenth of her friends' salaries. While Diễm embodied highly valued cultural competences recognized as foreign or cosmopolitan, she was also excluded economically because she was Vietnamese. She was located in a space in between the globalized and the national where middle classes are exposed to the judgement of others in marking their relative social positions (Liechty 2003, p. 67).

FINDINGS

White-collar occupations and professional careers are linked to achieving upward social mobility in Southeast Asia. This chapter has explored the working lives of a number of young educated professional in Ho Chi Minh City. It has demonstrated how, for Ho Chi Minh City's urban professionals, the workplace provides opportunities to express aspiration, realize achievements and produce status associated with relatively better social positions. While many graduates are unable to secure stable employment in Ho Chi Minh City's competitive labour market, high mobility between workplaces can offer benefits for skilled graduates who change jobs to improve their incomes and their working conditions as well as to gain different skills and experiences. By doing so, they are able to avoid downclassing by creating new opportunities even when they are under-employed. Working within these constraints enables them to accumulate enduring cultural capital through self-improvement that can be useful in the broader processes of social mobility and status production.

In this context, femininity can act effectively as embodied cultural capital. Jobs in Vietnam are not gender neutral and femininity has been naturalized as a workplace practice. An inherently feminine character continues to be associated with certain occupations that, in addition to being open to women, provide the conditions that can enable upward social mobility. Yet conforming to gender normalcy offers limited scope to move up socially and young educated women may seek to reconfigure their genderized behaviours. The value placed on performances of workplace femininity can 'rub off' on men who may benefit from reconfiguring their own genderized behaviours to conform to certain feminized ones also.

As different individuals have different abilities to move up socially, individual middle-class women seeking betterment, or a consolidation of a relatively better position, achieve qualitatively different outcomes. To combat the relative devaluation of qualifications and credentials that occurs as more and more graduates enter the job market, aspirational graduates aim to build their coffers of cultural capital with a range of new competences and skills, particularly foreign language skills, that can set them apart from others due to their scarcity value.

Focusing on achieving social mobility through a white-collar profession is a long-term strategy that involves an initial investment in education and relocation to a metropolitan area where, rather than the short-term economic rewards offered by unskilled labour migration, they are able to develop – through a lengthy process of socialization – the dispositions associated with an enduring social position that conveys status when they are recognized by others. In seeking careers in highly desired occupations which value workplace femininity, aspirational young urbanites consider not only the job requirements and conditions but also the associated lifestyle benefits that working in a professional career can generate. Workplaces can offer educated urban migrant women opportunities for exposure to new ways of living and new modes for expressing class culture.

CHAPTER FIVE

New middle-class leisure culture

L eisure culture can tell us much about upwardly mobile migrants in post-reform Ho Chi Minh City. The desires and strategies of new middle-class women for displaying acquired status and embodied dispositions through their social practices become apparent in their recreational choices. Like career options, higher incomes, higher levels of education, real estate and asset ownership as well as use of household technologies, greater access to leisure is an observable social transformation that stems from the economic development of post-reform urban Vietnam.

While recreational practices may be indicators of social differentiation and distinction, urban leisure practices also become a means for demonstrating status and social mobility via markers of class culture that are recognized, and responded to, by others. As recreational spaces move inside to more exclusive and contained arenas, leisure choices become an effective means of communicating social distance and producing social distinction not only between different social classes but also within new status groups. Conversely, leisure also offers opportunities to those who have achieved enduring status to express their belonging to a normative social life rather than an exclusive or gilded lifestyle.

A range of relationships between leisure and social mobility in women's chosen activities reveal that new middle-class interests are concerned with individualized recreational pleasures as well as a focus on the production of social identities in the space between localized and globalized cultural influences. Food preferences and eating are central to socializing in Vietnam. This chapter draws on the experiences of Liên, Tuyết, Nghĩa, Cúc, and Thu to explore how upward mobility can be demonstrated through culinary choices and leisure, practices that I describe as producing a new aesthetic language in urban leisure culture. In focusing on the practices of new middle-class women, their status as first-generation urban migrants is crucial in generating new ways of living and challenging conventional ideals and norms. Their leisure practices breathe new life into urban culture through reconfigurations of popular activities, entertainment and street culture.

HO CHI MINH CITY'S CULTURAL LANDSCAPE

Cities provide a unique cultural landscape for facilitating leisure and recreational activities. Postsocialist urban spaces have been viewed as unpredictable places that exhibit features of both third-worldly and western cities to create places where inequalities emerge as populations explode (Szelenyi 1996, pp. 288, 298). Postsocialist and global cities alike are 'crucibles of social change' that are characterized by cultural innovation and marked by enormous gulfs based on inclusion and exclusion. Stephen Castles and Mark Miller (2003, p. 287) describe how in these cities the 'included' fit the self-image of prosperous, technologically innovative and democratic society and the 'excluded' represent the 'shadow' side needed for the menial jobs in industry and services, but who do not fit the ideology driving the model. The parallels between a capitalist context and contemporary Ho Chi Minh City are remarkable in reflecting the influence of urbanization on emergent cultural practices.

While popular culture and the mass media account for some aspects of cultural innovation and the development of urban culture, migration and social mobility also play important roles in the revivification of urban culture in providing opportunities to integrate experiences from different regions of Vietnam and abroad into everyday social practices, particularly those that offer an exclusionary function. Rapid urbanization of Vietnam's Southeast has brought migrants from all over Vietnam and they bring their own localized practices with them. In Ho Chi Minh City, residents can be exposed to diverse experiences and new styles of living. New trends in eating, such as the development of downtown eateries specializing in regionalized local foods and seasonal delicacies, may preserve cultural traditions through certain dishes that often are no longer eaten at home. Participating in urban food culture also has value as local specialties are rare, partly as a result of seasonal availability but also due to environmental changes and a shortage of land for cultivation (Ton Nu Quynh Tran 2002, pp. 47, 51). While new migrants are able to influence the urban cultural landscape in this way, not all migrants have the material resources to do so. It is the relatively well-resourced and educated new middle class who are most enabled to influence urban culture and set new trends in urban culinary practice.

Beside local influences introduced through urbanization, other significant influences on Vietnamese urban culture originate outside Vietnam. Foreign influences, especially evident in the colonial and post-colonial periods (see Chapter 2), have been singled out by Vietnamese as a source in the emergence of distinct new cultural trends. For example, the introduction of café culture to Vietnam is popularly recognized as a contribution of French colonialism (Quách Thu Nguyệt et al. 2007, p. 53; Nguyễn Huy Tưởng 2011). Cultural innovations such as this became accessible to urban Vietnamese elites and were incorporated into their lifestyles (E. Peters 2012). Early twentieth-century Vietnamese cultural life was influenced significantly by colonial era French values and systems in urban centres. Urban women benefitted from access to education at all levels, including study abroad, and some were able to maintain economic independence through employment as teachers, nurses, pharmacists or administrative staff. As Vietnamese research records, in urban areas, young people married for love and lived separately from their parents after marriage. Coupled with higher levels of education and opportunities for wage employment, young urban women led a new 'mode of living' that also influenced the ways people dressed and the forms of entertainment (movie houses, theatres, dancing halls, western songs and music) they enjoyed (Le Thi 1999, pp. 41–3). The mid-1930s urban women's media caricaturized this urban 'new girl' as a sporty fashionista who loved to go dancing, bar-hopping or just settle down with a romantic novel. She 'fell in love easily', promoted equal rights and suffrage, and did her best to evade neo-Confucian responsibilities (McHale 1995, p. 188; Marr 1981). Globalized cultural influences were a source of new ways of living among well-resourced city residents that enabled them to challenge and reconfigure genderized social norms.

In the second half of the twentieth century, middle-class cultural life in Saigon was influenced by imported cultural practices and popular culture predominately from the US. Indeed post-war middle-class formation across Asia was profoundly influenced by American culture. As Shiraishi Takashi (2008, pp. 3–4) argues, in contrast to the US where post-war development involved forming middle classes at the same time as forming national subjects, in East Asian middle-class formation involved national citizens embracing an imported American way of life centred on consumer goods, mass communication and privatized nuclear family life in highly developed cities. Imported cultural influences associated with Northeast Asian economic investment have been also been noted in middle-class transformations across Southeast Asian mega-urban regions (Shiraishi 2008, p. 11). In post-reform Vietnam, East Asian popular culture, in the forms of cinema, television, online gaming and globalized fast food, has become an integral part of the urban Vietnamese cultural landscape (Thomas 2002; Nguyen and Thomas 2004). Consequently, in twenty-first century Ho Chi Minh City the cultural landscape is diverse and multi-faceted, incorporating globalized and regionalized cultural, leisure and culinary practices.

LEISURE AND URBAN VIETNAMESE WOMEN

Opportunities for leisure in Saigon / Ho Chi Minh City, as a cosmopolitan and dynamic social context, have been affected by political and economic conditions. For new middle-class women in the southern capital, leisure has centred on street culture and socializing as well as outings to specific recreational sites such as cinemas. In the past, as Vietnamese women's autobiographies demonstrate, middle-class girls experienced and pursued leisure and recreation far more so than their mothers. Much of their mothers' time, which was freed in part from household responsibilities by servants, was spent managing businesses and philanthropic programs. Their daughters' time, for the most part, was dedicated to study and later professional work, allowing ample free time for leisure and recreation with the advantage of disposable income from an allowance, scholarship or salary. After the demise of the post-colonial southern Republic in 1975, however, the urban environment changed and middle-class women's recreational lives became more restricted through their limited access to the social and economic capital that could allow the pursuit of a life of leisure. While leisure continued to be social in orientation, restrictions were also placed on women's use of time as well as social and geographic space.

In addition to losing access to the means for cultivating a dynamic social life, the recreational choices that became available to middle-class women in Ho Chi Minh City after 1975 were also different. There were fewer opportunities for individuals to make personal leisure choices as activities that were previously popular were banned, or restricted to the wealthy members of the socialist super-elite. The 1980s saw restricted geographic mobility further compromising leisure and recreation, including visiting and family rituals, such as a *đám giỗ*, a large and elaborate feast to honour a deceased ancestor.[1] At this time, to move between provinces, travel permits were required but difficult to negotiate and, although many vehicles and motorbikes could still be found in southern Vietnam, fuel was scarce. Shortages of cash wealth and of available goods limited essential shopping and virtually eliminated window-shopping, although black market trading continued (Beresford and Dang Phong 2000).

By the early 1980s, recreation began to be managed by the state via local institutions, such as the Youth Culture House (*Nhà Văn Hóa Thanh Niên*) and Women's Union 'Clubhouse' (*Nhà Văn Hóa Phụ Nữ*). During the 1980s, it was left to state institutions to facilitate sophisticated social gatherings, musical entertainment and even international travel for its members. One young woman whom I met in Ho Chi Minh City recalled travelling throughout southern Vietnam's provinces on tour with an orchestra based at the Children's Culture House (*Nhà Văn Hoá Thiếu Niên*). Another had travelled to Eastern Europe on an official children's delegation to an international Communist Youth meeting. Others I met had travelled for postgraduate study, workplace training, and for music, mathematics, chess or sporting competitions. Needless to say, eligibility for selection in southern Vietnam was affected by one's family's social standing and political record. In these examples, state-structured leisure was conflated with productive achievement but also relied on qualitatively different signals of cultural capital associated with the particularized context of reunified socialist Vietnam.

New configurations of leisure after 1975 were not only state-facilitated. Existing leisure practices also continued but underwent transformations stemming from new economic and political conditions. Despite the hardships of the years immediately after 1975, Saigon's café culture continued on the streets of Ho Chi Minh City, for example, at Teresa

---

1   *Ngàygiỗ* are more important than birthdays in celebrating the life and achievements of parents, grandparents, and ancestors as well as national heroes / heroines. In her autobiography, Lien Yeomans (2001, pp. 37–40) provides a detailed description of the preparations of the altar and the feast for a *đám giỗ*.

Nguyen's café in District Three (Nguyen and Knight 2004). However, café culture then was the realm of men. Now living with his family in Ho Chi Minh City, one friend recalled his first impressions of the city when he visited relatives there as a young man in the early 1980s. He recalled that, in the downtown areas of the southern metropolis, due to widespread male unemployment, the men in the family could spend their mornings reading a newspaper at a café with their friends while their wives worked to support the household. Leisure, in this example, was facilitated for men who lacked valued forms of capital since they had been revalued.

For Vietnamese women, opportunities for leisure vary not only with economic resources but also with gendered expectations around work and the use of social space. In the 1980s, an emphasis on socialist family values and on productive labour saw most women working regardless of their social backgrounds and their prior training. A collection of memoirs recalling the years of 're-education' in southern Vietnam after 1975 described the conditions faced by women in Ho Chi Minh City. Hoàng Ngọc Thanh Dung (1988, pp. 43–5) recalled that recruitment to work in the 'Association of Liberated Women' was virtually compulsory and extended women's working day from dawn until 10 or 11 pm. Women surveyed by the National Institute of Culture in 1987 reported they did not take part in cultural sessions or recreation organized by their workplaces due to restrictions on their time caused by a double shift of productive and domestic labour. This report concluded that, aside from women having restricted time and limited means for recreation, unlike men who knew how to utilize spare money, the majority of women in the study had requested guidance and organization as they did not know what to do for leisure, or even how to go about it (Lê Thị Nhâm Tuyết 1989).[2] Consistently, in Vietnamese state discourses, women have been blamed for their own lack of participation (Truong 2008). The hours women were expected to work also curtailed possibilities for their leisure and recreation.

The resulting situation for a generation of middle-class women, many of whom had experienced dramatic and sudden downward mobility in terms of a loss of social, economic and political capital, was new. It was,

---

2   In the report, the reasons given by the surveyed women – in defined occupational groups of workers, peasants, artists, and intellectuals – for their non-participation were having no money or means, tiredness after earning one's living, little leisure time, spare money used for husband and children, as well as a lack of guidance and organization (Lê Thị Nhâm Tuyết 1989, pp. 47, 55).

however, not the first time that twentieth-century middle classes had experienced rapid downward mobility due to political and economic change, as middle-class women's autobiographies demonstrate for those who fled the postcolonial urban North after 1954. Comparable to the late 1950s, in the early 1980s, women with formal education and work experience – including pharmacists and medical doctors – were perhaps better off than middle-class housewives who lacked formal training and were no longer regarded as bearers of valued cultural capital due to its revaluation. Saigonese housewives were mocked as bearers of decadent bourgeois values (Pettus 2003, pp. 198–9).

Prior to its reconfiguration in individualized urban and private contexts, women's leisure in post-reform Ho Chi Minh City continued to be structured by the state, the family or the workplace. An example is International Women's Day (*Ngày Phụ Nữ Quốc Tế*), which is held on 8 March annually and is a holiday for women in Vietnam and other – mostly socialist – countries. Outside Ho Chi Minh City homes, official celebrations with corporate backing and private sponsorship are organized each year to acknowledge women and celebrate their contributions to family and society through, for example, a free public aerobics class funded by an international health and beauty corporation. Inside homes, as married women visiting Xuân's shop in Tần Định informed me, husbands are invited to take over the household chores, including cooking, cleaning and caring, on Women's Day to highlight the importance and complexity of women's domestic responsibilities.

Throughout the rest of the year, Vietnamese women's domestic labour is clearly routinized and divided via status-based kin relations. Different social positions determine different tasks and chores for women in the home. At annual rituals and other feasts, older women are able to gossip with each other and relax because the younger women usually perform the chores. Unmarried daughters also may be able to escape much of the more strenuous labour if their brothers have brought wives – daughters-in-law – to the family. With the removal of travel restrictions, travel to and returning from the ancestral home for family rituals, which may involve a long journey outside the city, can provide an opportunity for leisure and recreation for women during the trip. Attending the rituals of other families as guests almost always allow women some leisure time if they are free to attend. In nuclear households, everyday household labour may not be distributed but can enable regular and predictable opportunities for socializing or recreation.

Like the state, the family is a powerful organizer of women's time and activities. In Vietnam, the centrality of women's domestic roles is communicated to children via socialization processes in the family and at school. Girls throughout Vietnam are encouraged to identify themselves primarily with future motherhood and the burdens of work in the household (Rydstrøm 2004, p. 78; Werner 2009). Ashley Pettus (2003, pp. 12–13) demonstrates that the urban middle-class housewife reproduces class society through her role within the family as mother and wife. This role centres on bearing cultural capital through the effective parenting of healthy and successful model children and satisfaction of a healthy and successful ideal husband. As Angela McRobbie (2004, pp. 100–1) argues in her study of the British mass media, forms of class antagonism are actively generated and legitimated between women both through their exemplary roles as wives and mothers and by them being standard bearers for middle-class family values. Women's family activities can be understood not only as bearing cultural capital but also as accumulating emotional capital through creating a loving disposition (Bourdieu 1976).

Beyond the family, the workplace is also effective in facilitating how women use their time. The flexibility of family-based work contrasts with opportunities for relaxation time for permanent and full-time employees. Vietnamese workplaces structure an employee's relaxation time, enabling them to have an annual vacation when they may otherwise not have the means or opportunity. Organized company annual vacations take staff away to popular hillside or coastal resort towns, including Đà Lạt, Nha Trang, Hà Tiên, or Mũi Né. Structured relaxation time at a foreign company, such as Minh's company, may be transformed into productive time. Non-state workplaces can also facilitate leisure time. For an employee who desires social mobility and seeks betterment, such as Tuyết, there are several clear advantages in pursuing professional occupations, where productive time in the workplace provides experience of how other people – particularly elites and expatriates – spend their non-productive and recreational time (see Chapter 4).

Middle-class urban leisure has continued to evolve beyond the consequences of reunification, years of 're-education', refugee exodus and macro-economic reform of the 1980s. Leisure practices, like tastes, are not independent of other dimensions of social practice (Bourdieu 1984, p. 193). A revaluation of the highly valued signals of cultural capital affects how leisure and recreation are used by new middle classes to demonstrate relative social position not only between classes in an increasingly differentiated social space but also between individuals within new status groups. New middle-class women, who have access to considerable resources, are enabled to pursue their leisure choices beyond state organization and outside the norms and ideals of conventional family life. For new middle-class women, leisure can operate as a resource for maintaining an enduring social position in a range of innovative ways in public and exclusive spaces, between individuals in different social classes and within new status groups.

CREATING AND MITIGATING SOCIAL DISTANCE

Achieving a relatively higher social position involves substantial long-term investment to develop the embodied signals of distinction that set an individual apart from others. Leisure activities are a recognizable realm of practice that enable aspiring individuals to create social distance between themselves and others through their choices which are assumed to be guided by taste which can be interpreted by others as representative of a desired social position (Bourdieu, 1990a, pp. 131–2). In a socially segregated city, such as Ho Chi Minh City, social distance is not always a desirable state as it provides an exclusionary function that can impede social interaction beyond an individual's status group. Leisure practices enable new middle-class women, such as Liên, to not only demonstrate distinction but also to mitigate social distance and demonstrate belonging to a neighbourhood.

The first evening we met Liên took me out to eat. As she was unmarried and did not yet have the children she desired, she had no reason to prepare meals and, with her relative wealth, was able to afford to eat out regularly near her office or home. By not cooking at home, Liên had no need to maintain an altar for the kitchen god (*Ông Táo*) so she had packed it into a cupboard under the gas stove. Her neglect of a Vietnamese custom reflected not only her busy lifestyle, but also her orientation towards a modern globalized mode of living freed from localized traditional practices.

It was late, around 10 pm, and neither Liên nor I had taken an evening meal yet. Eating at a late hour, she claimed, was a habit she learned when she was away studying in Europe. She proposed that we go outside to eat. I was still wearing my street clothes, but Liên was wearing a printed cotton suit (*bộ*) as she usually did inside the house. She only changed her shoes – from indoor plastic slip-on shoes (*dép*) to outdoor plastic slip-on shoes – and stepped out into the laneway, waiting for me to follow her so she could lock up the house. After doing so, we made our way along the laneway to find that Xuân, the jeweller and many other families had shut up their businesses for the day. Besides Liên and a few young men living in the laneway, the households retired early and woke before dawn.

Outside Liên's laneway, the neighbourhood streets in Tân Định were transformed and supported a diverse nightlife of seasonal food stalls and faddish entertainments that shifted with tastes and means. The area beside the local market and along the river temporarily housed itinerant traders, who could laugh together as they tallied their nightly takings, making gains towards their dream of a new house, education for their children, or obligation to look after their relatives. This vibrant street culture kept the neighbourhood busy with activity and relatively safe at night.

The makeshift stalls that had appeared on both sides of the road offered a vast range of local and regional dishes. The night owls in the neighbourhood seemed to gravitate to these stalls and to organize themselves by age and gender. Women, many of whom were traders rather than customers, were chatting together as they worked. There was nothing new in this. Women in Tân Định in the past preferred work that was social, especially trading due to its high degree of sociability (Hoskins and Shepherd 1965). Children, still awake, were hanging around the women, their mothers, aunts or grandmothers. Men – their fathers, husbands and sons – were drinking together. The younger men were at a noisy video café that was screening a Tiger Cup football game and the older men at low tables dotted along the roadside.

Despite Liên's laneway being asleep, a whole neighbourhood seemed to be out on the pavement. Communal living and shared space remain a significant part of Ho Chi Minh City neighbourhood life. Residents spend much of their day outside and they deal with private and personal issues – grooming, breastfeeding, arguing, crying, eating, sleeping – in full view of family, friends, neighbourhood peddlers, customers, and passing pedestrians and motorbike riders. Perhaps due to a lack of access to private space in cramped accommodations, residents of inner-city Ho Chi Minh City hang out in the evenings in outdoor areas, including street stalls, food vending stalls and the pavements in front of shops, houses and apartments. Unlike exclusive leisure and recreation places, these spaces require no membership or affiliation for entry beyond acceptance into the neighbourhood.

Liên led me along the road towards the river. We passed a pharmacy, a tailor shop, three groceries, a dairy, several hairdressers and a locked-up café before we stopped in front of a group of noodle stalls, where Liên planned for us to eat. For some new middle-class women like Liên, who did not cook at home, eating at local street stalls could provide a solution. But for others, eating on the street was not an option; they were repelled by a perceived lack of hygiene, concerned about a risk of food poisoning and discouraged due to a feeling of loneliness and social dislocation felt when eating beyond the sphere of kin.

Liên selected a stall based on the noodle dish offered there. The stall was operated by a group of good-mannered talkative girls. Three young women jumped to their feet when they spotted Liên, as they did for each new customer. 'Chào cô!' they greeted her as usual. Like Liên, the girls were from the Mekong Delta. Like Liên, they each wore a matching printed suit, plastic slip-on shoes and gold necklaces. Unlike Liên, each of the girls wore hoop earrings and an arm full of gold bangles. Between them they were looking after one baby.

Liên returned their greetings. They looked at me over Liên's head and slowly said, 'Chào cô!' to me, as though I were deaf. It was the first time we had met. In a flurry of hands, they assessed my height (taller), my feet (bigger), my nose (higher), my complexion (paler), my arms (with moles and hair), my earlobes (no gold), my wrists (no gold), and my fingers (no gold), attempting to discover something we had in common to establish a bond of some type. I returned their greetings and joined Liên at the low table she had chosen closest to their cart. The noodle seller began to prepare Liên's usual order, a dish she had enjoyed in the Mekong Delta as a child. Their small talk indicated familiarity but also a respect that distinguished Liên from the girls. They had no difficulty recognizing Liên as someone who occupied a relatively higher social position than themselves. Before long, a bowl was placed in front of both Liên and I and the seller invited us to eat.

Each new customer who arrived at the group of low tables noticed us: Liên, a sophisticated urban professional, and me, a foreigner. Initially, it was me who attracted more attention. The seller explained to them who I was. To her, I was a student who lived nearby, an Australian with a long name, not yet married, in Vietnam by myself, but staying for a long time, without my family. They watched me eat, commenting on what I did. (Like Liên and the other customers, I neatly spat gristle, fat and other rubbish on the ground nearby and, after dabbing, discretely dropped soiled tissue under the table to be swept up later.) Some customers nodded politely to me, but others waved with a greeting, asking my nationality and other details which caused a minor disruption to the usual noodle slurping and beer swilling. With their questions, as is typical in Vietnamese social interactions, they were seeking to form bonds of empathy or confirm social distance.

The slightest disruption became a potential source of entertainment and a diversion from the monotony of an evening of streetside drinking (*nhậu*).[3] At the next cart, one man stood to acknowledge me, both arms waving in my direction. Gaining the attention of his friends with an introductory call: 'Aus-tra-lia! *Úc, Úc, Úc! Ox-trây-lia!*'[4], the drunk man held his hands together in front of his chest and began bouncing up and down, waving at me and calling 'kan-gar-ooooooooo!' His friends collapsed into laughter. Our young noodle seller, however, looked at him blankly, an eyebrow raised in disapproval. Disappointed, he explained to her that the kangaroo had become very famous at the Sydney 2000 Olympic Games where Vietnam won its first Olympic medal. He had watched the winning taekwando bout on the nearby café television that was now showing the football game. The noodle seller smiled condescendingly at him and gestured over her shoulder to her

3 As a leisure practice, Bourdieu (1984, p. 193) would regard streetside drinking to not be independent of other dimensions of social practice. This is reflected in my fieldwork also. After more than a decade of fieldworking in middle-class Ho Chi Minh City, where I have experienced a wide range of urban leisure practices, I have never been invited to enjoy an evening of streetside drinking by a middle-class Vietnamese woman. This does not speak to a lack of widespread popularity of streetside drinking, but confirms gendered and classed dimensions of leisure practices such as *nhậu*. Nir Avieli (2011, p. 63) offers detailed comments on this topic.

4 I found that in Ho Chi Minh City, 'Australia' is increasingly referred to in Vietnamese via a transliteration as 'Oxtrâylia' rather than the Vietnamese 'Úc'.

house, saying she was too busy working and did not have time to watch television.[5]

The group of drunks seemed to take her serious manner as a challenge and in a pack stood up and began hopping back and forward as best they could. Aiming to cheer her up, they hopped in delight in front of her cart, yelling 'kan-gar-oooo-oooo-oooo!' between belly laughs and long after she began to ignore them. Around her, other women clucked disapprovingly at the group of misbehaving husbands. Liên said nothing as she finished her noodles.

Quickly bored with the symbolic stereotype of Australia that went unrecognized and thus had no enduring value among the traders or other customers, the group of men directed their attention to Liên. She was as interesting – if not more interesting – to the men and other customers than I had been. Liên's cheap printed suit and plastic shoes did not camouflage her. In the close proximity of the tables, well within earshot, they speculated. She was well-spoken and sophisticated, probably a teacher – they said to each other – certainly well-paid, and not like them. Always polite and tolerant, Liên allowed them to speculate as though she were out of earshot. We continued to ignore their comments. They continued to discuss her. Some had seen her going past on her motorbike: a highly desired and highly regarded imported Japanese model. She always seemed busy and was always well dressed. Tonight – they noted – she was dining with a foreigner, not in a fancy restaurant but – why? they asked – here away from the downtown at a local street stall. It was at this point that the noodle sellers claimed Liên as a regular customer who, like them, was from the Mekong Delta and who, like them, belonged to the neighbourhood as a local laneway resident.

The episode at Liên's local street stall highlights that a sense of belonging stems in part at least from establishing a connection and participating in communal and shared social life in the neighbourhood. Although Liên's lifestyle was obviously different, I realized that on this occasion Liên had consciously chosen to dress and behave in a manner

---

5 A World Bank time-use survey reports that the amount of time Vietnamese men spent doing unpaid housework is three quarters (75 per cent) that of women. But figures in a 1999 Vietnamese newspaper survey are more extreme, claiming Ho Chi Minh City women spend up to six hours a day on housework, while their husbands spend just 90 minutes (Long et al. 2000, pp. 84–5). Werner (2009, pp. 92–3) reports that gender differences in time use remain extreme, with much of the household labour performed by women, particularly in large and multi-generational families where men rarely assist.

not to set herself apart in the neighbourhood, but to demonstrate that she belonged in their particular habitus. By wearing her house clothes – the cheap suit and plastic shoes – and speaking in a Mekong Delta accent, Liên was able to draw on the highly valued signals of embodied cultural capital to establish loose bonds of empathy with the noodle sellers and, to some extent, mitigate the social distance between their relative social positions. By doing so, she indicated that she was at home at the street stall, taking a quick meal in an environment as familiar as a family kitchen.

Moreover, by taking me – a foreigner and new customer – along with her to eat at one of her regular spots, Liên was able to further consolidate her sense of belonging not only to the neighbourhood but also to Vietnam. Aside from creating loose bonds of empathy through her Mekong Delta origins, accent and taste in food, Liên created additional bonds of empathy with others by being Vietnamese in contrast to me, a foreigner and cultural outsider. My presence emphasized that Liên belonged. Recognized as a foreigner, my status contrasted with Liên's status on the basis of an assumed social distance between a cultural insider and a cultural outsider. Mary Beth Mills (1999, p. 24) reports on a comparable distance assumed by her status 'as a white, well-educated, presumably wealthy foreigner' which created social, cultural and emotional distance between herself and the community that she researched in Thailand. The bonds of empathy that Liên had created temporarily reduced social distance between herself and the others. Yet it was only in this context at this time that it was possible for her to offset the social distance that others recognized, although the loose bonds of empathy that she had created might have prevailed.

Liên's use of non-productive time spent in the neighbourhood where she resided enabled her to demonstrate social belonging through participating in local street life but also to maintain her social distance and a relatively better social position. Like Liên, Xuân and the neighbours in the laneway, the noodle seller and many of the other stall holders were all migrants to Saigon / Ho Chi Minh City. Their diverse backgrounds and different motivations did not overshadow that they were each seeking betterment and that the city was a place that could provide opportunities where they could work hard to build a new life and improve their future prospects.

When Liên and I had finished our supper, the noodle seller accepted payment, adding the notes to a stash that would help add another gold bracelet to her wrist and which might one day educate the baby. Smiling, she bade us farewell. We headed back to the house. The screening of the football game had not yet finished, so the street by the café was still lively. In contrast, the laneway was quiet and dark as we crept inside.

DYNAMIC URBAN STREET CULTURE AND IDENTITY IN THE CITY

Residents in the Tân Định laneway, such as Xuân who was from the Centre, and Liên who was from the Mekong Delta, reflected the diversity of Saigon / Ho Chi Minh City. Southern Vietnamese historian Sơn Nam (1992, pp. 72–86) viewed Saigon as a cosmopolitan zone of contact between cultures. To demonstrate his point of view, he tracked various influences of outsiders (regional Vietnamese and foreign) in twentieth-century Saigon, paying particular attention to Saigon's eating culture and dealing with the local appropriation of imported cooking styles as well as focusing on the sustained popularity of selected imported dishes and fashionable eating districts. Mid twentieth-century Saigon, as reported by Vietnamese cultural historian Thượng Hồng (2003, p. 9), was not as modern or civilized as today and the choice of cuisine on the streets was not as diverse, but the city had specific distinctive characteristics that were 'hard to forget' (*rất khó quên*). Influences imported from abroad began to affect local traditions. Perceived foreign and outside influences in many aspects of Vietnamese food culture, from ingredients to methods of cooking, are widely accepted by Vietnamese people. Yet, Vietnamese cuisine is highly regionalized and oriented to a sense of local identity, one that is imagined or invented (Anderson 1991; Hobsbawm and Ranger 2012; see also Avieli 2005b).

Like the leisure activities of Southeast Asian new middle classes, Vietnamese leisure remains profoundly social, centring on interactions with others and eating. A popular aspect of Saigonese street culture that continues to flourish in post-reform Ho Chi Minh City is snacking. Snacking outdoors at street stalls and portable cafés that appear on pavements after the midday heat has subsided typifies Ho Chi Minh City's dynamic street culture. Before or after organized activities, including classes, work, sporting events and other social gatherings, groups get together for informal socializing and snacking. The extraordinary range of snack dishes available reflects the diversity of regional influences in post-reform Ho Chi Minh City. Resembling French hors d'oeuvres or Spanish tapas (Thượng Hồng 2003, pp. 30–1), they range from everyday dishes to seasonal specialties, and an unspoken rule of snacking culture is that one continues to eat as long as finances permit. Sharing food reinforces a sense of belonging to a family, a neighbourhood and a community for Vietnamese. As sociologist Le Thi records in her memoir, taking her meals with other new Viet Minh recruits, and no longer at the same table as her kin, fostered a new sense of belonging to her new social group (Duong and Sidel 1998, p. 1026).[6]

Engaging in the culture of street snacking can be a daily activity that begins in childhood, with street sellers catering to children outside primary schools. Many of these stall holders seem to be older women, whom the children refer to using kinship terms of 'grandma' (*bà*) or 'aunty' (*cô*). Outside a house where I stayed in 2005 in a laneway in District Three, after classes at the neighbourhood school were dismissed, the children walking home together stopped at a favourite seller's stall where they gathered with their friends to snack on inexpensive fried fish balls (*cá chiên*), miniature fresh spring rolls (*bò bía*) or small rice dumplings (*bánh bèo*). Parents running late to collect their sons and daughters retrieved them from the street stalls where, while they snacked, they were under the temporary care of the stall holders. In addition to hanging around primary schools, street sellers also position themselves around markets, secondary schools and universities as well as near temples, bookshops and recreational parks. In the evenings, many of these places support makeshift restaurant strips as vendors set up their stalls sell regional specialties together, night after night.

Across the city's districts, scores of migrant cooks selling in food stalls as well as restaurants are locally famed for regional specialities associated with their faraway homes and urban migrants travel great distances within the city to sample their authentic dishes. The diversity of snacks available in the city can satisfy the nostalgic longing of migrants living away from home. In a short story, Ho Chi Minh City-based writer Vũ Tam Huê (2004, pp. 165–7) invokes her reader's emotions through

---

6   A connection to kin and a sense of belonging provided through sharing food is not only felt by migrants within Vietnam. Vietnamese-American journalist Andrew Lam (2005) describes his sense of belonging to the family in terms of his mother's love expressed in the meals she prepares for him and his own love for her shown by eating her meals.

recollections of the tastes and other sensory experiences of a rural childhood. Tam Huệ fondly remembers snacking on 'Mekong potato' pudding (*chè củ súng*)[7] at a small market in Mỹ Thọ (the provincial capital of Tiền Giang province in the central Mekong Delta). She recalls the grandmotherly sellers looking like they had been there forever, unlike the varieties of *chè* (puddings) they sold which always tasted sweet and 'untainted' (*thanh tân*). For migrants, the unforgettable snacks of childhood may also be the longed for snacks of home.

While shared eating creates a sense of belonging, food culture clearly connects Vietnamese with their origins and the widespread availability of regional specialities highlights that a sense of Vietnamese identity is highly regionalized. In Ho Chi Minh City, a connection to the tastes of a rural childhood is a shared experience among many urban residents, and also serves to distinguish between migrants originating from different regions of Vietnam, across the Mekong Delta or along the Central Coast. The difficulties that Vietnamese seem to have in leaving their origins behind, in food culture at least, affects urban identity making by complicating the process of transformation, or 'taking off', that allows aspiring and well-resourced urban migrants to distance themselves from the limited prospects of a rural life and achieve betterment by leaving the past behind (Bourdieu 1984, p. 337).

CULTIVATING A SENSE OF BELONGING

Across Ho Chi Minh City, there are many places in which to go snacking and many different kinds of food to snack on. Common snack foods are widely diverse and different areas within the city are famous for particular snacks that can be purchased there, some having origins as far away as Huế in central Vietnam and Hanoi in the north.

Snacking is an activity that can mark regional identity, but it also demonstrates participation in a typical urban social life. While snacking is often viewed as an activity for young people to enjoy in the years before the responsibilities of family life restrict their free time and require their participation in paid labour, the culture of snacking also provides

---

7 The *củ súng* is a small tuber vegetable that is black on the outside, white on the inside and grown only in the Mekong Delta. Because there is no equivalent in English, I have translated it as 'Mekong potato' in an attempt to distinguish it from more well-known types of potato and sweet potato but, more importantly, to indicate that it is a local speciality.

opportunities to socialize in order to develop friendships and relationships. Groups of young people do not necessarily go out to snack when
they are hungry, as snacking is primarily a social event where they are
able to hang out with their friends, often in the late afternoons after
daytime classes or at the end of the day after evening meals, work or
evening classes.

Typical snack outings involve a group of friends sharing food and
socializing. Tuyết invited me out to join her snacking one Saturday
afternoon before she had graduated and started working. She aimed to
educate me, introducing me to what she viewed as an essential activity in Vietnamese cultural life. The place she had chosen, *Chè 88*, was
a widely reputed snack café in trendy Phú Nhuận district of Ho Chi
Minh City. It was popular with groups of school friends and university
students, courting couples as well as young families with small children.
With everyone crammed into the shaded upstairs terrace of the shop, it
was crowded. With bursts of laughter and clinking of metal spoons on
porcelain bowls, it was noisy and chaotic. The waitresses, in matching
uniforms and sports shoes, constantly hurried. They hurried up the
steep spiralling staircase carrying trays of snacks and drinks. They hurried past tables delivering bowls, wiping up spills and collecting orders
as they went. They hurried downstairs to the kitchen with new orders
and trays piled high with used bowls, glasses and ashtrays.

We sat on low plastic stools around a low table. On the wall behind
us, a menu listed dozens of savoury and sweet snacks. There were all
types of rice dumplings and rice paper rolls (*bánh bao, bánh bèo, bánh
cuốn, bò bía*), quail and duck eggs, health drinks made from seaweed
(*rong biển*), ginseng (*sâm lạnh*), and pennywort (*rau má*), a variety of
popular puddings (*chè*), such as grapefruit rind, lotus seed, corn, green
bean, and taro, as well as a choice of seasonal fruit smoothies (*sinh tố*),
fresh coconut juice, ice creams, bottled fruit juices, and sodas.

Throughout the afternoon, in her comments and actions, Tuyết demonstrated that the inexpensive desserts, drinks and other snacks were
an important part of a typical student life and youth cultural identity.
Snacking involved not only eating, but also hanging out with friends,
sharing food and jokes, talking, listening to and singing pop songs, playing on their mobile phones as well as reading newspapers and magazines
together. Snacking has been a conventional part of modern Vietnamese

youth culture. Like Tuyết and other young people in post-reform Ho Chi Minh City, in postcolonial Saigon young people including Nguyễn Thị Thu-Lâm (1989, pp. 113–14) and Mai Elliott (1999, p. 264) used to spend their free time hanging out and snacking with their classmates and sisters. Demonstrating behaviour, attitudes and values which are recognizable as legitimate practices of social participation enables a young person to also demonstrate belonging to an identity (Bourdieu 1990a, p. 136). As Alan Warde (1997, p. 64) argues, sharing food in a recognizable, familiar and authentic practice, such as snacking, not only serves to conjure nostalgia between the participants, but also sustains the practice and its meaning in a particular social and culinary context. To Tuyết, eating and hanging out were part of the same activity. It was inconceivable to be social without sharing food.

Food preferences and culinary practices can be a significant means of cultural expression that addresses issues ranging from status, class and gender identities to the influences of tradition, migration and new technologies (Warde 1997, pp. 22–3). Snacking in Ho Chi Minh City offers a way for young people to demonstrate a range of aspects of urban identity making, including a conventional gender identity. By rejecting the fizzy sweetness of coca-cola, a 'hot' and globalized choice, and opting for a 'cooling' glass of pennywort (*rau má*) and a protein-, calcium- and iron-rich fertilized duck egg (*hột vịt lộn*), two localized Vietnamese offerings, Tuyết chose in line with norms that could be recognized by others as conventional choices for a young Vietnamese woman concerned about her weight, her appearance and her health. As a leisure practice, snacking is not independent of other realms of social practice (Bourdieu 1984, p. 193). The symbolic meanings of various popular cultural activities, such as snacking, only become apparent when the relative social positions of participating individuals are taken into account (Roose, van Eijck and Lievens 2012, p. 508).

Snacking was also a way for an educated young person to demonstrate middle-class ambitions. In contrast to the author Tam Huê, who fondly recalled the tastes of her childhood, Nghĩa avoided some of the local specialities he associated with his origins in Central Vietnam. Nghĩa, the second youngest child of a large village family, had arrived in Ho Chi Minh City to study at university. As the first person in his family to graduate high school, Nghĩa pressured himself to excel so as not to disappoint his older siblings who supplemented his modest income derived from a student stipend and casual employment with any additional funds that their small-scale produce and brewing businesses could generate.

One afternoon free from commitments, Nghĩa took me snacking on specialities from the Southeast. He chose a number of popular dishes for me to sample and selected dishes from the Centre for himself. However, he refused to take corn pudding (*chè bắp*), a very popular snacking dish. To dissipate the tense atmosphere that had quickly developed between Nghĩa and the seller, he explained his reasons so as not to cause her offence by refusing her dish. He refused the dish not because he felt too superior to eat her food, nor because he was afraid of being poisoned by street food. He refused the dish because it contained corn. For Nghĩa, corn did not evoke fond memories of childhood, but acted as a reminder of the extreme poverty he had endured when his widowed father could not afford to buy sufficient rice to feed his children. Refusing corn became symbolic of a divide between the impoverished life Nghĩa had left behind when he moved to Ho Chi Minh City and the new life he hoped to build in the future. Nghĩa's refusal to eat corn reflects a refurbishment of his culinary choices in line with his new pretensions (Bourdieu 1984, p. 150).

While Lisa Drummond (2012, p. 88) observes that street food in Vietnam may be seen by some as dirty, unhygienic and a last resort, for others street food symbolizes the tastes of childhood and offers an opportunity to mark a regionalized identity that could be oriented to a tradition of subsistence living within a kin group, or to an alternative new way of living. A transformation of identity necessitates a reconfiguration of values and dispositions. Food preferences offer a means of expressing identity through selecting or rejecting particular dishes and their symbolic associations. As Alex Rhys-Taylor (2013, pp. 239–41) argues, the selection and enjoyment of a particular meal – such as jellied eel and other street seafood dishes in London – is strongly associated with a lower-status (working-class) identity, while disgust at the sight and smell of the same meal is associated with relative privilege and distinction. Food preferences have long been a way not only to express markers of individual identity but also to transmit classed (and gendered) sensibilities from one generation to the next at the family table.

Refusing particular food – as unpalatable or disgusting – disrupts the intergenerational transmission of classed (and gendered) identities and enables identification with new and emerging status positions.

As cultural capital is dynamic and its relative value can change, the symbolic associations of a particular dish or style of eating can also be reconfigured. In central Vietnam throughout the 2000s, Nir Avieli (2011, pp. 65–9) observed a reconfiguration in the symbolic meaning of consuming dog meat, a dish strongly associated as masculine and as northern regional food. Initially, it was not disgust but fear of misfortune stemming from Buddhist beliefs that deterred locals from eating dog meat. With greater contact between elite and affluent northerners and aspirational locals, the dish became widely popular and imbued with a range of meanings including the rejection of Buddhist conventions and adoption of modernization, secularization, cosmopolitanism, sophistication and freedom associated with new exotic culinary choices.

For Nghĩa also, the symbolic meaning of corn had been reconfigured. The story he shared revealed that as a child he had eaten any corn offered to him by *chị Hai*, his eldest sister and the motherless family's primary carer, even if it had malformed kernels, was no longer fresh, or was taken in the form of a tasteless watery soup. According to him, his sister routinely gave up her own portion so that he might eat, reflecting her obligation to nurture the family and the sacrifice it involved. In a Confucian-influenced society, such as Vietnam, parents' investment in a child rests on an expectation of reciprocity. Merav Shohet (2013, p. 204) points out the debt Vietnamese children have to their parents is repayable via practices of filial piety comprising respect and nurturance. These practices overlap and intertwine with an ethic of 'sacrifice' (*hy sinh*) which operates both within and beyond the family. In Nghĩa's case, the debt was to his sister whose sacrifices were invested in raising him. The benefits Nghĩa's new urban status, and any wealth and power it conveyed, would be directed not only towards himself but also to the sister and their natal family through the obligation he has to repay his debt to them.

Yet, having eaten corn with his family was a connection that retained value as cultural capital associated with the authentic experience of a post-war Vietnamese cultural identity. Retaining valued signals of cultural capital, such as a connection to a normative loving family and authentic experiences of cultural life in a specific region, can enhance an aspiring urbanite's accumulated reservoir of cultural capital and consolidate their position amongst Ho Chi Minh City's new middle classes. This can be achieved by highlighting the positive moral associations of 'having roots' – or not 'losing roots' (*mất gốc*) – that deeply connect them to an authentic Vietnamese cultural identity. As Nir Avieli (2013, pp. 128–9) suggests, consumption of particular authentic cuisine not known to outsiders can distinguish locals as those richer in cultural capital.

EXCLUSION AND FUSION IN URBAN CULINARY PRACTICES

Historically, the majority of leisure and recreational activities in Southeast Asia took place outdoors and in public space, typified in dynamic street cultures. With the emergence of middle classes across Southeast Asia, popular leisure activities of the new rich such as shopping, cinema, and eating out may be given a 'middle-class touch' by shifting into purpose-built spaces or moving indoors into privatized space (Chua 2000b; Gerke 2000; Hooper 1998). As I have argued elsewhere (Earl 2004, p. 367), the shifting of café culture from the street into the private environment of air-conditioned cafés indicates an exclusivity that marks social distance associated with cultural capital in the form of taste rather than solely based on wealth. In upmarket cafés it is apparent that it is the choice of environment that is significant in displaying taste. An aspiring young person, such as Liên, may enjoy a familiar leisure activity but at the same time produce and display status via the choice of a privatized leisure space that excludes other status groups and individuals who do not possess the cultural, or economic, resources to participate. Within privatized spaces, urbanites may be exposed to new cultural influences and encounter new social practices that reconfigure familiar ways of being.

Street snacking has found its way from outdoor spaces into exclusive places patronized by middle classes. In 2004, a new downtown eatery promoted a street-style of eating in the luxury environment of a refurbished French colonial era villa. As it quickly gained in popularity and became one of the places to be seen in Ho Chi Minh City, *Nhà Hàng Ngon* (Delicious Restaurant) set a new standard for eating. The restaurant's courtyard had been paved and converted into a series of outdoor kitchens comprising modified street stalls, each of which specialized in a particular Vietnamese regional speciality. The restaurant reportedly hired locally renowned street cooks, many of whom were migrants who had brought with them to Ho Chi Minh City the knowledge of their regional culinary favourites. As a result, *Nhà Hàng Ngon* serves meals with strong associations with particular regions of Vietnam. The menu included a range of popular wet and dry noodle dishes such as *cao lầu*, the local specialty from central Vietnam reportedly made by three families in Hoi An (Avieli 2013, p. 124), as well as other recognized regional noodle dishes such as *mì quảng* from the Centre and *bún mắm* from the Mekong Delta. There were also a range of fresh and fried spring rolls, all kinds of cakes (*bánh*) and puddings (*chè*) as well as popular street snacks, such as fertilized duck eggs (*hột vịt lộn)*. Most of the dishes on the menu could be found at restaurants or street stalls outside, although some are not so common on Ho Chi Minh City's streets.

A concept of tradition in food cultures serves to locate the diner in a familiar, nostalgic and authentic culinary tradition that is often embellished or adapted (Warde 1997, p. 64). At *Nhà Hàng Ngon*, authentic culinary traditions are embellished by their relocation from the city's popular streetside stalls into an exclusive urban eatery whilst they retain their regionalized associations, associations which are imagined or invented. Inside the restaurant a diner will find a family atmosphere and a crowd that is usually a mixture of urbanite couples, young families, affluent businessmen, overseas Vietnamese, expatriates and foreign tourists. Its popularity led to its own upstairs extensions within a year of its opening, but also to other restaurants imitating its décor and style, using similar names and locations in nearby streets. The success of the *Nhà Hàng Ngon* chain and its imitators shows that the activity of street-style eating has been reconfigured by being relocated within an exclusive place where urbanites can demonstrate their familiarity and belonging within a mixed social crowd at the same time demonstrating their belonging to a particularized Vietnamese culture through their food orders or regional specialities (Earl 2008, p. 227). Middle-class Vietnamese diners are not only able to express their urbanite credentials in differentiating themselves from overseas Vietnamese visitors, expatriates and foreign tourists but also to distinguish themselves from others within the same relatively prosperous social middle.

One evening I met Cúc and her colleagues at *Nhà Hàng Ngon*. The five of them were in their late twenties and early thirties. They had come directly from work and were dressed in their daytime uniform of a straight black skirt, company blouse and heels. Each also wore a trendy jacket over her company shirt and carried a brightly coloured purse. Their hairstyles were short and fashionable. Holding each other's hands or forearms and sharing jokes together, they were obviously good friends as well as colleagues. They not only shared the same office job, they also shared a rural–urban migrant identity. Four, including Cúc, originated in the Mekong Delta. The other young woman came from the Central Coast. They had arrived in Ho Chi Minh City after graduating high school to study at university and had each won a job at the same company. Three of them had commenced work at the same time.

At the restaurant table, they expressed their shared identity though their food preferences. After studying the extensive menu and commenting on the range of dishes on offer, they walked around the stalls where the dishes were prepared to determine the freshness of ingredients as well as the origins and local reputation of the cook. After careful consideration, they selected the same noodle dish they had chosen on their previous visit. The four colleagues from the Mekong Delta ordered *bún mắm*. However, the colleague from the Central Coast objected to the strong taste of fermented shrimp paste that characterizes *bún mắm*, explaining that she had learned to eat some Delta cuisine, such as *bún nước lèo Sóc Trăng*, with her colleagues but was still unable to enjoy the distinctive taste of *bún mắm*. In support, her closest friend in the group switched her choice. Having agreed to order *bún nước lèo Sóc Trăng*, a milder noodle soup, they then turned to Cúc and me to question my ability – as a cultural outsider – to enjoy *bún mắm*. Based on their experience, they advised Cúc to recommend an alternative dish to me, assuming that my palate would be unable to tolerate the unfamiliar taste. Without discussion, Cúc selected a dish that we had previously shared. Her choice of *bún bò Huế*, a chilli noodle soup from central Vietnam, had been a new taste for her which she had acquired among a group of new friends at university years earlier. While the five young women were colleagues, they had not been classmates and the others rejected the suggestion that they also switch their choice to this unfamiliar dish.

In making their selections, the group was sharing food to affirm their belonging as colleagues but also to distinguish between themselves within the group. The first two colleagues from the Mekong Delta affirmed their belonging to their regional identity and the bonds of empathy that they shared with each other by sharing *bún mắm*, an authentic and familiar dish, one more time. The colleague from the Central Coast had developed an agreeable palate that could tolerate Delta cuisine, proving her compatibility with the group and reinforcing the closeness of the bonds she had with her friend who shared the same alternative culinary selection of *bún nước lèo Sóc Trăng*. Yet Cúc's preference for a dish from an outside region, one she had never visited, expressed her orientation to cosmopolitanized tastes, firstly, acquired through the contact with outsiders that only she had experienced during her college years and, secondly, through her friendship with me and our sharing of the same dish. In this way, Cúc not only demonstrated shared cultural capital associated with a Mekong Delta regional identity in her initial choice, a dish the group had shared on a previous visit, but also distinguished herself from her colleagues as one who possessed greater cultural capital expressed through familiarity and long-established connection to an authentic but outside and alien taste.

Alan Warde (1997, p. 118) observes that some people consciously express their identities and lifestyles through their selections of what they eat and where they dine when eating out. Their choices are determined according to their dispositions, which presuppose an understanding of the relation between certain practices or representations and analogous positions in the social space (Bourdieu 1990a, pp. 131–2). Yet, to assume a link between certain dishes and specific identities, as Nir Avieli (2005b, p. 168) reflects, may be 'simplistic and potentially misleading' when dealing with invented food traditions. But the imagined regional origins of food may become symbolically significant for urban migrants in a multi-dimensional social context as they can gain profits from cultural associations with a highly valued authentic culinary tradition.

When eating out, Ho Chi Minh City's new middle classes may search for authentic tasting, quality regionalized cuisine that symbolizes the dishes they remember from childhood. They may choose to enjoy a familiar, authentic dish and its symbolic meaning in an exclusive urban eatery, such as Cúc's colleagues from the Mekong Delta did. Others, such as Cúc or her colleague from the Central Coast, might adapt to a new identity by adopting a new taste that consciously reflects their belonging to a new group or new status position. Alternatively, like Nghĩa who refused to eat corn, they might retain their connection to the authentic dish and its symbolic meaning through social distance by consciously rejecting it as they orient themselves to a new status position.

For new middle classes, regional pronunciation and longing for the culinary palate of a distant home may be recognized as valued forms of embodied cultural capital that reflect positively on their acquired new middle-class status position because they have not made a complete break from the authentic cultural traditions of their pasts and have not 'lost their roots' (*mất gốc*). Rather, they reconfigure the value ascribed to having authentic Vietnamese roots. In doing so, the relative value associated with 'high-brow' and 'low-brow' tastes is also reconfigured as popular tastes are not displaced but assume a more prominent position as valued cultural capital. A revised idea of cultural capital is not inherently associated with specific attributes of high culture. Annick Prieur and Mike Savage (2011, p. 571) explain that because highly valued cultural capital is embedded in a specific and dynamic social context, it is subject to reconfigurations that have meanings locally. The cultural landscape of post-reform Ho Chi Minh City is diversified and characterized by competing and contradictory taste profiles stemming from a diverse palate of regionalized and globalized cultural influences.

CHANGING PATTERNS IN MIDDLE-CLASS EATING OUT

Within privatized spaces, urbanites may be exposed to new cultural influences and encounter new social practices that reconfigure familiar ways of being. Throughout the 2000s, Vietnamese café culture underwent a transformation as it shifted from flexible outdoor spaces to exclusive purpose-built indoor places. Vietnamese café culture was further transformed with the opening of American chain cafés, such as Gloria Jean's and Tea Leaf and Coffee Bean, which introduced a globalized concept of café culture. Customers place an order using their first name and pay the bill prior to service. They wait to pick up their own orders. They find their own tables and serve themselves. This contrasts with a Vietnamese expectation of full table service.

A foreign style of café culture adds to the diversity of the urban leisure landscape and has been embraced by Vietnamese urbanites who choose new or reconfigured leisure activities that reflect their pretensions (Bourdieu 1984, p. 150). Familiarity with a new way of doing things, on the one hand, demonstrates familiarity with and belonging to a globalized elite cultural context and, on the other hand, demonstrates familiarity with but distance from a parochial Vietnamese cultural context. As Yan Yunxiang (2006, p. 52) points out, the introduction of an iconic global fast food chain's outlets in Beijing provided new forms of dining and new patterns of behaviour that grew in popularity within urban middle classes. But these new social practices were dynamic and continued to evolve so that, as Gao Zhihong (2013) argues, over three decades discourses of McDonald's in China have gradually diversified. While they have retained associations with the US, these associations have been revalued in line with varying localized social and political contexts.

In Ho Chi Minh City, globalized cultural influences are welcomed and reconfigured in the local cultural landscape. The Park Son retail chain introduced a level of luxury to department store experiences across Ho Chi Minh City. Inside the downtown Park Son department store, Vietnamese chain stores occupied both retail and food court spaces alongside international chains from Northeast and Southeast Asia as well as North America and Europe. The food court offered a mixture of cuisine and fast food in an air-conditioned exclusive environment with the bustling crowded atmosphere of a street eatery. The food court catered to a diverse crowd of Vietnamese urbanites and their families, Vietnamese returnees, Northeast Asian expatriate university students, and foreign tourists. It offered more than globalized fast food options and their localized imitators. A number of food court retailers also provided popular Vietnamese snacking cuisine, such as *cơm tấm* (broken rice), *phở* (northern-style rice noodle soup), *bánh cuốn* (fresh rice paper rolls), *lẩu* (hotpot) and *sinh tố* (smoothies). The bustling atmosphere of the food court, which Thu found particularly exciting, contrasted with the echoing quietness of the other department store floors at meal times.

When Thu took me to visit the Park Son food court one Friday after work in 2012, it was crowded with young couples, families and teens. We had difficulty finding two seats and agreed to share a table with an elderly Vietnamese woman and her teenaged granddaughters, a practice typical in a busy streetside eatery. Faced with a diverse menu ranging from sushi, ramen and bibimbap to hamburgers, pizza and ice cream sundaes, Thu ordered us *lẩu* (hotpot), a typical Vietnamese family meal comprising a platter of meat or seafood, salad, herbs and other vegetables cooked at the table in a wide flat pot of soup. However, in the food court, our orders were supplied by *Cái tô*, a new franchised Vietnamese fast food store that specialized in miniaturized individual servings of '*lẩu 1 người (hotpot for one person)*' (bilingual slogan). Each of the pre-prepared *lẩu*-for-one dishes arrived on an individual tray mounted on its own mini burner and accompanied by an individual plate of greens.

Lẩu-for-one was a downtown innovation, a new trend especially popular among lunching office workers that contrasted sharply with conventional *lẩu*, which is typically a family meal shared by a large group at a special occasion such as a birthday or wedding. Single-serve hotpots were an adaptation of the traditional form catering primarily to new middle-class office workers in the city. *Lẩu*-for-one eateries provide small tables suitable for one or two diners. Especially during the lunch break, they tend to be very busy places. They offer about a dozen standard hotpots, such as meat, seafood or mushroom, a vegetarian option. The customers, who have limited time for lunch, receive pre-prepared hotpots which are already boiling to ensure almost no waiting time. An aim to provide a quicker, easier and cheaper cooking process are among the simplifications made to particular dishes, such as *mì quảng* noodles in Hoi An, when they are mass produced in tourist-oriented or fast food contexts (Aveili 2013, p. 127). Adapting specific dishes indicates a reconfiguration of local eating in line with globalized fast food practices.

Lẩu-for-one is a fast food version of a traditional Vietnamese dish. In this modified form, it was easily relocated from an eatery into a diversified food court environment. At the Park Son food court, our fellow diners were surprised to see the individualized *lẩu*-for-one servings arrive at our table. The server checked the two trays against the order slip, tore it and left us to our meals. The other meals soon arrived, too. The two granddaughters had ordered a combination of hamburgers, sushi rolls and Vietnamese broken rice, which they seemed very eager to share. But their grandmother eyed Thu's choice of a familiar Vietnamese family dish and, having assessed its adequate quality, asked for directions to the order counter.

Considering the range of dishes as either 'high-brow' or 'low-brow' choices was meaningless in the food court. In a context where openness to new or unfamiliar influences and behaviours is expected, or at least tolerated, very diverse social practices can be generated. The breadth of interests and scope of activities, as Roose, van Eijck and Lievens (2012, p. 508) contend, become more relevant than distinctions between high-brow and low-brow tastes. Attempting to categorize an adapted version of *lẩu*, a dish often served in its original form at weddings and feasts, as high-brow or low-brow in contrast to Vietnamese broken rice or globalized fast foods is lost as the symbolic meanings associated with culinary choices depend on the relative positions of individuals in the social space. The uses of culinary specialities, as Nir Avieli (2013, p. 129) observes, highlight that expressions of cultural sophistication in twenty-first century Vietnam are flexible, dynamic and contradictory. This reveals that there is more to class distinction than an ability to spend and consume. The choice of activity and location as well as how an activity is carried out are significant in setting oneself apart from others within a status group whose members are equipped to recognize the relative value of different modes of distinction. Hagen Koo (2006, p. 13) argues daily experience is required to expose oneself through the long process of socialization that enables the formation of an enduring class culture.

For new middle-class women, such as Thu, who are assumed to be familiar – to an extent at least – with globalized cultures, participating in a parochial activity demonstrates a desire to belong to a national cultural identity and a normative social life, the importance of which Bourdieu (1990a, p. 136) stresses for individuals to feel a sense of belonging and participate in a socially differentiated context. Demonstrating the same needs and same desires as everyone else in a group or neighbourhood enhances a sense of belonging through selective participation, rather than through direct or indirect social exclusion. As Cúc's colleagues' choice of noodles at an exclusive eatery served to establish bonds between themselves and affirm their compatibility with each other, Thu's choice connected her more closely with a Vietnamese identity and the palate of the grandmother with whom we shared a table. Thu demonstrated identity and belonging through her choice of food in a socially diverse but privatized context. As Liên's choice of noodles at her local street stall served to mitigate social distance between herself and her neighbours, Thu's choice of a Vietnamese family meal – albeit in an individualized serving and not shared with an actual family – served to connect her to Vietnamese culture in a globalized culinary context. At the same time, Thu's choice not to order globalized fast food was a means to distinguish herself from those around her. Her choice of parochial cuisine enabled her to set herself apart from the granddaughters at our table. In ordering a reconfigured *lẩu* dish rather than an exotic foreign dish such as a hamburger, Thu privileged the familiar traditional cuisine over the globalized option. The value associated with globalized cultural influences varies with local conditions and fast foods can be recognized by some, such as the granddaughters, as new and desirable, while they are recognized by others, such as Thu and the grandmother, as artificial and tasteless. Thu's choice reflected the dual façade of cultural capital, one that simultaneously valued certain globalized practices (such as fast food, imported wine or European classical music) and also certain localized practices (such as parochial cuisine or cultural festival traditions). Her choice of parochial cuisine displayed normality and belonging which compensated for the social distance that her sophisticated appearance and mannerisms conveyed. Through her culinary practices, she located herself in the space between the global and the local.

A NEW AESTHETIC LANGUAGE OF URBAN LIFESTYLING

The food practices of Ho Chi Minh City's new middle-class women, such as Liên, Tuyết, Cúc and Thu, reveal a tension between globalized and localized practices and their changing value as cultural capital. In mega-urban Southeast Asia, scholars have noted the contrasting value placed on globalized and local cultural influences by new middle classes. Brenda Yeoh (2004, pp. 2434–5) highlights a clear distinction in Singapore between cosmopolitanism and parochialism. English proficiency and skills in banking, information technology and science are valued as globalized and modern attributes. These are contrasted with living, working and training locally to play a role in maintaining core values and social stability. Abdul Rahman Embong (2002, p. 126) observes a western-oriented homogenizing process of cosmopolitanism among the new rich, the upper level of Malaysia's middle classes, that objectively and subjectively differentiates them from other Malay middle and lower classes who lack their exposure to western education, values and lifestyles as a process. A comparable tension is apparent in postsocialist Europe. In Serbia, Predrag Cvetičanin and Mihaela Popescu (2011, p. 449) identify a basic opposition, not between high-brow culture and popular culture, but between global and local cultures that enables the formation of two distinctive types of cultural capital. Local cultural capital relates to rites of passage and traditional folk culture, singing and dancing, while global cultural capital relates to high-brow opera and ballet, popular jazz and rock, foreign languages, knowledge of history, information technology and university education.

The lifestyle choices of Ho Chi Minh City's middle-class youth are greatly influenced by imported popular culture, which perpetuates an association of classiness with the outside world which originated in the colonial era. It is thus not a new phenomenon that young people are attracted to globalized cultural influences. While outside influences have not always been seen in a negative light, particularly in urban middle-class life, an ongoing fascination with imported practices, beliefs and ideals among aspirational young people has long been regarded by the Vietnamese state as threatening to displace Vietnamese cultural traditions. But social distance is not exclusively associated with the foreign, as relative social positions between – and within – classes are also determined by values, attitudes and behaviour that stem from Vietnamese, or indigenized, cultural traditions. In short, cultural capital plays a key role in claims to, and recognition of, relatively higher social positions within emerging status groups, even when an individual's choices seem inconsistent and contradictory.

Transformations of taste in middle-class Ho Chi Minh City occur in a context of globalized, localized, diversified, and cosmopolitan influences. This context affects individual dispositions by generating transformations that result in inconsistencies and contradictions between local and globalized cultural influences. Throughout the 1990s, Vietnamese authorities became concerned about the extent of the influence of globalized youth culture and other imported practices – labelled by the state as 'social evils' (*tệ nạn xã hội*) and 'poisonous culture' (*văn hóa độc hại*)

(Rydstrøm 2006; Taylor 2001) – in the social lives of Vietnamese youth. Historian David Marr points out that, in a group of 1,800 surveyed on famous personalities, a majority of Vietnamese youth in the 1990s could not identify a Vietnamese anticolonial hero or the mythical founding father of Vietnam, but successfully recognized Argentinean football hero Maradona and American pop star Michael Jackson. The survey results prompted authorities to call for more national history education in schools and society to reinforce – or reinstate – a sense of Vietnamese cultural identity (Marr 1997, pp. 339, 341). This pro-nationalism was a response to the effects of a decade of market reforms and the collapse of the Soviet Union. As Jayne Werner (2009, p. 76) observes, the concern of the state failed to recognize that their national narratives had lost relevance to the ideological needs of the post-reform era, an era that flourished through increasing globalization. Moreover, such a fear was not new, nor associated only with the post-reform state. It is reflected in the experiences of previous generations. In 1960s Saigon, for example, Mai Elliott (1999, p. 291) explained that, having grown up on a cultural diet of imported American popular and material culture during the war years, she was unable to answer even the most basic questions about Vietnamese Confucian heritage.

Yet other state strategies emphasized not only the 'pollution' of Vietnamese culture through a rejection of foreign influences, but also the adoption of selected, desirable foreign influences to enhance young people's cultural identities. David Marr, again, reports a contribution to a 1995 media forum, in the state-run newspaper *Tuổi Trẻ* (Youth), that called for young people to assimilate 'pride' in their origins with modern communications, technology and industry to form a meaningful contemporary identity that could be passed on to future generations (Marr and Rosen 1999, p. 200). This focus in the Vietnamese state media mirrors the perspective put forward in Vietnamese state research. In a book titled *The Role of the Family in the Formation of the Vietnamese Personality*, Le Thi (1999) asserts that the contemporary Vietnamese personality becomes whole through the absorption of a diverse range of influences incorporated with existing 'traditional' values. Drawing on an autobiographical essay (see below), Le Thi explains, she experienced rapid downward social mobility, having grown up among the urban middle classes before joining the revolution. The dissonance between these relative class subjectivities is the source of the diverse influences

166

that Le Thi suggests all Vietnamese need to incorporate into their personalities. One point worth noting here is that each generation of middle-class Vietnamese in the twentieth century has undergone a pattern of successive upward then downward social mobility, potentially enabling a comparable incorporation of contrasting values.

In the autobiographical essay, 'Some Recollections of My First Days Taking Part in the August Revolution of 1945', Le Thi described herself thus:

> [P]articipating in the revolution was truly a road to *changing my life*, in all its aspects – my spirit, my thinking, my worldview, the whole way of life of an 'urban petty bourgeois'… I learned to forge an ideology and a work style of the working class… In my heart, however, I am truly grateful to my parents for enabling me to study, for providing me with the valuable knowledge I needed for my revolutionary activities later, and especially for instilling in me a way of living, a sense of the special ethics of a family of teachers: an emphasis on humanity, on justice, on courtesy, on intellect, and on beliefs… Thus there is in me the influences of the culture of my family, among them some traditional [Confucian] ethical values, along with the influences of a new culture, of a Marxist revolutionary ethics. These influences do not conflict; they are woven together in me (Duong and Sidel 1998, p. 1028, original emphasis).

In weaving together these strands, Le Thi narrates a causal 'retrospective illusion' that comes to terms with competing cultural influences, rather than allowing an adopted culture of Marxist revolutionary ethics to fully displace her existing classed and gendered culture (see Bourdieu 1993b, p. 193). She goes on to explain that the 'most reasonable spectrum of values' can be first observed in the lifestyles of young urban couples who readily accommodate change in relationships, thinking, living, divisions of labour and solutions to family affairs (Le Thi 1999, pp. 80–2). Such a spectrum recognizes diversity across individual experience and places value on personal development and change in a particular time and a particular place. Dealing with relative social position in this way describes social change that is shaped by a transformation of dispositions, as individuals leave their old world behind and take up new lifestyles (Bourdieu 1990b, p. 68). Yet, in post-reform Vietnam, the old world is never fully left behind by educated urban migrant women of the new middle classes.

Central to Le Thi's claim is an internalization of the other that involves more than material culture and associated practices to include the ideas and values of moral culture. Following sociologist Ulrich Beck (2002, p. 18) on cosmopolitanism, this represents a dialogic imagination that describes 'the clash of cultures and rationalities within one's own life, the *"internalized* other"... correspond[ing] to the coexistence of rival ways of life in the individual experience'. Here, Beck's cosmopolitanism draws on Mitchell Cohen (1992, p. 483) to present 'a dialectical concept of rooted cosmopolitanism, which accepts a multiplicity of roots and branches and that rests on the legitimacy of plural loyalties, of standing in many circles, but with common ground'.

Conceptualizations of cosmopolitanism, as Beck (2002, p. 33) points out, have broadened not only from a western centre point but also from an elitist association *only* with middle classes to also incorporate the experiences and desires of underclasses and previously excluded others. Cosmopolitanism has become a 'transformative' condition of 'openness to the world' that is oriented to the particularized context in which it operates (Delanty 2012, p. 336). In post-reform urban China, as Lisa Rofel (2007, pp. 114, 133) explains, cosmopolitanism is connected to the importation of ideas and practices from abroad (the west) to create a new intellectual movement in major urban centres, but it is neither universal nor stable as in one context 'Chineseness' can denote the local and in another the cosmopolitan. In Russia, cosmopolitanism also does not represent a universalist concept and centres on oscillating interpretations. As Alexei Yurchak (2006, pp. 132, 163) explains, cosmopolitanism in the last Soviet generation was characterized by ambiguity, as it was difficult to know which cultural signals were valued and which were rejected by official ideology that varied with emerging social issues. Cosmopolitanism captured a state of being inside and outside at the same time.

Inconsistency and contradiction within cultural tastes, such as those demonstrated by Liên, Tuyết, Cúc and Thu in their culinary practices, was recognized by Bourdieu in later revisions to his original study of class dispositions (Bourdieu 1984; see also Bennett 2007; Lahire 2008). Bourdieu describes class tastes in *Distinction* in relatively homogenous terms; however, elsewhere he acknowledges that an equivalent class position does not necessarily imply that individuals hold a unified set of class cultural tastes (Bourdieu 1998a, p. 11) and that in class-divided societies, the efficacy and profits of symbolic capital are secured based on the fact that all agents do not have equal economic and cultural means for moving beyond their original position (Bourdieu 1997, p. 49). Building on this position, sociologist Tony Bennett's work in the UK demonstrates that members of a particular class cohort do not necessarily report actual consonant tastes and unified lifestyles. Bennett found that 'dissonant tastes' and 'cross-over tastes' characterize the taste profiles of occupationally-based classes among multi-dimensional communities in contemporary Britain. Bennett's findings demonstrate that taste profiles are not necessarily unified and globalized practices and technologies, including television, do not necessarily indicate low-brow tastes (Bennett 2007; Bennett et al. 2009). Bennett argues that Bourdieu did not anticipate that a 'divided habitus' or 'dissonant tastes' might be a cultural norm, rather than exception to the rule. In understanding this relation, and that changing social conditions affect the values ascribed to practices and positions, we begin to perceive what may constitute a new aesthetic language of urban leisure lifestyling in middle-class Southeast Asia.[8]

In a context such as Ho Chi Minh City, which is part of a rapidly growing, culturally diverse and socially differentiated mega-urban region, the significance of urbanization in the formation of new middle classes can be stressed. Rural–urban migrants bring varying culinary and cultural influences from other regions of Vietnam to Ho Chi Minh City and through their interactions they expose themselves and each other to new ideas and tastes. Additionally, increasing contact with imported popular culture and products provides greater exposure for Ho Chi Minh City urbanites to a diverse palate of globalized cultural influences. Bernard Lahire (2008, p. 174) argues that as urbanites 'rub shoulders' they retain a range of heterogeneous dispositions of varying strength. The mixing of diverse genres and dissonant cultural tastes becomes 'a generative formula for practices and representations' that defends and challenges previously established markers of distinction (p. 178). Regenerating, or reconfiguring, the cultural landscape of

---

8   The term 'new aesthetic language' was used by Michael Pinches (1999a, p. 36) in describing the cultivation of tastes in informal everyday life among middle classes in urban Southeast Asia.

distinction operates not only as a boundary between social classes but also to differentiate individuals within the same status group (p. 180). Further complicating the Vietnamese (and Southeast Asian) example is the feminization of migration which adds a gendered dimension to considerations of the development of encultured dispositions and the formation of middle classes.

FINDINGS

Greater access to leisure is one of many observable social transformations that educated urban women in post-reform Vietnam have experienced. This chapter has explored the re-emergence of middle-class culture through the context of leisure lifestyling and urban recreational practices among new middle-class women. The specific examples considered represent urban leisure practices that continue to be widely popular over time and between different social groups in order to demonstrate that individual dispositions and strategies that produce or mitigate social distance – rather than the choice of activity – distinguish aspirational middle classes from others. Beyond entertainment, the benefits of leisure lifestyling, like job-hunting, are also concerned with family social position and family plans for the future. As in the postcolonial past, leisure practices in the post-reform era indicate social differentiation and distinction whilst also demonstrating social mobility and acting as markers of social status which are recognized and deciphered by others.

Urban migrants play an important role in revitalizing urban culture through the influences that they exert on entertainment, recreational choices and street life. Their concerns in expressing self-identity and belonging to a group away from home are influential on the refurbishment of their pretensions. Transformations of taste in middle-class Ho Chi Minh City occur in a context of globalized, localized, diversified, and cosmopolitan influences. This context affects individual dispositions by generating transformations that result in inconsistencies and contradictions between local and globalized cultural influences. This cultural dissonance does not reflect high- or low-brow tastes, but the competing tastes of a diversified and dynamic cultural landscape. The adaptation of existing leisure practices for new purposes and into exclusive spaces are among the ways that aspirational migrants develop a new aesthetic language that enables them to benefit from the new conditions encountered in the city after reform. A new aesthetic language, which describes acts of judgement, valuation and appreciation within the social processes of urban middle-class cultural production, recognizes periodic revaluations of cultural capital in a changing and flexible social context. This new aesthetic language is dynamic and evolves over time. Its outcomes vary for different agents, some of whom are able to use the results to benefit from processes of social exclusion to produce social distance or mitigate its effects and express belonging.

CHAPTER SIX

Social mobility in a
multi-dimensional family

U rbanization in Asia provides opportunities for education and non-manual salaried work that enable some young people to exceed their parents' social positions, their levels of education and their earning capacities. As members of Asia's new middle classes, they are aspirational and they aim to build lifestyles marked by comfort, convenience and quality. Their acquisitions of a new class position are recognized by more than their possession of status-marking goods. Those who have made it are marked by a durable veneer of class culture that is recognizable to others. Within a multi-dimensional family, the lifestyles of younger, more highly educated members contrast with the lifestyles of the relatives they have left behind. Their migrations to the city, where they can access education and employment, represent a turning point individually and for the whole family. Through a singular field of interaction, new middle-class family members are able to extend benefits back home, although the rewards for family members are differential.

Urban migration does not only facilitate social mobility, it also allows for exploring new ways of living. Migration in Vietnam, as Christine White (1987, p. 228) points out, has been a strategy for young women to evade traditional obligations and family responsibilities whilst experiencing periods of relative autonomy. While at first educated urban migrant women may have experienced some economic hardship in the city, with employment they may be able to wield economic power not only to consolidate their independence from the family but also to extend the benefits of their new social power to others within the family and beyond. In this way their break from the past is symbolic as they maintain close contact. This chapter explores the consumption practices of new middle-class women, including Tuyết, Thu and her friend Hòa,

Cúc and Liên, by exploring the ways that they spend, what forms their remittances take, and where they direct them. The discussion moves beyond money and goods to explore their transmissions of knowledge and experience across a singular field of interaction that operates between them and their families in rural Vietnam.

MARKING AN URBAN MIDDLE-CLASS LIFE

Asia's ascending middle classes have sought betterment in terms of improved socio-economic standards of living. Abdul Rahman Embong (2001, p. 13) explains that rapid state-led economic growth since the 1970s and 1980s transformed Pacific Asian societies from 'agricultural backwaters' into 'economic powerhouses' where success is marked by a modern and technologically driven urban lifestyle. Affluence has been associated with a cultural veneer of suburban living, air-conditioned office work, car driving and endless access to consumer products. Knowledge and beliefs also underpin the material markers of a new middle-class lifestyle in reflecting the cultural sophistication that is essential to building an enduring class cultural position. The prosperity and expansion of middle classes have depended on the economic success of their countries and the achievements of new middle classes has offered the lower classes 'the promise of a life of plenty' (Shiraishi 2008, pp. 15–16). A desire for material goods has marked the achievement of relative upward mobility among new middle classes across Southeast Asia and China. Consumption practices represent an important means of expressing social identities and creating models for others to emulate.

In postsocialist cities, the pursuit of a consumer lifestyle marks new middle-class status and indicates a shift towards a mode of consumption identified more closely with the goods of capitalist consumption than the ideals of the socialist past (Bourdieu 1998c, p. 14; Lamont and Lareau 1988, p. 163). As standards of living in postsocialist Asia improved, different commodities were recognized as marking relative economic status. In China consumer products that symbolize social position have shifted as incomes and aspirations have escalated. Beverley Hooper (1998, p. 168) identified that in the 1970s, a radio, a bicycle and a sewing machine were the most desired products. By the 1980s, a television, a refrigerator and a washing machine in urban areas had displaced the previous set. The 1990s saw a VCR, CD player and air-conditioner as the recognized markers of social position, which were subsequently displaced by Chinese millennium desires for a telephone, privately owned apartment and a car. The markers of relative status are dynamic and shift as society develops, reflecting the process of gradually improving standards of living in China as the population pulls itself out of poverty in line with state-led reform (Kharas and Gertz 2010, p. 43; Rolandsen 2011, pp. 186–7).

Chua Beng Huat (2000a, p. 23) regards the status goods desired in China, while more modest than industrialized Asian countries, to mark the 'rungs of the consumption ladder' that enable a family to climb up when they possess the desired goods. But it is not only the ability to consume goods that expresses class culture. Mark Liechty (2003, pp. 6–7) observes the cultural processes of consumption to play a significant role in the formation of middle classness. Jean-Pascal Daloz (2008, p. 314) explains that, while it may seem 'stereotypical' to own certain goods, the prized commodities desired in a particular social context enable individuals to 'project' an image to others. The symbolic meaning of a commodity is what marks status. Chua Beng Huat (2000a, pp. 23–4) has reflected on the displacement of sewing machines as markers of status in Singapore. A sewing machine had been one of the most highly desired assets in Singapore in the 1970s because clothes were hand-made so learning to sew was an important step for all women. In the 1980s fewer women learned to sew as ready-made clothes became widely available. By the late 1980s, hardly any woman under thirty knew how to sew and it was difficult to find a machine repairer. Owning a sewing machine was no longer desired as a marker of class cultural status. The product itself was not status-producing. Rather, it was the appropriate use of the product and its symbolic meaning that had marked betterment and cultural sophistication. Highly valued signals of distinction are particularized to place and time and, importantly, they are dynamic, evolving as the stakes are increased. Changing markers of status reflect that post-authoritarian, post-reform and capitalist societies alike are dynamic and characterized by transformations and social differentiation.

Placing value on material goods as markers of social stratification in Vietnam is not new. Like postsocialist China, a range of desired material goods and other tangible markers of betterment have long indicated economic status and social prestige in Vietnam. In tracking the desirability of status-producing material goods in post-war Vietnam, David Marr (1988, p. 1) records that televisions, radios and refrigerators marked social status in the late 1970s. By the 1980s, attention centred on electronic equipment (stereos, televisions, VCRs, photocopiers, fax machines, computers), western music, kung fu movies from Hong Kong, translations of popular foreign novels, small business manuals, and 'the alleged magical properties of market forces in modern economics' (Marr 1993, p. 337). Both goods and knowledge associated with globalized culture were highly valued. In the 1990s the most desired asset among Vietnamese was an imported Japanese motorbike, an asset Liên prized. I have argued that a motorbike offered new freedoms to educated Vietnamese women at this time (Earl 2004, pp. 363–5). Allison Truitt (2008, pp. 3–4) regards motorbikes to do so by altering the boundaries of public and private to shape 'a new paradigm of urban mobility'. Private transport had become a marker of independence and affluence.

In the 2000s, a motorbike and a television were basic commodities in urban Vietnam. Almost all households in Vietnam's four major cities owned a motorbike and colour television, three in four a refrigerator, half a washing machine and a computer, and one in three had air-conditioning (GSO 2011c, p. 86).[1] Entertainment and communications technologies, such as flat screen televisions, smart phones, laptops and tablets, accessorized urban middle-class lifestyles. The majority of Ho Chi Minh City residents have cable television (80 per cent) and a mobile phone (70 per cent) (Ruwitch and Szep 2011, p. 5). New furnishings, interior decorations, artworks and modern household technologies, such as induction cook tops and bladeless fans, decorate better residences. But dissonance marks the urban Vietnamese cultural landscape. Elizabeth Vann (2012, pp. 162–3) observes that Vietnamese middle classes particularly value consumer goods they perceive to be hygienic, safe, secure and convenient but also goods associated with fashionable and cosmopolitan, local and globalized cultural influences. Other modern consumer practices including privatized recreation, commercial sex, and ultrasound tech-

---

1   Vietnamese state figures recorded that in 2009 91.1 per cent of metropolitan households owned a motorbike; 91.4 per cent a colour television; 72.6 per cent a refrigerator; 52.6 per cent a washing machine; 49.6 per cent a computer; and 31.7 per cent air-conditioning (GSO 2011c, p. 86).

nology also mark urban middle-class consumer lifestyles in Vietnam (Drummond 2012, p. 89).

Status-producing goods in post-war Vietnam have centred on technology and desired goods have changed as they became outmoded. The relative value of a motorbike decreased as ownership of a private car became a marker of social and economic achievement in urban Vietnam in the 2010s, mirroring that car ownership had previously displaced the value of motorbike ownership in Singapore, Kuala Lumpur and Bangkok (Embong 2001, p. 13; Howard 2011, pp. 136–8; PuruShotam 1998, p. 130; Shiraishi 2008, p. 5).

In the 2010s, a family home continues to be a key focal point of middle-class life in urban Vietnam. In addition to the desired commodities that indicate the cultural veneer of a middle-class lifestyle, owning a home consolidates one's social position. A renovated multi-storied house or a suburban villa continues to mark a relatively better social position in Ho Chi Minh City. Weekend cottages and holiday houses further differentiate those with enduring social and economic status from others (Drummond 2012, p. 85; To Xuan Phuc 2012; see also Tai and Sidel 2013). As I argued in Chapter 5, access to privatized space in Ho Chi Minh City offers an exclusivity that gilds widely practised leisure activities and enables new middle classes to show distance from other status groups but also to differentiate themselves from others within their own status group through a new aesthetic language of middle-class lifestyling that draws on globalized and localized practices that are deciphered in the particularized context in which an individual moves.

Cultural sophistication can be expressed through an individual's use of products so long as others recognize the value of their practices and are able to decipher their meanings. To do so, an individual must maintain contact with those who are equipped to recognize their rise from an original social position to a life of relative plenty. Writing on Indonesia, Solvay Gerke (2000, pp. 142–3) offers a useful explanation of how consumption can mark class stratification by differentiating between a poverty line that separates the very poor from the not-so-poor and a consumption line that separates the not-so-poor from the new middle class, who are those able to secure higher education and afford the symbolic items of middle-class consumption. Although not drawing on Bourdieu's sociology, Gerke's model is valuable as it implicitly recognizes that agents do not share equal abilities to move up social strata and that dissonant and contrasting tastes are possible in the social field.

RECOGNIZING ASPIRATION AND ACHIEVEMENT

While the distribution of economic capital through commodity consumption may indicate an aspiration for betterment, on its own it is not sufficient to demonstrate status in class culture. Possessing status-differentiating consumer goods and money does not alone indicate cultural sophistication. Socialization and daily experiences developed over time enable the formation of a middle-class culture and social identity, which incorporate self-improvement, lifestyling, social awareness and a globalized outlook (Koo 2006, p. 13; Hsiao 2010, p. 253).

Distinction may be recognized beyond the ownership of goods, yet lifestyle-oriented consumer products, such as an imported motorbike in Vietnam, have been integral to the construction and maintenance of a lifestyle that is recognized by others to be urban and middle-class. The meanings and value attached to lifestyle accessories as markers of social distance depend as much on the perceivers as on the producers. The reception of such products and goods indicates the relative social position of their owners and observers and, in doing so, marks the social landscape in observable and recognizable patterns. Distinctions between haves and have-nots reflect a changing position in relation to global markets, but also within Vietnam locally, where widespread ownership of a highly desired lifestyle accessory reduces its symbolic value in status production.

An imported motorbike has long been unchallenged as the most desired asset in urban Vietnam. At a specific time, having a particular model of motorbike conveys status or desire for upward mobility. As the stakes in intra-class competition are increased, the most desirable model changes. Imported Japanese models were the ultimate marker of status in the 1990s but had become normalized by the late 2000s as they were so widely owned among middle classes in Ho Chi Minh City. The reduction in symbolic value of a Japanese motorbike and what a motorbike signified about its rider was reflected in advertisements in the urban Vietnamese lifestyle media which, as Lisa Drummond (2004, pp. 173–4) suggests, provides a manual for how to be urban and middle-class. Further, Drummond (2012, p. 80) argues that the consumer-oriented practices of middle-class lifestyles have been naturalized as the 'urban normal'. However, Truong Thi Thuy Hang (2008 p. 19) points out that the Vietnamese mass media also feeds normative models of womanhood to women for emulation, models which deter women from asserting their own interests in line with historical gendered discourses of sacrifice and reciprocity as primary drivers of women's agency and behaviour.

State institutions, such as the mass media, can be credited with promoting idealized models for emulation and imitation by the population. In Bourdieu's sociology, social institutions, such as schools, families and the mass media, play a crucial role in the socialization of young people by shaping individuals according to models of social convention. The point of view of the institution represents a legitimate normative point of view which everyone within the limits of a particular society can recognize. Institutional discourses, which may be qualitatively different from one another, function to affirm individual identities, to ascribe appropriate appearances, behaviours, attitudes and values associated with these identities, as well as to record authorized accounts of normative social participation (Bourdieu 1990a, p. 136). The Vietnamese state mass media promotes models of idealized middle-class life as a promise to the lower classes that fosters their aspirations to pursue a higher standard of living and a better future.

The evolving relationships between desired goods and lifestyling are reflected in the imagery in Vietnamese women's magazine advertisements for Japanese motorbikes. In 2003, Yamaha's *SiriusV* motorbike was advertised with a bilingual slogan '*Mốt thời thượng I'm stylish*' (*Thế Giới Phụ Nữ*, 10 March 2003, p. 29). In the same issue, Suzuki's *Smash* motorbike was advertised as a 'new trend in motorbikes' (*mốt mới cho xe máy*). The model was pictured taking a fashionable young urban couple up an incline outside a new apartment building with residents overlooking from their balconies. Among them, a casually dressed urbanite man and a businessman observe 'it accelerates so easily!' (*tăng tốc dễ dàng!*) and 'it goes uphill so smoothly!' (*lên dốc nhẹ nhàng!*). A student on the ground floor concludes 'Oh! It truly surpasses everything!' (*Ồ! Thật vượt trội!*) (*Thế Giới Phụ Nữ*, 10 March 2003, p. 45). The Japanese motorbike symbolized the young couple's rise socially.

While owning a motorbike is ubiquitous in Vietnamese cities, a motorbike can also clearly signify wealth and status. The type, style, location, and usage of a motorbike indicates a wide breadth of information about the social background and aspirations of the rider. Aspiring young women may judge a young man by the type of motorbike he owns. Without one he is not a serious choice as a sweetheart (*người yêu*). So important is the desire for assets that reflect a promise of future social mobility that male undergraduates, such as Nghĩa, even take out loans to buy a motorbike before courting. Nghĩa worked in a number of casual and part-time jobs (selling ice-cream, as an extra on film sets, translating Sino-Vietnamese documents) in order to pay off his loans. A desire to demonstrate aspiration is so great in Ho Chi Minh City that street stalls sell inexpensive replacement labels which can superficially transform a relatively inexpensive Chinese motorbike into what appears to be an authentic Japanese model costing three times as much (Earl 2004, p. 363).

In the 2000s, as motorbike ownership became universal, Japanese motorbikes became a relatively affordable norm in well-off urban households. By 2012, two Honda models were advertised to young people as typical accessories of everyday urban life. Honda's *Vision* motorbike was advertised with the bilingual slogan 'Fully satisfied every day. Thỏa ước ao – Vui ngày mới' (*Thanh Niên Tuần San*, 6 April 2012, p. 66). Similarly, Honda's *Lead* motorbike was promoted with the slogan (in English) 'Lead to the next stage. Smart persons select smart things' (*Tiếp Thị & Gia Đình*, 2 April 2012, p. 3). These models had become typical choices for everyday use in urban life and were promoted in this manner in Vietnam's mass media.

From the late 2000s, European motorbikes set the standard of luxury and affluence among urbanites. Particularly popular among Ho Chi Minh City's super-rich twenty-somethings in the early 2010s were fully imported canary yellow Vespas. Even more exclusive was the Piaggio brand – with its slogan 'Art of the motorbike' (in English) – and its *Fly* model, which was promoted to connoisseurs in Vietnam's *Vogue* equivalent with the slogan 'Bay bổng cùng Fly' (Soar above all with the Fly) (*Đẹp*, 159, April 2012, p. 69). In contrast to imported Japanese models which had become symbolic of an everyday ride, an imported European model could set an urbanite apart from the rest.

Messages such as these in the mass media offer the promise that status in urban middle-class lifestyles is easily enhanced by possessing desired material goods which can be readily deciphered and admired by one's peers. But ownership of a branded motorbike operates like an academic qualification that acts as a certificate of cultural competence. The brand name, like institutional recognition, makes it possible to compare owners and the relative symbolic value of their ride by establishing conversion rates between cultural capital and economic capital based on guaranteed monetary values in a strict relationship between product, rank and remuneration (Bourdieu 1997, pp. 50–1, n. 10). The value placed on ownership of material goods or acquisition of academic qualifications that indicate cultural capital retain their value so long as they remain relatively scarce, due in part to their exclusivity and expense, which can be recognized as distinction for its owner (Bourdieu 1997, p. 49).

TRENDSETTING AND IMITATION

For new middle classes, who arrive in the city with a goal of improving their lives, investment in luxury commodities may be at first out of their reach. The inhibitive cost of the most highly desired material goods, such as a luxury motorbike, helps to differentiate aspirational social climbers from those who aim to achieve enduring social positions. Those who strive most for distinction, for example in purchasing a luxury motorbike to imitate a model life of comfort and affluence, are those who recognize their own lack in credentials (Bourdieu 1990a, p. 11). Different choices in resource allocation reflect differences in the efficacy of an individual's social position and subsequent power (Bourdieu 1993a, pp. 72–3). Jean-Pascal Daloz (2008, p. 312) points out that the efficacy of concealment and exposure in consumption depends on the particularized local conditions of the context. A new consumer in a modern city may seek more exposure to assert a social position because others know little about them.

While the super-rich can acquire authentic luxury goods and others can purchase modest imitations, new middle classes allocate their resources in order to maximize the accumulation of reservoirs of underlying cultural capital that may yield an enduring veneer of class culture that retains value. Elizabeth Vann (2006, p. 291) observes that Vietnam's new consumers direct their spending 'wisely' to purchases based on perceptions of quality, style and durability. They also participate widely in purchasing 'mimic goods'. Such goods are imitations or modelled in the style of an original brand, such as Sony, and are judged on their quality and popularity (Vann 2006, pp. 289–90). While an individual who can demonstrate a cultural veneer of taste based on a reservoir of underlying cultural capital is more successful than one who simply imitates the practices of others (Bourdieu 1984, p. 66), when resources are limited spending choices may become more significant. Bernard Lahire (2008, p. 177) observes that an individual may adopt a kind of reasoning that reflects the relative significance of their personal economic investment in becoming demanding about making selections and decisions when the purchase has taken the majority of their resources. Simply imitating historical or conventional forms is not reflective of cultural sophistication as 'it is the emergent that conveys cultural stakes' (Prieur and Savage 2011, pp. 557–8).

Trendsetting offers opportunities for new consumers to employ cultural literacy and taste to trump economic power in competition with Vietnam's super-rich. Nguyen-vo Thu-huong (2004, p. 184) observed that Ho Chi Minh City's aspirational garment workers did not simply imitate the behaviours of others but generated new trends and new ways of consuming that were recognized for their symbolic value in their local context. Creating a new trend based on underlying cultural capital may overcome a lack of economic capital in inter-class competition. Trendsetters, for David Goodman (1996, pp. 238–9), are those who set social and economic standards that others follow through their influence and in their constant appearances in the public eye. They are the ones who 'project' an image for others to emulate and the mass media to promote. Jean-Pascal Daloz (2008, p. 313) explains:

> [O]dd combinations seem possible without elite status necessarily becoming uncertain... A young lady wearing torn T-shirt and jeans, but with a sophisticated hair style, is very unlikely to be taken as a poor person. This calls attention to... giving a general impression through one or several attributes only.

Selecting certain attributes to flaunt can generate a new trend that does not consume all of an individual's economic resources but offers extensive benefits in terms of accumulating highly valued signals deciphered as cultural capital.

In the early 2000s, a motorbike was the most widely desired asset among Vietnamese, but it was beyond the reach of many aspirational young men. At this time, owning a retro Vespa in Hanoi enhanced an urbanite's social profile. Vespas were especially popular among young men, who 'cared for' (*chăm sóc*, nurtured) and 'indulged in' (*đam mê*) their restored vehicles (*Phụ Nữ*, 10 Feb 2003, p. 27). On the one hand, these retro rides were imported European motorbikes that were highly desired for their aesthetic appeal. As older models, their refurbishments required not only cash investment, but also the investment of technical skill and time. The individualized features of the restorations, particularly the paint and upholstery, possessed scarcity value that outweighed the appeal of a new mass produced model. As a trend recognized for its association with underlying cultural literacy, a renovated motorbike can mark a relatively higher status position in a similar way to making aesthetic choices in the home (Bourdieu 1984, p. 379). With an initial purchase as little as 10 per cent of a new Japanese motorbike, a restored older model could also overcome an economic handicap experienced by a young person with limited support from kin. This trend also evolved as the stakes increased. In the late 2000s, second-hand Honda Cubs or low-powered Charlys, painted purple or orange and trimmed in white leather upholstery, were fully restored and sold on to trendsetting young women in Ho Chi Minh City.

The influences of trendsetters in postsocialist Asia stem from a growing individualization in cultural life. In China, Yan Yunxiang (2009, p. 287) has observed the emergence of processes of individualization in 'DIY biographic work' that is influenced by globalization, while Unn Målfrid Rolandsen (2011, p. 185) has reported the diminishing power of local authorities to govern everyday lives which has enabled individuals to 'take possession' of their life choices. In Vietnam, Christina Schwenkel and Ann-Marie Leshkowich (2012a, pp. 379–80) note 'technologies of personhood' associated with 'neoliberal logics' located at the intersection of the global and the market. These processes are skewed towards one side of Mark Liechty's (2003, p. 67) 'space between' as they focus more on differentiation produced through alignment with modern and globalized relationships than with the traditional and local. Yet the conditions that give rise to individualization are fostered by state-led economic development and state-endorsed promotion of entrepreneurial strategies to build economic growth. As Annette Kim (2008, p. 32) points out, capitalism in Ho Chi Minh City is not 'natural' but has emerged through relationships with state institutions. In a functioning dynamic social world, periods of political or economic transition – and episodes of culture contact – may result in a questioning of accepted social convention and reconfiguring the interactive relationships between individuals and the state (Bourdieu 1977, pp. 168–9; Eyal, Szelenyi and Townsley 1998). Bernard Lahire (2008, p. 172) elaborates that when an individual moves beyond the sphere of influence of an institution and 'outside of the zone', social conventions do not necessarily impose themselves and resistance to the dominant cultural order may arise so long as a competing institutional logic is on offer, for example, from peer groups, professions, the family, or the mass media. The relative influence of socially structuring institutions, including the state, evolves but does not disappear. While the state and other institutions do not necessarily control individual life choices, individuals 'take possession' of their choices within structural constraints.

By the early 2010s, a motorbike had become a basic commodity in urban Vietnam and had lost its value as a commodity symbolizing affluence, in a similar process as having a sewing machine in Singapore in the 1980s. Rather than a motorbike, it was car ownership that enhanced urban middle-class social profiles in the 2010s. Choosing a relatively inexpensive second-hand model that had a unique aesthetic appeal, such as Tuyết did, could mark relative social distance within economic constraints. Tuyết had purchased a recent model of a Korean branded small family car. Buying the vehicle second-hand overcame the economic challenge that Tuyết faced as its purchase price was the equivalent of a mid-range motorbike. Having moved from the spacious house that she had built in Thủ Đức to a smaller one closer to her natal home in Bình Dương, Tuyết was able to consider buying a car. The lower cost of living there had enabled her to save more and the lower density living offered room for garaging. Further, the rural zoning at that time reduced the taxes associated with running a car.

Tuyết's decision to buy a car was a wise purchase which she regarded to be safe, secure and convenient, an attitude Vietnam's new consumers share (Vann 2006, pp. 162–3). Tuyết had never enjoyed riding a motorbike as, due to her petite size, she had found them difficult to control. She was not confident transporting a passenger, even a child, on a motorbike and she usually relied on her husband for a lift. With a car, she could safely transport her own and her sisters' children as well as her parents who were too elderly to travel by motorbike. Tuyết's desire for car ownership can be read in terms of emotional capital in caring for others in the family (Reay 2004, p. 71; Bourdieu 1998b). While Tuyết was asserting her own view in making the decision to buy a car, her intentions were to benefit the family. In this way, her reasoning conformed with an idealized model of Vietnamese womanhood, such as that promoted in the Vietnamese state mass media, by addressing the needs and interests of her family before herself. Tuyết's agency was directed to recreating and defending a normative gender identity (McNay 2004, p. 175). For women, conforming to naturalized femininity may go unrecognized as a strategy because gender normalcy offers them a limited form of capital (McDowell 1997, p. 207; Skeggs 2004, p. 22). However, when a woman, such as Tuyết, is seeking to move beyond her existing social position, conforming to normative womanhood may be an advantage in retaining a localized gender identity that can be recognized by others. Ann Marie Leshkowich (2011, p. 286) argues that appeals to feminine gender essentialism among Ho Chi Minh City's petty bourgeois market traders have 'defused' the problem of their class claims. Conforming to some localized gender norms can mitigate the social distance achieved by a new middle-class woman in a socially differentiated context to ensure a sense of belonging.

Although Tuyết never drove the car into Ho Chi Minh City, she regularly transported six adults and three children around the urban fringes in the candy-coloured two-door hatch. Despite being a less powerful and less desirable model, the car's appearance was idiosyncratic so that it drew attention from those around her for its scarcity value, which yielded profits of distinction for its owner (Bourdieu 1997, p. 49). Rather than imitating others, Tuyết provided a creative solution and cultural innovation that enabled her and her family to experience a relatively better lifestyle. Purchasing the car was a strategy to improve the standard of living of the whole family and to improve the family's social position. It enabled Tuyết to make plausible claims on a relatively higher social position whilst maintaining her normative identity as a good mother and responsible daughter. For Tuyết, producing emotional capital associated with her work in the family played an important role in her rise socially. Tuyết employed a new aesthetic language to locate herself in the space in between the globalized and the localized where she could express her relatively higher social position through her possession of a highly desired commodity and its use to fulfil a normative gender role in a reconfigured way. In this sense, Tuyết was a trendsetter who drew on her cultural literacy to trump an economic handicap.

FAMILY STRATEGIES FOR BETTERMENT

While there are signs that some middle classes in Vietnam's major cities are moving beyond government control (King, Nguyen and Nguyen 2008, p. 794), most are supportive of the state so long as their interests are being met. State-led economic development, in particular, offers the conditions in which the population can rise out of poverty. But more than state-led support is required for middle classes to flourish. The family plays an important role in providing the resources and support to build a better future. Vietnam's metropolitan areas do not only have high levels of economic development but also the highest proportion (34 per cent) of households with no dependents (GSO 2011a, p. 87). In such households, family resources can be concentrated on investing in the socialization process required to achieve an enduring middle-class position for adult children prior to marriage. As the children rise, the whole family may benefit from a higher standard of living and the material conditions that foster the development of middle-class culture.

Like Thu, Minh lived in Tân Bình (see Chapter 3). Unlike Thu, Minh lived with his natal family: his parents, a sister Hương (introduced in Chapter 7) and a brother Út. Each of the children was unmarried, bilingual and employed in lucrative positions in the foreign or private sectors. Another brother, Hai, lived abroad. Hai had signed up to a communist work program months before the fall of the Berlin Wall and later had secured European residency. Minh's family had pooled their resources to move across Ho Chi Minh City to a larger multi-storied house in a better area. It was not the first move the family had made. Years earlier, Minh's parents had migrated from Hanoi to the Central Coast, where the younger children were born and all were educated. Education was the first step up a metaphoric 'consumption ladder' that might lift the family out of poverty. In the mid-1990s, after Minh had successfully relocated himself to Ho Chi Minh City and found work in a foreign company, the whole family joined him in the city. Migration to Ho Chi Minh City was another step up the ladder that moved the

185

family away from a poverty line and towards a consumption line. In Ho Chi Minh City, Minh's parents had been enjoying their retirement, while their children had been building their careers. In addition to the graduate salaries of three adult children working in Ho Chi Minh City, Minh's household benefited from remittances of money, goods and knowledge sent by the brother living abroad to boost the family's economic resources and coffers of cultural capital. His migration offered an alternative strategy to mitigate the risk of relying on only one path or ladder to success. The two brothers each acted as a type of breadwinner in the family in line with gender normalcy.

In their new neighbourhood in Tân Bình, houses were protected by high gates and walls topped with broken glass. Some places had guard dogs which barked as we passed by. Unlike Thu's neighbourhood across Tân Bình, where neighbours chatted freely and walked in the streets, Minh's neighbours zoomed by on motorbikes and in vehicles with darkened windows. Like his neighbours' homes, Minh's family home was designed to garage a car in the front room. Although his family did not own a car, many of their neighbours did. From the terrace, I watched them painstakingly enter the narrow doorways from steep concrete ramps off the street.

Near Minh's place, the pavements were clear of vendors. Private kara-oke bars and cafés were air-conditioned and sound-proofed, not enter-taining the neighbourhood as they did in inner-city laneways in District One's Tân Định or District Three's Vườn Chuối. Privatized leisure places and living spaces marked Minh's neighbourhood as a relatively better area. While 'hyper-visibility' can reveal status in some contexts, Jean-Pascal Daloz (2008, p. 317 n. 17) reiterates that elsewhere privacy and an 'imagined presence' can convey distinction by concealing actual practices. Li Zhang (2008, p. 24) argues that the privatization of postso-cialist living space does not only reflect increasing social differentiation but also enables the formation of class cultures and subjectivities. In post-reform urban Vietnam an emerging emphasis on privacy has influenced urban ways of living. Privacy is not a phenomenon uniquely associated with postsocialism. As Jane Jacobs (1994, p. 69) points out, privacy is also highly desired in capitalist cities and regarded as 'precious' because urban residents 'in most places', regardless of income, gender, ethnicity, or housing type, cannot find it. However, access to private spaces and a focus on private lives is new and highly desired in Vietnam and formerly socialist contexts. The new focus on privacy in post-reform life in various contexts differs dramatically from representations of socialist and Soviet everyday life. Under socialism in China, private life was associated with love and intimacy and located in domestic space (Yan 2003). In Soviet Russia, private life was regarded as synonymous, not with 'real life', but with foreign, inauthentic behaviour, so much so that an opposition developed between 'private' life and 'Russian' life (Boym 1994, pp. 73–4). Privacy, in this sense, was located in between the national and globalized in the space where Mark Liechty (2003, p. 67) locates the middle class. Access to private living space enabled Minh and his family members to each explore and express their individualized identities and personal tastes.

While Thu lived in one small room packed with consumer commodities, Minh's family home was large so that, in addition to two spare bedrooms, each of the children had a separate bedroom. The children's rooms were furnished with a double bed, a wooden wardrobe, a study desk, and a television. The walls were decorated with framed posters of Vietnamese and foreign pop stars and each child had a collection of imported cosmetics and colognes. Their wardrobes were crammed with clothes and accessories. Their shoes were displayed on racks that lined the staircase landings. They shared a cable television subscription and they each owned their own fully imported motorbike. The family also kept a spare Japanese motorbike in case of an inconvenient breakdown. While the children lived in great comfort, with their busy work schedules and active social lives, they rarely spent time at home.

The parents' room was similarly furnished. The father, a retired Party official, spent his time in front of the television. He preferred factual documentaries about foreign cities and wildlife to popular melodramas that focused on the lives of unfortunate and unhappy people. Their mother had never worked outside the home and she spent her time in the kitchen or the guest room. The kitchen was spacious and modern, with a refrigerator, a washing machine, and other appliances. Upstairs, the centrepiece of the guest room was a generously decorated, three-metre tall, artificial Christmas tree, untouched for two years since the European brother had last visited. The walls displayed family photographs through childhood to graduations, tracking the family's progress.

A collection of English language books and mail order catalogues of Swedish home furnishings and German fashions were displayed on a bookshelf. Minh's mother's magazines were stacked on a small table next to the tea serving tray.

The very high standard of living achieved by Minh's natal family indicates their social mobility and economic security. While Party membership may have helped the family's rise through underlying reservoirs of political capital, Party membership or a father's administrative post has been found to have limited effect on occupational mobility in Vietnam and that effect was concentrated in the north (Kim 2004, pp. 199–200). As Lotte Thomsen (2011, p. 635) points out, being a former northerner in Ho Chi Minh City does not necessarily imply being well connected. Most families in southern Vietnam seem to have some close or tenuous kin connection to a Party official at one of the three levels of government. Since Minh's father had retired, the enduring value of his political capital had waned. The family had relied more on currently valued forms of economic and cultural capital accumulated by the children than the father's formerly valued political capital. As alternatives, economic and cultural capital mitigated the possibility of relegation, a form of indirect social exclusion, that may have been generated by clinging to an outmoded and devalued form of capital (Bourdieu and Passeron 1979, p. 14).

While it is challenged by other forms of more valued capital, political capital retains some significance in postsocialist social mobility. Political capital – in the form of politico-ideological socialization – is one of the four dimensions that Thomas Heberer (2003, p. 64) identifies as differentiating the strata within the middle class in postsocialist Vietnam and China. Predrag Cvetičanin and Mihaela Popescu (2011, p. 467) identify formal authority and informal powers stemming from social and political capital as pertinent influences in a 'complex social jigsaw puzzle' of middle-class formation in postsocialist Serbia. Party background may be a salient factor in mobility in postsocialist contexts, but enduring economic resources, such as high salary employment or financial investments, and valued cultural capital associated with globalization or provided from relatives abroad, are arguably more useful as they are more readily convertible into valuable symbolic privileges.

Having only a good background or a high bank balance is not enough to achieve an enduring status position. In Malaysia and China, a privileged background coupled with education credentials and access to bureaucratic power has enabled urbanites to achieve a better lifestyle (Buckley 1999, p. 210; Embong 2006b, p. 160). In Vietnam also, a combination of privileged background, education credentials and exposure to different ways of doing things has given rise to middle-class lifestyles (Gainsborough 2002, pp. 701–2). Any one attribute or credential alone is not sufficient to achieve and maintain a new status position. The greater range of highly valued and recognizable credentials an aspiring person, such as Minh, can accrue, the greater his potential to secure an enduring new middle-class position for himself and his family.

INTRA-URBAN MOBILITY

Moving across the city to a larger family home, as Minh's family had done, can further enhance a relatively higher social position. In Ho Chi Minh City spatial mobility also reflects social mobility. Patrick Gubry et al. (2010, pp. 75–6) report that one in five Ho Chi Minh City residents is on the move across the city from the inner city, where the standard of living is highest but neighbourhoods are densely crowded and housing is cramped and in short supply. Half of those on the move settle in the relatively recently occupied suburban areas of the outer north where standards of living are relatively lower but where they can start an independent household and be closer to work. The other half settle in the the urbanizing rural fringes to the west, such as Bình Chánh and Hóc Môn, where they can afford to become property owners. In these new suburbs, some areas are regarded as better than others and a desirable residential address can convey status.

Hierarchies of social segregation within cities are evident in spatial processes of differentiation which can distinguish between those with highly valued cultural competencies and those only with economic resources. In postsocialist cities, as Gyorgy Enyedi (1996, pp. 105–6) argues, relocation to better regarded areas is evident through housing applications and escalating land prices which sustain social segregation by reinforcing the relative prestige of different areas. In *Surburban Beijing*, Friederike Fleischer (2010, p. 109) observes that urbanites purchase houses on a real or perceived association offered by desirable residential addresses. In Beijing, the consumption of space has turned into a marker of difference. In Ho Chi Minh City also the address conveys distinction.

Buying into an exclusive gated community, such as Phú Mỹ Hưng in Ho Chi Minh City's District Seven, is an indicator of exclusivity and afflu-ence associated with Vietnam's super-rich and expatriates (Douglass and Huang 2007, p. 26). Part of the appeal in the opulence of gated communi-ties across mega-urban Southeast Asia is the juxtaposition with the poor quality of housing and lacking amenities of other city areas (Douglass et al. 2008, p. 290; Embong 2006b, pp. 160–1). Another part of the appeal of exclusive areas is a greater homogeneity of the neighbourhood, which also contrasts with other areas of the city, such as inner-city laneways, which are marked by their social and cultural diversity.

Spatial distance from an established community can produce social distance, which may enable the absent members to pursue new identities and new ways of living without facing sanctions generated by failing to conform to the norms and encultured expectations that bind a diverse neighbourhood by emphasizing the bonds they share. Among ascending Vietnamese groups in Sydney, social mobility is determined in part by intra-urban mobility as individuals and families who move away from ex-isting kin and community networks to better regarded suburban areas are recognized for their improved social position and higher status (Thomas 1999). In global cities in Europe and Japan, Chinese and Singaporean international students differentiate themselves from communities of expatriate and migrant workers (Cheng 2002, pp. 167–8; Li Minghuan 2002, p. 173; Piper and Roces 2003a, p. 8). Having left a community, so long as they stay away, it is possible to create and maintain a new relatively higher social position. While a physical absence can ensure their new position, they maintain contact in order to transfer the benefits that their new positions confer to those left behind. Without contact the new status position may go unrecognized and thus have no enduring value.

In Ho Chi Minh City, a move across the city into a gated community or better regarded area can reflect an achievement of social mobility. For Minh's family, their 'imagined presence' inside privatized living space conveyed status by concealment but, for Hòa, hyper-visibility became an important part of her strategy to rise (Daloz 2008, p. 312). Hòa, a friend of Thu's and a successful businesswoman, had purchased a house in Phú Mỹ Hưng, the exclusive planned development to the south of Ho Chi Minh City centre. She invited us to visit the new house. It was one of a number of identical houses that sat side by side along the street, evenly spaced and regularly numbered. The side streets were cordoned off into enclaves accessible from an entry way off the main thoroughfare and were patrolled by roving security guards. As a result, she sometimes did not lock her front door although she always chained and padlocked the high front gate. Inside the gate there was space for the family's two cars in the small open courtyard. A low-maintenance garden and water feature led to the front steps, which were cluttered with the family's shoes.

The front door was opened by *dì Ba*, an elderly widowed aunt who worked for the family of four as housekeeper, babysitter and cook (not driver), but it was Hòa's husband who welcomed us in. Inside neutral tiles and papered walls contrasted with elaborate chrome and glass light fittings. The ground floor was open plan. Visible from the front door, dry goods were piled high along the wall next to the dining table, where Hòa and her family were entertaining relatives. We were ushered into the guest room next to the front door. We sat on a beige leather lounge suite and admired a synthetic shag rug, a plasma TV in its own cabinet and a transparent polymer coffee table. We discussed the items on the table: a box of wine bought in Europe and labelled with the family's name, a small clock mounted in Perspex with a preserved Malaysian scorpion, a set of cocktail forks with handles in the shape of the Petronas Twin Towers, and a copy of that day's newspaper. A staircase led to the family's bedrooms and a home office on the second floor.

Desiring a place of her own, Thu loved Hòa's place in Phú Mỹ Hưng. What initially appealed to her was the regularity, cleanliness and safety of the neighbourhood and its streets. She also liked the house and its spaciousness, modern decorating and tokens of transnational experience. What did not appeal to her was the different lifestyle Hòa described that living in an exclusive gated community demanded. Hòa found that matching the lifestyles of her neighbours was financially crippling. Like her neighbours, her children were schooled privately and paying the school fees was a significant cost that was exacerbated by the additional financial and time burden of their compulsory extra-curricular activities. Transporting the children to their after-school classes, music and sporting commitments also cut into her working day.

Hòa concealed the economic burden of maintaining her lifestyle in the new suburb. The cost of living in Phú Mỹ Hưng was high and Hòa could not afford to shop locally at the nearby supermarket, so she travelled to

District One each week to buy fresh food, clothing and household items. Driving a car was convenient within the wide boulevards of Phú Mỹ Hưng but Hòa found it was inconvenient to travel by car to work or to socialize in other districts of Ho Chi Minh City. This also made shopping a chore. Car parking was provided in Phú Mỹ Hưng but elsewhere in the city was difficult to find and costly. Congested roads made the journey to visit friends outside Phú Mỹ Hưng time consuming and also caused her social isolation. Without a knowledge of English, which was spoken daily by the Vietnamese neighbours and their children, Hòa found it was difficult to socialize locally among her neighbours. Hòa revealed certain attributes of her lifestyle to her neighbours, such as owning two cars and having a busy schedule, but concealed other aspects, such as where she shopped and where her close friends and kin lived.

Moving into Phú Mỹ Hưng marked a break from the past as Hòa and her family had left their old lives behind. In class-divided societies, the efficacy and profits of symbolic capital are secured based on the fact that individuals do not have equal economic and cultural means for moving beyond their original position (Bourdieu 1997, p. 49). Awareness of the different social outcomes achieved in processes of social ascension can generate insecurity and a fear of falling for those with the most to lose, but it can also enable them to mobilize other lower-ranked members in their family through remittances of economic, material and knowledge resources. Absence from the family and community becomes an important factor in realizing social mobility and maintaining new social position as opportunities for betterment are not available at home. In post-reform Vietnam, as in new rich Indonesia and the Philippines, migrants must remain away from home and family to guarantee their new found status, but also to enjoy the benefits of their new position (Antlov 1999, p. 201; Dang Nguyen Anh 2002, pp. 93–4; Pinches 2001, pp. 187, 200). While benefits cannot be realized at home, they may be recognized there by those remaining behind so long as contact is maintained. Vietnam's social climbers maintain their connections with their past as a way to ensure that the progress they are making is recognized.

Hòa's resources were stretched by the move to Phú Mỹ Hưng which conveyed status and enabled her to achieve a relatively higher social position. Yet Hòa faced a cultural handicap. She was required to invest relatively more than others to achieve the same cultural privileges. Hòa faced overselection in her attempt to 'pass' as an equal with her neighbours (Bourdieu and Passeron 1979, p. 14). Attempts to increase one's cultural capital in this manner do not necessarily change one's original class placement and a lack of 'fit' always leads to non-inclusion (Silva 2005, p. 87; see Bourdieu 1984, 1996). However, Hòa was able to recognize the 'telling markers' of cultural coding and determine what to reveal and what to conceal. In doing so, she did not reveal that she was 'out of touch' or lacking the appropriate background knowledge to rise socially in her new suburb (Prieur and Savage 2011, p. 578). Thus, despite some anxiety about maintaining her new social position, Hòa can be regarded to be successful in achieving her claims on a place among Phú Mỹ Hưng's elites and super-rich as she convincingly embodied and expressed the right messages that indicated her cultural sophistication.

VỀ QUÊ, RETURNING HOME

A desire for betterment has been a characteristic of middle classes in twentieth-century Vietnam in periods of colonialism, postcolonialism and socialism. In the post-reform era, aspiration is also characteristic of Ho Chi Minh City's re-emerging urban middle classes. A move to the urban Southeast or across Ho Chi Minh City is not the only path to upward social mobility. In Vietnamese multi-dimensional families, members have differential access to avenues for social mobility. They are located across urban and rural areas and they participate in both urban and rural economies. Maintaining 'invisible' loyalties between family members has been assumed to interfere with adaptation and assimilation processes as migrants are torn between home or host (Espin 1999, p. 33). Rather than regarding the migrant's location as the key factor that determines self-identity (in line with an official household registration system, for example), it is useful to consider connections to kin. Absent family members maintain relationships with their families, their homes and their communities from afar. Contact between migrants and their families comprise far-reaching social networks which Michelle Lee and Nicola Piper (2003, p. 126) describe as operating as 'a singular field of interaction' that is marked by the exchange of communication, remittances and emotion. A desire to maintain emotional connections is based on bonds of solidarity within the Vietnamese family (Phạm Văn Bích 1999). While staying away from home is required to gain education and employment that can guarantee a higher social position, having a desire to return is one thing that all Vietnamese migrants seem to share. A family member who never returns home is regarded as a failure (Sơn Nam 1992, p. 9).

Like other educated young women originating from the Mekong Delta, Cúc and her sisters maintain strong links with their birthplace and regularly return home for Buddhist festivals and family feasts as well as for an occasional weekend escape from the city. The preparations for such journeys are often time consuming and expensive and take priority over all other commitments in their lives. On one of these occasions, Cúc invited me to join her family and their friends to celebrate the anniversary which commemorated her paternal grandfather's death (*đám giỗ*). The elaborate feast was the most important of their annual ritual days, more significant even than Tết.

We headed back to Cúc's house to make final preparations for the feast and the journey from the city. Back at her place, the atmosphere was strangely tense. The family had obviously been disagreeing, but the argument had been silenced by my arrival. The heaviness was interrupted by the phone. It was Hồng, an older sister, wondering when we would be ready to leave. From the repetition of her name, it became clear that the dispute had centred on their sister Hạnh. The family disagreement had interrupted Cúc's preparations. With Hạnh now gone out, Cúc could continue to prepare. As she stirred a cooling pot, she challenged me to guess the ingredients. I leaned over. It was sweet-smelling. A scolding reminded me to take care that my ponytail did not fall in the pot as I leaned over it. A pale yellow, thick and chunky soup was bubbling away. Cúc interrupted my inspection by announcing the key ingredients were pomelo rind, white beans and sugar. It was a pomelo 'sweet soup' pudding (*chè bưởi*), a special dessert. Cúc stopped stirring and looked up at me. She told me that everyone else planned to meet us in the morning at Hồng's place. Putting on a serious face, she began to study my arms, pressing them to gauge their strength. Gesturing to the cooking pot, still near boiling, she warned me she was going to ask me to help her transport the dessert. She grinned, and with her arms out, mimed me sitting on the back of her motorbike balancing buckets of steaming liquid as she dodged through imaginary traffic. She raised her eyebrows asking me: could I ride pillion and carry a plastic bucket of pomelo pudding from her house across the northern districts of Ho Chi Minh City to her sister's house without spilling or spoiling it? Indeed without any dire consequences, we arrived at Hồng's place later that night after the children had already fallen asleep.

The family had hired a mini-bus to make the journey home to Tiền Giang province (in the central Mekong Delta). The bus would leave from Hồng's house in Gò Vấp in the north of Ho Chi Minh City. At the time (in 2001) this was an extravagance; only two of the family in the city were working, the remaining siblings were studying or unemployed. The main reasons for the expenditure were practical as newly implemented traffic laws would require motorbike helmets to be worn on highways, so that each family member would have to buy a helmet, even though throughout the year they could share one or two.[2] Guests might get lost trying to find the village. Once home, there would be a lot of motorbikes to park and watch over. Travelling together on a bus would be more pleasant and no one would feel tired after arriving. A bus would also be more convenient to transport pre-prepared food, including the buckets of pomelo pudding.

The next morning, after several delays, we began the journey. The bus, already nearly full with family members, stopped at Hồng's workplace to pick up her colleagues and finally we headed westwards out of Ho Chi Minh City past the new subdivisions, which had expanded in the short time since we had previously travelled this route. Ongoing pavement works on the highway did not hold us up and before long we crossed the province border between Ho Chi Minh City and Long An. Here, we stopped for breakfast at a roadside traveller's restaurant where we were mobbed by vendors hocking cured pork (*nem*), salted sticky rice (*xôi mặn*), bread rolls and other travelling food. We breakfasted on southern-style noodle soup (*hủ tiếu nam vàng*) or sweetmeat porridge (*cháo lòng*) at a large round table at the rear of the restaurant away from the road.

Back on the bus, we dozed on full stomachs for the second leg of the journey. After crossing from Long An into Tiền Giang province, we followed the highway west at the provincial capital Mỹ Thọ. Getting closer

---

2   Since then, helmet wearing laws have been extended to all journeys and for all adult riders and passengers so adult riders in Vietnam now own their own helmet. Not owning a helmet these days is indicative of diverse poles of wealth or poverty; a non-rider might be a person who travels in luxury by private car, on the one hand, or by the inexpensive public bus, on the other.

to home improved the atmosphere in the stuffy bus. We took a break at the first village for a brief family visit before continuing down the sandy track. As the track narrowed, the bus faced the danger of becoming wedged. It was scraped on the top and sides by branches and bumped from below by potholes. The hired driver refused to continue despite encouragement. In compromise, Hồng hailed a passing motorized cart (*xe lôi*) and negotiated to take us through the next village, around a kilometre from the house. The men dusted off the dirty wooden cart and helped the women climb up. Each of the prepared dishes was handed up to us on the cart. Perching on its wooden bench, each bump jarred smiles out of us until we reached the canal. At the steep and narrow bridge, the driver cut the engine. He could take us no further. In front of us, two village women were loading baskets of freshly picked rambutan from a canoe into a small truck which would transport them into the city to be sold. Obviously city folk, we passengers alighted and stood watching them.

In the morning heat, the task of delivering the prepared food and other fresh goods became urgent. Some of the men hurried ahead to pick up motorbikes. The rest of us crossed the canal and began to walk along the dusty path towards the house. At the gate, the dust suddenly became mud. For some time, the driveway had been a muddy mess due to a leak in the rice paddy or lotus pond or both. By the time we reached the house, each of us needed to dust off our clothes and wash down our shoes and feet. The homecoming was an exciting time and, once we had changed out of our city clothes and into printed cotton suits, we joined a group of boisterous nieces and nephews and their parents in the kitchen.

These were the elders who had invested in the sisters' migration to the city and their education. Their investment was made with the expectation that it would be a long-term strategy for building a better future in which their family's material standard of living would be improved and they would be cared for in old age. Underpinning this is an assumption that new status, and any wealth and power it conveys, would be directed not only towards the sisters but also back to the natal family through the obligation that children have to repay a debt to them. In a Confucian-influenced society, such as Vietnam, parents' investment in their child rests on an expectation of reciprocity, a moral ethic that is learned by Vietnamese children along with dispositions and behaviours in the family (Rydstrøm 2003; Shohet 2013).

196

The family remains one of the primary sites for the intergenerational transmission of classed (and gendered) modes of living. Bourdieu (1998b, p. 68) argues that the work of enhancing cultural capital within the family falls upon women, who are responsible for the accumulation and transmission of economic, cultural and symbolic privileges in the creation of a normal family. But, as Jean-Pascal Daloz (2008, p. 315) warns, we should not assume the signals of distinction of one generation 'trickle down' to the next and societies may be unable to 'escape the "shackles" of tradition'. While the intergenerational transmission of dispositions and moral ethics is assumed to be directed from the parents, especially the mother, to the children, in Confucian-influenced society, reciprocity – in various forms – circulates from younger members of the family to their elders. The transmission of class cultural dispositions in multi-dimensional families, where close contact is maintained between educated urban migrants and their natal families at home, operates in both directions.

FUTURE HOMECOMINGS

While a family member may maintain a physical absence, a significant economy operates within family networks, where family members residing in the city distribute a proportion of their income, assets and other non-material resources to their natal family outside the city. Across Pacific Asia, the contributions of migrants enhance the living standards of families. Cynthia Bautista (2006, p. 167) highlights that connections with (and remittances from) relatives abroad have a great impact on upward social mobility for those in both rural and urban areas in the Philippines. In Hong Kong, daughters remit regularly between a third and half their incomes to their natal families and plan to continue doing so throughout their parents' lifetimes (Jackson, Ho and Na 2013, p. 679). In Vietnam, female labour migrants send almost twice as much money home than men (17 and 10 per cent of incomes, respectively) and it is directed by the household head to health and education costs (Marx and Fleischer 2010, pp. 41–2). Educated urban migrant women also send remittances of varying types to their natal families; however, their contributions are not always in the form of cash or commodities. Further, the rewards the natal family receives are not in the same form as when the investment was made, since the valued signals of cultural capital associated with a relatively higher social position are dynamic and evolve over time.

Close contact between urban migrants and their families enables them to appreciate the different rates of change in levels of development and standards of living between urban and rural areas and to determine their families' material needs in rising out of poverty as well as their desires in moving beyond a consumption line. Since they had moved to the city, Cúc and her sisters maintained close contact with their family and regularly visited their parent's home. In the city, they had graduated and won jobs. They had become familiar with city life and had met new friends originating from different places, such as Cúc's friends from the Centre who taught her how to eat *bún bò Huế* (see Chapter 5). Cúc and her sisters provided lodging for their parents and relatives when they visited the city. For their visiting nieces and cousins, they not only housed them but also offered them advice on education and future employment opportunities. But the most visible contribution they made was to the development of their parent's home.

Another trip I accompanied them on, made less than a decade later, revealed the extent their remittances and advice had improved the standard of living and social status of their natal family. On this occasion, we were driven in an air-conditioned car by Cúc's brother. He took the Ho Chi Minh City–Trung Lương Expressway out of the city, a tollway that despite its name was a poor quality road interrupted by traffic lights and an uneven surface which at times necessitated vehicles passing at a walking pace. Nevertheless, the journey to the village was quicker and more comfortable than a bus or motorbike, taking less than two hours. As we approached it become obvious that the village itself was more developed. Most of the houses had permanent roofs and were connected to electricity. The village was also much greener since the trees lost in earlier major flooding had been replaced. Roads had been sealed and the car was able to travel directly from Ho Chi Minh City to the gates of Cúc's parent's house. The gates were also new and were open as our arrival was expected. At the end of the concrete drive way, the yard had been extended and paved to create a parking area where Cúc's brother reversed the car. Cúc's father still kept his bicycle on the side of the house next to the canal.

The parents' home had been repaired and its décor updated. The floor plan remained the same, but the interior tiling on floors and walls had been replaced. The kitchen had been updated, and while the solid fuel stove remained, a gas cooker had also been installed. A family-size refrigerator was in constant use storing vegetables from the re-established garden and water produced by the new water filter. The plumbing had also been improved and an eight-kilogram automatic washing machine stood in a new internal laundry area in front of the bathroom. Besides the re-established garden, an extensive orchard that had drowned in flood waters had been replanted and was well established.

The remittances that the children sent home repaid their moral debt and supplemented the incomes of their retired parents and older rural siblings, thus enabling the renovation of their parents' home. Remittances to rural households across Vietnam, when not ear-marked for education, are often directed to material assets and resources that are widely available in urban areas. While not all rural development can be attributed to the influence of remittances from urban or overseas Vietnamese relatives, remittances make a considerable difference to standards of living in Vietnamese villages. One in five rural households have refrigerators, compared to three in five urban households, and one in twenty rural households have washing machines, compared to one in three urban households (GSO 2011c, p. 87). A higher standard of living was one result of investing in a daughter's education. However, the symbolic meanings associated with the new commodities did not necessarily extend from the particularized context of the urban social world to the rural one.

Because Cúc's elders preferred hand washing, they did not use the new washing machine which remained wrapped in plastic. Because they preferred cooking on a solid fuel stove, which did not risk leaking gas or spoiling the food with fumes, they seldom used the gas cooker. The elders seemed to appreciate the efforts to look after them, but they did not abandon their way of living and adopt a new city lifestyle. The modifications made to their home were recognized by themselves, their relatives and neighbours as the reciprocity that children are obligated to demonstrate in hierarchical family relationships (Shohet 2013, p. 204). The children's gifts conferred status on their parents in the context of village life, even though the parents retained their old way of living. The gifts reflected a higher standard of living and a promise to others of the advantages of long-term investment in children's education, but as commodities they symbolized different things. The shifting meaning of commodities between urban and village contexts reflects that their meanings are polysemic and dynamic. As Nir Avieli (2013, p. 129) demonstrates, the symbolic meanings associated with different cultural signals change in different contexts. Jean-Pascal Daloz (2008, p. 310) explains that people use material possessions to express their own identities and judge those of others so long as they are socially shared as symbols and comprehensible by everyone. This does not necessarily mean that the elders were unable to recognize and decipher the highly valued signals of an urban symbolic world, which they had been exposed to, but that the symbolic value of commodities is particularized to a specific context and the possession of commodities convey qualitatively different messages in urban and rural symbolic worlds.

SUPPORTING FAMILY FROM AFAR

Urban migrants, such as Cúc, Liên, Tuyết and Thu, are able to repay the moral debt incurred to the natal family through their past investment in their daughters' move to the city and their education. They are able to improve their families' standard of living through financial remittances as well as improve the prospects of their younger relatives through financing their education and transmitting valuable knowledge and advice. As daughters, their roles in decision making in the natal family may have become more prominent with their supplies of remittances. On the one hand, the rural renovations funded by urbanized daughters reflect their traditional gendered obligations to look after their families. In contemporary Vietnam, female migrants are expected to maintain connections with their families back home through visits and telephone contact on account of their naturalized roles as carers, particularly wives and mothers (Agergaard and Vu 2011, p. 409; Ha and Ha 2001). Daughters similarly share a traditional obligation to reciprocate and care. On the other hand, as Robbie Peters (2012, p. 563) outlines, rural–urban migrant women in Ho Chi Minh City exercise more autonomy beyond the family than is conventionally anticipated in normative ideals of Vietnamese womanhood. Migrant daughters are able to earn high incomes and contribute to decisions concerning the economic security and material circumstances of the natal family. Their supply of remittances transfers economic power in the family and it is possible that they may become the main family breadwinner. Migrant daughters are no longer simply dependents of the natal family and they may be consulted in decision making (Bélanger and Tran 2011, pp. 65–6; Hòang 2009, p. 15). While most daughters comply with the obligation to remit funds to their natal families, as Mary Beth Mills (1999, p. 135) observes, rural daughters working (in Bangkok) can gain control of family finances to some extent by controlling when and how much they send home. Besides remittances of cash and assets, which can generate new configurations of economic power in the natal family, remittances of knowledge and advice supplied by daughters can reconfigure expectations linked to normative gender roles.

Daughters not only invest cash but also provide advice and knowledge about various aspects of cultural life and other social practices. These opportunities are especially available to younger family members, particularly their older siblings' children and their cousins. Like Cúc and her sisters, Liên was in a position to support her family through financial and knowledge remittances. Liên hosted a niece and her friends in the city whenever there was a book fair, exam swot session or university open day. On these visits, she took them shopping and eating to teach them how to live in Ho Chi Minh City where they were planning to study and work later. The girls were exposed to new fashion, urban leisure, Liên's circle of friends, and their tips about emerging fields of employment and strategies for winning high paid office jobs, such as which economics or accounting course to study and which foreign language to learn. During their visits, the leisure they engaged in became a resource to increase their competence and skills and further their personal development and potential career trajectory (Rolandsen 2011, p. 184). This experience gave them a head start by beginning the long process of socialization to an enduring new middle-class position earlier than their peers (Bourdieu 1990a, p. 136; Koo 2006, p. 13). Yet, their choices fell in line with genderized fields of work and study in that they discussed general office work and administration which were deemed suitable positions for women. In this way, they defended gendered expectations and reproduced gender hierarchy by conforming to genderized norms (see Chapter 4).

In addition to passing on knowledge, advice and experience to her niece, Liên also provided the capital for an extensive renovation of her mother's house in the central Mekong Delta. The renovation repaired flood damage at her mother's wooden single room dwelling and added a five-room brick extension that included an internal kitchen and bathroom with plumbing and electricity, as well as window glass throughout. The new house was furnished with raised wooden beds, new plump mattresses with 'Saigonese style' cotton sheets (not woven sleeping mats), wooden wardrobes, desks and chairs, a dining suite, and window drapes. Upholstered chairs and drapes were unusual in the dusty and humid heat of the Mekong Delta, where wooden or plastic chairs and thin synthetic curtains replaced before Tết are more typical. As the drapes were drawn to cut down the daytime heat, elaborate light fittings decorated each room. Liên's niece was able to confirm her aunt's choices in decoration based on her own limited experiences in Ho Chi Minh City. Aunt and niece focused on accumulating cultural capital on behalf of the family through work associated with wives and mothers in investing time and resources in the lives of others (Bourdieu 1998b; Nowotny 1981; Reay 2004).

Outside the house, the removal of fruit trees solved a problem concerning their ongoing upkeep for Liên's ageing mother. Harvesting the fruit had cost more in labour than it generated in income and the trees had also lost their relative value as assets in contrast with the renovated house. Landscaping created a new front yard with pots of bonsai and other plants in an attractive geometric design that complemented a new concrete driveway. This provided a smooth and less dusty surface for playing badminton in the mornings. The renovation was a tangible means of displaying the family's connections with wealth and cultural capital associated with urban and globalized choices, such as the cotton sheets, westernized furniture and heavy drapes, each of which the niece had admired on visits to homes in Ho Chi Minh City.

After the renovation was complete, Liên's mother continued to use the old wooden part of the house during the day for watching television in the mornings and resting in a hammock in the afternoons. Liên's mother complained the soft mattress of the new bed hurt her back and she also preferred using the old semi-internal bathroom, which was fresher than the new airless tiled wet room. Despite her mother maintaining her old way of living, the new commodities were manifestations of Liên's obligation to care for her mother and repay her debt. The presence of desired commodities communicated this to the neighbours and visiting relatives and represented the promise of a better life that long-term investment in a daughter's education could provide in the future. Moreover, by conforming to a traditional genderized role as a dutiful daughter Liên consolidated a sense of belonging that mitigated the social distance she had achieved. She employed a new aesthetic language to locate herself in a relatively higher social position without being directly excluded from her family and her mother's neighbourhood.

The house became a way to reveal a higher standard of living to which others could aim to aspire. Since she had moved to this area, Liên's mother had displayed the trinkets she had collected from around the world. The large glass cabinet in which she displayed her collection also remained in the old house where she spent most of her time. She had not travelled herself; the tokens came from Liên and the children of her friends and relatives who had studied, worked or travelled abroad. When they returned, they brought small gifts – a teddy bear in national dress, a miniature statue or a replica building – which Liên's mother displayed in the glass cabinet. Hai Ren (2013, p. 118) reports that his informants in China shared travel experiences including information about prices, food, climate and the built environment as a life lesson for others who did not have first-hand experience of other cultures. Although she had no direct experiences, Liên's mother recounted an encyclopaedic knowledge about the origin and symbolism of each item in her cabinet, the climate and any unique customs of the country they originated from, as well as the biography of the young person who had gifted it to her and how the travel had impacted on their future prospects. She offered life lessons for others who lacked knowledge and experience.

While Liên's mother refused to use the new part of the house, like the cabinet of trinkets, the renovated rooms enabled her to continue introducing new globalized styles of interior decoration as well as new technological commodities to her neighbours, friends and relatives. Liên complied with her traditional obligation to repay her natal family, but her mother was a trendsetter in setting a standard for others to follow. For Liên's mother, it was neither age nor a rural location that indicated the shape of her dispositions, which were skewed towards the globalized and away from tradition. While Liên concealed her experience studying abroad, her mother revealed her knowledge about new experiences and social practices not only to distinguish herself from those around her, but to offer them a head start in the long process of socialization that marks an enduring class status position. For Liên's mother, a new aesthetic language enabled her to position herself in a relatively superior position located in between the traditions of a rural context and the globalized influences symbolized in her new house and the cabinet of trinkets.

Knowledge transmission and house renovation are among the most anticipated contributions an absent family member can make. Like Liên, Thu played a key role in her family's economic security. Thu funded the renovation and refurbishment of her parents' home. With a new roof and tiling on the walls and floors, the bathroom became an internal room. She had a hot water machine and washing machine installed into the new bathroom. Similarly, new walls made the kitchen internal. The house was painted and floors retiled throughout. These modifications raised her parents' standard of living and helped lift them out of poverty. Thu had a large flat screen television and new refrigerator installed into the guest room downstairs. Thu's father particularly enjoyed staying home to watch football matches and live music concerts. The second floor was divided into three bedrooms which were furnished with western-style beds. The upstairs altar room at the front of the house was also refurbished. These additions lifted their way of living towards a consumption line that marks the not-so-poor (Gerke 2000, pp. 142–3). Further to this, Thu supplied her cousins with school and university books as well as clothing, shoes, handbags, accessories and cosmetics. Some of these were her own unused items, while others she bought on sale in Ho Chi Minh City. She often took calls from them and gave them advice about education, employment and financial investment. While this advice was free, it was highly valuable for them to build their futures. Thu's greatest monthly expenses were the cash remittances she regularly transferred to her mother. These supported a wholesale seasonal produce business and funded their annual family rituals and anniversaries, such as *ngày giỗ*. Unlike Nghĩa, the young man who borrowed money to buy a desirable model of motorbike, Thu went without a new motorbike in order to meet these financial expectations and pay off her study loans.

In Pacific Asia, women labour migrants direct significant resources to their families. Women migrants in Beijing go without a mobile phone, the comfort of air-conditioning and the convenience of a motorbike so that they can purchase a computer for their children's study and pay expensive school fees (Fleischer 2010, p. 119). Filipina transnational labour migrants endure short-term hardships, abuses and loneliness so that they can support their children to enjoy a better future (Pinches 2001, p. 197; Bautista 2006). In Hong Kong and Vietnam, daughters routinely go without modern comforts so they can remit significant proportions of their incomes home (Jackson, Ho and Na 2013, p. 679; Marx and Fleischer 2010, pp. 41–2). Like them, Thu sacrificed to support her family, sending money, goods and knowledge to her parents and cousins. Writing on Thailand, Mary Beth Mills (1999, p. 158) points out that it is less common for low-skilled labour migrants to invest in their own education and training or to direct resources to a long-term goal and future plan, such as Thu had done in financing her own study.

Daughters are regarded to be more responsible in directing a proportion of their incomes back to the family. In larger families than Thu's, the youngest members, such as Cúc and Hạnh, are often the ones who contribute most. Like them, Tuyết also rebuilt her parents' house, redecorated and refurnished it with traditional wooden furniture and modern household appliances. She invested in land in her natal village with a view to relocating her ageing parents into a more spacious modern home. These contributions aimed to raise their standard of living and provide them greater comfort in their old age. Tuyết supported a family member serving a prison sentence. Each month she provided a stipend that covered daily food and hygiene needs. She returned the living support to her natal family that she had previously received from them when she was a student. She took on the responsibility of educating a young niece and nephew and contributed to the costs of their schooling including fees, uniforms, shoes and books. For an older niece, she provided a second-hand motorbike so the girl could remain living at home and commute to a suburban selective-entry school. The gift was practical, not intended for leisure. It reflected a long-term investment strategy that could benefit Tuyết's children in the future when this niece was grown up and working and could reciprocate the support she had received. Further, Tuyết was philanthropic and preferred to give money to organized funds for specific causes that published her name as a benefactor rather than directly to beggars or to the anonymous donation boxes in supermarkets that supported annual flood relief or public health campaigns. Revealing her donation publicly was important in the city where few people knew her name or her family. All of Tuyết's activities were directed to caring for her family, or for needy others, in line with a normative discourse of Vietnamese womanhood that sees women as dependent wives and nurturing mothers. Her role as a daughter was reconfigured due in part to her greater earning capacity and stable income, but also as her family had no sons and her parents were no longer economically productive due to their advanced age.

While renovations provide a higher standard of living for family members, it is not simply the ownership of assets that marks relative social distance. Consuming experiences is also important in distinguishing status in Vietnamese middle-class lifestyles. Experiences such as studying for a car driving licence, not succumbing to travel sickness on car journeys, or overcoming a fear of flying, can represent familiarity with middle-class leisure lifestyling. Such experiences can hold scarcity value and set one apart, even without actually owning a car or an aeroplane. This knowledge is based on experience and is not dependent on ownership of a commodity to express familiarity with attributes of an urban lifestyle and the globalized cultural practices associated with elites and middle classes.

Tuyết and her sister enrolled themselves and their husbands in a car driving licence course. The four attended evening classes as they had attended classes in economics and foreign languages in the past. Knowing how to drive a car was a differentiating skill that held scarcity value. Tuyết's husband was not interested in car driving himself, but he had studied the courses and he praised his wife for her patience and care whenever she drove. Having patience and paying attention to details are feminine attributes associated with a gendered division of labour stemming from an understanding of gendered character and behaviour as inherent and naturalized. A female taxi driver in Ho Chi Minh City once told me that women are better drivers than men because of their female nature, making a claim similar to the one Tuyết's husband offered.

Tuyết eventually bought a small second-hand candy-coloured car (discussed above). The vehicle enabled Tuyết to take her family on day outings on the weekends to meals, swimming, day spas, and fun parks. She exposed them to new ideas and experiences which they could enjoy together but which conveyed differential rewards to different family members. Tuyết repaid her debt to her elders through the transfer of knowledge and experience as well as by providing greater comfort and a higher standard of living through better quality housing and material assets. At the same time she was investing in the future of her niece and younger relatives who could repay their debt to her in forms that might benefit the couple or their children in the future.

The flow of dispositions was transmitted not only from her elders to Tuyết during her childhood socialization and schooling, but also from her to them and other members in the multi-dimensional family through a singular field of interaction. She had not made a complete break from the past and by pooling the family's resources she was able to mark out a new status position for herself and eventually help the others step further up the metaphoric consumption ladder that marks class status. Her actions helped raise the others to a new standard of living in pursuit of a promised life of plenty.

FINDINGS

The arrival of migrants to a city can have an impact on urban social life and create new social interests. Daughters from multi-dimensional families living in Ho Chi Minh City are able to explore new ways of living through a symbolic break with their past lifestyles. While urban migration increases the social diversity across a city, this chapter has revealed that it also increases the diversity within the family of a migrant. While it is the younger members who benefit from opportunities available in the city to undergo a desired status transformation, parents and older siblings who remain in rural areas do not necessarily share in benefits beyond material support. The symbolic value of goods, knowledge and experiences that are transmitted by educated urban migrants to their family members are deciphered in their own particularized social contexts.

A singular field of interaction in multi-dimensional families is characterized by close and frequent contact between new middle-class family members and others who may benefit from distributions of wealth, resources and knowledge, especially advice about education and employment in city. The transmission of class cultural resources across families can become circular in criss-crossing generations. The intergenerational transmission of dispositions and capital does not only flow from well-resourced elders to younger members, but also from younger members who possess greater reservoirs of cultural and economic capital to their elders. Pooling resources across a multi-dimensional family can have benefits for those in rural as well as urban areas.

The varying outcomes achieved by social climbers highlights the differential influences of a range of different social conditions. Lower-ranked, particularly younger, members of multi-dimensional families who also remain outside the city can draw on remittances of economic, material and knowledge resources and attempt to build a new class position so long as they are willing to enter the long socialization process required to develop enduring class culture. Early exposure can give them a head start; their access to direct experience of highly valued cultural signals enables them to expand an underlying reservoir of cultural capital more readily or more rapidly than their peers. A focus on education as an initial stepping stone to new class positions enables social climbers from different backgrounds to achieve a comparative entry level. Desires for education and employment, which are most readily available in cities, drive urbanization and create new dynamics in the natal family centring on resource distribution and decision making. Absent daughters become agents of change who are able to achieve new gender status in the natal family as a consequence of the new economic and social status that they have achieved in the city. They employ a new aesthetic language to express their social positions as relatively better without directly excluding themselves from the family, neighbourhood and community.

CHAPTER SEVEN

Delaying and desiring marriage

*A*n assumption of change in all aspects of social life after reform risks overlooking continuities that mark new middle-class lifestyles and shape twenty-first century urban culture in Vietnam. This chapter explores the desires and expectations of educated women in contemporary urban Ho Chi Minh City who delay marriage and childbirth, including Liên, Hạnh, Cúc and their niece Vân, Minh's sister Hương, Xuân's sisters Yến and Chi, and Diễm. Despite their achievements in education, their careers and lifestyles, marriage and family continue to be central to middle-class Vietnamese women's identities. Indeed marriage is virtually a universal expectation in Vietnam and most Vietnamese women are married by forty (GSO 2011a, p. 100). Historically marriage offered Vietnamese middle-class girls a chance to improve their lot in life, or at least maintain their existing social position. But in twenty-first century Vietnam, marriage offers less opportunity for aspirational women to achieve mobility when compared with other strategies such as education and salaried employment.

Educated women in Vietnam face difficulties finding suitable marriage partners. This may be due to a number of reasons ranging from having a higher level of education or a higher salary than a man, being over thirty, being regarded as too independent, or having expectations that could not be met. For new middle-class women, unlike career, marriage does not necessarily provide future security but may involve a loss of newly acquired social, economic and gender status. Remaining single can provide women with relative autonomy and a high degree of economic independence even with unstable employment in a highly competitive urban job market. Even so, a woman who fails to marry or fails to produce a child in Vietnam suffers stigma. It would be rare for a stigmatized person, who experiences direct social exclusion, to successfully achieve social mobility within the zone of influence of Vietnamese cultural expectations.

The urban labour market is not the only opportunity available to women seeking to move up socially or to find economic security for themselves and members of their natal families. New middle-class women experience new configurations of gender at work, wider access to leisure choices and new gender roles in the natal family. Expectations of marriage in Vietnam, however, largely remain normative and have evolved little. Educated young women are faced with fewer options for starting a family and maintaining status, which can create a dilemma in choosing between a focus on career and the enduring status it can facilitate, or on marriage which may come with an expectation that a husband's social position and career are more important than a wife's. Daughters, who have achieved new economic, social and gender power, may be unwilling to revert to traditional gender roles.

PRESSURE TO MARRY

The desire to marry among new middle-class women in Vietnam is strong. Despite achieving relatively higher social status through education and employment, educated young women have the lower social status of 'perpetual minors' because they remain unmarried (Tai 1992, p. 92). Thu had long focused on her career and, having turned thirty, she was also seeking a suitable husband. She regularly dated via the Internet with Vietnamese, overseas Vietnamese and foreign men and kept in touch with former classmates who sometimes provided introductions for her. One promising romance with a foreign beau had been thwarted by his mother and another romance with a Vietnamese man abandoned by Thu after she discovered that he was already married. While for Thu it was difficult to find a suitable man, one of her former classmates had and the couple was celebrating their wedding. As I had been staying at Thu's apartment I accompanied her to the wedding party, which was the second one she had attended that weekend.

We were running late. We ran downstairs, carrying our heels, an extra motorbike helmet and an envelope of cash for the couple. Half an hour later we arrived at the White Palace, a suburban function centre in Ho Chi Minh City's north. It was a busy place and there were a number of weddings and other family functions scheduled that day. At the top of the escalator, an MC directed us to the right function room. The wedding party were already by the door preparing to make an entrance. The bride and groom, arm in arm, stood behind an MC and six bridesmaids in identical white bridal gowns. It was more than ten minutes before they entered, giving us enough time to find spare seats at a table beside the massive speakers inside.

Two MCs introduced each performance. On the stage, professional singers belted out duets and, on the elevated catwalk stretching from the stage to the dance floor at the centre of the room, a dance troupe dressed as brides and grooms began a contemporary waltz routine. The dancing couples on the catwalk were fenced in by tall poles supporting tiny candles. One row of candles led to a six-tiered frosted wedding cake on the left of the stage and the other to a pyramid of flat champagne glasses on the right. Above the stage, the couple's studio wedding photographs and photographs taken of the guests arriving played on two stadium-size flat screens.

Finally, with a clash of symbols, the couple entered. A militarized wedding march played and the dancers and waiters flanked both sides of the stage clapping in time to the music. The wedding party posed on the stage for the group of photographers and cameraman who were recording the event. Next, the couple walked to one side of the stage and cut the cake for the cameras. The MC popped the corks of two bottles of champagne and, having moved to the other side of the stage, the couple emptied them onto dry ice in the glasses on top of the pyramid. Five minutes after the couple had entered the room, their parents thanked the guests and invited us to eat. The food was served swiftly, course by course in under an hour. Then, the MC came to the microphone and gathered a group of single women in their late teens and early twenties to the dance floor at the end of the catwalk.

The bride took centre stage and walked solo along the catwalk towards the frenzied mob of girls. They wore towering heels and skimpy satin cocktail dresses. They were all heavily made-up and wore their hair streaked in fashionable red or brown. At the end of the catwalk, the bride turned her back on them and pitched her bouquet of blood-orange coloured rose buds over her head and into the throng. A desperate grappling of hands tore the bouquet apart and the bound stem of the posy landed heavily on the floor at the feet of a girl in a simple cream mini dress. After a moment of stunned silence, another girl in a leopard skin print party frock grabbed the broken bouquet and held it above her head proudly waving it about for the others to congratulate her. The bride had turned around to see who had won her flowers and smiled at the girl. The pile of petals was forgotten as the girls stepped through them to return to their table with the trophy. The desperation of this crowd of young single women attests to the enduring importance of marriage and pressure not to fail in finding a husband.

For Vietnamese, marriage remains as an important step to adulthood. Hạnh and Liên were among those who felt the pressure to marry. For a single woman in Ho Chi Minh City, to remain alone and be 'left on the shelf' (*ế chồng*) did not become a serious concern until she was over thirty. After thirty, there was a risk that singlehood might become permanent. That risk created pressure on single women who made attempts to avoid exposure to family scrutiny. Some new middle-class women skipped family Tết celebrations by taking a tour of Bangkok or Singapore over the new year holiday. Others limited visits to their natal families if they had vacation time or a busy schedule at work.

At Tết, educated urbanized women like Hạnh avoided the more conservative women in their villages in order to evade their questions. During one of my visit to her village over Tết, Hạnh used me to distract her aunts and divert their attention away from herself and her unmarried status. Hạnh also invited me to join her on a customary visit to her former primary school teacher. The teacher had retired soon after teaching Hạnh, so by the time her younger sister Cúc had started school, there was a new, younger teacher. Unlike Cúc's teacher, Hạnh's teacher was not interested in her students' career successes. She wagged her finger and scolded Hạnh for failing to start a family. Hạnh was made to feel the pressure to marry more acutely than Cúc as she was older. While Hạnh and other professional women have fulfilled the educational expectations of their parents, they have not been able to fulfil their own expectations for marriage and children.

Like Hạnh, Liên rarely reunited with her former classmates. I accompanied Liên the second time her entire class had met after their graduation to a wedding party held in the evening at the glamorous Hotel Continental, an icon of French colonial Saigon. The bride was a former classmate of Liên. Liên knew that some of the men in the class had already married, but she was one of those who had missed parties and other reunions because she had been abroad studying.

Entering the Hotel Continental was like entering another world. Two billboard-sized portraits of bridal couples standing on opposite sides of the lobby made it easy for Liên to recognize which banquet room her friend's wedding party would be held in. Next to their portrait, the couple was standing with their families welcoming their guests. Although Liên did not say so, the bride's family was obviously prosperous and relatives had returned from the US to attend the wedding.

In the banquet room, Liên and I sat with her former classmates. Having brought partners but not children, they pulled up chairs to cram the expanded group around two tables. Like the bride, the classmates were also obviously well-off: economics graduates, managers and directors. They spoke amongst themselves in a lingua franca of technological Business English and Vietnamese, comparing the latest models of mobile phone and flight times between Singapore, Bangkok and Ho Chi Minh City.

Their conversation was briefly interrupted by the arrival of the bride at our table. She showed photographs taken that morning at the formal marriage ceremony, where she had worn the first of three hired dresses, a slim-fitting *áo dài* traditional dress that, instead of being the conventional red of wedding garments, was a fashionable hot pink. She circulated the room serving drinks and thanking guests, until the formalities began. The speeches and singing did not fully interrupt the conversations at the guests' tables. After the cake was cut, Liên quietly asked me to join her outside for some fresh air. She suggested I bring my camera to appreciate how beautiful the city could be at night. I was surprised, because she knew I had seen the city at night scores of times. When the others noticed us leaving, Liên gestured towards me and the camera she was holding. She told them I wanted to take a photograph in front of the hotel. We left directly without stopping to greet people at their tables as we passed.

Outside, the warm evening air was a relief after the chill of the air-conditioning. Despite her smile, Liên was upset. We took several photographs, taking turns to pose for the camera. Liên attempted to hide what she felt. She had found out for certain that she was the last unmarried person in her class, a fact she had not expected. At the time, I failed to grasp the significance of this for Liên. She usually relied on her education and employment as an explanation for her temporarily delayed marriage. However, with all her classmates and peers having already established a career and been married, her single status now seemed to be becoming permanent, at least in their eyes. She did not regard herself in these terms; she did not want to remain alone.

Liên was feeling trapped by social pressures to conform to cultural traditions of conventional family life. I was reminded of Liên's concerns the night I moved into her house, when our first conversation had become uncomfortable and Liên's eyes had flashed at me as she explained the freedoms that – as a foreigner – she perceived I had, and which – as a Vietnamese – she perceived she lacked. Her present concerns were not with legal rights to gender equality in the workplace, nor with sexual harassment at work, but with issues of love. She was concerned about the freedom to choose a partner, or a series of partners, for love even against the family's wishes and about the freedom to have a child, or many children, with or without a husband, or one permanent partner. Her time studying abroad had opened her eyes to the possibility that a woman might juggle a career, a relationship and a family. On this issue, she considered most of Vietnam – even Ho Chi Minh City – to be lagging behind.

For other educated urban women in Liên's position, reasserted tradition in the role of a dutiful daughter can only last for so long before relatives and neighbours begin to wonder what is wrong. Was an unmarried woman in her mid-thirties too self-centred to marry? Was there some other problem? Why had she not met a man? For years, indeed since the end of high school, Liên had been introduced to potential suitors, men whom her relatives, classmates, colleagues, friends, neighbours – or whoever made the introduction – had assessed to be ideal. But none of these men had been suitable. At the time, none of them had seemed able to fulfil the right needs and this had not been a problem. Now, there was the possibility of never finding a husband and never having the joys of family life or the responsibilities of housework and childcare. Remaining single would mean not having to compromise to suit his needs or those of anyone else. Remaining single would mean being an aunt, but not a mother. Remaining single would cement her career and lifestyle as more important than family life. Remaining single would mean no longer waiting for love.

SINGLE LIFE IN POST-REFORM VIETNAM

For Vietnamese, marriage is an integral part of a model life. Regarded as a stepping stone to adulthood, marriage is seen as a virtual social rule and one of the most important life achievements. A single woman in Vietnam is judged to be an incomplete person and labelled as 'left on the shelf' or as 'a delayed-action bomb' (Williams and Guest 2005, pp. 172–3). As David Marr (1981, pp. 248–9) advises, marriage for Vietnamese women is conventionally believed to provide a secure base for living and acting, so that without a marriage a woman risks being stigmatized.

Despite recognizing that singlehood 'should be regarded as a *normal phenomenon of human life*' (Le Thi 2008, p. 18, original emphasis), Vietnamese state discourses portray single women (*phụ nữ đơn thân*) as vulnerable and as those they are without access to capital and resources, without education and employment, and living outside urban areas. Of course many women identified as single have been at some time married, but live alone because they have been widowed, divorced or abandoned by their husbands or lovers. Others choose not to marry. Danièle Bélanger and Khuất Thu Hồng (2002, pp. 103, 105–6, 109) observe that never-married women (in rural northern Vietnam) identified a turning point in their lives when they realized that their unmarried state was no longer temporary. Some reported having chosen to remain single – and more often than not living with their natal families – in preference to agreeing to a less desirable marriage, explaining that the right man did not appear at the right time. Vietnamese state research discourses do not acknowledge women's agency, but report that the majority of single women in Vietnam are not single by choice and that their singlehood results from 'compromises' and 'misfortune'. They recognize that single women do not suffer only 'sadness and deprivation' but also 'experience joy' in their lives (Le Thi 2008, pp. 4, 35, 115). Educated and professional young urban women who are recognized for their achievements do not seem to be classified as 'single' as this refers to vulnerable women. This may be because single life is feared due to practical concerns about economic survival. As Philip Martin (2010, p. S7) observes, single women in Vietnam are viewed as victims of the socio-economic context and not as agents of change.

Single mothers and their children are subjected to stigmatization and public humiliation in post-war Vietnamese state discourses. Women raising a family without a husband are seen to have 'valiantly confronted' enduring social prejudices as well as material difficulties stemming from life without a breadwinner husband (Nguyen Thanh Tam 1996, pp. 87–8). State discourses on single mothers similarly fail to recognize women's agency. In a study of village life, Jayne Werner (2009, p. 86) highlights an isolated case of a single mother who had been supported by both her own and her fiancé's families to have her child after he was killed in an accident. The stigma most single mothers attract reveals the enduring value placed on marriage and patrilineal kinship in Vietnam (Phinney 2008).

The risks of public humiliation and inferior social status seem to be more acute in village life. In urban areas, many young Vietnamese women consciously choose to delay marriage in order to complete their education, to establish a professional career, or at least to work in some type of labour program for future benefit. Young women in Ho Chi Minh City and the Mekong Delta are among those who wait the longest to marry (GSO & UNDP 2001, pp. 9–10; GSO 2011c, p. 13). Never marrying is highest in highly industrialized areas such as the Southeast (GSO 2011a, p. 117). Educated urban women starting a career may become relatively independent in economic and social terms and, importantly, retain potential to marry. They are not yet *permanently* single.

This phenomenon is not unique to post-reform urban Vietnam. In postcolonial southern Vietnam, East and Southeast Asia, and the post-socialist world, as well as Western Europe and North America, educated young women choose to delay marriage. Japan's 'parasite singles', for example, represent an emerging type of female agency among urban professionals, who stay with their parents as daughters even after they have graduated and begun working professionally. While their lifestyles are understood in terms of luxury consumption, entertainment and leisure lifestyling, they are also viewed as more 'traditional' in remaining at home until marriage and being available to arrange for their parents' care in old age (Dales 2005, pp. 133–6). In their roles as daughters, parasite singles reassert aspects of traditional responsibilities in family life, although as educated professionals, they reject conventions of submissive feminine behaviour and especially hierarchical, unequal spousal relationships.

One product of rapid urbanization in Vietnam's Southeast is a comparable generation of educated and professional single women. The success of this generation of single women not only affects family life but raises questions of why, who and when they might marry. Young educated women, including Thu, Liên and Hạnh (above) and Cúc, Hương and Diễm (see below), are conscious of the social stigma associated with remaining single. Their awareness of their failure to enter a marriage becomes most apparent at their classmates' wedding parties and at Tết when extended families reunite and family members visit their former teachers.

A HAPPY REUNION

Unlike Thu, Hạnh and Liên, Cúc's reunion with her classmates was a happy event. Her former high school classmates usually gathered in the village to visit their teacher as a class. To find out when to go and where to meet, Cúc needed to catch up with one of her classmates in the provincial town. One of them had a mother who ran a café there. Like many other mothers of her age, she was a war widow. We woke her as we pulled in under the café verandah out of the sun. She had been taking a rest in a deck chair. Her feet had been tucked up off the ground and her arms thrown back over her head. When she heard the motorbike throttle off, she immediately jumped up from her chair. At this time of day, there were usually no guests in her café; most people were at home sleeping off their midday meals. In an instant, she was standing with the ubiquitous machete in her hand, gesturing towards a couple of deck chairs in a dark corner where it would be cool to rest. Cúc had removed her helmet, but otherwise did not move. The café owner stopped in surprise at her guest's reluctance, at the same time noticing me: taller and foreign. Cúc grinned broadly and giggled her greetings. Recognition suddenly animated the woman's face, softening her features and her business mannerisms. She grabbed Cúc and squeezed her shoulders, waist and arms. She called out to someone resting in the house behind the café, as she patted Cúc's hair and straightened her blouse, neatening its creases. Impatiently, Cúc called out much louder than the older woman had. The voice of a man – Huy, Cúc's classmate – answered from the far side of the darkened doorway.

Huy's mother's café / home was made of wood, greyed with age and wear. The building sagged on one end away from the canal over which it was built and towards a vacant block of land where café guests could park their motorbikes. Coloured bulbs that hung across the verandah were, even during the day, brightly decorative and welcoming. Hammocks hung across each end between the verandah posts. A cigarette counter housed several brands of cigarettes as well as useful items like cigarette lighters, light bulbs, pens, and batteries. A small row of empty cans advertised the brands and flavours that were sold there. A blackboard listed the prices of a range of home-brewed alcohols. The floor was earthen and the smell of stagnant canal water lingered in the afternoon heat. Huy appeared in shorts and a crumpled t-shirt spattered with water that dripped from his clean face. He scuffed his plastic *dép* as he came across the floor towards us. His hair was wet, but uncombed. His handshake was firm and his nails neatly manicured. Strangely, he greeted us in fluent English. Quickly, I realized he was a sophisticated urban businessman. With that realization, he seemed out of place in his mother's café.

In the following hours, Huy spread the word that Cúc had returned home. The class set a date and time to pay a visit to their former teacher, who, since her marriage, had moved to her husband's village nearby. The teacher's house was hidden from the road by two parallel hedges. To enter we followed a well-worn track that led us first to the left. We walked along the length of the hedge until we found a gap that acted as a doorway. Then we turned to the right and continued until we found our way into a small courtyard. The class had already arrived for the visit. The women were seated in the front room of the two-room wooden house and the men were standing in the courtyard. They were all waiting to greet Cúc and catch up with news from the city. She was the only woman who had not arranged a lift with a husband or a trustworthy male classmate. The men were scolded for not escorting her. Cúc seemed insulted and embarrassed by this judgement and quickly changed the subject, inquiring after the teacher's new baby. While she did so, I discovered that Cúc was the only woman from her class living in Ho Chi Minh City. Huy was considered the most successful classmate, as he worked in a foreign company and spoke two foreign languages. Another young man – Thiệu

– worked in the city, but did not speak foreign languages. Both remained single. Cúc had graduated from university in the city and continued to study English, although she was unmarried and, at new year, still unemployed. One other young woman – Huệ – had studied at a teacher's college in the city, but had since returned home to marry. High school sweethearts Mỹ Trân and her husband were the only members of the class with a child. Tấm was the only one absent.

Although Tấm had not visited the teacher, she had been persuaded to visit Cúc. At Cúc's place, she had kicked off her sandals at the doorway when she arrived and greeted Cúc's mother like her own. She was heavy with makeup but seemed happy and bright as she rolled up the hems of her jeans and made her way into the kitchen. Throughout the meal, Tấm remained in the kitchen so that she and Cúc could catch up. Their absence gave Huệ and Mỹ Trân an opportunity to quietly fill me in on Tấm's misfortunes. Tấm avoided social contact because she felt ashamed. She had urgently wanted to marry and, even though she was pretty, she had trouble finding a man. The previous year, as a last resort, she had consulted a matchmaker in order to find a good husband and finally marry. But the husband she had found was violent and after only three months she had returned herself to her parent's house. Because of this, her husband's parents did not visit her parents on Mùng Một, the first day of the new year, an action which severs social ties. In-laws in southern families usually maintain close connections to ensure the stability of the couple (Đỗ Thái Đồng 1991, p. 80). The consequence for Tấm is that she will find it difficult to remarry in Vietnam and may remain in her father's house for the rest of her life due to the shame she has brought onto her family.

Huệ and Mỹ Trân hoped that Tấm's misfortunes would not affect Cúc. Although her classmates acknowledged her successes, they also mentioned how sad she must be since she had lost her special someone (*người yêu*) and lived a lonely life. They explained that Cúc should have married Thiệu, the most popular boy in their class. No one knew what had happened to the romance. Later, Cúc complained about Thiệu: he was always hungry, he always smoked cigarettes, and he was always drunk.

Huệ and Mỹ Trân could not imagine their lives without their husbands, both of whom were side by side at the other end of the table toasting each other and their classmates. Mỹ Trân had worked in the market since finishing school, but had recently taken over her mother's stall, where she sold women's underwear and sleepwear. Her house faced out to the square where the market stalls were set up early each morning. She looked as glamorous as any market woman, with her toenails shaped to a point and painted silver, her eyebrows plucked thin, and sets of thick gold bracelets on her arms. She wore her long hair clipped back in a plastic bow and large hoop earrings, which her son tugged. She was educated, having completed high school, and ran a successful business. Her achievements exemplified that it was women with education or entrepreneurial skills who were able to benefit from the opportunities of economic reform in Vietnam (Tran and Le 2000, p. 94; Leshkowich 2011).

Mỹ Trân had married her high school sweetheart, one of the other classmates, the year after they graduated from school. They had had a son, their only child, less than a year after that. As Cúc predicted, when we visited, Mỹ Trân played their wedding video. On the video, Mỹ Trân was made-up like an opera diva and floated between the tables, serving her guests food and drink. Each classmate had aged a decade, but the video showed that Cúc was one of the few women who had worn a western-style business suit at the wedding. Although Mỹ Trân had what Cúc told me she craved – a husband, a house of her own, and a son – Cúc was critical of Mỹ Trân's choices, her appearance and lifestyle. According to her, Mỹ Trân was flashy and uneducated. She could not make a good home for her son and did not know how to bring him up properly. In Cúc's view, the teacher Huệ and her husband would be much better parents.

Like Mỹ Trân and her husband, Huệ and her husband had also been high school sweethearts. Unlike Mỹ Trân and her husband, Huệ and her husband had delayed their marriage until they had stable jobs and enough resources to build a house. Their house was new. The interior painting had been finished just three weeks earlier in time for Tết. In the front courtyard was a small garden of potted plants and a fish pond, next to which the classmates parked their motorbikes. The other classmates were helping Huệ to sweep and hand wash the tiled front room floor when we entered the house. Huệ apologized, explaining that the house needed cleaning because it was only occupied on Sundays.

During the week Huệ boarded with her husband's relatives in the Delta city of Mỹ Thọ, where she taught English, and her husband spent the week at his mother's house in the village. Huệ returned home each week on Saturday afternoons to spend time with her husband and clean her house, before returning to work early Monday mornings. Huệ's career meant that she spent most of her week away from her husband. Their loving separation, although less common in the younger generation, was not unheard of among the older generation of women. 'Visiting marriages' such as these have been a recognized family pattern in Vietnam, which varied over time and between places, but usually occurred due to economic reasons and especially due to (the husband's) labour migration (Phạm Văn Bích 1999, pp. 174–6).

Huệ left the others to finish cleaning and escorted Cúc and me through her house. We admired both downstairs rooms – front room and kitchen – before popping our heads up the ladder into the sleeping loft. We admired Huệ's wedding album which she proudly showed off, pointing out each of the classmates as they appeared in her photographs. Back in the front room, the women had finished cleaning and had laid newspapers onto the tiles to act as a tablecloth. At the end the meal, Huệ served watermelon and then, in her doorway arm in arm with her husband, bid us farewell.

THE PERFECT PARTNER

Husbands seemed to loom large in the minds of educated young women in their twenties, even when a husband remained a future dream. Although Vietnamese women's roles in the family were traditionally defined in terms of relationships with men, the success of their relationships with senior women in the family, especially the mother-in-law, continued to be important in their daily lives (Werner 2009, p. 136). Relationships with husbands have become more central in urban women's ideas about family life than in multi-generational village households, indicating an emphasis on romantic love that emerged with the widespread nuclearization of urban households and suggesting the increasing prominence of gender status among educated young women who desire greater independence and autonomy. Despite Vietnamese state researchers claiming that wives were emancipated from submissive family relationships in Vietnam after reform, family roles are fraught with contradictions between conventional and new arrangements and between ideals and realities (Lê Thị Nhâm Tuyết 1989, 2002; Werner 2009).

In Vietnam, daughters sending remittances are able to contribute to decisions about the household and lead a relatively autonomous life away from home prior to marriage. But, after reform, ideals of a future wife remained closely wedded to traditional stereotypes of submission. In a survey of young Vietnamese people seeking partners, young men reported that their ideal wife would be, firstly, an attractive, morally and physically healthy woman who is capable of making a living; secondly, faithful to her husband; thirdly, good at doing housework; and lastly, respectful and understanding of her husband (Lê Thị Nhâm Tuyết 2002, p. 258). These attributes desired in an ideal wife correspond fairly evenly with the four traditional feminine virtues (*tư đúc*) (Ngô Thị Ngân Bình 2004).[1]

A reassertion of traditionalized gender roles that occurred in post-reform Vietnam also characterized postsocialist countries where, as a result of reform, notions of femininity have tended to revert back to pre-socialist norms (Werner and Bélanger 2002, p. 16). In post-reform China, a state newspaper article reported to women the qualities modern men would seek in a wife. The most-liked Chinese woman was one who listens respectfully, shows her appreciation, and worships her man. The least-liked was a fearless, brave and loud woman who likes to joke, gamble and swear (Johansson 2001, pp. 99, 108–9). The postsocialist Russian mass media also fed contradictory messages to women about reproductive and productive roles which were 'hardly ideal', but which focused on a woman's physical appearance over her intellect; on her obedience to male superiors; on female caring and giving roles; on women's domestication and removal from the labour market; and on a woman seeking an ideal partner and desiring male attention (Kay

---

1   At the beginning of the new millennium, ideals of post-reform womanhood in Vietnam were constructed in terms that resemble the hierarchical relationships and dependency on the household familiar in the earlier Confucian heritage. A modified interpretation of traditional virtues – presented in an excerpt from an interview published by *Thanh Niên* (Youth) newspaper reporter Nguyễn Thùy with Nguyễn Thị Lập, the Vietnam Women's Union (VWU) Chairperson from Ho Chi Minh City – not only reinforced Confucian influences in family life, but also reinforced a double burden for women. The VWU's reinterpreted set of virtues included the contribution of industrious women not only to housework, but also to society (*công,* industry); the responsibility of women to take care of their physical appearance, but also their health (*dung,* appearance); the ability of women to refine their speech, but also to be assertive (*ngôn,* speech / interpersonal communication); and the requirement of women to be faithful and unselfish (*hạnh,* behaviour), although – for the first time in state discourse – they were advised to remarry so as to avoid single life (Nguyễn Thùy 2002, p. 6).

1997, pp. 77, 81–7). In Southeast Asia too, middle-class men preferred submissive and lower-ranked wives. In Malaysia, new middle-class men tend to marry women with lower qualifications, and the higher the man's qualifications, the lower his wife's (Embong 2002, p. 82).

Yet, for Southeast Asia's new middle classes, marriage does not necessarily secure upward social mobility. Rather than marriage in Bangkok a career offers the most important stepping stone to upward social mobility (Limmanee et al. 2001, p. 471). For new middle-class women in the Philippines, education provides an avenue to social mobility. More females across class categories have college diplomas than males, and young women are significantly better educated than their mothers. Three out of four outrank their fathers in terms of occupation. The children of farmers move up higher than others even though they start from a lower base (Bautista 2001b, p. 278). For new middle-class women in Southeast Asia, the benefits offered by education and employment seem less risky, or at least more predictable, than those offered through marriage.

In Vietnam, a desire for change in family life was stressed even before reform and expressed in aspirations for non-agricultural work and a new type of husband in the post-reform era. Young women reported that their ideal husband would be, firstly, faithful to his wife; secondly, employed, earning enough to support a family; and lastly, willing to share the burden of family affairs (Lê Thị Nhâm Tuyết 2002, p. 260). Vietnamese survey results suggested that both young men and young women imagined an understanding spouse who contributes to the household and family life. Men were expected by women to contribute financially, but also share housework while women were expected by men to not only make a living but also take responsibility for the housework and childcare. In reality, even though women expected a husband to support the family, many men reported un- or under-employment forcing their dependence on their wife's income (Lê Thị Nhâm Tuyết 2002, p. 257).

Since the 1980s, urban women hoping to balance their working and family lives relied on a contribution from their husbands at home. Although access to resources and individual character were advantages, professional women could not have succeeded without a husband's help with shopping, meal preparation, childcare and housework (Lê Thị

Nhâm Tuyết 1989, pp. 96–8). Working women's desires for change were assisted in Ho Chi Minh City in the early 1980s by high male unemployment which freed husbands to help around the house (Hoàng Ngọc Thanh Dung 1988, pp. 43–5). Socialist debates on women's emancipation did not generally focus on the effects on men (see Le Thi 1998). In the post-reform era, however, changing masculinities – such as those in Russia and China (e.g. Kay and Kostenko 2006; Rofel 1999) – indicate that changing expectations of womanhood necessarily impact on men. New configurations of gender in urban Vietnamese family relationships have brought new expectations of men as husbands and fathers (Bui 2010; Martin 2010; Horton and Rydstrøm 2011).

Unlike expectations of women's submission in Vietnam's past, post-reform equality debates emphasized that women's participation in social and family life no longer involved 'passive' roles (Lê Thị Nhâm Tuyết 1989, pp. 26, 37–8). Growing competition and changing expectations in partners was reflected in the state mass media. Young women in the post-reform era were portrayed not only as aggressive in pursuing love, but also in fierce competition with each other to find the more perfect match. A 2003 article in *Phụ Nữ* (Women) newspaper raised a concern that young women might tend not to seek permanent relationships, but pursue superficial and temporary liaisons, where there is no trust (*lòng tin*). In these relationships, a young woman might be attracted to a handsome, illustrious (*nổi tiếng*), and vivacious (*lanh lợi*) boy because other girls pay attention to him. Based on what others say and feel about him, she can develop a clear sense of him becoming her boyfriend and she might aim to become the one who triumphs (*chiến thắng*) and 'carries off the prize' (*đoạt giải*). But, the article argued, the relationship will not go anywhere if it is shallow or based only on physical beauty. Anxiety or boredom will prematurely break them up. If she does not try, she might become a 'choosy old maid' (*bà ghen khó tính*). To avoid that, a girl needs to realize that a boyfriend is not perfect. She needs to understand that he can be loving, quick-witted, smart and funny, but sometimes he can also be silly (*ngố hết sức*). When she feels really comfortable with him, she also does not have to pretend to be perfect (*Phụ Nữ*, 5 May 2003, p. 7, p. 9). This article reflects a desire for a new configuration of urban femininity that rejects women's submission and recognizes their agency.

A LESS-THAN-IDEAL HUSBAND

The night we discussed Cúc's high school sweetheart was very hot with little breeze. Cúc, Hạnh, their niece Vân and I had been left alone, although the responsibility of our care had been delegated to the oldest Hạnh by their brother (Vân's uncle) who had wanted to go drinking with his school friends from the village. The sisters were used to Vân's company and often advised and guided her regarding schooling and city life.

Vân had grown up in a nuclear family and had close contact with both her father's and her mother's extended families. As a student, she had excelled, particularly in English classes, and with her aunts' guidance, she put her eye on a career in finance with the possibility of using her language skills to earn a very good living in a foreign company based in the city. With her high grades, she had won a university place and had moved to live with relatives in a rapidly urbanizing rural-zoned district on the urban fringe of Ho Chi Minh City. Their house had the disadvantage of being far from her downtown campus and away from her favourite hangouts, but it offered low-cost living and the support of family life. Vân was required to do the housework every morning before classes. In the evenings and on Sundays, she studied extra classes.

Vân's initial arrival in the city had been difficult, but with the advice and support of her aunts Cúc and Hạnh, she learned the city lifestyle. Then, at the beginning of her second year, when she was twenty, she inherited the responsibility of caring for her younger brother, who had moved to Ho Chi Minh City to begin primary school. Vân then became his primary caregiver, responsible for looking after him, as well as feeding and clothing him. At mealtimes, in the kitchen or wherever he might be, she spoon fed him as her mother had instructed her to do. But while eating, he was regularly distracted by computer games, television programs, visitors, or mischief. Sometimes he spat his food in Vân's face or, worse, over his school uniform, which Vân would later have to hand wash. Vân also had the duty of delivering her brother to and retrieving him from school. To do so, a relative had supplied a second-hand motorbike, which also allowed her some degree of freedom and the flexibility to get to and from her own classes. Gradually, Vân managed a balance between her domestic responsibilities, her social life and her study commitments.

Vân had not grown up in the house where we were staying, but had completed high school there. Spread out on the cool floor tiles, we eventually gave up a one-sided card game which Hạnh usually won and lay waiting for a breeze and sleep. It was so hot that the window had to be opened. Once opened, the neighbourhood sounds of night could freely enter. In the house below the open window a woman was being beaten by her husband. This momentarily stopped our conversation and delayed the possibility of sleep. According to Vân, these neighbours often fought which made her grateful that she lived in the city and, in recent years, only heard their disputes rarely. After the husband had finally left, the wife at first sobbed and then anger overwhelmed her and she screamed out her troubles in a broad Mekong Delta accent. Cúc and Vân relayed her loneliness, her loss of gold and assets, her husband's gambling and adultery, her son's disappearance and suspected death, her miserable destiny, an anticipated lack of fortune for the coming year, and an overview of her various injuries. Vân speculated that if the neighbour lived in the city, she might be able to divorce her husband, but in the countryside with no independent income, it was simply not practical. For the neighbour to survive the added social stigma of divorce in her vulnerable economic position would not be possible.

Cúc agreed. To abandon a husband is far worse than being abandoned by a husband, as the misfortunes of Cúc's friend Tắm demonstrated. Cúc confessed that Tắm had wanted to ask me to find an Australian husband for her, but she was too shy to do so. Tắm had heard village stories about foreign marriage and believed that, unlike a Vietnamese man, a foreigner would not worry about her age, nor that she had already been married and had failed. If she escaped her life in the village by moving abroad, she believed she would also escape all her problems. Cúc soberly recommended that none of us marry a husband like the one her school friend had married. But to avoid a husband like Tắm's or like the neighbour's, who would they marry? Would it be worse to marry an unsuitable man than to be alone? What type of man would be suitable? Who would make an ideal husband?

AN IDEAL HUSBAND

Ten years younger than us and yet to receive her first kiss, Vân had a very clear image to share. In her mind, an ideal husband would be Vietnamese and would want to live in Vietnam. Vân's ideal husband is an honest and good-natured man, who is physically strong, handsome, and taller than his wife. While it is important to read his facial features for personality traits, it is not important to read his horoscope for compatibility.[2] An aunt's marriage indicated to her that it was not necessary to rely on astrological beliefs to make a successful match. That aunt had misled her superstitious parents and parents-in-law about the degrees of compatibility between herself and her fiancé. As their years together attested, astrological incompatibility had not affected the happiness of an actual relationship. The couple had rejected traditional views in preference for modern ones that centred on romantic love.

Cúc interrupted to contribute additional criteria. He should be five years older than his wife, to give him the advantage of maturity and time to have established himself financially in a good position for marriage. She did not mention the hierarchy and submission that an age difference implies. Cúc's ideal husband should also have a new and preferably imported motorbike to show he is practical, responsible and serious (as well as fashionable and on the move up?).

Vân continued. As a minimum, he must have education and employment. He should not just be educated, but preferably have sophistication. He should be well enough employed to provide for his wife and children, as well as his ageing parents and other relatives. Although he has parents and maintains a close relationship with them, he does not live with them. He lives independently in his own house, away from the ancestral homeland and away from his mother, the mother-in-law. He must be willing to visit his in-laws and his wife's family, whom she should not be expected to give up. He must want to live independently of both families in Ho Chi Minh City after marriage, where both partners can have access to better jobs, better incomes and a higher standard of living.

---

2   Vietnamese astrological signs follow the lunar calendar (*âm lịch*), a Chinese calendarical system popularized across East Asia and comprising a sexagenary cycle of ten 'heavenly stems' (*can*) and twelve 'earthly branches' (*chi*), the latter of which are represented by the set of animals popularly understood in the west as the 'Chinese zodiac'. This astrological system can be used to determine personality characteristics and flaws according to the year, month, day and hour that each person is born. In Vietnam, it is most commonly used to forecast the destiny of an infant at birth, to explain degrees of compatibility between people before marriage, and to predict degrees of fortune or misfortune at specific points on an individual's life path, particularly before major decisions, such as marriage or international travel, and also at the beginning of each new year.

Vân continued. He should not be the eldest son in his family. It would be convenient if he has an older brother who is already married, preferably with a son of his own. This would mean that there will be less pressure on his wife to be a daughter-in-law and look after his ageing parents, but also less pressure to interrupt or cease a career to have a child straight away. Her experience caring for her brother had taught her how much work raising a child created.

Vân's ideal man is open-minded and supportive of women's rights, education and employment. A husband with a positive attitude towards women's advancement would tolerate a modern and ambitious wife and encourage her to foster and fulfil her own goals and ambitions as well as work together to achieve a solid marriage partnership. He would be willing to help at home. He should be house-trained and can look after himself and the children if needed. This capacity would be useful if he was to be left behind overnight or longer due to inter-regional or international business trips, shift work or other work commitments. Cúc speculated on the potential hazard of a husband left alone. Vân suggested that while he should love his wife, he must not miss her too much when she is busy at work as he would be busy with his own job and he would have no time for mischief. He was, like Minh, expected to behave in a considerably more feminized manner than that of a conventional Vietnamese ideal of masculine character (see Chapter 4).

I wondered out loud how they might meet this man. Cúc and Vân thought meeting an ideal husband might be difficult. He may be too busy at work or rarely in Ho Chi Minh City due to work commitments. He may prefer a stay-at-home wife who can look after him, his children and his busy lifestyle. Alternatively, the ideal man might be married already or he might have a significant flaw explaining why he remains unmarried, such as a violent temper, drinking or gambling.

Vân had a clear image of her ideal man outlined in the physical, intellectual, financial, attitudinal, and familial characteristics she found desirable. If Vân were to meet a man with these qualities, as his wife she would not have to give up her career, economic and social status. Nor, residing in an urban nuclear household, would she necessarily have to compromise the new found gender status daughters may achieve in contributing to decisions taken in their natal families. Vân's expectations of adapting to changing family relationships did not centre on her own sacrifices for marriage but on expectations of gender equality in spousal relationships that were widespread in post-reform Vietnam (Thai 2008, p. 119; see also Werner 2009, pp. 80–8).

MAINTAINING STATUS AFTER MARRIAGE

For a woman to reach her mid-thirties without successfully finding a partner – as Hạnh, Liên and Minh's sister Hương, had done – marriage might suddenly loom as more important than a career. Like Hạnh and Liên, Hương had a career, but unlike them, she was determined to be married. Because she worked long hours, her mother actively encouraged her to find a suitable husband through her workplace. Hương worked in the international airport terminal where she was able to meet many men each day.

Minh described his sister Hương as a hard-working and goal-oriented girl. When she committed herself to her endeavour, she soon found a husband. The husband she found was a Vietnamese-American businessman who regularly travelled to Vietnam. They had met at a ticketing counter and an administrative delay had enabled them to get to know each other a little and arrange a meeting. Hương had noted down the important details from his passport – full name, date of birth, birthplace, home address, number and duration of visits to Vietnam, visits to other countries, type of business – which she had brought home to her mother and together they had looked on a map to find his home state and consulted an astrologer regarding his compatibility, temperament and fortunes.

Their romance had been abrupt due to his flight schedule. Between his visits to Vietnam, mother and daughter planned the details of the ceremony, housing, finances and began to talk of children. They hoped that the marriage would stop the neighbour's negative comments about Hương's advancing age and single status, although it was possible that marriage to an overseas Vietnamese man would start a new series of criticisms. The couple married within months and spent a four-day honeymoon at home in Tân Bình. Hương was saving for a trip to the US to meet her parents-in-law and begin the process for applying for residency papers. Meanwhile, she intended to remain at home in Vietnam working in her job while her husband would do the same in the US and visit Vietnam several times each year. She was not concerned about being lonely because – just as now – she would have her work, her friends, her family, and soon enough a baby to keep her busy. Hung Cam Thai (2008, p. 35) refers to this time as a waiting period that can be indefinite due to restrictive US immigration processes.

In the longer term, the marriage could provide opportunities for the family to move to the US and for the parents to join their old friends now living there. They might grow used to the idea of ageing in greater comfort and with access to better health care. In her mother's eyes, Hương was a dutiful daughter and a responsible girl. She was an educated young woman who had remained at home with her parents, studying to improve herself and achieve a better job through which she could improve the family economy. Hương's lifestyle was like a Japanese parasite single (Dales 2005). A transnational marriage offered Hương a means to achieving married status as well as maintaining her existing lifestyle. During the waiting period at least, Hương and others like her could maintain their newly achieved economic, social and gender power in the natal family after marriage. In this regard, they are unlike state media portrayals of Vietnamese transnational brides who are portrayed as young, ignorant and naïve (Bélanger, Khuất and Tran 2013, p. 95).

Transnational marriage offers more than a solution to a potential loss of independence and autonomy for single women who have delayed marriage too long. Divorced or widowed women, such as Cúc's classmate Tấm (above) and Xuân's sisters Chi and Yến (see below), also look to transnational marriage as a possible solution to their reduced status positions in Vietnam. For them, marriage becomes an alternative to education and employment in achieving social mobility and a relatively higher standard of living. Yet, marriage does not figure prominently in the social mobility of young and single new middle classes as it may not be a less risky means of advancing social position (cf. Bourdieu 1976). Those women who use marriage as a strategy for mobility tend to leave Vietnam. For them, transnational marriage can free them from Vietnamese traditional obligations of patriarchal marriage and offer something more for their children in terms of an enduring status position. In this way, they challenge Vietnamese conventions and break down normative ideals of womanhood that centre on a Vietnamese wife's submission to her breadwinner husband.

MITIGATING STIGMA THROUGH TRANSNATIONAL MARRIAGE

The evening Liên and I were going to the wedding at the Continental Hotel (discussed above), we took a long time getting ready. When we were both finally ready, Liên locked up the house and we walked along the laneway to the street. Our emergence onto the street interrupted Xuân, who was as usual under her shop awning. Xuân had been talking to her older sisters, who had dropped in to show off some photographs and to cuddle the baby. They looked, first at Liên and then at me, inspecting us from head to toe. They commented favourably on our hair and our shoes, the baby echoing their compliment: *Đẹp!* (Beautiful!). Xuân held her son's arms back to prevent him stroking the velvet and silk of our party frocks.

Liên stepped closer to the curb and looked along the street in case a taxi happened to be passing. As we waited for one to appear, Xuân's sisters took the opportunity to question me. They wanted to know if this would be my first wedding party. Each question they asked me, they also asked the baby. He giggled at the extra attention, repeating their words and grabbing with his sticky fingers. They wanted to know if I was married, why I was not yet married, if my parents were unhappy, when I would marry, and how many babies I would have. They were as curious about me as I was about them.

I already knew the youngest and eldest of the sisters. The youngest – Xuân – was married and had a son. The eldest – Yến – was single then. She had two teenage children, a son and a daughter, who lived with her in their widowed grandmother's house near the local market. Their grandfather had died when their mother was young. Their father had never shared a house with Yến due to work commitments that took him outside the city. Although he had visited his family regularly for years, he eventually abandoned them. The children still remembered him.

Yến was petite. She usually wore an *áo bà ba* blouse and loose dark pants. Her long dark hair was almost always tied back from her face in a simple plastic clip. She worked long hours as a restaurant cook and had not been interested in marrying again, despite her children having no father or grandfather. They had an uncle (*cậu*), the only son in the family. He lived with Yến's family in their mother's house near the market. His mother and sisters were pleased that he had married two years earlier and had already produced a son. His wife did not need to work, but stayed home to look after the boy, her husband and her mother-in-law. Because she was often too busy with the baby, Xuân took her mother's lunch to the morning market stall where she worked each day.

The second sister – Trang – had followed her mother into business. She was broad shouldered and straight talking. Her mother had attempted to conceive a boy and was initially disappointed to receive a second daughter. Despite this disappointment, she had taken her under her wing and fostered her talent in business. Trang had been so successful that she had opened her own stall, becoming independent of her mother's business until she left the market.

After leaving the market, Trang had opened a coffee stall in the city centre. Her stall was set up from early morning until late at night at the top of a narrow laneway that led to her apartment building. Trang spent most of her day with her husband, who ran his business next to hers. Together, they served customers or rested side by side in deck chairs. Most of their customers lived in nearby apartments or worked in the nearby city office buildings. They had married two decades ago, as soon as Trang had finished high school. She was 18. He was 34. It is said that Vietnamese believe when the husband is a few years older than the wife, harmony and stability can be ensured because she will respect him and he will pamper her (Phạm Văn Bích 1999, pp. 141–2). However, because it had been a whirlwind romance, and because he was so much older than Trang, their match had caused a minor scandal. As a result, everyone had expected a baby. The baby – a boy – did not arrive for eight years. By then, it had become apparent that they were fated to be together. Their happiness overshadowed any disapproval and it was forgotten. The second child – a girl – arrived eight years after the first. She was sweet, about six years old and shyly clinging to her mother as we chatted. To combat the evening heat, Trang offered me her newspaper to use as a hand fan.

Unlike Trang, the third sister – Chi – lived with Yến's family and her brother's family at her mother's house. Chi was tall. She had permed her hair and almost always wore short sundresses. She worked in a beauty salon near the market. When she was young, she had been married to a Vietnamese man. That husband was a wild and hot-tempered man. No one in the neighbourhood was surprised when she divorced him and returned to her mother's house. She had recently remarried.

Because Xuân's family members frequently dropped by, I commented that I had not yet met Chi's new husband. My comment made Chi and her sister Trang laugh out loud. They showed me the photographs they had brought for Xuân. Chi's new husband was a foreigner and he lived abroad. They had been introduced through an aunt (*dì*), who had moved abroad years earlier. Chi's husband was much older than her and a widower. His first marriage had produced children old enough to be Chi's younger brothers and sisters. He had recently retired from work due to ailing health but because he shared Chi's adventuresome spirit and bawdy sense of humour, they were a good match.

The husband was young at heart and wanted a new companion. Chi was still young and wanted a family of her own but was unable to have children after a severe beating from her first husband. As a solution, Chi had created a family by adopting two street children to share the happiness of the new marriage and the benefits of a life abroad. Her new husband had visited Vietnam to finalize the departure paperwork for Chi and the children. They had been waiting for passports and visas to be approved for five months. The process was a complicated one that involved a series of interviews, character assessments, language tests, and scrutiny of the whole family. Chi's marriage overcame the stigma she had experienced as a divorced and childless woman.

After meeting Chi's husband, Yến re-evaluated her own future and that of her children. Without a father, they had experienced social and economic disadvantage and had been teased at school. Their education was important to Yến so the overseas aunt, who had acted as matchmaker for Chi, had explained the benefits of the education system in her local area. With her family's encouragement and support, Yến consented to marrying a neighbour of her aunt, a foreign man more than twenty years her senior. The agreement meant that Yến would be expected to work as housekeeper, cook and personal care attendant in exchange for her children's education at state secondary and post-secondary institutions.

In contrast to labour migration, marriage migration is often condemned in Vietnam as exploitative of women (Bélanger and Tran 2011, p. 64). Yet, some Vietnamese women value maternal love over conjugal love despite the social stigma mothers without husbands and children without fathers attract (Phinney 2008). Transnational marriage not only offered Yến an alternative to stigmatized gender status in Vietnam, but also a better future for her fatherless children. Her desire for international education in an English speaking context for her children reflects the value placed on education and foreign language competence in achieving social and economic success among Vietnamese. The children would also become familiar with life in an industrialized modern city where, even in unskilled work, their future employment prospects would be better than in Ho Chi Minh City. Further, Yến's teenaged daughter would be freed from Vietnamese gender expectations and any possible social stigma her future circumstances might attract, such as that her mother had suffered as a result of her failed marriage.

Yến had a change of heart after her sister's marriage to a foreigner. Moving abroad would enable her to make a long-term investment in her children's futures with the expectation that they would repay the debt at a later time and care for their mother in her advanced years. In doing so, Yến demonstrated that she was not ignorant nor naïve, which contrasted with Vietnamese state media portrayals of transnational brides, although she did employ a transnational strategy to mitigate stigma and conform to Vietnamese gender norms about the role of a wife-mother centred on emotional capital and caring for others. For Yến, a new aesthetic language involved drawing on a transnational strategy to ensure her relative autonomy and independence in line with westernized concepts of the self at the same time as conforming to localized ideals of responsible motherhood in sacrificing her own desires to foster the future prospects of her children.

Divorced or widowed women, such as Chi and Yến, can benefit from transnational marriage as a strategy to overcome the stigma associated with their reduced status positions. Their choices demonstrate that transnational marriage is a more effective alternative than education or employment in overcoming a less desirable status position generated by a stigmatized gender identity, i.e. being a single mother or failed wife, particularly for a woman over thirty who had returned to live with her natal family. While marriage does not seem to figure as prominently in the strategies for social mobility of the young and single among Ho Chi Minh City's new middle classes, women who have family responsibilities may benefit from transnational marriage solutions. For them, marrying transnationally may be less risky than taking no action to mitigate social stigma with regard to the prospects of their children who may gain new opportunities for achieving social mobility and a relatively higher standard of living beyond the structural constraints of Vietnamese society and inside the zone of influence of the competing discourses of other qualitatively different social institutions (Lahire 2008, p. 172).

WHAT ABOUT LOVE?

Among the many influencing factors, love was also a consideration for marriage. Like Hương and her mother, Diễm and her mother were conscious of finding the right man for her. The man Diễm's mother thought would make a suitable husband for her daughter resembled Vân's ideal husband (above), but Diễm had her own ideas about her future man. One evening, I met Diễm in front of the Youth Culture House (*Nhà Văn Hóa Thanh Niên*) and from there we walked along Đồng Khởi Street to a fashionable downtown café where we ordered coke floats and talked.

Diễm outlined her problem. She and her mother held contrasting views about the type of man a woman could marry without losing status. While her mother had a checklist of social and economic criteria that she applied to her daughter's potential partners, Diễm herself had only five criteria: love, admiration, passion, physical attraction, and mental attraction. Diễm explained that their different views stemmed from her mother being an educated Saigonese person who had grown up in a middle-class household in postcolonial Saigon. After 1975 her family had experienced downward mobility, so she idealized the good life that she had lived in her childhood and imposed the associated values on her daughters (see Hess 1977; Hoskins 1976).

Discussing her mother's ideas made Diễm roll her eyes; she found her mother's views outdated and conservative. Her views about middle-class girls were like those in literary templates such as *Truyện Kiều* (Tale of Kiều) (see Nguyễn Du 2000).[3] In 'The Traditional Roles of Women',

3 *Truyện Kiều* (Tale of Kiều) is regarded as the most widely known narrative poem in Vietnam and many Vietnamese, even the young, can recite its popular stanzas and passages. Composed in the early nineteenth century from Chinese sources, Kiều's story is one of an unfortunate daughter who experiences love, loss, trickery, kidnapping, abuse, slavery, revenge, and eventually happiness. In the course of the narrative, women are recognized in both capital-bearing and capital-accumulating roles that are enabled by social background, circumstance and access to resources. Kiều herself experiences a lifetime of unstable social position caused by periodic upward and downward mobility connected to her marital/sexual status. Although some aspects of Kiều's tale – such as Kiều choosing her own love interest, loving two men, and being tainted by prostitution – might seem to lend themselves to a

a literary exploration of class dispositions embodied by Vietnamese women, Công Huyên Tôn Nữ Thị Nha Trang (1973, pp. 83–155) identified a unified set of embodied attributes and social behaviours valued among elites and the middle classes. Nha Trang's reading outlines the importance of physical appearance and feminine behaviour in bearing cultural capital on behalf of the family. The role of education credentials is downplayed as secondary and paid employment is irrelevant because, as mothers, middle-class women would be responsible for socializing children and maintaining harmonious family relationships. Importantly, middle-class parents should aim to raise their daughters to achieve an enduring, preferably higher, status position through strategically arranged marriages. Embodied cultural capital and emotional capital outweigh all other forms of capital in this ideal of middle-class women's lives. Templates for middle-class girls are characterized by values and practices that aim to maintain the status quo by defending normative behaviours and reinforcing existing social positions (Bourdieu 1977, p. 169; see also Bourdieu 1998b). In other words, such models reinforced patrilineal kinship as the salient structure for women to advance socially.

As Jayne Werner (2009, pp. 2–3) reflects, communist discourses promoted ideals of equality in the family and, while Confucian family structures had been undermined, gender hierarchies remained. In *Between Sacrifice and Desire,* a study on urban femininity in Hanoi, anthropologist Ashley Pettus (2003, pp. 12–13) locates the middle-class housewife at the centre of the modern nuclear household where she is responsible for proper nutrition, hygiene, economic discipline, birth control, marital 'democracy' and good parenting, while also being expressly distanced from both the countryside and the market place. Pettus observes that, rather than employment, marriage was long favoured as the less risky means of achieving maximum profits in middle-class families. In Bourdieu's (1976) terms, Pettus' study demonstrates the narrow view that middle-class marriage is the business of the clan and community and that middle-class women reproduce class society through their roles within the family as mother and wife.

---

negative interpretation, her lot in life is regarded in Vietnamese tradition as fated and she is admired for surviving the difficult circumstances and personal challenges she faces. Because of this, Vietnamese women read randomly selected lines of *Truyện Kiều* to tell fortunes and make predictions for their own lives.

While the views expressed by Diễm's mother corresponded to literary and historical ideals of patrilineal kinship, they did not correspond with the views expressed in the autobiographies of other middle-class women in postcolonial Saigon. Against her father's wishes, Mai Elliott (1999, p. 307), for example, expressed a desire to pursue a free-choice marriage, to marry a foreigner for love and to marry a man of a lower social position. Elliott valued love over social status. Diễm's own views were more closely aligned with Elliott's views – or those of Shawn McHale's (1995, p. 188) modern urban 'new girl' – than those of her mother. Unlike her mother, Diễm foremost wanted to marry for love and desired gender equality between partners in a marriage. Like Cúc's friend Tấm, Diễm was attracted to the idea of marrying a foreigner who would not be preoccupied with Vietnamese traditions, nor worry about her advancing age. Such a marriage would be outside the zone of influence of Vietnamese genderized norms but would be constrained by other competing social logics with which Diễm was willing to conform.

Diễm circulated in an expatriate social world and her contact with (male) expatriates – the partners of her (Vietnamese) girlfriends – taught her that foreigners valued love over all else in a marriage. Diễm had been dating a Vietnamese man who had emigrated to the US, but she had not yet agreed to follow him as she did not want to leave her family nor Vietnam. Transnationalism could offer her secure status that she might risk losing if she remained in Vietnam. As Hung Cam Thai (2008, p. 119) points out, avoiding marriage with local men is a way for highly educated Vietnamese women to resist patriarchal arrangements and the oppression of a dominating husband. But it was also a way to maintaining new gender, social and economic status that might otherwise be lost. Marrying a Vietnamese man who shared the same familiar cultural dispositions and symbolic world but who lived abroad and beyond the structural constraints of Vietnamese society might offer a very desirable solution.

Mother and daughter were both concerned with finding a suitable husband, although their views about how this could be achieved were different. Diễm's mother defended Vietnamese conventions of marriage by focusing on normative ideals of patrilineal kinship, while Diễm herself challenged them by pursuing a modern ideal of love beyond the constraints and 'outside the zone' of influence of Vietnamese social institutions. However, Diễm's modern ideal of love was not new in middle-class urban Vietnam as it had been popularized in the twentieth century. For Diễm, a new aesthetic language drew on Vietnamese cultural traditions and modern westernized values to locate her in a space between the national and the global where she could be recognized by others for the status she had achieved without losing her Vietnamese self-identity. For her, marriage could function as an effective strategy to achieve a better future if she left Vietnam but only if the match was one based on romantic love.

FINDINGS

Marriage is a recognized strategy for women to gain social status, economic security and new experiences beyond the sphere of the natal family. In post-reform Vietnam, marriage strategies alone can be more risky for young middle-class women in realizing their desires for a better future. This chapter has explored changing values among educated urban migrant women concerning family life. It has outlined a range of attitudes to married life and single life in urban and rural social groups to highlight that there are diverse experiences of family life and changing perceptions about family roles which are evolving as families become more fragmented. Conventional models of femininity and womanhood represented in the state mass media are typically oriented to emotional capital and other forms of feminine gender normalcy. Conforming to gender normalcy offers limited means to move up socially, but new or fragmented family forms can provide more opportunities for accumulating cultural capital (Silva 2005, p. 100).

Evading Vietnamese gender norms, particularly expectations of women's submission, is important in new middle-class women's strategies to achieve social mobility. Absence from their natal families enables them to evade oppressive norms and live relatively autonomously but also to meet obligations to care and reciprocate in their natal family. Daughters can retain a decision-making role in their natal family after marriage especially if they have no brother or father, or if their husband is a foreigner and outside the zone of influence of Vietnamese cultural norms that relocate a wife's obligations to her husband's household. Engaging in a transnational marriage can overcome social stigma that derives from a less-than-ideal, or non-normative, gender status, such as divorce or delayed marriage, although it is not the only option available to new middle-class women in Ho Chi Minh City.

What is crucial to a new middle-class woman in her twenties differs from what is salient to her in her thirties and later. For young new middle-class women, the symbolic privileges of cultural capital achieved through education and employment are so effective that they can displace the benefits of emotional capital accumulated through marriage and children's achievements. For new middle-class women who have delayed marriage, ideas of marriage centre on maintaining or improving social status by not losing the gender status they have acquired through reconfigured social roles in the natal family. For other middle-class women who already have children, ideas of marriage also consider the future prospects of their children as much as their own personal happiness.

Despite social stigma derived from remaining single, in post-reform Ho Chi Minh City cultural capital in the form of education credentials and cultural competences is more enduring and more valuable for new middle-class women than emotional capital associated with family life. Nevertheless, family remains central in the process of socialization that forms encultured dispositions and reproduces class culture. When the intergenerational transmission of dispositions is multi-directional and criss-crosses generations (see Chapter 6), the conventional role of a wife and mother can also be reconfigured as the relative value of emotional capital decreases. Differential access to privileges enables individuals to transform themselves and exert an influence on others across multi-dimensional families, so long as the forms of capital they embody are deciphered as signals of cultural sophistication. In this sense, the reconfiguration of the role of a new middle-class wife and mother is one that contrasts with the ideology of the Vietnamese state.

CHAPTER EIGHT

Conclusion

T his book has revealed what it is like to become middle-class in Vietnam's mega-urban Southeast region, an inquiry that was centred within the daily lives of educated urban migrant women living and working in post-reform Ho Chi Minh City. I set out to explore the extent of change they experience in their lives and to investigate the nature of middle-class formation through their lifeworlds. In this chapter I present the resulting snapshot of new middle classes in Vietnam's Southeast. I also compare post-reform and postcolonial Saigonese middle classes as well as analyse similarities and differences between Vietnam's middle classes to those in East and Southeast Asia. Throughout the book, I have aimed to redress the gender blindness of class analysis to some extent by considering class in Vietnam through a gender-conscious lens in terms of agency in educated urban migrant women's lifeworlds. The following discussion sums up a number of reflections on the form and development of Vietnam's new middle classes in historical and globalized contexts.

A SNAPSHOT OF HO CHI MINH CITY'S NEW MIDDLE CLASS

The individual cultural portraits of new middle-class lifeworlds that I have explored incorporate a diverse range of embodied practices, tastes, attitudes and values that may be contradictory, but which are recognized by others to hold scarcity value and indicate cultural competence and relative betterment. As long as they are recognized, they can be understood as applying to some and not to others in order to differentiate and produce social distance. Not all individuals have the same access to resources, nor to the conditions that might enable them to achieve upward social mobility. The results of attempts to rise socially are different for different individuals. Those who come from relatively prosperous families, or families that are able to pool resources to fund the urban migration of their junior members for education and employment, are the ones who are most readily able to achieve a new status position. Individuals who comprise the emerging status groups of the urban middle classes in Vietnam are aspirational. For them, the advantage of cash wealth is less important than access to resources coupled with education and free time that can be spent on self-improvement and status production.

As I moved within the lifeworlds of educated urban middle-class women, the relative importance of cultural capital over economic capital was reflected in the changing value of capital-bearing and capital-accumulating practices in their family and working lives. In post-reform Ho Chi Minh City, strategies of urban migration and education enabled them to achieve new social positions, while a range of other social practices enabled them to consciously distinguish themselves and exclude others in order to produce social distance. The daily lives of Liên, Cúc, Hạnh, Thu, Tuyết, and others illustrate that established social processes and familiar cultural practices flourish in post-reform urban Vietnamese society, a context which has been assumed to encompass some of the most far-reaching social transformations of recent history. The insights offered in the experiences of these educated urban migrant women have allowed me to contribute to an understanding of social differentiation, social change and cultural adaptation after reform in Vietnam. Their experiences highlight the importance of continuities in managing social change and understanding that lived social relations operate within contexts characterized by contradictions, especially when family forms are fragmented or do not conform to an ideologically driven ideal. Faced with new conditions after reform, these individuals demonstrated that they could adapt by drawing on existing and recognizable modes of living. Participation and inclusion in a community is important for individuals who may desire to set themselves apart from each other but are also committed to remaining part of a family, neighbourhood, alumnae, or some other community where they are able to maintain a sense of belonging. Yet their absences from their family or community also became important in breaking from the past to realize the new prospects that a different path could offer.

Re-emerging middle classes and emerging urban status groups in post-reform Ho Chi Minh City reflect an increasing social differentiation of urban society, as well as the continuing engagement of Vietnamese with a variety of global networks. These engagements influence daily life on official and unofficial levels to impact on what it is like to live in contemporary urban Vietnam, a context that is highly differentiated not only socially and economically but also in terms of cultural influences. Recognizing these influences, whether direct or indirect, is analytically important in locating Vietnam's emerging middle classes within wider national and regional trends, including Southeast Asia's new rich and new middle-class status groups, and a history of colonial and postcolonial urban culture in Vietnam (see below). What also becomes apparent in recognizing these influences is that Vietnamese state discourses do not readily acknowledge the diversity of daily experience among the population. This is particularly apparent in genderized discourses, which are strongly shaped by ideologically driven norms.

In Ho Chi Minh City, it seems that a gap is evident between official state discourses centred on Vietnamese social life and the lived experience of aspirational and affluent city residents. The advice neighbourhood women gave me, when they recommended that I pay less attention to books and more attention to local opinions and attitudes, ultimately guided the approach that I took in investigating Ho Chi Minh City's emerging middle classes as it highlighted such a gap. Living among and spending time with educated urban migrant women revealed to me the textures, moods, rhythms and tastes of their daily lives, and shed light on how aspirational young women negotiate their participation in contemporary urban Vietnamese life. This approach emphasized the importance of finding out – as person-centred ethnographers aim to do – what it is like to live in post-reform Ho Chi Minh City and to differentiate between life lived and life talked about (Desjarlais 2003, p. 6; LeVine 1982, p. 293). In fieldwork I followed a rich source of connections, associations and relationships that continue to shape the lives of educated urban migrant women (Marcus 1995, p. 109). In doing so, I was led by the informants through the daily activities of their lifeworlds, an approach that involved being on the move rather than dwelling in a single field location, such as a cloth market (cf. Leshkowich 2000; Pettus 2003). The resulting snapshot of new middle-class life in Ho Chi Minh City highlights the experiences of the group of educated urban migrant women and exposes that, for the most part, they are not represented in official Vietnamese state discourse. This oversight is not only apparent for middle classes; neither is it apparent for educated urban women, for single women, for women with economic power, nor only in southern Vietnam. New middle-class women are one of the many socio-cultural groups that are not recognized by the state. There is a gap in the state's 'aerial map' of Vietnamese social life with respect to gendered, classed and metropolitan experience.

Like other emerging status groups in contemporary Vietnam, such as working-class labourers or entrepreneurs, Ho Chi Minh City's new middle classes neither represent a defined and officially recognized status group nor do they share a class consciousness. However, they do share a desire to live a better life and aspirations to build a more comfortable and more economically secure future. It is important to stress the influence of urbanization on social differentiation and new status group formation in post-reform Vietnam. Urbanization in Vietnam, a country characterized by its rural hinterland, is a salient factor in raising the population out of poverty through state-led development. The significance of class practices in post-reform Vietnamese society has come to the fore during a period of social transformation associated with the economic transition from state socialism to a market-oriented economy which has been accompanied by a greater awareness of the diversity of social structure, increasing social inequalities, and the continuing expansion of the urban Southeast. The transformation of post-reform urban Vietnamese society is assumed to have been widespread, profound, and dramatic. Yet it is not the first time that mass migration to Vietnam's Southeast has impacted on social life in the region, nor the first time that economic transformation has made its mark. The extent of change, as Martin Gainsborough (2010) notes, is perhaps over-stated.

Educated urban migrant women, in contrast with others in their neighbourhoods, especially low-skilled labour migrants, are well resourced, relatively autonomous and highly mobile in their daily lives. To explore the re-emergence of middle classes, I drew on concepts from Pierre Bourdieu's sociology which, in contrast to Marxian accounts of inequality, recognize that interacting axes of inequality are complex, historical and fundamentally cultural. By not singling out any one influential social condition over others, my reading of Bourdieu's sociology allows for a more complex analysis of the social world, where processes of social differentiation exert qualitatively different effects on an individual's ability to move up socially. Social institutions play a central role in classifying and 'gilding' individuals, initially through socialization processes in the family and later in education institutions. Under the influence of a normalizing social institution, it is possible for individuals to 're-classify' themselves in new higher status positions indicated by 'better' lifestyles.

I discovered that members of the emerging new middle class employ a new aesthetic language that draws on processes of social exclusion and makes challenges to social convention in the production and mitigation of social distance. This shows that a new aesthetic language paradoxically embodies change and draws on continuities in dispositions, tastes and particularized highly valued cultural signals. It seems to be generated among aspirational members of the new middle class during social upheaval, such as migration or economic reform, and especially when motivated by a desire to improve, or to re-establish, their social positions. Although developing during social change, a new aesthetic language employs the particularized highly valued cultural signals of that location and historical time. Common to it is the emergence of new ways of living and of dissonant tastes, reflecting changing attitudes and increasing diversity in social and cultural life. While some of the strategies employed within a new aesthetic language challenge existing ideals to compel social change, other strategies attempt to reinforce or reassert a sense of belonging through selective participation in conventional social life.

Understanding what it was like for educated urban migrant women to live in post-reform Ho Chi Minh City reveals the significance of migration to changing urban culture and the benefits that a social upheaval, or a 'turning point' in their life, may convey so long as the participating individual can adapt to the new conditions. Post-reform educated migrants moved individually and maintained contact with a multi-dimensional family back home through flows of communication, emotion and remittances. Because of this ongoing contact, their adaptations to urban life and their self-improvements are recognized at home, even though opportunities for making a professional white-collar career and living a middle-class leisure lifestyle are near impossible currently outside metropolitan areas and the largest urban centres in Vietnam. While the 'presence' of middle classes and social climbers might have a 'collective impact' on the urban landscape, as Lisa Drummond (2012,

p. 80) observes, small urban areas are not readily able to provide the conditions in which middle classes can flourish. Well-resourced rural residents may well be more able to move up socially than residents in small urban areas, especially if they have robust transnational resource networks in place. The major cities of Vietnam, particularly the mega-urban region of the Southeast, most readily provide the conditions for new middle classes to flourish. It is not just an urban but a metropolitan context that is important in the formation of new status groups.

Aspirational migrants arrive in the city to take up opportunities for education and work that are not possible at home in rural or small urban centres. In the city, they are able to access new types of leisure and recreation as well as witness new ways of living and engage in different forms of marriage, particularly late marriage. Living alone in the city – away from elders in the natal family – young women may gain relative autonomy in choosing how to live, even though they are initially supported by their elders. Their rise from relatively humble social origins involves a long-term investment in education and professional career that will provide the conditions to rise socially through the gradual development of the enduring dispositions of class culture not simply greater economic capital. Their gradual construction of a better life for themselves and their natal families is a process of re-socialization that involves making a break from the past and developing new tastes and preferences compatible with the desired future position. The results of this process vary for different individuals as they have different access to avenues for social mobility.

Life in Ho Chi Minh City may be less stable and less certain than the life that educated migrants left behind in the natal family home. Notwithstanding some risk, the opportunities available in the metropolitan area potentially offer greater rewards than those they could otherwise have achieved. Some families, such as the laneway shopkeeper Xuân's, had experienced downward mobility and, through migration to Ho Chi Minh City, they aimed to rebuild lost social position. In other families, such as Liên's and Thu's, which were fragmented having no surviving sons, a daughter took on a breadwinner role to lift the family out of poverty and improve their material comfort and status position. The younger members of larger families, such as Cúc and Tuyết, were supported by their older siblings to make a move to the city and extend the family's coffers of cultural and economic capital. For them also, it was a daughter who took on this responsibility. In families that lacked a father or sons, daughters could assume their roles. For these young women, the responsibilities they assumed in their adult lives contrasted with the roles they had been brought up hoping to fulfil. Rather than improving their individual positions through marriage, education and employment offered them a means for lifting themselves and their natal families out of impoverished or average circumstances to a relatively better social position. The instability and uncertainty that is generated by change in the form of economic reform may become an opportunity for them to join the ranks of the urban middle classes.

New middle classes negotiate instabilities and uncertainties in post-reform urban life in ways that may seem surprising. Graduate employees take advantage of unstable conditions in professional urban employment to better their positions by increasing their mobility within and between workplaces. By constantly renegotiating position and salary, as well as upgrading their qualifications, graduate employees are able to relatively improve their conditions, but also extend their social and professional networks to enhance their prospects for mobility. Unstable employment and under-employment can provide opportunities to move up socially. In working life, some graduate professional women benefit from reject-ing the embodied practices of conventional workplace femininity, while some graduate professional men benefit from adopting characteristics associated with femininity and the affective ties of emotional capital (Bourdieu 1998b; Reay 2004). Reconfigurations of gender normalcy can also provide opportunities to move up socially.

In family life, educated urban migrant women also negotiate insta-bilities and uncertainties in surprising ways. Because they focus on further education and developing a professional career, which while it might be lucrative might also be unstable, educated urban women tend to delay marriage and childbirth, in many cases until they are aged thirty or older. Young unmarried women may be able to free themselves from a double burden of professional and family work, suggesting that cultural capital accumulated outside the home is actually more valuable to young educated women than emotional capital accumulated through their relationships with a husband and children. This tendency seems to be incompatible with reassertions of traditional womanhood which have emerged in societies coping with dramatic social change. While they do not conform to normative gender expectations centred on mother-hood, educated urban migrant women do conform to other traditional female roles. As with Japan's parasite singles, they maintain loyalty to their parents in fulfilling the traditional role of a dutiful daughter by providing care and support to their natal family. Nevertheless, they reject, temporarily at least, hierarchical spousal relations and the role of a submissive daughter-in-law who cares and supports her husband's family. Even though educated women may achieve a relatively higher professional status, the choice to remain a daughter rather than become a wife and mother involves accepting a relatively low-rank status in the family and neighbourhood, as Vietnamese women traditionallly are not regarded to be complete adults until marriage. For an older woman, an alternative solution is to enter a transnational marriage which may en-able her to maintain her social, economic and gender status within the natal family and mitigate social stigma associated with single life within the zone of influence of Vietnamese social institutions. Moving beyond this zone of influence might also free a woman's own daughter from stigma stemming from the choices she might make in the future.

However, the new economic power of new middle-class women may enable them to claim new social power as daughters who contribute to decisions taken in the natal family, particularly if the family is fragmented, comprising few men or a foreign husband who lives abroad. This new economic power is reflected in their consumption practices. Class culture can be expressed through consumption practices and spending patterns, although, as Mark Liechty (2003, p. 67) observes, it is difficult to distinguish between classes solely on the basis of consumption. The family home is central to middle-class consumption in Vietnam; a middle-class life is family-oriented and centres on the home. Directing spending towards a family home that provides material comforts and a high standard of living marks a middle-class lifestyle. Spatial mobility is linked to upward social mobility and buying into an exclusive area can also mark class status. However, the desirability of particular assets and residential addresses is not stable. Ownership of a desired material object or asset operates like an academic qualification that acts as a certificate of cultural competence. Its value is recognizable to others but decreases as it gains in popularity and the stakes increase. The material benefits associated with an urban middle-class life are transmitted by daughters to their natal families where their symbolic value may be qualitatively different. Spending is not the only strategy that new middle-class women employ to build a new status position. Re-socialization through a long process of exposure to encultured dispositions marks cultural sophistication.

Single life in the city has other benefits. The lifestyling choices of educated urban migrant women demonstrate how they negotiate leisure and adapt to the changing urban landscape and emerging recreational spaces. Unexpectedly, they adapt their established and recognizable recreational practices to new social spaces, rather than creating new leisure options, in order to set themselves apart from others in the community and produce social distance. To differentiate themselves within their status groups, new middle-class women demonstrate aspiration and the capacity to achieve distinction through processes that involve the recognition of cultural competence to determine who has achieved, who is able to develop, and who merely imitates a cultural veneer. While these practices aim to distinguish, other practices they employ aim to enhance a sense of belonging. They may selectively participate in popular neighbourhood activities to claim a place within their surroundings and demonstrate that they continue to belong to the community. Some middle-class practices aim to mitigate social distance.

New middle-class culture in Ho Chi Minh City is a migrant culture that challenges urban conventions and introduces new practices as rural connections are maintained and regionalized culture may be celebrated. In this way, new middle classes do not 'take off' completely as they remain anchored to their families and reliant not only on their resources but also selected dispositions of their childhood. Such dispositions may be recognized as highly valued cultural signals of authentic regionalized culture reflecting that new middle classes, while physically absent from home, have not completely rejected their origins to 'lose their roots' (*mất gốc*). At the same time, they engage with globalized and foreign cultural influences that 'rub off' on them in the socially and culturally diverse context of a mega-urban region. Consequently, a diverse palate of social and cultural practices characterizes their daily experience. The dispositions of their cultural palate may be deciphered by others as conveying status. It is not the first time that migrants have played a significant role in revivifying urban culture in Saigon / Ho Chi Minh

City, a context that has been regarded as cosmopolitan at least since the mid twentieth century. Inconsistencies and contradictions in tastes are typical of a modern globalized urban context. Cultural dissonance results from the diversity of practices that can be recognized for what is valuable at a particular time and place, indicating that class culture is not characterized by a cultural homophily but by being dynamic, polysemic and flexible. Its instability might be a source of anxiety for some, but can also be a source of excitement and adventure for others.

A snapshot of new middle classes in Ho Chi Minh City reveals that they enjoy a good life characterized by a high level of material comfort and better economic prospects than many. They may not have economic security and may rely on loans to make major purchases or investments. They may be particularly vulnerable to periods of unemployment and the effects of global economic crisis. Nevertheless, they have no shortage of funds for day-to-day living. They are able to mitigate risk by relying on a family network through which they can draw on resources but also contribute to the family's coffers. They possess high levels of formal education as well as diverse experiences of, and knowledge about, regionalized traditions and globalized cultural influences. Education, experience and knowledge is expanded for new middle classes through contact primarily with metropolitan areas, especially the mega-urban Southeast which offers the best opportunities for study, work and social contact. Urban migration is one of the ways that aspirational families equip junior members to rise socially. These families tend to be simultaneously outward looking and supportive of the state so long as their interests are maintained. The rise of their young people has been facilitated in part by state education, although they are beginning to voice criticisms of its perceived limitations. New middle classes express class culture through leisure, consumption and embodied practices, which have taken new forms for young educated women. Middle-class culture in Vietnam is family-oriented; however, marriage is no longer the most salient means for younger women to move up socially. But transnational marriage may have become the most effective means for mature women to overcome social stigma stemming from delayed marriage or divorce. New middle-class women are able to achieve new gender status on a basis of their increased economic power and relative autonomy from the family, status which has not reverted back to pre-reform norms.

VIETNAM'S MIDDLE CLASSES IN THE LATTER TWENTIETH AND TWENTY-FIRST CENTURIES

Understanding what it was like to live among middle classes in postcolonial Saigon in the mid to late twentieth century reveals a number of continuities with what it is like to live among middle classes in post-reform Ho Chi Minh City. Autobiographical memoirs of life in postcolonial Saigon written by educated middle-class women provide a snapshot that reveals their lifeworlds (see Chapter 2). While I am mindful of the limitations of comparing a handful of autobiographies with a handful of individual cultural portraits, comparisons of these snapshots are useful in mapping the paths the development of Vietnam's middle classes has taken.

Urbanization is an important condition for the rise of middle classes. Postcolonial and post-reform urban middle classes were migrants, although their motivations to migrate differed. In the postcolonial era, as a result of war when whole families were forced to flee, they lost their wealth, assets and social status. In the southern capital, where many ended up, they were faced with adapting to new ways of living in order to cope, belong and achieve. For young people, in particular, this social upheaval interrupted, dislocated and often destroyed the dreams and aspirations that they had held for themselves and which their natal families had held for them. Postcolonial Saigon provided opportunities for them to rebuild their lives. In the post-reform era, as a result of economic reform new opportunities for employment and education became available in Ho Chi Minh City and individual migrants were attracted to the industrializing zones of the Southeast. The majority were young women equipped with education and skills and they left their natal families prior to marriage when they set out for the Southeast. The opportunities generated by economic reform expanded their horizons and offered a new future to them individually as well as to members of their families who remained in their natal villages.

The snapshots of Vietnamese middle-class life provided in postcolonial women's self-writing and in the post-reform lifeworlds of educated urban migrant women reveal a number of important overlaps in their experiences. They share a sense of self-identity centred on home and family that is not simply aligned with national culture but also imbued with regionalized variants associated with tastes and desires stemming from their childhood memories of a particular place in a particular time before change. Since they are young and not yet married, the influence of the natal family on their individual selves is the most significant, although their schooling and the messages of the mass media are also important. While they are relatively autonomous in their daily lives, living beyond the physical location of the natal family, their individual agency continues to operate within the zone of influence and structural constraints of these social institutions. In postcolonial and post-reform urban Vietnam, a range of genderizing social norms remain powerful but operate with differential efficacy. Considering that gender is a lived social relation, the extent of influence of normative discourses and individual responses to them change over time and with respect to any new circumstances they face. As Lois McNay (2004, p. 185) argues, normative discourses can be defended, challenged and reconfigured by individuals to meet their differing needs. Some women might achieve new social power stemming not only from social conditions but also from individual circumstances.

The individual circumstances of and social conditions faced by middle classes in postcolonial Saigon and post-reform Ho Chi Minh City differ in several important aspects. Their origins contrast. Some of the authors of the autobiographies, such as Ho Xuan Huong (2002), originated in the rural south but most, such as Mai Elliott (1999) and Nguyễn Thị Thu-Lâm (1989), were from the urban North and their flight involved transnational migration from postcolonial North to South. While urban migrants in post-reform Vietnam arrive in the Southeast from nearly every other province in Vietnam, the educated urban migrant women came from the Mekong Delta, like Cúc and Liên, and the Central Coast, like Thu. The combined impact of their migrations has contributed to building the mega-urban region in Vietnam's Southeast. Its origins stem from wartime evacuations to the city, where migrants lived with poor infrastructure and overcrowding. Its expansion was facilitated by economic reform, where migrants no longer settled in the inner city but occupied formerly agricultural land in the developing urban fringes. Many migrants initially lived with poor infrastructure but benefited from the new opportunities available in the booming southern economy.

They had different motivations to move to the urban Southeast, but once they had arrived they faced new social conditions that required them to adapt in order to make the most of their situations. The young women had left behind a familiar world and found a qualitatively different world. The postcolonial refugees encountered this new world with their families, while the post-reform migrants faced it alone, without their parents but sometimes with a sibling, cousin or niece. For them, migration was not forced but formed part of a long-term strategy that involved planning, resourcing and participation of various members of the natal family.

Both postcolonial and post-reform middle classes share an aspiration to improve their social positions; the former seek to rebuild their lost status, wealth and material assets and the latter seek to acquire new status, economic security and a higher standard of living. Their resources are invested directly for this purpose and rewards are distributed to individuals across the natal family. Some families may be content to achieve a relatively good standard of living, such as the shopkeeper Xuân's family had done. While the family's social standing in post-reform Ho Chi Minh City was modest in contrast with their prior position, they were safe, comfortable and healthy. The family's loss of social and economic capital was caused by war and their regaining of it was enabled by state-led economic reform. They had experienced a pattern of mobility that involved the rapid loss and slow regain of their social position.

When the position of the family becomes relatively stable, even if it has not yet reached its peak and even if some family members are still on the rise individually, resources can be directed outside the family to others in more needy circumstances. A commitment to charity and philanthropy was evident among many of the middle-class women in the autobiographies as well as in the post-reform city. Tuyết, for example, was able to direct resources within her natal family as well as outside. Achieving an enduring status position may take longer for larger families, but they may have better circumstances from which to ascend as they have a greater capacity to pool resources. However, if they start from a lower position their ascension would involve greater investment and might also take longer to achieve and more resources to maintain.

Family backgrounds of postcolonial and post-reform middle classes are comparable. Almost all come from non-military and non-political backgrounds. The majority of the families represented in the autobiographies were large urban nuclear families, such as Nguyễn Thị Thu-Lâm's

(1989), that had been supported by a breadwinner father who worked in the postcolonial civil service or in business. The natal families of the educated young women in the post-reform era, such as Hạnh's and Cúc's, relied on more diverse sources of income stemming from agricultural and other fresh produce businesses. After relocation to Saigon / Ho Chi Minh City, the nature of household incomes changed as daughters and junior family members were no longer simply dependents but also contributed significantly to family finances. It is worth noting that across the examples from postcolonial and post-reform eras, the families were, or became, fragmented; many comprised of women – mother, aunts, daughters – with few or no men. Some families had many daughters and few sons. For others, family members were physically separated. This resulted not only from the imprisonment, loss or military service of a father and/or brothers and sisters, but also from their temporary absences due to work commitments involving travel or long hours as well as international study. Transnational marriage was another way that family members were separated, although this affected more daughters than sons.

The fragmentation of families meant that daughters had opportunities to take up different roles. Their responsibilities were extended beyond childhood study and recreation to include higher education or advanced training for a profession that, in the postcolonial era, would help alleviate a wartime labour shortage and boost household income to rebuild family coffers and, in the post-reform era, would help staff the growing enterprises that emerged with industrialization of the Southeast. Daughters could take up new responsibilities to contribute to funding improved living standards and building enduring social status within the natal family. The new opportunities available to young women in the wartime and post-reform economies sprung up to address an immediate need but became ingrained so that social expectations changed. The new responsibilities that women were able to take up did not simply disappear but became part of a new way of living. Nira Yuval-Davis and Floya Anthias (1989) argue that new opportunities presented to women during dramatic social change which reconfigure their social roles rarely revert back to original expectations. The earning capacity of educated urban women in Saigon / Ho Chi Minh City outstripped that of men which potentially reconfigured an idea of a male household breadwinner. Even when this was the case, Vietnamese men may continue to expect to control the household (Thai 2008, p. 87).

In the labour markets of postcolonial and post-reform Saigon / Ho Chi Minh City, there are notably comparisons in the consequences of employment for young and single middle-class women. The jobs that they filled were feminized in line with cultural expectations about feminine character and suitable fields of work for junior ranked and unmarried women. In the postcolonial era, the civil service expanded to provide new positions for young women, such as Mai Elliott (1999), and with a high turnover of staff jobs were widely available for middle-class women to secure. In the post-reform era, the non-state sector offered the most lucrative and rewarding opportunities for young women, such as Thu, and they pursued work in a range of fields that, like civil service work, included general office work such as secretarial, interpreting and administrative positions. The growth of the service sector and office-based work did not displace the wide availability of petty trade and artisan family enterprises but created new opportunities for alternative sources of employment for young women.

Education was one of the steps bringing new opportunities to young middle-class women in the city in the postcolonial and post-reform eras. Many opportunities available in urban workplaces required an underpinning level of education. In a competitive job market with an oversupply of educated workers, the stakes may increase so that higher levels of minimum qualifications are necessary to win a position. In both contexts, graduates faced high rates of un- and under-employment, young women might also be faced with part-time, insecure, or irregular work. Employers and their staff conformed to a gender division of labour based on inherent genderized characters that saw women placed in particular, often lower-skilled, positions and men in positions comprising more seniority, more responsibility and more opportunity for promotion.

Nevertheless, some women – especially young and unmarried women – had some advantages at work and were able to earn salaries as well as take on new challenges and experiences. Possessing the valued skills of office communication and administration offered young women remarkable opportunities through their workplaces not only to earn relatively high and/or relatively stable salaries which might convey economic power, but also to expand their social networks beyond the sphere of kin which could transform their potential to accumulate cultural capital by exposing them to new cultural influences and new ways of living. Even with powerful normative discourses of appropriate womanhood circulating, some middle-class women were able to evade the restrictions of a patrilineal culture to reconfigure their gender roles. Wartime conditions played an important role in this change during the postcolonial era for middle-class women such as Thinh Hoang (1989), while in the post-reform era it was the expansion of the sectors most dominated by women that was among the most significant effects for women such as Hạnh. It is worth questioning what impact such transformations might have on the men with whom they work, live and love.

Social change stemming from political reform and war during the postcolonial era and driven by economic reform in the post-reform era was reflected in the value parents placed on education, especially the education of daughters. The purpose of women's education evolved as women were mobilized to meet labour supply needs in the wartime economy and in the industrializing zones of the Southeast. Urban schools and universities were expanded and places became widely available for women. Moreover, parents understood the value of educating daughters not only in terms of their possible contributions to the household economy. Educating daughters potentially enabled them to gain independence in travelling beyond the home unaccompanied, their own economic security if they later built a career, and equality as they could be judged on their own skills and merits. An educated young woman, such as Le Kwang Kim (1963, p. 464), might come to exist in her own right. A family comprising educated daughters was one that possessed greater coffers of cultural capital and its accumulation conferred status on the family, as Ngàn Hac Tráng's (1995, p. 75) father realized. Even when a daughter did not rely on her education for employment, it could gild her. The gilding of daughters with institutionalized cultural capital – in addition to the embodied form – was new.

While education might enable young women to be judged in their own right, the family remained significant in defining their self-identities. One of the most noticeable transformations in young middle-class women's lives was that marriage in Vietnam seemed to lose its efficacy in facilitating social status. In their autobiographies, middle-class women in postcolonial Saigon reported delaying marriage, separating from or divorcing their Vietnamese husbands, or marrying foreign men who were outside the zone of influence of Vietnamese social norms. Marriage to a foreigner could free a middle-class woman, such as Uyen Loewald (1987) or Nguyễn Thị Thu-Lâm (1989), from the stigma of her past status in postcolonial Saigon. Le Kwang Kim (1963, p. 468) did not remarry but worked and took on the breadwinner role to support her child and mother, as Yến had initially chosen to do. In the post-reform era, young middle-class women delayed marriage until their thirties at least. A few, such as Tuyết, married Vietnamese men who were also aspirational urban migrants from large rural families. Other middle-class women, particularly those who were facing stigmatized social positions stemming from divorce, separation and single parenthood, opted for transnational marriages with foreign men. Marriage was favoured as less risky strategy for middle-class women to move up socially only for those who experienced stigma that resulted from having delayed marriage too long or failed at a previous relationship. This indicates that middle-class women may reject submission and hierarchical spousal relationships but they may conform to marriage based on an ideal of equality, such as Diễm did. By rejecting a norm of early marriage and remaining in the natal home, middle-class women could become agents of social change and exert an influence on family structure and social roles. Postcolonial urban households were increasingly nuclear, but this was affected by restrictions on urban space imposed by overcrowding and the fragmentation of families as members were lost or absent. Post-reform urban households were also ideally nuclear, but as families also became fragmented, other configurations were also apparent, for example, when adult daughters, such as Yến or Chi, had returned to the natal home.

In the twentieth and twenty-first centuries, Saigon / Ho Chi Minh City has represented a place of hope but also a place of some risk. The influence of the city extends beyond its limits to rural areas and many Vietnamese are familiar with an idea of the southern capital without necessarily having visited there. Such an idea of Saigon, which contrasts with the hardships of an honest rural life, is associated with material assets and embodied practices as well as attitudes, dispositions, knowledge and experience. On the one hand, city life is bustling and exciting. It offers new people to meet, new activities to enjoy and new places to visit.

On the other hand, it is sprawling and potentially threatening involving strangers, pollution, noise, overcrowding and traffic.

In the city, middle-class lives are marked by material comfort in the forms of basic household infrastructure, such as electricity and plumbing, and modern appliances in the home, private forms of transport and the latest trends in entertainment and technology. The knowledge and experiences available in metropolitan areas – such as translated foreign literature and national classics; knowledge of elaborate and expensive traditional ceremonies and kinship rituals; foreign language learning; and direct contact with cultural outsiders from other regions of Vietnam and abroad – can mark an individual imbued through a long process of class cultural socialization to an enduring status position. In their interactions with others, they can be exposed to cultural dispositions that might 'rub off' on them, such as when Nguyễn Thị Thu-Lâm (1989, pp. 113–14) learned to sing the memorized lyrics of foreign pop songs, or Diễm imitated a Canadian boyfriend taking home restaurant leftovers. These practices might seem strange to some, but to others who are able to recognize their value, they may be deciphered as indicating cultural sophistication.

The signals of cultural sophistication are not stable and evolve over time. Within a particularized context, globalized and localized cultural influences are differentially valued. The attitudes and dispositions that middle-class women embody reflect their orientations to globalized and localized cultural influences associated with class status. Class cultural attitudes and dispositions can be expressed through fashion and appearance. Embodied practices are imbued with cultural meanings that are recognizable to others who share in a particularized symbolic world. A young middle-class woman can express her choices to embrace or reject a modern and globalized appearance or a traditional and localized one through her clothing and physical appearance. Traditional Vietnamese feminine norms value white skin and sleek long black hair, which contrast with a westernized femininity comprising makeup and curly hair as worn by Mai Elliott (1999) or Tuyết. Clothing also reflects encultured dispositions. Vietnamese traditional garments, such as a peasant blouse and loose fitting trousers worn daily by Xuân or a simple printed suit worn to the late night noodle stall by Liên, contrast with a westernized appearance that ranges from a straight skirt or jeans worn in the workplace by Cúc, a blazer worn by her to a rural classmate's wedding party, or an evening gown worn by Liên to an urban classmate's wedding party. Unless these choices are recognizable to others as cultural signals they hold little value and may even convey the wrong status. Modern and westernized appearances might be more difficult for those beyond the middle classes to decipher. Urban middle-class women at first appeared to Le Ly Hayslip (1989, p. 113) as no different from low-class bar girls and she had to learn the highly valued signals of class culture that they embodied in their appearances. Recognizing a westernized appearance not as reflecting cultural sophistication but prostitution was also noted by Mai Elliott (1999, p. 307) in the postcolonial era and by Jayne Werner (2009, p. 4) of the state mass media in the post-reform era. Conforming to gender normalcy, including appearance norms, conveys limited status for women as it may go unrecognized as a strategy (Skeggs 2004, p. 22). But challenging or rejecting gender normalcy risks being deciphered incorrectly by others.

Embodying class culture involves more than simply following the lead of others and imitating their appearances. Beyond the family, young educated women might become agents of change through their paid employment. Educated women in Ho Chi Minh City seem to benefit most from opportunities for employment in the foreign and private sectors, particularly when they remain single. Their opting out of the state sector and delaying marriage can generate new configurations of gender which may set the standard for others to follow. Young women might resist gendered expectations by rejecting gender norms in their workplaces, as they did in the mid-1980s when they avoided teaching and other feminized professions (Marr 1988, p. 19). They might conform to some but reject other aspects of workplace performances of femininity, such as Tuyết did when she adhered to Vietnamese norms but avoided the globalized femininity of her colleagues. By relegating herself, she received incentives to 'catch up' and compete equally with her peers. For new middle-class men, adopting qualities of naturalized femininity in performances of workplace gender may confer status through highly valued cultural signals associated with a global-oriented middle-class culture. New status positions have been increasingly defined by mobile relationships to gender performance, with more flexible gender codes evident among urban middle classes (Adkins 2001, p. 691). These examples mirror an observation made by Ann Marie Leshkowich (2011, p. 284) that femininity has become 'a marketable skill' among entrepreneurs and traders in post-reform Ho Chi Minh City. Femininity as cultural capital can be recognized in embodied practices through appearance norms as well as dispositions that are expressed through behaviours.

Vietnam's middle classes are aspirational and share a desire to rise. For postcolonial middle classes, this was a desire to rebuild lost status, while post-reform middle classes desired to achieve a new status position and relatively better standard of living. Their positions were threatened by competition from outsiders and those with greater economic or political capital. While those with rapidly acquired wealth did not generally challenge the cultural sophistication of middle classes, the social power they could exercise as a result of their significant economic capital threatened to displace the social power accumulated by educated and cosmopolitan new middle classes. A fear of falling indicates that their positions are not yet secure and they are vulnerable not only to the consequences of individual action but also to structural constraints, such as political upheaval, war or financial crisis.

The path that characterizes the development of Vietnam's middle classes from the mid twentieth to the early twenty-first centuries is one of modulation. Urban middle classes began to rise socially and were faced with a loss of social, economic and political capital that saw them fall temporarily at the end of the colonial era. In postcolonial Saigon, they once again rose as they rebuilt their lost status, or acquired new status. They faced another loss of social, economic and political capital that again saw them fall temporarily at the end of the war. In the post-reform era, urban middle classes began to rise again with the conditions of state-led economic reform that aimed to lift the population out of poverty. New attention has been focused on Vietnam's urban middle classes in the twenty-first century, which contrasts with the state's omission of urban middle-class experience in the latter twentieth century.

HO CHI MINH CITY'S NEW MIDDLE CLASS AS AN ASIAN MIDDLE CLASS

Pacific Asia's middle classes are very diverse but share a range of salient features. It is useful to analyse to what extent new middle classes in Vietnam's Southeast resemble other Asian middle classes. While exposure to war, conflict and revolution differed across Southeast Asia in the twentieth century, up to half a century of post-war economic development has enabled the emergence of small but influential middle classes in cities across the region. Shiraishi Takashi (2008, p. 4) observes that Thai, Filipino, Malay and Indonesian middle classes have all developed in different political and social structures, by different paths, and with different successes. Middle-class formation in mega-urban Bangkok, Metro Manila, the Klang Valley and Jakarta Metropolitan Area has been viewed as a third wave subsequent to the formation of colonial Asian and post-war Northeast Asian middle classes. In this path-dependent pattern, middle-class formation in coastal cities of China follows Southeast Asia as a latecomer. This raises the question of where Vietnam would fit in this pattern: To what extent is class formation in Vietnam's mega-urban Southeast akin to the emergence of Southeast Asia's middle classes and to the case of China with which it shares a Confucian-influenced society and a socialist past?

While patterns in the formation of Asian middle classes have been identified, the diversity of Asia's middle classes cannot be overlooked. Historical conditions, including experiences of colonialism and achievement of independence as well as economic conditions stemming from nation building and post-authoritarian development are among the most influential factors that have generated diversity among Southeast Asian middle classes. Hattori, Funatsu and Torii (2003, p. 130) stress the diverse characteristics that middle classes in Pacific Asia acquired in the course of their development: Singapore and Hong Kong are unique contexts in lacking a rural hinterland; Thailand and the Philippines saw slow rural–urban migration, while South Korea and Malaysia experienced rapid rural–urban migration. On this point, Vietnam's Southeast can be similarly differentiated from its industrialized neighbours due to its particularized historical and economic development but also grouped with Greater Seoul (South Korea) and the Klang Valley (Malaysia) in that Vietnam's Southeast has also experienced waves of rapid urbanization.

Definitions of class based on occupational status and consumption practices have become the central approaches to analysing Asian middle classes. Distinguishing between new status groups based on their education credentials, employment security and standard of living provides a foundation for interpreting their lifestyle preferences, attitudes and outlook. As Cynthia Bautista (2001b, p. 270) summarizes, in Metro Manila the individuals who are most able to achieve social mobility and maintain enduring new status positions belong to the urban service class or new middle class. Members of the new middle class are predominantly metropolitan-based and they rely on education to gain secure employment, particularly in regular salaried positions as professionals, administrators, officials, managers and supervisors of non-manual employees in the non-state sector. Their education and employment underpins the lifestyle that enables the development of their outlook which other employment conditions cannot readily achieve. But, as Bautista (2001b, pp. 270–1) qualifies, occupations are not necessarily determinants of lifestyles and attitudes, and white-collar employees do not automatically share class identities. In contrast to new middle classes, the petty bourgeoisie comprising small proprietors and artisans (or old middle class) and other routine non-manual workers (or marginal middle class) find it much more difficult to achieve and maintain comparable social positions. This observation has also been made in urban China where education and secure employment characterize new middle classes with traders and entrepreneurs not regarded to be really middle-class (Li Chunling 2010, p. 145). Thomas Heberer (2003, p. 64) also distinguishes traders and entrepreneurs from political and professional middle classes in China and Vietnam.

Locating middle classes in the middle of urban society between the new rich and entrepreneurs who occupy relatively higher positions and working classes who occupy relatively lower positions seems straightforward, as Michael Hsiao (2010, pp. 255–6) suggests for well-off urbanites in China's middle. But, there is more to middle-class lifestyling than a middle income, average education and typical white-collar occupation. Lifestyles and consumption practices play a part in the differentiation of urban classes, as observed in Thailand and across Asia (Limmanee et al. 2001, p. 471; Vorng 2011; see also Koo 2006). Mark Liechty (2003, p. 67) regards middle classes to locate themselves in the space in between globalized and nationalist consumption practices aligned with other status groups. Chua Beng Huat (2000a, p. 23) suggests that, with the possession of desired status goods, aspirational status groups can climb up 'rungs of the consumption ladder' into a middle-class position. Indonesian new middle classes in Yogyarkarta and Padang report a simplified consumption ladder stemming from a folk model of social differentiation based on two rungs: a poverty line and a consumption line. This three-fold division separates the absolute poor and new rich and differentiates 'those with enough' in the middle in real and symbolic terms (Gerke 2000, pp. 142–3). Locating middle classes in the middle of society places them in a space where others can observe and imitate their practices as a strategy to move up to join them, or ridicule and mock them as a strategy to remain socially superior to them.

Across Asia, middle classes are heterogeneous. Dealing with the diversity of Southeast Asia's middle classes in analysis has presented several issues. In Academia Sinica's East Asia and Southeast Asia Middle Class projects, for example, India, China and Indonesia were excluded as their size and diversity made it difficult to develop a cogent case of middle-class formation across the whole Pacific, postsocialist and South Asian region (Hattori, Funatsu and Torii 2003, p. 130). Despite this, recent research on the rise of global middle classes centres particularly on India and China due in part at least to the size and power of their new consumers and middle classes (e.g. Donner 2011; Fernandes 2006; Hsiao 2013; Lange and Meier 2009; Li Cheng 2010; Rolandsen 2011).

In analysis of Southeast Asian middle classes, dichotomies also present a problem. A lack of dialectical engagement is evident when traditional culture is contrasted with modernity, national culture is contrasted with globalization, and rural life is contrasted with urban life as though there is no connection between them, even when middle classes are located in the middle of society in the space 'between'. Such contrasts fail to explain observable social phenomena, for example, in Thailand where circular urban migration between cities and villages overcomes a rural–urban divide (Hattori, Funatsu and Torii 2003, pp. 137–8; see also Mills 2012; Vorng 2011). A rural–urban divide loses its relevance also in Vietnam when 'in between' identities are generated for migrants moving between rural families and urban employment (Nguyen Tuan Anh et al. 2012, p. 1105). These dichotomies assume that identities are imbued by a cultural homophily that is generated through particularized social space or geographic location. In urban middle-class women's lives, too, modern and traditional lifestyles are contrasted as though they are not connected. For example, in China images in the women's mass media contrast an adorned modern women with a traditional virtuous wife (Hooper 1998, p. 167). Vietnamese state ideology also contrasts women's choices, demonizing their engagement with globalized influences often exemplified by prostitution and promoting wholesome nation-oriented womanhoods of the reform era (Werner 2009, p. 4). The problem presented by dichotomies can be overcome by recognizing cultural dissonance as a feature of the field and addressing social practices that take place between individuals across geographic locations in terms of a singular field of interaction that incorporates diversity and encompasses rural and urban, traditional and modern, male and female (Lee and Piper 2003, p. 126).

It is the young and single with education that are regarded to achieve most readily new middle-class status across Southeast Asia and China. For Chua Beng-Huat (2000a, p. 14), a window for building an urban middle-class lifestyle through unlimited consumption opens in the years between adolescence and marriage for twenty-something singles in Singapore. For Annie Hau-Nung Chan (2000, p. 105), new middle classes in Hong Kong are also singles aged between 25 and 35. They are locally born, highly educated and financially independent. They hold secure non-manual salaried jobs and command higher than average incomes. While these examples from the Asian city-states contrast with industrializing nations of Southeast Asia with a rural hinterland where some members of multi-dimensional families are located, they highlight a lack of gender-consciousness in analysis of middle-class experience. In contrast, Laura Dales (2005, pp. 133–6) recognizes an emerging type of female agency among educated urban professionals in Japan – 'parasite singles' – who, even after they have graduated and begun working professionally, remain living with their parents. They are located between the modern and globalized consumer-oriented lifestyles of the middle class and the traditional role of an unmarried daughter who cares for her parents in their old age. Unlike the singles of Asia's cities, single women in Vietnam are portrayed by the state as victims, not agents of change (Martin 2010, p. S7). Further, young women who choose to become transnational brides in Vietnam are represented in the state mass media as ignorant and naïve (Bélanger, Khuất and Tran 2013, p. 95).

Considerations of class in Southeast Asia do not only overlook gender agency; some overlook agency in general. Richard Robison (1998, p. 63) regards middle classes in Asia to be 'products of sets of social and economic dynamics that require change', but not as agents of change. Yet educated urban migrant women in Vietnam's Southeast play a key role in rebuilding family status or achieving new status. Urbanized daughters in multi-dimensional families may become agents of change and influence the structures that previously ensured their subordination. The burden of reproducing new status positions is regarded to be the work of women, as Bourdieu (1998b, p. 68) observed. But Nirmala PuruShotam (1998, p. 127) argues while maintaining a better life 'imprisons' women, it also 'brings access' to knowledge enabling them to question their subordination and pressure the state for a new place in an established social order. As women move up the social hierarchy, they are less pressured to conform to gender norms (Bourdieu 1984, pp. 382–3). A fear of falling and losing newly achieved independence, autonomy and status can generate new ways of being middle-class also (PuruShotam 1998, p. 130; Ehrenreich 1989).

Rather than only focusing on themselves, new middle-class women are concerned with improving the status of their families as well. Gendered experiences of middle-class lifestyles are family-oriented, as Nirmala PuruShotam (1998, p. 137) highlights for Singapore where middle-class women's lifestyles are oriented to family life and their spending is directed by wives to improving material comfort of the family home and maintaining their own physical and sexual attractiveness. In Metro Manila, middle-class life is a family-oriented life also. There, middle classness is neither associated with singlehood nor non-productive women (Bautista 2001b, p. 280). Like them, new middle classes in Vietnam's Southeast are family-oriented and direct their spending to their families, even when they remain single, to improve their material circumstances and future prospects.

Members of the first-generation new middle class in Southeast Asia, as Abdul Rahman Embong (2002, p. 62) explains, generally come from lower-class backgrounds. Even though they have achieved a new class position, their experiences of poverty and hardship during childhood make them empathetic towards peasants and working classes, including their own kin. Despite becoming urbanized, they foster close links between themselves and their extended kin (Embong 2002, p. 93). In a multi-dimensional family, knowledge remittances from new middle-class members of the family can provide exposure to highly valued cultural signals that are recognized as cultural capital. This exposure can provide daily experience as part of the long process of socialization through which enduring class culture is formed (Koo 2006, p. 13). In Ho Chi Minh City, educated urban migrant women transmit their knowledge and experience to members of their natal families, especially to cousins and nieces who also hope to move to the city. This exposure can give them a head start in developing dispositions that can be recognized as indicating class culture. Directing their resources to the benefit of others reflects an accumulation of emotional capital uniquely associated with the work of women in the family.

New middle classes in Ho Chi Minh City share features with first- and second-generation middle classes in mega-urban Southeast Asia and urban middle classes in China. Social change and economic development gave rise to Asia's middle classes. While first-generation middle classes in Southeast Asia benefit from ties to the state and they support the state so long as their interests are maintained, with the rise of democratic movements in capitalist Southeast Asia, their loyalties can no longer be guaranteed (Hsiao 2006, pp. 7–8). Urban middle classes may resist the state in the form of opting out. In Vietnam, new middle-class professionals opt out of poorly paid but secure state sector jobs to focus on opportunities in the non-state sector. In Vietnam's non-state sector, it can also be difficult to achieve stable employment and economic insecurity. Those who are unable to compete might opt out of salaried employment to pursue work in private business (Leshkowich 2006; Turner and Nguyen 2005). Women who marry well might opt out of professions and into homemaking after marriage, as suggested by a relatively high proportion of housewives in Ho Chi Minh City (Gubry et al. 2010, p. 74).

New middle classes in Vietnam are beginning to show signs of less reliance on the state education system, which no longer matches their pretensions, not only through the teaching of socialist ideology but also through a perceived lack of quality in education. Their resistance is evident in a shift into local private schooling, off-shore international programs, or international schooling. This shift reflects an increase in the education stakes as the relative prestige of state qualifications has lost value due to greater numbers of individuals possessing degrees and diplomas. The level and field of qualifications and the prestige of an in-stitution that a student seeks have value when they are based not only on coffers of economic capital in the form of fee-paying university courses, but also on cultural capital and gilding that stems from dispositions acquired through the process of study and which mark the graduate as one with cultural sophistication and learning.

Relying less on the state is an indicator of the consolidation of middle classes in enduring social positions in Southeast Asia. As in Ho Chi Minh City, Jakarta's new middle class are independent of the state or only indirectly dependent on government-related occupations (Dhakidae 2001, p. 508). But this situation contrasts with Malaysia, where Embong (2006a, p. 148) notes a 'remarkable' difference between first-generation new middle classes who relied on government jobs and second-generation new middle classes who have a preference for private sector employment or setting up a private business. In Malaysia, new middle-class parents preferred their sons to become doctors, engineers or IT professionals and their daughters to study medicine, education or accountancy and to work in the private sector or their own businesses. State employment was a 'last resort' (Embong 2002, pp. 90–1). Across Southeast Asia, urban middle classes diversify their sources of employment to achieve greater income security. In the Philippines, for example, research by Cynthia Bautista (2001b, pp. 271–2) revealed downtown corporate managers in Metro Manila who were also employed in family businesses and non-manual workers in the government sector who moonlighted to boost their incomes. While new middle classes depend on the state – initially through state-led development, state education and perhaps state employment – the family also is a reliable source of support for new middle classes in Asia, particularly through businesses operated within a multi-dimensional family.

Vietnamese new middle classes have relied on state-led development and state education in pursuing their aspirations for upward social mobility. They have remained supportive of the state so long as their interests have been maintained. In Vietnam's major cities, there are growing signs that middle classes are becoming restless and moving beyond state control (King, Nguyen and Nguyen 2008, p. 794). Their opting out of state sector employment and state-funded education may be regarded as a challenge to the state in the form of resisting structures that ensure subordination. While it is unlikely that this will lead to a political challenge to the state in Vietnam in the short term, as participation in political and democratic institutions is considerably lower than other Southeast Asian nations (Douglass et al. 2008, pp. 314–17), it may set the standard for others to follow. Middle classes can become trendsetters for others to emulate and imitate, as David Goodman (1996) points out concerning urban lifestyling and Michael Waibel (2009) suggests concerning sustainable living practices in Ho Chi Minh City.

Southeast Asia's first generation of new middle classes argues Abdul Rahman Embong (2001, p. 16) were 'beholden to the state'. In Vietnam, social change experienced and initiated by middle classes has been linked to a privileged background, education credentials, travel abroad and exposure to different ways of doing things (Gainsborough 2002, pp. 701–2). However, as Ben Kerkvliet (1995, pp. 399–400) observed, the relationship between the state and society in Vietnam became a continuous, dynamic interaction that varied in intensity from 'lethargic' to 'animated'. Even for those with close ties to the state, Ashley Carruthers (2002, p. 429) noted, it was extremely difficult for Vietnamese nationals to accumulate valued types of cultural capital, including foreign university degrees, bilingualism and cosmopolitanism. Political connections convert to limited opportunities for occupational mobility in Vietnam and those opportunities are concentrated in the north (Kim 2004, pp. 199–200; Thomsen 2011). While Victor King (2008, p. 97) assessed that the Vietnamese state plays an 'inordinately important' role in moulding the social class structure in Vietnam, it seems that the state has not fully kept up to date with urban class development. As Jayne Werner (2009, p. 76) noted, Vietnamese state discourses no longer meet the needs of post-reform society.

One point that the Vietnamese state emphasizes which remains relevant is that education can be a step towards a better future. Education is the most important predictor of success for rural–urban migrants in mega-urban regions of the developing world (Koo 1978, p. 297). First-generation new middle classes come from diverse social origins but possess homogenous education (Hattori, Funatsu and Torii 2003, p. 138). Education enables individuals from all sectors of society to move up socially. In China, the expansion of higher education has allowed the new middle class to come from any family or community (Lin and Sun 2010, p. 217). In Manila, Kuala Lumpur, Jakarta and Bangkok, the accumulation of cultural capital in the form of education credentials is the factor that distinguishes new middle classes from their parents (Bautista 2001a, p. 111; Dhakidae 2001, pp. 509–10; Embong 2002, p. 69; Limmanee et al. 2001, p. 471). Also in Vietnam, education is the key avenue to achieving a better life (Bélanger and Pendakis 2009, p. 280).

Education alone is not enough to achieve a new class position. While education offers the possibility of lifting the population out of poverty, the actual outcomes of education are not the same for all. Different individuals enter institutions from different starting points and education credentials from different institutions are differently valued. Further, wider access to education decreases the symbolic value of credentials and increases the minimum entry requirements. In urban China, for example, higher education has become a minimum condition for employment as almost all government officials and professionals are graduates (Lin and Sun 2010, p. 219). Alvin So (2006, pp. 30–1) predicts that second-generation middle classes in Southeast Asia will be relatively disadvantaged in the job market by the eroded value of credentials which may result in their status positions being more 'precarious' and 'insecure' than their parents. Middle classes face insecurity and uncertainty because the value of their coffers of cultural capital changes. Their 'shared project' of marking out a space in between other status groups and cultural influences, as described by Mark Liechty (2003, p. 67), is never finished; status production is an ongoing process. Some middle classes find the process generates insecurity and anxiety, while others find this uncertainty exciting and full of the hope of a better future.

To distinguish themselves as privileged from others who are stable or vulnerable, Hagen Koo (2006, p. 10) suggests that new middle classes need to rely not only on salaried income but also on job security and durable investments. To remain competitive in the job market, Abdul Rahman Embong (2006a, p. 149) suggests that the second generation will need to supplement their university education with other highly valued competences such as language and communication skills. This is already the case in Ho Chi Minh City, where graduates supplement their qualifications with skills and experience that sets them apart from others. Learning a second foreign language, or acquiring native speaker fluency, are among the communication skills that a graduate might develop to get ahead in Ho Chi Minh City's competitive non-state labour market.

Gaining work experience in a new or emerging field, such as human re-source management or public relations, is an alternative to embellishing formal qualifications with practical and desirable skills. In this regard, the highly competitive job market encountered by second-generation Malay middle classes is comparable to the job market in Vietnam's urban Southeast. In post-reform Ho Chi Minh City, first-generation middle classes share some similarities with second-generation Southeast Asian middle classes. Even though Vietnam has been labelled a 'latecomer' (e.g. Chua 2009, p. 102), aspects of middle-class mobility in Ho Chi Minh City appear to have been somehow accelerated. The formation of middle classes in Vietnam, while taking a qualitatively different path to development, have more in common with the rise of middle classes across Southeast Asia than expected or presumed.

New middle classes in Malaysia and China remain optimistic about the future. In Malaysia, professionals with secure employment are not only adventurous in seeking better jobs that offer higher salaries, experience and job satisfaction, but also confident in securing new employment (Embong 2006a, p. 150). China's new middle classes are generally satisfied and optimistic; however, they remain somewhat uncertain about their future health, happiness, lifestyles and prospects. The uncertainty that new middle class professionals in China feel is much lower than entrepreneurs and similar to that of blue-collar work-ers (Hsiao 2010, p. 257). As in Malaysia and China, new middle classes in Vietnam, Mexico, Chile and Spain are generally optimistic happy and satisfied (King 2008, p. 95). However, there is little sense of optimism in *Reinvention of Distinction*, an edited volume centred on Vietnam's urban middle classes. Lisa Drummond (2012, p. 80) describes urban lifestyles in Vietnam's capital Hanoi as 'precarious, experimental, testing, grasp-ing, aspirational, uneasy, consumerist, uncomfortable'. For her, they are imbued with a 'sense of tentativeness' deriving from an ambiguous relationship between the socialist state and an urban middle class. A sense of tentativeness extends across various practices of Vietnam's mid-dle classes. For Erica Peters (2012, p. 55), Vietnam's colonial middle classes demonstrated it when they 'could never be sure' that their claims on status were recognized in a constantly renewing culinary landscape of taste. For Elizabeth Vann (2012, p. 166), middle-class consumption in Vietnam 'has always been an uncertain enterprise' as consumption practices are 'fragile, difficult, complicated, contradictory, and even political'. Recognizing that cultural dissonance is a feature of the field goes some way to overcoming the problems that stem from assuming a cultural homophily and interpreting the changing value of cultural capital as difficult, complicated and contradictory.

There is no doubt that urban middle class in Vietnam have been growing in size and social power in the post-reform era. Martin Gainsborough (2002, p. 700) observed that Ho Chi Minh City's middle classes were yet to 'flex their muscles' in the 1990s. In the 2000s, Vietnam's urban middle classes began to attract increasing attention due in part to their new economic role but also due to the wide circulation of their practices as social and cultural influences. While the political priorities of market reform in Vietnam focused on continuity with the socialist past, the case of middle-class development in Vietnam's Southeast is further complicated by its asynchronous political history and unique contemporary social context. Indeed both aspects of postcolonial differentiation and mega-urban development have not been the focus of Vietnamese state discourses (Nguyen-Marshall 2004, p. 157; Werner 2009, p. 76). This presumes that the influence of particularized historical context and social conditions are salient to class formation. Yet, acknowledging the diversity of social, cultural, ethnic and political contexts across Southeast Asia leads to a realisation that while particularized dispositions – in the form of highly valued cultural signals – are recognized to mark status within certain cultural landscapes, their particularity is not shared across all middle classes and does not retain its value in qualitatively different contexts. Within Vietnam, middle classes are diverse and their dispositions are characterized by cultural dissonance whether they are located in Ho Chi Minh City, Hanoi or the provincial city of Buôn Me Thuột in the Central Highlands. Ho Chi Minh City's new middle classes, although qualitatively different, are aspirational new status groups that share features with other middle classes across Southeast Asia and postsocialist China.

References

Adkins, Lisa 2001. 'Cultural Feminization: "Money, Sex and Power" for Women', *Signs: Journal of Women in Culture and Society,* Vol. 26, No. 3, pp. 669–95.

—— 2004. 'Reflexivity: Freedom or Habit of Gender?', in Lisa Adkins and Beverley Skeggs (eds), *Feminism After Bourdieu.* Oxford: Blackwell Publishing, pp. 191–210.

Agergaard, Jytte and Vu Thi Thao 2011. 'Mobile, Flexible, and Adaptable: Female Migrants in Hanoi's Informal Sector', *Population Space Place,* Vol. 17, pp. 407–20.

Anderson, Benedict 1991. *Imagined Communities: Reflections on the Origin and Spread of Nationalism,* rev. ed. New York: Verso.

Avieli, Nir 2005a. 'Roasted Pigs and *Bao* Dumplings: Festive Food and Imagined Transnational Identity in Chinese–Vietnamese Festivals', *Asia Pacific Viewpoint,* Vol. 46, No. 3, pp. 281–293.

—— 2005b. 'Vietnamese New Year Rice Cakes: Iconic Festive Dishes and Contested National Identity', *Ethnology,* Vol. 44, No. 2, pp. 167–87.

—— 2011. 'Dog Meat Politics in a Vietnamese Town', *Ethnology,* Vol. 50, No. 1, pp. 59–78.

—— 2012. *Rice Talks: Food and Community in a Vietnamese Town.* Bloomington: Indiana University Press.

—— 2013. 'What is "Local Food?" Dynamic Culinary Heritage in the World Heritage Site of Hoi An, Vietnam', *Journal of Heritage Tourism,* Vol. 8, No. 2–3, pp. 120–32.

Balaban, John (ed. and transl.) 2000. *Spring Essence: The Poetry of Ho Xuan Huong.* Port Townsend, WA: Copper Canyon Press.

Balaban, John and Nguyen Qui Duc (eds) 1996. *Vietnam.* San Francisco: Whereabouts Press.

Barsegian, Igor 2000. 'When Text Becomes Field: Fieldwork in "Transitional" Societies', in Hermine De Soto and Nora Dudwick (eds), *Fieldwork Dilemmas: Anthropologists in Postsocialist States.* Madison: University of Wisconsin Press, pp. 119–29.

Bautista, Cynthia 2001a. 'Composition and Origins of the Middle Classes', in Hsin-Huang Michael Hsiao (ed.), *Exploration of the*

Middle Classes in Southeast Asia. Taipei: Program for Southeast Asian Studies, Academia Sinica, pp. 91–149.

—— 2001b. 'Images of the Middle Classes in Metro Manila', in Hsin-Huang Michael Hsiao (ed.), *Exploration of the Middle Classes in Southeast Asia*. Taipei: Program for Southeast Asian Studies, Academia Sinica, pp. 267–98.

—— 2006. 'Beyond the EDSA Revolts: The Middle Classes in Contemporary Philippines Development and Politics', in Hsin-Huang Michael Hsiao (ed.), *The Changing Faces of the Middle Classes in Asia-Pacific*. Taipei: Academia Sinica, pp. 167–86.

Beck, Ulrich 2002. 'The Cosmopolitan Society and Its Enemies', *Theory, Culture and Society*, Vol. 19, No. 1–2, pp. 17–44.

Bélanger, Danièle and Khuất Thu Hồng 2002. 'Too Late To Marry: Failure, Fate or Fortune? Female Singlehood in Rural North Việt Nam', in Jayne Werner and Danièle Bélanger (eds), *Gender, Household, State: Doi Moi in Viet Nam*. Ithaca: Cornell University Southeast Asia Program, pp. 89–110.

Bélanger, Danièle, Khuất Thu Hồng and Trần Giang Linh 2013. 'Transnational Marriages between Vietnamese Women and Asian Men in Vietnamese Online Media', *Journal of Vietnamese Studies*, Vol. 8, No. 2, pp. 81–114.

Bélanger, Danièle and Katherine Pendakis 2009. 'Daughters, Work, and Families in Globalizing Vietnam', in Magali Barbieri and Danièle Bélanger (eds), *Reconfiguring Families in Contemporary Vietnam*. Stanford: Stanford University Press, pp. 265–97.

Bélanger, Danièle and Tran Giang Linh 2011. 'The Impact of Transnational Migration on Gender and Marriage in Sending Communities of Vietnam', *Current Sociology*, Vol. 59, No. 1, pp. 59–77.

Bélanger, Danièle, Lisa B. Welch Drummond and Van Nguyen-Marshall 2012. 'Introduction: Who Are the Urban Middle Class in Vietnam?', in Van Nguyen-Marshall, Lisa B. Welch Drummond and Danièle Bélanger (eds), *The Reinvention of Distinction: Modernity and the Middle Class in Urban Vietnam*. Dordrecht: Springer, pp. 1–17.

Bennett, Tony 2007. 'Habitus Clivé: Aesthetics and Politics in the Work of Pierre Bourdieu', *New Literary History*, Vol. 38, No. 1, pp. 201–28.

Bennett, Tony, Mike Savage , Elizabeth Silva , Alan Warde , Modesto Gayo-Cal and David Wright 2009. *Culture, Class, Distinction*. London: Routledge.

Beresford, Melanie 1993. 'The Political Economy of Dismantling the "Bureaucratic Centralism and Subsidy System" in Vietnam', in Kevin Hewison, Richard Robison and Garry Rodan (eds), *Southeast Asia in the 1990s: Authoritarianism, Democracy and Capitalism*. St Leonards: Allen and Unwin, pp. 215–36.

Beresford, Melanie and Dang Phong 2000. *Economic Transition in Vietnam: Trade and Aid in the Demise of a Centrally Planned Economy*. Cheltenham: Edward Elgar.

Bourdieu, Pierre 1974. 'The School as a Conservative Force: Scholastic and Cultural Inequalities', transl. by J.C. Whitehouse, in John Eggleston (ed.), *Contemporary Research in the Sociology of Education*. London: Methuen.

—— 1976. 'Marriage Strategies as Strategies of Social Reproduction', in Robert Forster and Orest Ranum (eds), *Family and Society: Selections from the Annales: Economies, Sociétiés, Civilisations*. Transl. by Elborg Forster and Patricia M. Ranum. Baltimore: Johns Hopkins University Press, pp. 117–44.

—— 1977. *Outline of a Theory of Practice*. Transl. by Richard Nice. Cambridge: Cambridge University Press.

—— 1984. *Distinction: a Social Critique of the Judgement of Taste*. Transl. by Richard Nice. London: Routledge and Kegan Paul.

—— 1990a. *In Other Words: Essays Towards a Reflexive Sociology*. Transl. by Matthew Adamson. Stanford: Stanford University Press.

—— 1990b. *Logic of Practice*. Transl. by Richard Nice. Cambridge: Polity Press.

—— 1993a. *Sociology in Question*. Transl. by Richard Nice. London: Sage.

—— 1993b. *The Field of Cultural Production: Essays on Art and Literature*. Ed. by Randal Johnson. Cambridge: Polity Press.

—— 1996. *State Nobility: Elite Schools in the Field of Power*. Transl. by Lauretta C. Clough. Cambridge: Polity Press.

—— 1997. 'The Forms of Capital', transl. by Richard Nice, in A.H. Halsey, Hugh Lauder, Phillip Brown and Amy Stuart Wells (eds), *Education: Culture, Economy, and Society*. Oxford: Oxford University Press, pp. 46–58.

—— 1998a. 'Social Space and Symbolic Space', transl. by Gisele Sapiro, ed. by Brian McHale, in *Practical Reason: On the Theory of Action*. Cambridge: Polity Press, pp. 1–13.

—— 1998b. 'The Family Spirit', transl. by Richard Nice, ed. by Randal Johnson, in *Practical Reason: On the Theory of Action.* Cambridge: Polity Press, pp. 64–74.

—— 1998c. 'The "Soviet" Variant and Political Capital', transl. by Gisele Sapiro, ed. by Brian McHale, in *Practical Reason: On the Theory of Action.* Cambridge: Polity Press, pp. 14–18.

—— 2001. *Masculine Domination.* Transl. by Richard Nice. Cambridge: Polity Press.

Bourdieu, Pierre and Jean-Claude Passeron 1979. *The Inheritors: French Students and Their Relation to Culture.* Transl. by Richard Nice. Chicago: University of Chicago Press.

Boym, Svetlana 1994. *Common Places: Mythologies of Everyday Life in Russia.* Cambridge, MA: Harvard University Press.

Bradley, Mark Phillip 2009. *Vietnam at War.* Oxford: Oxford University Press.

Buckley, Christopher 1999. 'How a Revolution Becomes a Dinner Party: Stratification, Mobility and the New Rich in Urban China', in Michael Pinches (ed.), *Culture and Privilege in Capitalist Asia.* London: Routledge, pp. 208–29.

Bui Thu Huong 2010. 'Let's talk about sex, baby': Sexual Communication in Marriage in Contemporary Vietnam', *Culture, Health and Sexuality,* Vol.12, No. S1, pp. S19–S29.

Butler, Judith 1990. *Gender Trouble: Feminism and the Subversion of Identity.* New York: Routledge.

Butler, Judith 1999. 'Performativity's Social Magic', in Richard Schusterman (ed.), *Bourdieu: A Critical Reader.* Oxford: Blackwell, pp. 113–28.

Carruthers, Ashley 2002. 'The Accumulation of National Belonging in Transnational Fields: Ways of Being at Home in Vietnam', *Identities: Global Studies in Culture and Power,* Vol. 9, No. 4, pp. 423–44.

Castles, Stephen and Mark J. Miller 2003. *The Age of Migration: International Population Movements in the Modern World,* 3rd ed. Houndmills: Palgrave Macmillan.

Chan, Annie Hau-Nung 2000. 'Middle-Class Formation and Consumption in Hong Kong', in Chua Beng Huat (ed.), *Consumption in Asia: Lifestyles and Identities.* London: Routledge, pp. 98–134.

Cheng, Xi 2002. 'Non-Remaining and Non-Returning: The Mainland Chinese Students in Japan and Europe since the 1970s', in Pal Nyiri and Igor Saveliev (eds), *Globalizing Chinese Migration: Trends in Europe and Asia*. Aldershot: Ashgate, pp. 158–72.

Chua Beng Huat 2000a. 'Consuming Asians: Ideas and Issues', in Chua Beng Huat (ed.), *Consumption in Asia: Lifestyles and Identities*. London: Routledge, pp. 1–34.

—— (ed.) 2000b. *Consumption in Asia: Lifestyles and Identities*. London: Routledge.

—— 2009. 'From Small Objects to Cars: Consumption Expansion in East Asia', in Hellmuth Lange and Lars Meier (eds), *The New Middle Classes: Globalizing Lifestyles, Consumerism and Environmental Concern*. Dordrecht: Springer, pp. 101–15.

Clifford, James 1997. 'Spatial Practices: Fieldwork, Travel, and the Disciplining of Anthropology', in Akhil Gupta and James Ferguson (eds), *Anthropological Locations: Boundaries and Grounds of a Field Science*. Berkeley: University of California Press, pp. 185–222.

Cohen, Mitchell 1992. 'Rooted Cosmopolitanism: Thoughts on the Left, Nationalism and Multiculturalism', *Dissent*, Vol. 39, No. 4, pp. 478–83.

Collins, Ngan 2005. 'Economic Reform and Unemployment in Vietnam', in John Benson and Ying Zhu (eds), *Unemployment in Asia*. London: Routledge, pp. 176–93.

Công Huyền Tôn Nữ Thị Nha Trang 1973. 'The Traditional Roles of Women as Reflected in Oral and Written Vietnamese Literature', Unpublished Ph.D. Thesis, University of California, Berkeley.

Coughlin, Richard 1950. 'The Position of Women in Vietnam', Unpublished paper, Southeast Asian Studies, Yale University.

Cvetičanin, Predrag and Mihaela Popescu 2011. 'The Art of Making Classes in Serbia: Another Particular Case of the Possible', *Poetics*, Vol. 39, pp. 444–68.

Dales, Laura 2005. 'Lifestyles of the Rich and Single: Reading Agency in the "Parasite Single" Issue', in Lyn Parker (ed.), *The Agency of Women in Asia*. Singapore: Marshall Cavendish, pp. 133–57.

Daloz, Jean-Pascal 2008. 'Towards the Cultural Contextualization of Social Distinction', *Journal of Cultural Economy*, Vol. 1, No. 3, pp. 305–20.

Dân Số Thành Phố Hồ Chí Minh: Kết Quả Tổng Điều Tra Ngày 01-04-1999 [Population of Ho Chi Minh City: Census Results 01-04-1999]. 2000. Ho Chi Minh City: Ban Chỉ Đạo Tổng Điều Tra Dân Số và Nhà ở Thành Phố Hồ Chí Minh.

Dang Nguyen Anh 2002. 'Migration Patterns and Economic Development in Viet Nam', *Vietnam Social Sciences,* No. 3, pp. 89–96.

Dang Nguyen Anh 2008. 'The Mega-Urban Transformations of Ho Chi Minh City in the Era of Doi Moi Renovation', in Gavin W. Jones and Mike Douglass (eds), *Mega-Urban Regions in Pacific Asia: Urban Dynamics in a Global Era.* Singapore: NUS Press, pp. 185–213.

Đặng Thanh Trúc 1996. 'Môi Trường Đô Thị và Hành Vi Phạm Pháp của Thanh Thiếu Niên' [The Urban Environment and Delinquent Behaviour of Youth], in Trịnh Duy Luân (ed.), *Tìm Hiểu Môn Xã Hội Học Đô Thị* [Understanding Urban Sociology]. Hanoi: Nhà Xuất Bản Khoa Học Xã Hội.

Đặng Thùy Trâm 2007. *Last Night I Dreamed of Peace: The Diary of Dang Thuy Tram.* New York: Harmony Books.

Dapice, David, Jose Gomez-Ibanez and Nguyen Xuan Thanh 2010. *Ho Chi Minh City: The Challenges of Growth.* Ho Chi Minh City: United Nations Development Programme in Vietnam.

Delanty, Gerard 2012. 'A Cosmopolitan Approach to the Explanation of Social Change: Social Mechanisms, Processes, Modernity', *The Sociological Review,* Vol. 60, No. 2, pp. 333–54.

Desjarlais, Robert 2003. *Sensory Biographies: Lives and Deaths Among Nepal's Yolmo Buddhists.* Berkeley: University of California Press.

Dhakidae, Daniel 2001. 'Lifestyles and Political Behaviour of the Indonesian Middle Classes', in Hsin-Huang Michael Hsiao (ed.), *Exploration of the Middle Classes in Southeast Asia.* Taipei: Program for Southeast Asian Studies, Academia Sinica, pp. 475–513.

Đỗ Thái Đồng 1991. 'Modifications of the Traditional Family in the South of Vietnam', in Rita Liljestrom and Tuong Lai (eds), *Sociological Studies on the Vietnamese Family.* Hanoi: Social Sciences Publishing House, pp. 69–83.

Donner, Henrike (ed.) 2011. *Being Middle-class in India: A Way of Life.* New York: Routledge.

Douglass, Mike and Huang, Liling 2007. 'Globalizing the City in Southeast Asia: Utopia on the Urban Edge: The Case of Phu My Hung, Saigon', *International Journal of Asia Pacific Studies,* Vol. 3, No. 2, pp. 1–42.

Douglass, Mike, Trung Quang Le, Cameron Kawika Lowry, Hao Thien Nguyen, Anh Nguyen Pham, Nghi Dong Thai and Hernani Yulinawati, 2008. 'The Livability of Mega-Urban Regions in Southeast Asia: Bangkok, Ho Chi Minh City, Jakarta and Manila

Compared', in Gavin W. Jones and Mike Douglass (eds), *Mega-Urban Regions in Pacific Asia: Urban Dynamics in a Global Era.* Singapore: NUS Press, pp. 284–319.

Drummond, Lisa 2004. 'The Modern "Vietnamese Woman": Socialization and Women's Magazines', in Lisa Drummond and Helle Rydstrøm (eds), *Gender Practices in Contemporary Vietnam.* Singapore: Singapore University Press, pp. 158–78.

Drummond, Lisa 2012. 'Middle Class Landscapes in a Transforming City: Hanoi in the 21st Century', in Van Nguyen-Marshall, Lisa B. Welch Drummond and Danièle Bélanger (eds), *The Reinvention of Distinction: Modernity and the Middle Class in Urban Vietnam.* Dordrecht: Springer, pp. 79–93.

Duong Thi Thanh Lien 1973. *Vietnamese Dishes.* Tacoma: Golden Dragon Trading Company.

Duong Thi Thoa (Le Thi) and Mark Sidel 1998. 'Changing My Life: How I Came to the Vietnamese Revolution', *Signs: Journal of Women in Culture and Society,* Vol. 23, No. 4, pp. 1017–29.

Earl, Catherine 2004. 'Leisure and Social Mobility in Ho Chi Minh City', in Philip Taylor (ed.), *Challenges to Reform: Social Inequality in Vietnam.* Singapore: ISEAS, pp. 351–79.

—— 2008. 'Longing and Belonging: An Ethnographic Study of Migration, Cultural Capital and Social Change among Ho Chi Minh City's Re-emerging Middle Classes', Unpublished PhD thesis, Victoria University.

—— 2010. 'Vietnam's "Informal Public" Spaces: Belonging and Social Distance in Post-Reform Ho Chi Minh City', *Journal of Vietnamese Studies*, Vol. 5, No. 1, pp. 86–124.

Edwards, Anastasia (ed.) 2003. *Saigon: Mistress of the Mekong: An Anthology.* New York: Oxford University Press.

Ehrenreich, Barbara 1989. *Fear of Falling: The Inner Life of the Middle Class.* New York: Pantheon.

Elfick, Jacqueline Tse-Mui 2010. 'Transnational Consumer Culture and Middle Class Professionals: An Ethnographic Account of Consumption and Identity in Post-Reform China.' Unpublished PhD thesis, The Hong Kong Polytechnic University.

Elliott, David W.P. 2003. *The Vietnamese War: Revolution and Social Change in the Mekong Delta, 1930–1975.* Armonk: M.E. Sharpe.

Elliott, Mai Van Duong 1999. *The Sacred Willow: Four Generations in the Life of a Vietnamese Family.* New York: Oxford University Press.

Embong, Abdul Rahman 2001. 'Introduction', in Abdul Rahman Embong (ed.), *Southeast Asian Middle Classes: Prospects for Social Change and Democratization.* Bangi, Selangor: Penerbit Universiti Kebangsaan Malaysia, pp. 13–30.

——2002. *State-Led Modernization and the New Middle Class in Malaysia.* Houndmills: Palgrave.

—— 2006a. 'Between Optimism, Contestation and Caution: The Second Generation Middle Classes in Malaysia', in Hsin-Huang Michael Hsiao (ed.), *The Changing Faces of the Middle Classes in Asia-Pacific.* Taipei: Academia Sinica, pp. 133–54.

——2006b. 'Malaysian Middle Classes Studies: A New Research Agenda', in Hsin-Huang Michael Hsiao (ed.), *The Changing Faces of the Middle Classes in Asia-Pacific.* Taipei: Academia Sinica, pp. 155–65.

Enyedi, Gyorgy 1996. 'Urbanization Under Socialism', in Gregory Andrusz, Michael Harloe and Ivan Szelenyi (eds), *Cities After Socialism: Urban and Regional Change and Conflict in Post-Socialist Societies.* Cambridge: Blackwell, pp. 100–18.

Espin, Oliva M. 1999. *Women Crossing Boundaries: A Psychology of Immigration and Transformations of Sexuality.* New York: Routledge.

Eyal, Gil, Ivan Szelenyi and Eleanor Townsley 1998. *Making Capitalism Without Capitalists: Class Formation and Elite Struggles in Post-Communist Central Europe.* London: Verso.

Fahey, Stephanie 1998. 'Vietnam's Women in the Renovation Era', in Krishna Sen and Maila Stivens (eds), *Gender and Power in Affluent Asia.* London: Routledge, pp. 222–49.

Fernandes, Leela 2006. *India's New Middle Class: Democratic Politics in an Era of Economic Reform.* Minneapolis: University of Minnesota Press.

Fleischer, Friederike 2010. *Suburban Beijing: Housing and Consumption in Contemporary China.* Minneapolis: University of Minnesota Press.

Forbes, Dean 1990. *Urbanisation and Urban Growth in Vietnam, 1979–1989.* International Population Dynamics Program Research Note No. 111, 14 June. Canberra: Australian National University.

Friedmann, John 2002. 'Placemaking as Project? Habitus and Migration in Transnational Cities', in Jean Hillier and Emma Rooksby (eds), *Habitus: A Sense of Place.* Aldershot: Ashgate, pp. 299–316.

Gainsborough, Martin 2002. 'Political Change in Vietnam: In Search of the Middle-Class Challenge to the State', *Asian Survey*, Vol. 42, No. 5, pp. 694–707.

—— 2010. *Vietnam: Rethinking the State.* London: Zed Books.

Gammeltoft, Tine 1999. *Women's Bodies, Women's Worries: Health and Family Planning in a Vietnamese Rural Community.* Richmond: Curzon Press.

General Civil Service Commission 1967. 'Vietnamese Women in Civil Service', in *Women in Vietnam: Selected Articles from Vietnamese Periodicals, Saigon, Hanoi, 1957–1966.* Transl. by Chiem T. Kiem. Honolulu: Center for Cultural and Technical Interchange Between East and West, University of Hawai'i, pp. 1–22.

Gerke, Solvay 2000. 'Global Lifestyles Under Local Conditions: the New Indonesian Middle Class', in Chua Beng Huat (ed.), *Consumption in Asia: Lifestyles and Identities.* London: Routledge, pp. 135–58.

Giang Thanh Long, 2010. *Taking Advantage of the Demographic Bonus in Viet Nam: Opportunities, Challenges, and Policy Options.* Hanoi: United Nations Viet Nam.

Goodman, David S.G. 1996. 'The People's Republic of China: the Party-State, Capitalist Revolution and New Entrepreneurs', in Richard Robison and David S.G. Goodman (eds), *The New Rich in Asia: Mobile Phones, McDonald's and Middle-Class Revolution.* London: Routledge, pp. 225–42.

GSO (General Statistical Office) 2001. *1999 Population and Housing Census: Census Monograph on Marriage, Fertility and Mortality in Viet Nam: Level, Trends and Differentials.* Hanoi: Statistical Publishing House.

—— 2008. *Ho Chi Minh City Statistical Yearbook, 2007.* Hanoi: Statistical Publishing House.

—— 2011a. *Age–Sex Structure and Marital Status of the Population in Viet Nam,* Hanoi: General Statistics Office of Vietnam.

—— 2011b. *Education in Vietnam: An Analysis of Key Indicators.* Hanoi: General Statistics Office of Vietnam.

—— 2011c. *Migration and Urbanization in Vietnam: Patterns, Trends and Differentials,* Hanoi: General Statistics Office of Vietnam.

—— 2011d. *The 1/4/2011 Population Change and Family Planning Survey: Major Findings.* Hanoi: General Statistics Office of Vietnam.

GSO & UNDP (General Statistical Office and United Nations Development Program) 2001. *1999 Population and Housing Census: Census Monograph on Internal Migration and Urbanization in Viet Nam.* Hanoi: Statistical Publishing House.

Gubry, Patrick, Le Thi Huong, Tran Thi Thanh Thuy, Nguyen Thi Thieng, Pham Thuy Huong and Vu Hoang Ngan 2010. 'Intra-Urban Mobility in Ho Chi Minh City and Hanoi', in Patrick Gubry, Franck Castiglioni, Jean-Michel Cusset, Nguyen Thi Thieng and Pham Thuy Huong (eds), *The Vietnamese City in Transition*. Singapore: Institute of Southeast Asian Studies, pp. 63–100.

Gupta, Akhil and James Ferguson 1997. 'Discipline and Practice: "The Field" as Site, Method, and Location in Anthropology', in Akhil Gupta and James Ferguson (eds), *Anthropological Locations: Boundaries and Grounds of a Field Science*. Berkeley: University of California Press, pp. 1–46.

Ha Thi Phuong Tien and Ha Quang Ngoc 2001. *Female Labour Migration: Rural–Urban*. Hanoi: Phu Nu Publishing House.

Hardy, Andrew 2003. 'Migrants in Contemporary Vietnamese History: Marginal or Mainstream?', in Abu Talib Ahmad and Tan Liok Ee (eds), *New Terrains in Southeast Asian History*. Athens: Ohio University Press, pp. 328–53.

——2004. *Red Hills: Migrants and the State in the Highlands of Vietnam*. Copenhagen: NIAS Press.

Harms, Erik 2011. *Saigon's Edge: On the Margins of Ho Chi Minh City*. Minneapolis: University of Minnesota Press.

Hattori, Tamio, Tsuruyo Funatsu and Takashi Torii 2003. 'Introduction: The Emergence of the Asian Middle Classes and their Characteristics', *The Developing Economies*, Vol. 41, No. 2, pp. 129–39.

Hayslip, Le Ly (with Jay Wurts) 1989. *When Heaven and Earth Changed Places: A Vietnamese Woman's Journey from War to Peace*. New York: Plume.

Hayslip, Le Ly and James Hayslip 1993. *Child of War, Woman of Peace*. New York: Doubleday.

Heberer, Thomas 2003. *Private Entrepreneurs in China and Vietnam: Social and Political Functioning of Strategic Groups*. Leiden: Brill.

Heberle, Mark (ed.) 2009. *Thirty Years After: New Essays on Vietnam War Literature, Film, and Art*. Newcastle upon Tyne: Cambridge Scholars Publishing.

Heryanto, Ariel 1999. 'The Years of Living Luxuriously: Identity Politics of Indonesia's New Rich', in Michael Pinches (ed.), *Culture and Privilege in Capitalist Asia*. London: Routledge, pp. 159–87.

Hess, David Lazear 1977. 'The Educated Vietnamese Middle Class of Metropolitan Saigon and their Legacy of Confucian Authority, 1954–1975', Unpublished PhD thesis, New York University.

Higgins, Rylan 2008. 'Negotiating the Middle: Interactions of Class, Gender and Consumerism among Middle Classes in Ho Chi Minh City, Vietnam', Unpublished PhD thesis, The University of Arizona.

Higgs, Peter 2003. 'Footpath Traders in a Hanoi Neighbourhood', in Lisa B.W. Drummond and Mandy Thomas (eds), *Consuming Urban Culture in Contemporary Vietnam*. London: RoutledgeCurzon, pp. 75–88.

Hitchcox, Linda 1994. 'Relocation in Vietnam and Outmigration: The Ideological and Economic Context', in Judith M. Brown and Rosemary Foot (eds), *Migration: The Asian Experience*. New York: St Martin's Press, pp. 202–20.

Ho Xuan Huong [pseud.] 2002. 'Weaving a Double Cloth', in Myra-Jean Bourke, Suzanne Holzknecht and Annie Bartlett (eds), *Weaving a Double Cloth: Stories of Asia-Pacific Women in Australia*. Canberra: Pandanus Books, pp. 5–23.

Hoang, Carina 2010. *Boat People: Personal Stories from the Vietnamese Exodus 1975–1992*. Cloverdale, Western Australia: Carina Hoang Communications.

Hoàng, Lan Anh 2009. 'Gender and agency in migration decision making: evidence from Vietnam.' Asia Research Institute Working Paper No. 115, http://www.ari.nus.edu.sg/docs/wps/wps09_115.pdf.

Hoàng Ngọc Thanh Dung 1988. 'To Serve the Cause of Women's Liberation', in Huỳnh Sanh Thông (ed. and transl.), *To Be Made Over: Tales of Socialist Re-Education in Vietnam*. New Haven: Yale Center for International and Area Studies, pp. 43–77.

Hobsbawm, Eric and Terence Ranger (eds) 2012. *The Invention of Tradition*. Cambridge: Cambridge University Press.

Hochschild, Arlie Russell 1983. *The Managed Heart: Commercialization of Human Feeling*. Berkeley: University of California Press.

Hollan, Douglas 2001. 'Developments in Person-Centred Ethnography', in Carmella Moore and Holly Mathews (eds), *The Psychology of Cultural Experience*. Cambridge: Cambridge University Press, pp. 48–67.

Hooper, Beverley 1998. '"Flower Vase and Housewife": Women and Consumerism in Post-Mao China', in Krishna Sen and Maila Stivens (eds), *Gender and Power in Affluent Asia*. London: Routledge, pp. 167–94.

Horton, Paul and Helle Rydstrøm 2011. 'Heterosexual Masculinity in Contemporary Vietnam: Privileges, Pleasures, and Protests', *Men and Masculinities*, Vol. 14, No. 5, pp. 542–64.

Hoskins, Marilyn W. 1976. 'Vietnamese Women: Their Roles and Their Opinions', in David J. Banks (ed.), *Changing Identities in Modern Southeast Asia*. Chicago: Aldine, pp. 127–46.

Hoskins, Marilyn W. and Eleanor Shepherd 1965. *Life in a Vietnamese Urban Quarter*. Carbondale: Center for Vietnamese Studies, Southern Illinois University.

Howard, Michael C. 2011. *Transnationalism and Society: An Introduction*. Jefferson: McFarland.

Hsiao, Hsin-Huang Michael 2006. 'Prioritizing the Middle Classes Research in Asia-Pacific', in Hsin-Huang Michael Hsiao (ed.), *The Changing Faces of the Middle Classes in Asia-Pacific*. Taipei: Academia Sinica, pp. 3–8.

—— 2010. 'Placing China's Middle Class in the Asia-Pacific Context', in Li Cheng (ed.), *China's Emerging Middle Class: Beyond Economic Transformation*. Washington: Brookings Institution Press, pp. 245–63.

—— 2013. *Chinese Middle Classes: China, Taiwan, Macao and Hong Kong*. New York: Routledge.

Hsiao, Hsin-Huang Michael and Hong-Zen Wang 2001. 'The Formation of the Middle Classes in Southeast Asia: An Overview', in Hsin-Huang Michael Hsiao (ed.), *Exploration of the Middle Classes in Southeast Asia*. Taipei: Program for Southeast Asian Studies, Academia Sinica, pp. 3–38.

Hutchison, Jane and Andrew Brown (eds) 2001. *Organising Labour in Globalising Asia*. London: Routledge.

Huỳnh Đình Tế 1962. 'Vietnamese Cultural Patterns and Values as Expressed in Proverbs', Unpublished Ph.D. Thesis, Columbia University.

Huỳnh Ngọc Trảng, Trương Ngọc Tường, Nguyễn Đại Phúc, Đỗ Văn Anh and Phạm Thiếu Hương 1997. *Sài Gòn – Gia Định Xưa: Tư Liệu và Hình Ảnh* [Saigon – Gia Dinh in the Past: Documents and Photographs]. Ho Chi Minh City: Nhà Xuất Bản Thành Phố Hồ Chí Minh.

Hy Van Luong 2006. 'Structure, Practice, and History: Contemporary Anthropological Research on Vietnam', *Journal of Vietnamese Studies*, Vol. 1, No. 1–2, pp. 371–410.

—— 2009. 'Urbanization, Migration, and Poverty: Ho Chi Minh City in Comparative Perspectives', in Hy Van Luong (ed.), *Urbanization, Migration and Poverty in a Vietnamese Metropolis: Hồ Chí Minh City in Comparative Perspective*. Singapore: NUS Press, pp. 1–28.

Jackson, Stevi, Petula Sik Ying Ho and Jin Nye Na 2013. 'Reshaping Tradition? Women Negotiating the Boundaries of Tradition and Modernity in Hong Kong and British Families', *The Sociological Review*, Vol. 61, pp. 667–87.

Jacobs, J. Bruce 1979. 'A Preliminary Model of Particularistic Ties in Chinese Political Alliances: Kan-ch'ing and Kuan-hsi in a Rural Taiwanese Township', *The China Quarterly*, No. 78, pp. 237–73.

Jacobs, Jane 1994. *The Death and Life of Great American Cities*. Harmondsworth: Penguin.

Jerneck, Anne 2010. 'Globalization, Growth and Gender: Poor Workers and Vendors in Urban Vietnam', in Helle Rydstrøm (ed.), *Gendered Inequalities in Asia: Configuring, Contesting and Recognizing Women and Men*. Copenhagen: NIAS Press, pp. 99–123.

Johansson, Perry 2001. 'Selling the 'Modern Woman': Consumer Culture and Chinese Gender Politics', in Shoma Munshi (ed.), *Images of the 'Modern Woman' in Asia: Global Media, Local Meanings*. Richmond: Curzon, pp. 94–122.

Kay, Rebecca 1997. 'Images of an Ideal Woman: Perceptions of Russian Womanhood through the Media, Education and Women's Own Eyes', in Mary Buckley (ed.), *Post-Soviet Women: From the Baltic to Central Asia*. Cambridge: Cambridge University Press, pp. 77–98.

Kay, Rebecca and Maxim Kostenko 2006. 'Men in Crisis or in Critical Need of Support? Insights from Russia and the UK', *Journal of Communist Studies and Transition Politics*, Vol. 22, No. 1, pp. 90–114.

Kelly, Gail 1984. 'The Presentation of Indigenous Society in the Schools of French West Africa and Indochina, 1918 to 1938', *Comparative Studies in Society and History*, Vol. 26, No. 3, pp. 523–42.

Kerkvliet, Benedict J. Tria 1995. 'Village-State Relations in Vietnam: The Effect of Everyday Politics on Decollectivization', *Journal of Asian Studies*, Vol. 54, No. 2, pp. 396–418.

Kharas, Homi and Geoffrey Gertz 2010. 'The New Global Middle Class: A Crossover From West to East', in Li Cheng (ed.), *China's Emerging*

Middle Class: Beyond Economic Transformation. Washington: Brookings Institution Press, pp. 32–51.

Khuat Thu Hong 2004. 'Sexual Harassment in Vietnam: A New Term for an Old Phenomenon', in Lisa Drummond and Helle Rydstrøm (eds), *Gender Practices in Contemporary Vietnam.* Singapore: Singapore University Press, pp. 117–36.

Kim, Annette Miae 2008. *Learning to be Capitalists: Entrepreneurs in Vietnam's Transition Economy.* New York: Oxford University Press.

Kim, Jee Young 2004. 'Political Capital, Human Capital, and Intergenerational Occupational Mobility in Northern Vietnam', in Philip Taylor (ed.), *Social Inequality in Vietnam and the Challenges to Reform.* Singapore: ISEAS, pp. 166–207.

King, Victor, 2008, 'The Middle Classes in Southeast Asia: Diversities, Identities, Comparisons and the Vietnamese case', *The International Journal of Asia Pacific Studies*, No. 4, pp. 73–109.

King, Victor, Nguyen Phuong An and Nguyen Huu Minh 2008. 'Professional Middle-Class Youth in Post-Reform Vietnam: Identity, Continuity, Change.' *Modern Asian Studies*, Vol. 42, No. 4, pp. 783–813.

Koo, Hagen 1978. 'Rural–urban Migration and Social Mobility in Third-World Metropolises: A Cross-National Study', *Sociological Quarterly*, Vol. 19, No. 2, pp. 292–303.

——— 2006. 'Globalization and the Asian Middle Classes', in Hsin-Huang Michael Hsiao (ed.), *The Changing Faces of the Middle Classes in Asia-Pacific.* Taipei: Academia Sinica, pp. 9–24.

Lahire, Bernard 2008. 'The Individual and the Mixing of Genres: Cultural Dissonance and Self-Distinction', *Poetics*, Vol. 36, pp. 166–88.

Lam, Andrew 2005. *Perfume Dreams: Reflections on the Vietnamese Diaspora.* Berkeley: Heyday Books.

Lamont, Michèle and Annette Lareau 1988. 'Cultural Capital: Allusions, Gaps and Glissandos in Recent Theoretical Developments', *Sociological Theory*, Vol. 6, No. 2 (Autumn), pp. 153–68.

Lange, Hellmuth and Lars Meier (eds) 2009. *The New Middle Classes: Globalizing Lifestyles, Consumerism and Environmental Concern.* Dordrecht: Springer.

Lawrence, Mark Atwood and Fredrik Logevall (eds) 2007. *The First Vietnam War: Colonial Conflict and Cold War Crisis.* Cambridge, MA: Harvard University Press.

Le Kwang Kim 1963. 'A Woman of Viet-Nam in a Changing World', in Barbara Ward (ed.), *Women in the New Asia: The Changing Social Roles of Men and Women in South and South-East Asia*. Paris: UNESCO, pp. 462–70.

Lê Minh Quốc 1999. *Các Vị Nữ Danh Nhân Việt Nam* [Celebrated Women of Vietnam]. Ho Chi Minh City: Nhà Xuất Bản Trẻ.

Lê Minh Quốc 2001. *Các Vị Nữ Danh Nhân Việt Nam: Phần Hai* [Celebrated Women of Vietnam: Volume Two]. Ho Chi Minh City: Nhà Xuất Bản Trẻ.

Lê Quốc Sử 2001. *Chuyện Kể Lê Hồng Phong và Nguyễn Thị Minh Khai* [The Story of Lê Hồng Phong and Nguyễn Thị Minh Khai]. Bến Tre: Nhà Xuất Bản Thanh Niên.

Le Thi 1995. 'Women's Labour and Socio-Economic Status in a Market-Oriented Economy', in Irene Nørlund, Carolyn L. Gates and Vu Cao Dam (eds), *Vietnam in a Changing World*. Richmond: Curzon Press, pp. 207–18.

—— 1998. *Phụ Nữ và Bình Dẳng Trong Đổi Mới ở Việt Nam* [Women and Gender Equality in Doi Moi in Vietnam]. Hanoi: Nhà Xuất Bản Phụ Nữ.

—— 1999. *The Role of the Family in the Formation of the Vietnamese Personality*. Hanoi: The Gioi Publishers.

—— 2001. *Employment and Life of Vietnamese Women During Economic Transition*. Hanoi: The Gioi Publishers.

—— 2008. *Single Women in Việt Nam*, 3rd ed. Hanoi: Thế Giới Publishers.

Lê Thị Nhâm Tuyết 1989. *Vietnamese Women in the Eighties*. Hanoi: Foreign Languages Publishing House.

—— 2002. *Images of the Vietnamese Woman in the New Millennium*. Transl. by Cao Thi Lien. Hanoi: The Gioi Publishers.

Lê Trưng Ngọc [n.d. 196?]. *Nữ Lư[u] Phận Sự / Devoirs De La Femme Annamite* (The Duties of Vietnamese Women). Hanoi: Imprimerie Ngo Tu Ha.

Lê Tuyết Thanh (ed.) 1993. *Phụ nữ miền Nam* [Southern Vietnamese Women]. Ho Chi Minh City: Bảo Tàng Phụ Nữ Nam Bộ.

Le Van Hòang and Truong Nhu Hien 1965. 'La Stratification et la Mobilite Sociale au Viet-nam'. Tokyo: Working paper for the UCRP international conference.

Lee, Michelle and Nicola Piper 2003. 'Reflections on Transnational Life-Course and Migratory Patterns of Middle-Class Women – Preliminary Observations from Malaysia', in Nicola Piper and Mina Roces (eds), *Wife or Worker? Asian Women and Migration*. Lanham: Rowman and Littlefield Publishers, pp. 121–36.

Leshkowich, Ann Marie 2000. 'Tightly Woven Threads: Gender, Kinship, and "Secret Agency" among Cloth and Clothing Traders in Ho Chi Minh City's Ben Thanh Market (Vietnam)', Unpublished Ph.D. Thesis, Harvard University.

—— 2006. 'Woman, Buddhist, Entrepreneur: Gender, Moral Values and Class Anxiety in Late Socialist Vietnam', *Journal of Vietnamese Studies*, Vol. 1, No. 1–2, pp. 277–313.

—— 2011. 'Making Class and Gender: (Market) Socialist Enframing of Traders in Ho Chi Minh City', *American Anthropologist*, Vol. 113, No. 2, pp. 277–90.

—— 2012. 'Finances, Family, Fashion, Fitness, and… Freedom? The Changing Lives of Urban Middle-Class Vietnamese Women', in Van Nguyen-Marshall, Lisa B. Welch Drummond and Danièle Bélanger (eds), *The Reinvention of Distinction: Modernity and the Middle Class in Urban Vietnam*. Dordrecht: Springer, pp. 95–113.

LeVine, Robert A. 1982. *Culture, Behavior, and Personality: An Introduction to the Comparative Study of Psychosocial Adaptation*, 2nd ed. New York: Aldine.

Li Cheng (ed.), 2010. *China's Emerging Middle Class: Beyond Economic Transformation*. Washington: Brookings Institution Press.

Li Chunling 2010. 'Characterizing China's Middle Class: Heterogeneous Composition and Multiple Identities', in Li Cheng (ed.), *China's Emerging Middle Class: Beyond Economic Transformation*. Washington: Brookings Institution Press, pp. 135–56.

Li Minghuan 2002. 'A Group in Transition: Chinese Students and Scholars in the Netherlands', in Pal Nyiri and Igor Saveliev (eds), *Globalizing Chinese Migration: Trends in Europe and Asia*. Aldershot: Ashgate, pp. 173–88.

Liechty, Mark 2003. *Suitably Modern: Making Middle-Class Culture in a New Consumer Society*. Princeton: Princeton University Press.

Limmanee, Anusorn, Chantana Banpasirichote, Prudhisan Jambala and Surichai Wun'Gaeo 2001. 'Middle classes in Bangkok', in Hsin-Huang Michael Hsiao (ed.), *Exploration of the Middle Classes in Southeast Asia*. Taipei: Program for Southeast Asian Studies, Academia Sinica, pp. 415–72.

Lin, Jing and Xiaoyan Sun 2010. 'Higher Education Expansion and China's Middle Class', in Li Cheng (ed.), *China's Emerging Middle Class: Beyond Economic Transformation.* Washington: Brookings Institution Press, pp. 217–42.

Loewald, Uyen 1987. *Child of Vietnam.* Melbourne: Hyland House.

Loftus, Ronald P. 2004. *Telling Lives: Women's Self-Writing in Modern Japan.* Honolulu: University of Hawai'i Press.

Long, Lynellyn D., Le Ngoc Hung, Allison Truitt, Le Thi Phuong Mai and Dang Nguyen Anh 2000. 'Changing Gender Relations in Vietnam's Post Doi Moi Era', Policy Research Report on Gender and Development, Working Paper Series No. 14, World Bank, http://siteresources.worldbank.org/INTGENDER/Resources/wp14.pdf.

Lovell, Terry 2000. 'Thinking Feminism With and Against Bourdieu', *Feminist Theory*, Vol. 1, No. 1, pp. 11–32.

Lũ Huy Nguyên 2004. *Hồ Xuân Hương: Thơ và Đời* [Hồ Xuân Hương: Life and Poetry]. Hanoi: Nhà Xuất Bản Văn Học.

Marcus, George 1995. 'Ethnography In/Of the World System: The Emergence of Multi-Sited Ethnography', *Annual Review of Anthropology*, Vol. 24, pp. 95–117.

Marr, David 1971. *Vietnamese Anticolonialism, 1885–1925.* Berkeley: University of California Press.

—— 1981. *Vietnamese Tradition on Trial, 1920–1945.* Berkeley: University of California Press.

—— 1988. 'Tertiary Education, Research, and the Information Sciences in Vietnam', in David G. Marr and Christine White (eds), *Postwar Vietnamese Dilemmas in Social Development.* Ithaca: Cornell University Southeast Asian Program, pp. 15–44.

—— 1993. 'Education, Research, and Information Circulation in Contemporary Vietnam', in William Turley and Mark Seldon (eds), *Reinventing Vietnamese Socialism: Doi Moi in Comparative Perspectives.* Boulder: Westview Press, pp. 337–58.

—— 1995. *Vietnam 1945: The Quest for Power.* Berkeley: University of California Press.

—— 1997. 'Vietnamese Youth in the 1990s', *The Vietnam Review*, No. 2 (Spring–Summer), pp. 288–354.

—— 2000. 'Concepts of 'Individual' and 'Self' in Twentieth-Century Vietnam', *Modern Asian Studies*, Vol. 34, No. 4, pp. 769–96.

Marr, David and Stanley Rosen 1999. 'Chinese and Vietnamese Youth in the 1990s', in Anita Chan, Benedict J. Tria Kerkvliet and Jonathan Unger (eds), *Transforming Asian Socialism: China and Vietnam Compared*. St Leonards: Allen and Unwin, pp. 176–203.

Martin, Philip 2010. 'These days virginity is just a feeling': Heterosexuality and Change in Young Urban Vietnamese Men', *Culture, Health and Sexuality*, Vol. 12, No. S1, pp. S5–S18.

Marx, Veronique and Katherine Fleischer 2010. *Internal Migration: Opportunities and Challenges for Socio-Economic Development in Viet Nam*. Hanoi: United Nations Viet Nam.

Megarrity, Lyndon 2007. 'Regional Goodwill, Sensibly Priced: Commonwealth Policies Towards Colombo Plan Scholars and Private Overseas Students, 1945–72', *Australian Historical Studies*, Vol. 38, No. 129, pp. 88–105.

McDowell, Linda 1997. *Capital Culture: Gender at Work in the City*. Malden: Blackwell.

McHale, Shawn 1995. 'Printing and Power: Vietnamese Debates Over Women's Place in Society, 1918–1934', in Keith W. Taylor and John K. Whitmore (eds), *Essays Into Vietnamese Pasts*. Ithaca: Cornell Southeast Asia Program, pp. 173–194.

McNay, Lois 2004. 'Agency and Experience: Gender as a Lived Experience', in Lisa Adkins and Beverley Skeggs (eds), *Feminism After Bourdieu*. Oxford: Blackwell Publishing, pp. 175–90.

McRobbie, Angela 2004. 'Notes on 'What Not to Wear' and Post-Feminist Symbolic Violence', in Lisa Adkins and Beverley Skeggs (eds), *Feminism After Bourdieu*. Oxford: Blackwell Publishing, pp. 99–109.

Mills, Mary Beth 1999. *Thai Women in the Global Labor Force: Consuming Desires, Contested Selves*. New Brunswick: Rutgers University Press.

Mills, Mary Beth 2012. 'Thai Mobilities and Cultural Citizenship', *Critical Asian Studies*, Vol. 44, No. 1, pp. 85–112.

Minh-Loan 1969. *Cẩm Nang Để Trở Thành Người Phụ Nữ Đẹp* [Manual for Becoming a Beautiful Woman]. [Saigon?]: Nhà Xuất Bản Bằng Đoàn.

Ministry of Planning and Investment & General Statistical Office 2011. *Population Projections for Vietnam, 2009–2049*. Hanoi: General Statistical Office.

Moi, Toril 1991. 'Appropriating Bourdieu: Feminist Theory and Pierre Bourdieu's Sociology of Culture', *New Literary History*, Vol. 22, No. 4, pp. 1017–49.

Myers, Norman, and Jennifer Kent 2003. 'New Consumers: The Influence of Affluence on the Environment', *PNAS – Proceedings of the National Academy of Sciences of the United States of America*, Vol. 100, No. 8, pp. 4963–8.

Nagengast, Carole 1991. *Reluctant Socialists, Rural Entrepreneurs: Class, Culture, and the Polish State.* Boulder: Westview Press.

Ngàn Hac Tráng [pseud.] 1995. 'Ngàn Hac Tráng', in Adrienne Jansen (ed.), *I Have In My Arms Both Ways,* 2nd ed. Wellington: Bridget Williams Books, pp. 67–82.

Nghiem Lien Huong 2004. 'Female Garment Workers: The New Young Volunteers in Vietnam's Modernization', in Philip Taylor (ed.), *Social Inequality in Vietnam and the Challenges to Reform.* Singapore: ISEAS, pp. 297–324.

Ngô Thị Ngân Bình 2004. 'The Confucian Four Feminine Virtues (*tu duc*): The Old Versus the New – *Ke thua* Versus *Phat huy*', in Lisa Drummond and Helle Rydstrøm (eds), *Gender Practices in Contemporary Vietnam.* Singapore: Singapore University Press, pp. 47–73.

Ngo Vinh Long 1974. *Before the Revolution: Vietnamese Peasants Under the French.* New York: Columbia University Press.

Nguyen Anh Tuan 1987. *South Vietnam Trial and Experience: A Challenge for Development.* Athens: Ohio University Center for International Studies and Center for Southeast Asian Studies.

Nguyen Bich Thuan and Mandy Thomas 2004. 'Young Women and Emergent Postsocialist Sensibilities in Contemporary Vietnam', *Asian Studies Review,* Vol. 28, No. 2, pp. 133–49.

Nguyễn Đình-Hòa 1999. *From the City Inside the Red River: A Cultural Memoir of Mid-Century Vietnam.* Jefferson: MacFarland.

Nguyễn Du 2000. *Truyện Kiều Bằng Tranh* [An Illustrated Tale of Kiều]. Ed. by Trần Kim Lý Thái Thuận. Hanoi: Nhà Xuất Bản Văn Hóa Dân Tộc.

Nguyen Duy Hinh and Tran Dinh Tho 1980. *The South Vietnamese Society.* Washington: U.S. Army Center of Military History.

Nguyen, Duy Long and James Knight 2004. *The Dragon's Journey: From Saigon to Sydney, the compelling story of a boy who eventually came to realise his mother's dream.* Sydney: Harper Collins.

Nguyễn Huy Tưởng 2011. 'Có Một Chút Paris…' [A little bit of Paris…] in *Sài Gòn Tản Văn: Hẻm Phố Thong Ra Thế Giới* [Saigon Prose: The

Streets and Lanes Open to the World]. Hanoi: Nhà Xuất Bản Hội Nhà Văn, pp. 37–52.

Nguyen, Nathalie Huynh Chau 2001. 'Writing and Memory in Kim Lefèvre's Autobiographical Narratives', *Intersections* [online], No. 5, http://intersections.anu.edu.au/issue5/nathalie.html.

—— 2005. *Voyage of Hope: Vietnamese Australian Women's Narratives*. Altona, Vic: Commond Ground.

—— 2009. *Memory Is Another Country: Women of the Vietnamese Diaspora*. Santa Barbara: Praeger.

Nguyen Pham Thanh Nam, Phuoc Minh Hiep, Mai Van Nam, Bui Van Trinh and Pham The Tri 2000. 'Human Resources Development in the Mekong Delta', CAS Discussion Paper No. 31. Antwerp: Centre for ASEAN Studies and Centre for International Management and Development, http://webh01.ua.ac.be/cas/PDF/CAS31.pdf.

Nguyễn Quang Vinh 1996. 'Thành Phố Hồ Chí Minh: Các Khía Cạnh Xã Hội và Nhân Văn của Quá Trình Đô Thị Hóa' [Ho Chi Minh City: Social and Human Aspects of the Process of Urbanization], in Trịnh Duy Luân (ed.), *Tìm Hiểu Môn Xã Hội Học Đô Thị* [Understanding Urban Sociology]. Hanoi: Nhà Xuất Bản Khoa Học Xã Hội.

Nguyen Thanh Tam 1996. 'Remarks on Women Who Live Without Husbands', in Kathleen Barry (ed.), *Vietnam's Women in Transition*. New York: St Martin's Press, pp. 87–92.

Nguyen Thi Dieu 2013. 'A Mythographical Journey to Modernity: The Textual and Symbolic Transformations of the Hùng Kings Founding Myths', *Journal of Southeast Asian Studies*, Vol. 44, No. 2, pp. 315–37.

Nguyen Thi Dinh 1976. *No Other Road to Take: Memoir of Mrs. Nguyen Thi Dinh*. Transl. by Mai Elliott. Data Paper No. 102, Southeast Asia Program. Ithaca: Cornell University.

Nguyen Thi Huo 1967. 'Modern Society Interviews Women: An interview with Mrs Nguyen Thi Huo', in *Women in Vietnam: Selected Articles from Vietnamese Periodicals, Saigon, Hanoi, 1957–1966*. Transl. by Chiem T. Kiem. Honolulu: East-West Center, pp. 58–64.

Nguyen Thi Khoa 1997. 'Vietnamese Female Intellectuals on the Threshold of the 21st Century', in Le Thi and Do Thi Binh (eds), *Ten Years of Progress: Vietnamese Women from 1985 to 1995*. Hanoi: Phu Nu Publishing House, pp. 262–8.

Nguyễn Thị Thu-Lâm (with Edith Kreisler and Sandra Christenson) 1989. *Fallen Leaves: Memoirs of a Vietnamese Woman from 1940 to 1975*. New Haven: Council on Southeast Asia Studies, Yale Center for International and Area Studies and Boston: William Joiner Center.

Nguyen Thi Tuyet Mai 1994. *The Rubber Tree: Memoir of a Vietnamese Woman who was an Anti-French Guerrilla, a Publisher and a Peace Activist*. Ed. by Monique Senderowicz. Jefferson: McFarland.

Nguyễn Thùy 2002. 'Four Virtues and Women Today', in Lê Thị Nhâm Tuyết (ed.), *Images of the Vietnamese Woman in the New Millennium*. Transl. by Cao Thị Liên. Hanoi: The Gioi Publishers, pp. 5–8.

Nguyen Trieu Dan 1991. *A Vietnamese Family Chronicle: Twelve Generations on the Banks of the Hat River*. Jefferson: McFarland.

Nguyen Tuan Anh, Jonathan Rigg, Luong Thi Thu Huong and Dinh Thi Dieu 2012. 'Becoming and Being Urban in Hanoi: Rural–Urban Migration and Relations in Viet Nam', *Journal of Peasant Studies*, Vol. 39, No. 5, pp. 1103–31.

Nguyen Xuan Hoang 1995. 'The Autobiography of a Useless Person', transl. by Thai Tuyet Quan, ed. by Wayne Karlin, in Wayne Karlin, Le Minh Khue and Truong Vu (eds) *The Other Side of Heaven: Postwar Fiction by Vietnamese and American Writers*. Willimantic: Curbstone Press, pp. 235–44.

Nguyen-Marshall, Van 2004. 'Oral History and Popular Memory in the Historiography of the Vietnam War', in Paul Budra and Michael Zeitlin (eds), *Soldier Talk: The Vietnam War in Oral Narrative*. Bloomington: Indiana University Press, pp. 141–66

Nguyen-vo Thu-huong 2004. 'The Class Sense of Bodies: Women Garment Workers Consume Body Products In and Around Ho Chi Minh City', in Lisa Drummond and Helle Rydstrøm (eds), *Gender Practices in Contemporary Vietnam*. Singapore: Singapore University Press, pp. 179–209.

——2006. 'The Body Wager: Materialist Resignification of Vietnamese Women Workers', *Gender, Place and Culture*, Vol. 13, No. 3, pp. 267–81.

——2008. *Ironies of Freedom: Sex, Culture, and Neoliberal Governance in Vietnam*. Seattle: University of Washington Press.

Nguyệt Tú 1976. *Chị Minh Khai: Truyện* [Our Sister Minh Khai: A Story]. Hanoi: Nhà Xuất Bản Phụ Nữ.

Nowotny, Helga 1981. 'Women in Public Life in Austria', in Cynthia Fuchs Epstein and Rose Laub Coser (eds), *Access to Power: Cross-National Studies of Women and Elites*. London: George Allen and Unwin, pp. 147–56.

Nữ Sĩ Vân Đài: Một Thời Thanh Lịch [The Poetess Van Dai: An Era of Refinement] 1999. Hanoi: Nhà Xuất Bản Van Học.

Nữ Sinh Sài Gòn Một Thời Để Nhớ: Ký Sự Truyền Thống của Nữ Sinh 5 Trường Nữ Trung Học Gia Long, Marie Curie, Đức Trí, Trưng Vương, Lê Văn Duyệt (1945-1975) [Saigon Schoolgirls of the Past: Traditional Chronicle of Schoolgirls from the 5 Girls Secondary Schools Gia Long, Marie Curie, Đức Trí, Trưng Vương, and Lê Văn Duyệt (1945-1975)]. 2002. Ho Chi Minh City: Nhà Xuất Bản Trẻ.

Ockey, Jim 1999. 'Creating the Thai Middle Class', in Michael Pinches (ed.), *Culture and Privilege in Capitalist Asia*. London: Routledge, pp. 231–51.

Ong, Aihwa and Li Zhang 2008. 'Introduction: Privatizing China: Powers of the Self, Socialism from Afar', in Li Zhang and Aihwa Ong (eds), *Privatizing China: Socialism From Afar*. Ithaca: Cornell University Press, pp. 1–19.

Pelley, Patricia M. 2002. *Postcolonial Vietnam: New Histories of the National Past*. Durham: Duke University Press.

Pelzer, Kristin [Christine White] 1993. 'Love, War, and Revolution: Reflections on the Memoirs of Nguyen Thi Dinh', in Jayne S. Werner and Luu Doan Huynh (eds), *The Vietnam War: Vietnamese and American Perspectives*. Armonk: M.E. Sharpe, pp. 95–112.

Perkins, Mandalay 2005. *Hanoi, Adieu: A Bittersweet Memoir of French Indochina*. London: Fourth Estate.

Peters, Erica J. 2012, 'Cuisine and Social Status Among Urban Vietnamese, 1888–1926', in Van Nguyen-Marshall, Lisa B. Welch Drummond and Danièle Bélanger (eds), *The Reinvention of Distinction: Modernity and the Middle Class in Urban Vietnam*. Dordrecht: Springer, pp. 43–57.

Peters, Robbie 2012. 'City of Ghosts: Migration, Work, and Value in the Life of a Ho Chi Minh City Saleswoman', *Critical Asian Studies*, Vol. 44, No. 4, pp. 543–70.

Peterson, Richard A. 1992. 'Understanding Audience Segmentation: From Elite and Mass to Omnivore and Univore', *Poetics*, Vol. 21, pp. 243–58.

Peterson, Richard A. and Roger M. Kern 1996. 'Changing Highbrow Taste: From Snob to Omnivore', *American Sociological Review*, Vol. 61, pp. 900–7.

Pettus, Ashley 2003. *Between Sacrifice and Desire: National Identity and the Governing of Femininity in Vietnam*. New York: Routledge.

Pham, Andrew X. 2008. *The Eaves of Heaven: A Life in Three Wars*. New York: Harmony Books.

Phạm-Cao-Tùng 1954. *Người Lịch Sự: Phép Xã-Giao và Ăn, Mặc Theo Đời Sống Mới (Có Phần Phụ Về Phép Lịch-Sự Tây)* [Refined Individuals: The Rules of Propriety, Eating, and Dressing Following the New Way of Life, With an Appendix on Western Style Manners]. Saigon: Nhà Xuất Bản P. Văn Tươi.

Phạm Minh Hạc 1998. *Vietnam's Education: The Current Position and Future Prospects*. Hanoi: The Gioi Publishers.

Pham Thi Hoai 1997. *The Crystal Messenger*. Transl. by Ton-That Quynh-Du. South Melbourne: Hyland House.

Phạm Văn Bích 1999. *The Vietnamese Family in Change: the Case of the Red River Delta*. Richmond: Curzon Press.

Pham Xuan Nam 2002. 'Some Preliminary Ideas on the Change of Social Structure and Classes in Vietnam during the Transition to a Socialist-Oriented Market Economy', *Vietnam Social Sciences*, No. 6, pp. 31–42.

Phinney, Harriet 2008. 'Objects of Affection: Vietnamese Discourses on Love and Emancipation,' *Positions*, Vol. 16, No. 2, pp. 329–56.

Phương Lan [n.d. 1975?–1985?]. *Anh Thư Nước Việt Từ Lập Quốc Đến Hiện Đại* [Vietnamese Heroines from the Foundation of the Nation to Today]. Glendale: Đai Nam.

Pinches, Michael 1999a. 'Cultural Relations, Class and the New Rich of Asia', in Michael Pinches (ed.), *Culture and Privilege in Capitalist Asia*. London: Routledge, pp. 1–56.

—— (ed.) 1999b. *Culture and Privilege in Capitalist Asia*. London: Routledge.

—— 2001. 'Class and National Identity: The Case of Filipino Migrant Workers', in Jane Hutchison and Andrew Brown (eds), *Organising Labour in Globalising Asia*. London: Routledge, pp. 187–213.

Pincus, Jonathan and John Sender 2008. 'Quantifying Poverty in Vietnam: Who Counts?', *Journal of Vietnamese Studies*, Vol. 3, No. 1, pp. 108–50.

Piper, Nicola and Mina Roces 2003a. 'Introduction: Marriage and Migration in an Age of Globalization', in Nicola Piper and Mina Roces (eds), *Wife or Worker? Asian Women and Migration*. Lanham: Rowman and Littlefield, pp. 1–22.

—— (eds) 2003b. *Wife or Worker? Asian Women and Migration*. Lanham: Rowman and Littlefield.

Prieur, Annick and Mike Savage 2011. 'Updating Cultural Capital Theory: A Discussion Based on Studies in Denmark and in Britain', *Poetics*, Vol. 39, pp. 566–80.

PuruShotam, Nirmala 1998. 'Between Compliance and Resistance: Women and the Middle-Class Way of Life in Singapore', in Krishna Sen and Maila Stivens (eds), *Gender and Power in Affluent Asia*. London: Routledge, pp. 127–66.

Quách Thu Nguyệt et al. 2007. *Hỏi Đáp về Sài Gòn Thành Phố Hồ Chí Minh* [Saigon Ho Chi Minh City Questions and Answers]. Vol. 4. Ho Chi Minh City: Nhà Xuất Bản Trẻ.

Reay, Diane 2004. 'Gendering Bourdieu's Concept of Capitals? Emotional Capital, Women and Social Class', in Lisa Adkins and Beverley Skeggs (eds), *Feminism After Bourdieu*. Oxford: Blackwell Publishing, pp. 57–74.

Ren, Hai 2013. *The Middle Class in Neoliberal China: Governing Risk, Life-Building, and Themed Spaces*. London: Routledge.

Rhys-Taylor, Alex 2013. 'Disgust and Distinction: The Case of the Jellied Eel', *The Sociological Review*, Vol. 61, No. 2, pp. 227–46.

Rimmer, Peter J. 1995. 'Moving Goods, People, and Information: Putting the ASEAN Mega-Urban Regions in Context', in T.G. McGee and Ira M. Robinson (eds), *The Mega-Urban Regions of Southeast Asia*. Vancouver: UBC Press, pp. 150–75.

Robison, Richard 1998. 'The Emergence of the Middle Classes in Southeast Asia and the Indonesian Case', in Johannes Dragsbaek Schmidt, Jacques Hersh and Niels Fold (eds), *Social Change in Southeast Asia*. Edinburgh Gate: Longman, pp. 60–77.

Robison, Richard and David S.G. Goodman 1996a. 'The New Rich in Asia: Economic Development, Social Status and Political Consciousness', in Richard Robison and David S.G. Goodman (eds), *The New Rich in Asia: Mobile Phones, McDonald's and Middle-Class Revolution*. London: Routledge, pp. 1–16.

—— (eds) 1996b. *The New Rich in Asia: Mobile Phones, McDonald's and Middle-Class Revolution*. London: Routledge.

Rodan, Garry (ed.), 1996. *Political Oppositions in Industrialising Asia*. London: Routledge.

Rofel, Lisa 1999. *Other Modernities: Gendered Yearnings in China after Socialism*. Berkeley: University of California Press.

—— 2007. *Desiring China: Experiments in Neoliberalism, Sexuality, and Public Culture.* Durham: Duke University Press.

Rolandsen, Unn Målfrid 2011. *Leisure and Power in Urban China: Everyday Life in a Chinese City.* New York: Routledge.

Roose, Henk, Koen van Eijck and John Lievens 2012. 'Culture of Distinction or Culture of Openness? Using a Social Space Approach to Analyze the Social Structuring of Lifestyles', *Poetics*, Vol. 40, pp. 491–513.

Ruwitch, John and Jason Szep 2011. 'Vietnam's Capitalist Roaders: Special Report', Thomson Reuters, http://graphics.thomsonreuters.com/AS/pdf/VietCapitalists.pdf.

Rydstrøm, Helle 2003. *Embodying Morality: Growing Up In Rural Northern Vietnam.* Honolulu: University of Hawai'i Press.

—— 2004. 'Female and Male "Characters": Images of Identification and Self-Identification for Rural Vietnamese Children and Adolescents', in Lisa Drummond and Helle Rydstrøm (eds), *Gender Practices in Contemporary Vietnam.* Singapore: Singapore University Press, pp. 74–95.

—— 2006. 'Sexual Desires and 'Social Evils': Young Women in Rural Vietnam', *Gender, Place and Culture* Vol. 13, No. 3, pp. 283–301.

—— 2010. 'Compromised Ideals: Family Life and the Recognition of Women in Vietnam', in Helle Rydstrøm (ed.), *Gendered Inequalities in Asia: Configuring, Contesting and Recognizing Women and Men.* Copenhagen: NIAS Press, pp. 170–90.

Sachs, Dana 2010. *The Life We Were Given: Operation Babylift, International Adoption, and the Children of War in Vietnam.* Boston: Beacon Press.

Salemink, Oscar 2003. *The Ethnography of Vietnam's Central Highlanders: a Historical Contextualization, 1850–1990.* Richmond: Curzon Press.

Sawyer, Anh Vu and Pam Proctor 2003. *Song of Saigon: One Woman's Journey to Freedom.* New York: Warner Faith.

Schwenkel, Christina and Ann Marie Leshkowich 2012a. 'Guest Editors' Introduction: How is Neoliberalism Good to Think Vietnam? How is Vietnam Good to Think Neoliberalism', *Positions*, Vol. 20, No. 2, pp. 379–401.

—— (eds) 2012b. 'Neoliberalism in Vietnam', a special issue of *Positions*, Vol. 20, No. 2, pp. 379–667.

Sen, Krishna 1998. 'Indonesian Women at Work: Reframing the Subject', in Krishna Sen and Maila Stivens (eds), *Gender and Power in Affluent Asia*. London: Routledge, pp. 35–62.

Sen, Krishna and Maila Stivens (eds) 1998. *Gender and Power in Affluent Asia*. London: Routledge.

Shamsul, A.B. 1999. 'From *Orang Kaya Baru* to *Melayu Baru*: Cultural Construction of the Malay "New Rich"', in Michael Pinches (ed.), *Culture and Privilege in Capitalist Asia*. London: Routledge, pp. 87–111.

Shellshear, Iphigénie-Catherine 2003. *Far From the Tamarind Tree: A Childhood Account of Indochine*. Double Bay: Longueville Books.

Shiraishi Takashi 2008, 'Introduction: The Rise of Middle Classes in Southeast Asia', in Shiraishi Takashi and Pasuk Phongpaichit (eds), *The Rise of Middle Classes in Southeast Asia*. Kyoto: Kyoto University Press, pp. 1–23.

Shohet, Merav 2013. 'Everyday Sacrifice and Language Socialization in Vietnam: The Power of a Respect Particle', *American Anthropologist*, Vol. 115, No. 2, pp. 203–17.

Silva, Elizabeth B. 2005. 'Gender, Home and Family in Cultural Capital Theory', *The British Journal of Sociology*, Vol. 56, No. 1, pp. 83–103.

Skeggs, Beverley 1997. *Formations of Class and Gender*. London: Sage.

—— 2004. 'Context and Background: Pierre Bourdieu's Analysis of Class, Gender and Sexuality', in Lisa Adkins and Beverley Skeggs (eds), *Feminism After Bourdieu*. Oxford: Blackwell Publishing, pp. 75–95.

Smith, R. B. 1972. 'The Vietnamese Elite of French Cochinchina, 1943', *Modern Asian Studies*, Vol. 6, No. 4, pp. 459–82.

So, Alvin Y. 2006. 'Historical Formation, Transformation, and the Future Trajectory of Middle Classes in Asia-Pacific', in Hsin-Huang Michael Hsiao (ed.), *The Changing Faces of the Middle Classes in Asia-Pacific*. Taipei: Academia Sinica, pp. 25–38.

Sơn Nam 1992. *Người Sài Gòn* [The Saigonese]. Ho Chi Minh City: Nhà Xuất Bản Trẻ.

Soucy, Alexander 2000. 'The Problem with Key Informants', *Anthropological Forum*, Vol. 10, No. 2, pp. 179–99.

Szelenyi, Ivan 1996. 'Cities Under Socialism – and After', in Gregory Andrusz, Michael Harloe and Ivan Szelenyi (eds), *Cities After*

Socialism: Urban and Regional Change and Conflict in Post-Socialist Societies. Cambridge: Blackwell, pp. 100–118.

Szemere, Anna 2000. '"We've Kicked the Habit": (Anti)Politics of Art's Autonomy and Transition in Hungary', in Daphne Berdahl, Matti Bunzl and Martha Lampland (eds), *Altering States: Ethnographies of Transition in Eastern Europe and the Former Soviet Union.* Ann Arbor: The University of Michigan Press, pp. 158–80.

Tai, Hue-Tam Ho 1992. *Radicalism and the Origins of the Vietnamese Revolution.* Cambridge, MA: Harvard University Press.

—— 2010. *Passion, Betrayal, and Revolution in Colonial Saigon: The Memoirs of Bao Luong.* Berkeley: University of California Press.

Tai, Hue-Tam Ho and Mark Sidel (eds) 2012. *State, Society and the Market in Contemporary Vietnam: Property, Power and Values.* New York: Routledge.

Tait, Janice 2005. *The Devil's Snare: A Memoir of Saigon.* Toronto: McGilligan Books.

Taylor, Philip 2001. *Fragments of the Present: Searching for Modernity in Vietnam's South.* Crows Nest: Allen and Unwin.

—— 2004a. *Goddess on the Rise: Pilgrimage and Popular Religion in Vietnam.* Honolulu: University of Hawai'i Press.

—— (ed.) 2004b. *Social Inequality in Vietnam and the Challenges to Reform.* Singapore: ISEAS.

Thai, Hung Cam 2008. *For Better or For Worse: Vietnamese International Marriages in the New Global Economy.* New Brunswick: Rutgers University Press.

Thinh Hoang 1989. *My Long Journey: A Vietnamese Woman's Story.* Transl. by Dep Thi Nguyen. Canberra: Curriculum Development Centre.

Thomas, Mandy 1999. *Dreams in the Shadows: Vietnamese-Australian Lives in Transition.* St Leonards: Allen and Unwin.

—— 2002. 'Re-Orientations: East Asian Popular Cultures in Contemporary Vietnam', *Asian Studies Review,* Vol. 26, No. 2, pp. 189–204.

Thomas, Mandy and Lisa Drummond 2003. 'Introduction', in Lisa B.W. Drummond and Mandy Thomas (eds), *Consuming Urban Culture in Contemporary Vietnam.* London: RoutledgeCurzon, pp. 1–17.

Thomsen, Lotte 2011. 'Business–State Relations in the Differentiated Private Sector in Vietnam: Access to Capital and Land', *Asian Journal of Social Science,* Vol. 39, pp. 627–51.

Thrift, Nigel and Dean K. Forbes 1986. *The Price of War: Urbanization in Vietnam, 1954–1985.* London: Allen and Unwin.

Thượng Hồng 2003. *Món Ngon Sài Gòn: Ký Sự Chọn Lọc* [The Food of Saigon: A Selected Chronicle]. Ho Chi Minh City: Nhà Xuất Bản Thanh Niên.

To Xuan Phuc 2012. 'When the *Đại Gia* (Urban Rich) Go to the Countryside: Impacts of the Urban-Fuelled Rural Land Market in the Uplands', in Van Nguyen-Marshall, Lisa B. Welch Drummond and Danièle Bélanger (eds), *The Reinvention of Distinction: Modernity and the Middle Class in Urban Vietnam.* Dordrecht: Springer, pp. 143–55.

Ton Nu Quynh Tran 2002. 'Culture Change in Urbanized Areas in Ho Chi Minh City at the End of the 20th Century', *Vietnam Social Sciences,* No. 4, pp. 45–52.

Tran, Angie Ngoc 2004. 'What's Women's Work? Male Negotiations and Gender Reproduction in the Vietnamese Garment Industry', in Lisa Drummond and Helle Rydstrøm (eds), *Gender Practices in Contemporary Vietnam.* Singapore: Singapore University Press, pp. 210–35.

Tran, G. B. 2010. *Vietnamerica: A Family's Journey.* New York: Villard.

Tran Thi Van Anh and Le Ngoc Hung 2000. *Women and* Doi Moi *in Vietnam,* 2nd ed. Hanoi: Women's Publishing House.

Trịnh Duy Luân 1996a. 'Chân Dung Một Khu Phố Đông Dân Cư Nghèo ở Thành Phố Hồ Chí Minh' [A Portrait of a Ward in Ho Chi Minh City Densely Populated With Underprivileged Migrants], in Trịnh Duy Luân (ed.), *Tìm Hiểu Môn Xã Hội Học Đô Thị* [Understanding Urban Sociology]. Hanoi: Nhà Xuất Bản Khoa Học Xã Hội.

—— 1996b. 'Tác Động Xã Hội của Đổi Mới ở Các Thành Phố Việt Nam' [The Social Impact of Doi Moi in Vietnamese Cities], in Trịnh Duy Luân (ed.), *Tìm Hiểu Môn Xã Hội Học Đô Thị* [Understanding Urban Sociology]. Hanoi: Nhà Xuất Bản Khoa Học Xã Hội.

Truitt, Allison 2008. 'On the Back of a Motorbike: Middle-Class Mobility in Ho Chi Minh City, Vietnam', *American Ethnologist,* Vol. 35, No. 1, pp. 3–19.

Truong Nhu Tang (with David Chanoff and Doan Van Toai) 1985. *Journal of a Vietcong.* London: Jonathan Cape.

Truong Thi Thuy Hang 2008. 'Women's Leadership in Vietnam: Opportunities and Challenges', *Signs: Journal of Women in Culture and Society,* Vol. 34, No. 1, pp. 16–21.

Turley, William S. and Brantly Womack 1999. 'Asian Socialism's Open Doors: Guangzhou and Ho Chi Minh City', in Anita Chan, Benedict J. Tria Kerkvliet and Jonathan Unger (eds), *Transforming Asian Socialism: China and Vietnam Compared.* St Leonards: Allen and Unwin, pp. 73–97.

Turner, Sarah and Phuong An Nguyen 2005. 'Young Entrepreneurs, Social Capital and *doi moi* in Hanoi, Vietnam', *Urban Studies,* Vol. 42, No. 10, pp. 1693–710.

Vân-Đài 1968. *Thanh Lịch: Cuốn Sách Xã-Giao Cho Tất Cả Bạn Gái* [Refinement and Politeness: An Etiquette Book for All Girls]. [Saigon?]: Hoa Tiên Phát Hành.

Văn Thị Kim Cúc 2002. 'The Parents' Conceptions on the Education of their Children (Case of Vietnamese Children)', *Vietnam Social Sciences,* No. 4, pp. 101–6.

Vann, Elizabeth F. 2006. 'The Limits of Authenticity in Vietnamese Consumer Markets', *American Anthropologist,* Vol. 108, No. 2, pp. 286–96.

—— 2012. 'Afterword: Consumption and Middle-Class Subjectivity in Vietnam', in Van Nguyen-Marshall, Lisa B. Welch Drummond and Danièle Bélanger (eds), *The Reinvention of Distinction: Modernity and the Middle Class in Urban Vietnam.* Dordrecht: Springer, pp. 157–70.

Veblen, Thorstein 1994 [1899]. *The Theory of the Leisure Class.* New York: Dover.

Viviani, Nancy 1996. *The Indochinese in Australia, 1975–1995: From Burnt Boats to Barbecues.* Melbourne: Oxford University Press.

Võ Phiến 1992. *Literature in South Vietnam, 1954–1975.* Transl. by Võ Đình Mai. Melbourne: Vietnamese Language and Culture Publications.

Vorng, Sophorntavy 2011. 'Beyond the Urban–Rural Divide: Complexities of Class, Status and Hierarchy in Bangkok', *Asian Journal of Social Science,* Vol. 39, pp. 674–701.

Vũ Tam Huê 2004. *Miếng Nhớ Miếng Thương* [Something Remembered, Something Loved]. Ho Chi Minh City: Nhà Xuất Bản Thanh Niên.

Waibel, Michael 2009. 'New Consumers as Key Target Groups for Sustainability before the Background of Climate Change in Emerging Economies: The Case of Ho Chi Minh City, Vietnam', in World Bank (ed.), *Proceedings of the 5th Urban Research Symposium of the Cities and Climate Change: Responding to an Urgent Agenda.* 28–30 June 2009, Marseille, France.

Wang, Lingzhen 2004. *Personal Matters: Women's Autobiographical Practice in Twentieth-Century China.* Stanford: Stanford University Press.

Warde, Alan 1997. *Consumption, Food and Taste: Culinary Antinomies and Commodity Culture.* London: Sage.

Watson, Rubie 1994. 'Memory, History and Opposition Under State Socialism: An Introduction', in Rubie Watson (ed.), *Memory, History and Opposition Under State Socialism.* Seattle: University of Washington Press, pp. 1–20.

Werner, Jayne 2002. 'Gender, Household, and State: Renovation (*Đổi Mới*) as Social Process in Vietnam', in Jayne Werner and Danièle Bélanger (eds), *Gender, Household, State: Doi Moi in Viet Nam.* Ithaca: Cornell University Southeast Asia Program, pp. 29–48.

Werner, Jayne 2009. *Gender, Household and State in Post-Revolutionary Vietnam.* New York: Routledge.

Werner, Jayne and Danièle Bélanger 2002. 'Introduction: Gender and Việt Nam Studies', in Jayne Werner and Danièle Bélanger (eds), *Gender, Household, State: Doi Moi in Viet Nam.* Ithaca: Cornell University Southeast Asia Program, pp. 13–28.

White, Christine 1987. 'State, Culture and Gender: Continuity and Change in Women's Position in Rural Vietnam', in Haleh Afshar (ed.), *Women, State and Ideology: Studies from Africa and Asia.* London: Macmillan, pp. 226–34.

Williams, Lindy and Guest, Michael Philip 2005. 'Attitudes Toward Marriage Among the Urban Middle-Class in Vietnam, Thailand, and the Philippines', *Journal of Comparative Family Studies,* Vol. 36, pp. 163–86.

Winkels, Alexandria 2012. 'Migration, Social Networks and Risk: The Case of Rural-to-Rural Migration in Vietnam', *Journal of Vietnamese Studies,* Vol. 7, No 4, pp. 92–121.

Wolf, Diane 1996. 'Situating Feminist Dilemmas in Fieldwork', in Diane Wolf (ed.), *Feminist Dilemmas in Fieldwork.* Boulder: Westview Press, pp. 1–55.

'Women and Their New Responsibility' 1967, in *Women in Vietnam: Selected Articles from Vietnamese Periodicals, Saigon, Hanoi, 1957–1966.* Transl. by Chiem T. Kiem. Honolulu: East-West Center, pp. 26–7.

Xuan Phuong and Danièle Mazingarbe 2004. *Ao Dai: My War, My Country, My Vietnam.* Transl. by Lynn M. Bensimon, ed. by Jonathan E. Myers. New York: Emquad International.

Yan Yunxiang 2003. *Private Life under Socialism: Love, Intimacy, and Family Change in a Chinese Village, 1949–1999.* Stanford: Stanford University Press.

Yan Yunxiang 2006. 'McDonald's in Beijing: The Localization of Americana', in James L. Watson (ed.), *Golden Arches East: McDonald's in East Asia,* 2nd ed. Stanford: Stanford University Press, pp. 39–76.

—— 2009 *The Individualization of Chinese Society.* Oxford: Berg.

Yarborough, Trin 2005. *Surviving Twice: Amerasian Children of the Vietnam War.* Washington DC: Potomac Books.

Yeoh, Brenda S. A. 2004. 'Cosmopolitanism and its Exclusions in Singapore', *Urban Studies,* Vol. 41, No. 12, pp. 2431–45.

Yeomans, Lien 2001. *Green Papaya: New Fruit from Old Seeds.* Milsons Point: Random House.

Yurchak, Alexei 2006. *Everything Was Forever, Until It Was No More: The Last Soviet Generation.* Princeton: Princeton University Press.

Yuval-Davis, Nira and Floya Anthias 1989. *Woman, Nation, State.* Houndmills: Macmillan.

Zhang, Li 2001. *Strangers in the City: Reconfigurations of Space, Power, and Social Networks Within China's Floating Population.* Stanford: Stanford University Press.

—— 2008. 'Private Homes, Distinct Lifestyles: Performing a New Middle Class', in Li Zhang and Aihwa Ong (eds), *Privatizing China: Socialism from Afar.* Ithaca: Cornell University Press, pp. 23–40.

Zinoman, Peter 2001. *The Colonial Bastille: A History of Imprisonment in Vietnam, 1862–1940.* Berkeley: University of California Press.

Index